BTEC FIRST

IT Practitioners

BTEC FIRST

IT Practitioners

K. Mary Reid, Alan Jarvis and Tracey Stump

Heinemann Educational Publishers
Halley Court, Jordan Hill, Oxford OX2 8EJ
Part of Harcourt Education

Heinemann is the registered trademark of Harcourt Education Limited

© K. Mary Reid, Alan Jarvis, Tracey Stump 2003

First published 2003

08 07 06 05 04
10 9 8 7 6 5 4 3 2

British Library Cataloguing in Publication Data is available from the British Library on request.

ISBN 0 435 45469 2

Designed by Kamae Design
Typeset by Saxon Graphics Ltd, Derby

Original illustrations © Harcourt Education Limited, 2002

Printed and Bound by CPI Bath

Cover photo: © Getty

Picture research by Peter Morris

Acknowledgements
Every effort has been made to contact copyright holders of material reproduced in this book. Any omissions will be rectified in subsequent printing if notice is given to the publishers.

Websites
Please note that the examples of websites suggested in this book were up to date at the time of writing. It is essential for tutors to preview each site before using it to ensure that the URL is still accurate and the content is appropriate. We suggest that tutors bookmark useful sites and consider enabling students to access them through the school or college intranet.

Tel: 01865 888058 www.heinemann.co.uk

Contents

INTRODUCTION

The BTEC First Diploma for IT Practitioners is a collection of three related qualifications:

BTEC First Diploma for IT Practitioners (General)
BTEC First Diploma for IT Practitioners (Software Development)
BTEC First Diploma for IT Practitioners (ICT Systems Support)

This book includes sufficient material to enable you to achieve any one of the three qualifications.

Whichever qualification you choose, you must pass six units;

- *two* compulsory core units, which are the same for all three qualifications
- *two* compulsory specialist units, which are specific to each qualification (Bank A*)
- *two* optional specialist units selected from a list specific to each qualification (Bank B*)

*Edexcel refers to the specialist lists as Bank A (compulsory) and Bank B (optional)

Units in this book

This book covers all the units shown in this table:

	General	Software	ICT System Support
Compulsory core	Unit 1: Introduction to Computer Systems		
	Unit 2: Uses of IT		
Compulsory specialist units (Bank A)	Unit 3: Information Systems	Unit 5: Software Development	Unit 4: User Support
	Unit 7: Introduction to Databases	Unit 20: Visual Programming	Unit 15: Networking Essentials
Optional specialist units (Bank B)	Unit 8: Business Applications	Unit 3: Information Systems	Unit 3: Information Systems
	Unit 13: Web Development	Unit 13: Web Development	Unit 13: Web Development

The *Tutor Resource File* provides additional material for all these units.

Units not in this book

There are some more optional specialist units in Bank B which are not included in this book. You may enter for a unit from the Bank B lists shown below, in place of any of the optional units that may appear in this book.

	General	Software Development	ICT System Support
Extra optional specialist units (Bank B) *Not covered in this book*	Unit 6: Communications and Organisations	Unit 12: Graphical User Interfaces	Unit 14: Numerical Systems
	Unit 9: E-commerce	Unit 21: Software Support	Unit 16: Introduction to Network Administration
	Unit 10: Financial Modelling	Unit 22: Software Development Project	Unit 17: Introduction to Network Design
	Unit 11: Business IT Project	Unit 23: Numerical Operations	Unit 18: Network Software
	Unit 12: Graphical User Interfaces	Unit 24: Website Programming	Unit 19: Network Development Project

The *Tutor Resource File* does provide guidance for the three project units, Units 11, 22 and 19, shown shaded in the table.

Assessment

You will find assessment guidance at the end of each unit in this book.

One unit from each qualification is assessed through an **Integrated Vocational Assignment** (IVA) which will be set and assessed by Edexcel.

IVA assessed units

- General
- Software Development
- ICT Systems Support

Unit 7: Introduction to Databases
Unit 5: Software Development
Unit 4: User Support

All other units are assessed internally. Your tutor will probably develop scenarios for you, provide you with case studies and set a mixture of assessment tasks for you to complete.

Acknowledgements

We would like to thank Matt Jackman and Gillian Burrell at Heinemann for their encouragement, wise advice and patience. We are also very grateful for the help and support given us by Neela Soomary, Rob Lee (of Telenor), and Yvonne Samuels.

K. Mary Reid

April 2003

The authors and publisher would like to thank the following for permission to reproduce material and photographs;

About.com – page 375

Amazon – page 357

Apple – page 44

Audit Bureau of Circulations – pages 331–332

Autodesk – page 86 (Autodesk, the Autodesk logo, AutoCAD are registered trademarks of Autodesk Inc in the USA and/or other countries)

Cern Photo – page 364

Certance – page 135

Channel 4 Television Corporation – page 251

Trevor Clifford – page 44

Clubrunner – page 93

Creative Sound Blaster – page 15

Decotech Design Software – page 74, 88, 89

Disneyland® Resort Paris – page 359

Epson – page 46

Hemera Photo Objects – page 49, 136

Kingston Theatre – page 302

Last Minute Network – page 376

Netscape – page 301

NHS Direct – page 360, 369

Oxford Internet Institute – page 113

Peter Morris – page 275, 289

Photodisc – page 115

Rex Features – page 120, 251

Tesco – page 377

Scout Association – page 361

Camilla Thomas – page 136

Yahoo! – page 378

UNIT 1: INTRODUCTION TO COMPUTER SYSTEMS

Success in this unit

What are the learning outcomes?

To achieve this unit you must:

- demonstrate an understanding of basic computer principles
- demonstrate an understanding of the functions of software
- interpret computer hardware specifications
- describe how various categories of user may interact with computer systems.

How is this unit assessed?

This unit is internally assessed. You must provide evidence in the form of a variety of documents that show that you meet the learning outcomes.

How do I provide assessment evidence?

Your evidence will probably be a mixture of the following:

- written reports
- answers to set questions
- printouts from software packages.

All your evidence should be presented in one folder, which should have a front cover and a contents page. The section headed *Assessment tasks* towards the end of this unit gives you more detailed advice about how to prepare for the assessment.

Introduction

About this unit

This unit introduces you to the basic concepts of computing. Most of the topics are dealt with in more depth in other units.

If you have taken courses in ICT before you may find that you already know some of the theory. You are still advised to study this unit carefully, as it does require you to apply your knowledge in practical contexts.

As you work your way through, you should be asking some questions about the computer systems in use at your centre, and a discussion with the technical staff would be very beneficial. If you own your own computer then you will probably want to experiment with some of its facilities.

1.1 Basic computer principles

Logical computer configuration

What are the main components in a computer system?

You will probably be familiar with the main components that make up a computer system (see Figure 1.1).

- The *Central Processing Unit (or processor)* carries out the instructions in a program, and controls all the other components. The CPU is normally stored on one chip.
- The *main memory*, which is usually referred to as RAM (Random Access Memory), holds all the data that is being used by a computer system whilst it is active. Main memory requires power to work, so it is emptied when the computer is switched off. Main memory is normally provided on one or more RAM semiconductor chips.
- *Input devices* transfer data to the CPU. Input devices include keyboard, mouse and microphone as well as a variety of specialised devices like barcode readers and scanners.
- *Output devices* receive data that is transferred to them from the CPU. Output devices include screen, speakers and printer. Some devices, such as a modem, can act as both input and output devices.
- *Backing store devices* are used to store data, but unlike the main memory, do not lose the data when they are switched off. Backing store devices include various types of disk and tape drive. All backing store devices store data on **storage media**, such as disks and tapes. Most backing store devices allow the system to write new data to the storage media as well as read it back; an exception to this is a CD-ROM drive which can only read disks.
- *Connectivity* is the term for all the cables and other channels that carry the data communications between the parts of the system.

?

What does it mean?

Storage media – these are the actual disks or tapes that are used to store digital data. Storage media are placed in a disk or tape drive, which then reads the data or writes new data to the medium. Storage media include hard disks, floppy disks, Zip disks, CDs, DVDs and digital tapes.

Note that 'media' is the plural for 'medium'.

The arrows in Figure 1.1 indicate the *dataflows* in the system – that is, the direction in which data passes between one component and another.

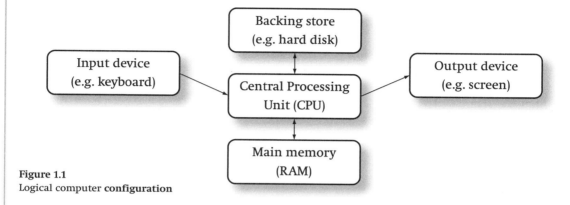

Figure 1.1
Logical computer **configuration**

?

What does it mean?

Configuration – we can talk about both computer (hardware) configuration and software configuration. In both cases we are talking about the choice of components and how they are connected to each other. There are many ways of configuring both a computer system and a software package, and each can be customised to suit the needs of the user.

How does the CPU control computer system resources?

The CPU controls the whole computer system. The computer has a number of physical resources including:

- main memory
- input devices
- output devices
- backing store.

None of these resources can do anything unless it is in communication with the CPU. All the input and output ports on a computer receive control signals from the CPU. Any resource that has to pass data to or from the CPU can only do so under the control of the CPU.

These resources all work at different speeds, and the CPU has to ensure that they all receive signals at the right time and in the right order.

You will learn more about the CPU later in this section. But before you do, you need to understand how a computer manages to store data in main memory and transfer it from one part of the system to another.

Case study – Writing a letter

We can see how all the components in a typical computer configuration are used in the task of writing a letter.

- The user views the screen (an output device).
- The user uses the mouse (an input device) to select the word processing application.
- The word processing program is loaded (that is, copied) from hard disk (backing store) to main memory.
- The word processing edit window is displayed on the screen.
- The user keys in characters on a keyboard (an input device), which are stored in a temporary file in main memory.
- The characters are also displayed on the screen.
- The user saves the file, which transfers (copies) it from the temporary file in main memory to hard disk.
- The user uses the mouse and/or keyboard to issue the print command.
- The print dialogue is displayed on the screen and the user uses the mouse and/or keyboard to complete this.
- The file is copied from main memory to the printer, where it is printed out.

Throughout all this, every action is the result of a program instruction. Instructions in the word processing program allow the user to edit the document. All the other actions happen as a result of program instructions in the operating system. So we can add:

- Every single program instruction is interpreted and carried out by the CPU.

Computer data representation

How is data represented in a computer system?

Computers store incredibly large amounts of data. This data can represent:

- numbers
- **characters** – that is, the letters and symbols on a keyboard
- instructions – from which whole programs are made
- many other kinds of data, such as colours and sounds.

What does it mean?

Character – a character is any letter or symbol that can be stored in a computer system. The standard characters include all the letters of the alphabet (both upper and lower case), the digits from 0 to 9, and all the punctuation marks and symbols shown on a normal keyboard (including the space). Additional characters can be stored as well, such as letters and symbols used in other languages, like é, β, ¥.

Although the data can be complex, it is all stored in a simple fashion. Our alphabet has 26 characters and our number system uses ten digits, but the computer has only two 'characters' to play with. These are known as *bits*. We refer to these two bits with the symbols 0 and 1.

So how can the computer store so much information with only two characters? Think about our number system for a moment – we have only ten digits and yet we can combine them in different ways to represent billions of numbers. Obviously, the position of each digit is important, so that the number 372 is a different number from 723, even though they both use the same digits. In the same way, even though the computer only has two bits, they can be combined to give billions of arrangements. These patterns of bits are known as **binary patterns**.

? What does it mean?

Binary (or bit) pattern – a binary (or bit) pattern is any combination of bits in a sequence.

Each of these binary patterns can be used to represent a different piece of data. Whenever binary patterns are used to store data, we describe it as **digital data**.

? What does it mean?

Digital – digital data is any data which is stored or transmitted using binary patterns.

Binary patterns are also transferred from one part of a computer to another. Whenever a computer is running, many millions of pieces of data are being moved around inside the processor every second. And every time data is transferred to or from one of the devices that make up the computer system (such as a keyboard, disk drive or printer) then binary patterns are sent as signals.

What are binary patterns?

Binary patterns are combinations of bits.

We can create four different binary patterns with exactly two bits. Here they are:

00

01

10

11

Next, how many binary patterns can be made with exactly three bits? They are:

000

001

010

011

100

101

110

111

The answer this time is 8. Note that $8 = 2 \times 2 \times 2$

Can you predict how many binary patterns you can make with four bits? Write down all the patterns systematically, and you should find 16. Note that $16 = 2 \times 2 \times 2 \times 2$

Can you now predict how many binary patterns you can make with 5, 6, 7 or 8 bits?

Look at this table:

Number of bits	Number of binary patterns	
2	4	$4 = 2^2 = 2 \times 2$
3	8	$8 = 2^3 = 2 \times 2 \times 2$
4	16	$16 = 2^4 = 2 \times 2 \times 2 \times 2$
5	32	$32 = 2^5 = 2 \times 2 \times 2 \times 2 \times 2$
6	64	$64 = 2^6 = 2 \times 2 \times 2 \times 2 \times 2 \times 2$
7	128	$128 = 2^7 = 2 \times 2 \times 2 \times 2 \times 2 \times 2 \times 2$
8	256	$256 = 2^8 = 2 \times 2 \times 2 \times 2 \times 2 \times 2 \times 2 \times 2$
9	512	$512 = 2^9 = 2 \times 2 \times 2 \times 2 \times 2 \times 2 \times 2 \times 2 \times 2$
10	1,024	$1024 = 2^{10} = 2 \times 2 \times 2 \times 2 \times 2 \times 2 \times 2 \times 2 \times 2 \times 2$
...		
16	65,536	$65,536 = 2^{16}$
...		
24	16,777,216	$16,777,216 = 2^{24}$
...		
32	4,294,967,296	$4,294,967,296 = 2^{32}$

Figure 1.2 Number of bit patterns that can be created with a fixed number of bits

You will see that the number of binary patterns doubles each time. In general, if there are n bits then these can be combined to give 2^n different binary patterns.

32 bits can be combined to give over four thousand million binary patterns – far more than we could ever need.

What are bytes and Kb?

Binary patterns are usually stored and transmitted in groups of 8 bits. An 8-bit pattern is known as a *byte*. For example, the binary pattern 10010111 is one byte in length. From the table above you can see that there are 256 ways of combining the 8 bits in one byte.

We measure the amount of data stored in a computer by counting how many bytes are used.

You will remember the standard ways of measuring metric units, as shown in this table:

Metric units	Name	Abbreviation
1,000	kilo	k
1,000,000	mega	M
1,000,000,000	giga	G

Figure 1.3 Metric units

Sometimes the abbreviations are used, and sometimes the full word is given. For example, when measuring distance, 1,000 metres (m) = 1 kilometre (km), and when measuring power, 1,000 watts (W) = 1 kilowatt (kW), and 1,000 kilowatts = 1 gigawatt (GW).

But when it comes to digital data, bytes are never counted in thousands. They are always counted in groups of 1,024 bytes. This is because of the way they are physically stored and accessed. You will have realised that powers of 2 feature very heavily in computer storage, and $1,024 = 2^{10}$.

1,024 is close to 1,000, so the accepted convention is that 1,024 bytes = 1 kilobyte (abbreviated to 1 Kb, or 1 Kbyte – note the capital K now, to distinguish it from k = 1000).

Metric units	Name		Computing units
1,000	kilo		1,024
1,000,000	mega		$1,048,576 = 1,024 \times 1,024$
1,000,000,000	giga		$1,073,741,824 = 1,024 \times 1,024 \times 1,024$

Figure 1.4 Computing units

The right-hand column of the table shows that in a computer system the terms Mega, and Giga mean *approximately* 1 million and 1 thousand million respectively. But for all everyday purposes you can think of 1 Mb as 1 million bytes, and 1 Gb as 1 thousand million bytes.

How can binary patterns be used to represent data?

As we saw before, binary patterns can be used to represent any data that is stored or transmitted digitally. In a computer the data could be numbers, characters or program instructions. The numbers themselves can stand for ordinary numbers as we use them, or for the elements that make up pictures and sound.

So one byte, such as 01100011, could represent a number, or a character, or part of a program instruction, or something in an image, or a fraction of a sound. How then does the computer know which one it means? That is actually a very profound question, and it may take several years of study to fully grasp the answer. But we can say that whenever a computer system is doing anything at all it is running a program, and that the program will be expecting to receive data of a particular type, so will interpret the data in a particular way.

Check your understanding – Wrongly interpreted data

Have you ever opened a document in a word processor and seen something like this?

DHH? B Î|Y:ôLßiúÔc?®?w=º{µ=çöTí÷êªê?\?oMÓ‹Ï˜u™^Mÿüâe?ÿ1ÿ÷ñôz?ÿÓå 2}c?üöÓo¿üã—¿?óô‹
¿ûéí»7—WÓ›üóû˜ÿüáï¿wû?¶÷s?æÏwOÓt"õüüütÛÿÉü?[ë˜Ÿ} Ó ´î?Ü÷?è...Œ§ËÓ?Û?—
ï}öáO?/æ—ÿk?f?˜?öƒß}üïÿ?áËŸßÛ?ößt?pJm?˜˜?T _ ,?Î\»ÎÚ¢–?ÙL?-è? q?dM
"£...#*ëòç—ÿœ'y_<X·Ù?|?£ñ

This may look like nonsense, but what has happened is that perfectly valid data has been interpreted wrongly by the software. The data represented by the binary patterns was, in fact, instructions in Microsoft® Word for laying out the document, but the software has interpreted the patterns as characters. This happens when documents have been stored in the format used by one software package and then loaded into another package which works with a different format.

Most of the time the software does interpret the bit patterns correctly.

Have you come across other examples of the wrong interpretation of data?

Binary patterns for characters and numbers

How are characters represented in a computer system?

Many years ago the computing community agreed on a standard method for representing characters in binary patterns. This is known as the American Standard Code for Information Interchange (ASCII). Each character is allocated 8 bits (1 byte), and these bit patterns are used whenever text is being stored or transmitted.

Binary pattern	Character
01000001	A
01000010	B
01000011	C
	...
01100001	a
01100010	b
01100011	c
01100100	d
01100101	e
	...
01110010	r
01110011	s
01110100	t
	...
00110000	0
00110001	1
00110010	2
	...
00100000	space
00100001	!
00100010	"

Figure 1.5 Some ASCII binary patterns

Notice that the upper-case (capital) and lower-case letters are treated as different characters. But can you see the relationship between the bit patterns for each?

Check your understanding – ASCII binary patterns

Work out what this message means. Each byte of data represents one character in ASCII.

01000010 01100101 00100000 01100001 00100000 01110011 01110100 01100001 01110010 00100001

Further research – Calculating the size of text files

A text file consists entirely of characters, using the ASCII coding system. An example of a text file could be a simple e-mail or a text message.

If the words in this book were all stored in a text file, how many kilobytes would it take up?

To answer the question, estimate how many characters there are in the book. Don't forget to include the spaces. Since each character needs one byte to store the character code, you can see immediately how many bytes are needed.

In practice, this book contains a great many illustrations and these use up far more storage space than the text on its own, but you could do a similar exercise with a novel without any illustrations.

How are numbers represented in a computer system?

We have already seen that the digits from 0 to 9 can be stored as characters using the ASCII binary patterns. However, these are no use at all if we want the computer system to do calculations with the numbers. So numbers are usually stored using another method.

As we saw earlier, binary patterns are stored in bytes. Binary patterns can be used to store numbers as well as characters, but numbers are not as simple as characters, mainly because there are several ways in which we can write a number.

We can start by looking at **denary numbers**. We can write a denary number in several different ways. For example, the number three hundred and fifty seven can be written as 357 or 357.0 or even 3.57×10^2 (in scientific notation). Each of these serves a different purpose.

What does it mean?

Denary numbers – denary numbers are the ordinary numbers that we use. A denary number which includes a decimal point, such as 13.56, is called a *decimal number*. A denary number which is a simple whole number without a decimal point is known as a *denary integer*. Denary numbers can be positive (greater than zero) or negative (less than zero).

In the same way, we can represent a number in more than one way in a binary pattern. The main methods are:

- binary **integers**
- Binary Coded Decimal
- sign and magnitude
- two's complement
- fixed point representation
- floating point representation.

We shall be looking only at the first two methods in this unit; the others have just been included in the list for completeness.

What does it mean?

Integer – an integer is a whole number. Integers include:

- all the negative whole numbers, that is,–1, –2, –3, –4, –5, etc.
- 0 (zero)
- all the positive whole numbers, that is, 1, 2, 3, 4, 5, etc.

What are binary integers?

Computer systems use one, two, three or even four bytes to store a single integer.

In Figure 1.2 we saw that 1 byte (8 bits) can hold 256 different binary patterns, whereas 2 bytes (16 bits) can store 65,536 different binary patterns.

We will start with 1 byte. Each of the 256 different binary patterns can be made to represent a different denary integer (whole number). We want to include the number 0, so we use 1 byte to represent the numbers 0, 1, 2, 3, 4, ... 255.

We could, of course, allocate the binary patterns at random to the denary integers, but as you might imagine computer engineers use a systematic method for doing this. It is important that the same method is used by everyone and that the bit patterns are easy to understand and manipulate. The binary integer method shown in Figure 1.6 is a very common way of using bit patterns to represent positive denary integers.

Denary integer	Binary integer
0	00000000
1	00000001
2	00000010
3	00000011
4	00000100
5	00000101
6	00000110
7	00000111
8	00001000
9	00001001
10	00001010
11	00001011
12	00001100

Figure 1.6 Binary integers

You should be able to see a pattern emerging. Can you work out what the binary integer is for 13? – and for 14, 15 and 16?

But what about 67, or 130, or 221? And can you say what denary integer is represented by the bit pattern 10010100? To answer these questions you either need a very long table, or you need a method to do the calculations.

You should notice that we always write all 8 bits when writing a binary integer.

How can I calculate which denary integer is represented by a given binary integer?

To understand the method, you need to think again about denary integers. Denary integers are numbers based on the number 10. The value of each digit in a denary integer depends on its position, as shown here.

$10{,}000=10^4$	$1{,}000=10^3$	$100=10^2$	$10=10^1$	1	Denary integer
4	7	0	9	2	47,092

$47{,}092 = 4 \times 10{,}000 + 7 \times 1{,}000 + 0 \times 100 + 9 \times 10 + 2 \times 1$

In the same way, binary integers can be thought of as numbers based on the number 2. A binary integer can be analysed like this:

Binary integer								Denary integer
$128=2^7$	$64=2^6$	$32=2^5$	$16=2^4$	$8=2^3$	$4=2^2$	$2=2^1$	1	
1	0	0	1	0	1	0	0	?

10010100 (binary) $\quad = 1 \times 128 + 0 \times 64 + 0 \times 32 + 1 \times 16 + 0 \times 8 + 1 \times 4 + 0 \times 2 + 0 \times 1$ (denary)

$\qquad = 128 + 16 + 4$ (denary)

$\qquad = 148$ (denary)

So using the binary integer method, 10010100 represents the denary number 148, and we can write the answer in the table:

Binary integer								Denary integer
$128=2^7$	$64=2^6$	$32=2^5$	$16=2^4$	$8=2^3$	$4=2^2$	$2=2^1$	1	
1	0	0	1	0	1	0	0	148

So if you want to convert a binary integer into its denary equivalent, just write it in a table like this and add up the values in the columns which have a bit value of 1.

Check your understanding – Converting binary integers to denary

Can you work out which denary integers are represented by these binary integers?

1   00111010
2   11101111
3   01000011
4   10010100
5   00000000
6   11111111

How can I calculate which binary integer represents a given denary integer?

If you want to convert denary integers to their binary integer equivalents, you simply work in reverse.

Binary integer								Denary integer
$128=2^7$	$64=2^6$	$32=2^5$	$16=2^4$	$8=2^3$	$4=2^2$	$2=2^1$	1	
?	?	?	?	?	?	?	?	205

Start on the left. Check whether the denary number (205) is greater than the number in the first column (128). In this case it is, which means that we need 128 in the number, so place 1 in the column:

Binary integer								Denary integer
$128=2^7$	$64=2^6$	$32=2^5$	$16=2^4$	$8=2^3$	$4=2^2$	$2=2^1$	1	
1	?	?	?	?	?	?	?	205

205 − 128 = 77, so that leaves 77 to fit into the table.

Moving from left to right, check whether 77 is greater than the number in the next column (64). It is, so the table becomes:

Binary integer								Denary integer
$128=2^7$	$64=2^6$	$32=2^5$	$16=2^4$	$8=2^3$	$4=2^2$	$2=2^1$	1	
1	1	?	?	?	?	?	?	205

77 − 64 = 13, so we now have to fit 13 into the table.

Moving to the next column we ask whether 13 is greater than the number at the top (32), and as it is not needed we place 0 in the column:

Binary integer								Denary integer
$128=2^7$	$64=2^6$	$32=2^5$	$16=2^4$	$8=2^3$	$4=2^2$	$2=2^1$	1	
1	1	0	?	?	?	?	?	205

We are still working with 13.

We continue to move along the columns until the number we are working with has been completely used up:

Binary integer								Denary integer
$128=2^7$	$64=2^6$	$32=2^5$	$16=2^4$	$8=2^3$	$4=2^2$	$2=2^1$	1	
1	1	0	0	1	1	0	1	205

As a final check, convert the binary integer back to denary to make sure that no mistakes have been made:

11001101 (binary) $= 1 \times 128 + 1 \times 64 + 0 \times 32 + 0 \times 16 + 1 \times 8 + 1 \times 4 + 0 \times 2 + 1 \times 1$ (denary)

$= 128 + 64 + 8 + 4 + 1$ (denary)

$= 205$ (denary)

Check your understanding – Converting denary integers to binary integers

Can you work out which binary integers are used to represent these denary integers?

1   204
2   51
3   136
4   15
5   243

What is Binary Coded Decimal (BCD)?

The binary integer method of representing denary integers is very useful if the software needs to do arithmetic with the numbers. But sometimes the computer system simply needs to store the values of each denary digit (0 to 9), so that it can display them correctly (on a scoreboard, for example.

The binary coded decimal system uses 4 bits to represent each denary digit. This means that 1 byte can store 2 digits and 2 bytes can store 4 digits. Each set of 4 bits holds the binary integer for a digit from the range 0 to 9.

Binary Coded Decimal				Denary digit
$8=2^3$	$4=2^2$	$2=2^1$	1	
0	0	0	0	0
0	0	0	1	1
0	0	1	0	2
0	0	1	1	3
0	1	0	0	4
0	1	0	1	5
0	1	1	0	6
0	1	1	1	7
1	0	0	0	8
1	0	0	1	9

Figure 1.7 Binary Coded Decimal

In the example below, the leftmost 4 bits represent the digit 8, and the rightmost 4 bits represent the digit 5.

Leftmost BCD				Denary digit
$8=2^3$	$4=2^2$	$2=2^1$	1	
1	0	0	0	8

Rightmost BCD				Denary digit
$8=2^3$	$4=2^2$	$2=2^1$	1	
0	1	0	1	5

Denary integer
85

1000 0101 (BCD) = 85 (denary)

Using 1 byte, BCD can represent denary integers from 00 to 99. You will notice that this only uses 100 out of the 256 bit patterns that could be made with one byte.

✓ **Check your understanding** – Binary Coded Decimal

Which denary numbers do each of these BCD codes represent?

1   0100 0010
2   0001 1001
3   0101 0011
4   0000 0111

How would each of these denary integers be represented in BCD?

5   27
6   94
7   15
8   3 (note that you do need to write this as 03)
9   10

Shorthand coding

Help! How do I remember binary patterns?

You don't have to.

Normally, whenever you key in a number or character the software generates the correct binary pattern. The only people who need to work with the binary patterns directly are programmers (who create the software in the first place) and systems administrators (who have to work with the operating system).

But even they do not have to know the actual binary patterns, as they can use a shorthand code instead.

There are two widely used shorthand codes for binary patterns:

- denary integers
- hexadecimal numbers.

How are denary numbers used as shorthand for binary patterns?

ASCII binary patterns are normally referred to by a denary integer, which is known as the ASCII code. This is calculated by treating each bit pattern as though it were a binary integer, and converting it to the corresponding denary integer. The table below gives the ASCII codes for some of the characters used before.

Binary pattern	ASCII code	Character
01000001	65	A
01000010	66	B
01000011	67	C
		...
01100001	97	a
01100010	98	b
01100011	99	c
		...
00110000	48	0
00110001	49	1
00110010	50	2
		...
00100000	32	space
00100001	33	!
00100010	34	"

Figure 1.8 Denary ASCII codes

Check your understanding – Using ASCII codes

You can, in fact, enter ASCII codes from the keyboard. Try this:

When you are creating text, hold down the Alt key whilst keying in the number 65 on the numeric keypad to the right of the keyboard. When you release the Alt key the character 'A' should appear.

Repeat with other ASCII codes.

How are hexadecimal numbers used as shorthand for binary patterns?

Sometimes you will see hexadecimal numbers used as an alternative shorthand code for binary patterns. These are mainly used by programmers and technical users who work directly with operating systems. 'Hexadecimal' is sometimes shortened to 'hex'.

The window in Figure 1.9 shows some of the technical settings for a sound card. The Input/Output Range is expressed as two hexadecimal codes, CC00 and CC3F. (You do not have to understand what this is for.)

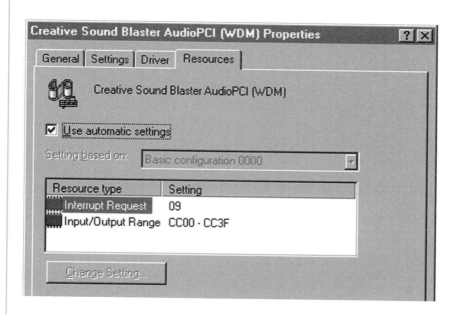

Figure 1.9 Hexadecimal codes used by a sound card

The term *hexadecimal* means 'based on 16', just as binary means 'based on 2' and denary means 'based on 10'. So hexadecimal codes use 16 'digits', which have the same values as 0 to 15 in denary integers. These 16 digits are shown in the table on the next page.

Binary integer				Hexadecimal digit	Denary integer
$8=2^3$	$4=2^2$	$2=2^1$	1		
0	0	0	0	0	0
0	0	0	1	1	1
0	0	1	0	2	2
0	0	1	1	3	3
0	1	0	0	4	4
0	1	0	1	5	5
0	1	1	0	6	6
0	1	1	1	7	7
1	0	0	0	8	8
1	0	0	1	9	9
1	0	1	0	A	10
1	0	1	1	B	11
1	1	0	0	C	12
1	1	0	1	D	13
1	1	1	0	E	14
1	1	1	1	F	15

Figure 1.10 Hexadecimal digits

This means that 1 hexadecimal digit can act as shorthand for a set of 4 bits, and 2 hexadecimal digits can act as shorthand for 1 byte.

How do I convert binary patterns to hexadecimal form?

Here is a binary pattern that we met before:

Binary integer								Denary integer
$128=2^7$	$64=2^6$	$32=2^5$	$16=2^4$	$8=2^3$	$4=2^2$	$2=2^1$	1	
1	1	0	0	1	1	0	1	205

We treat the leftmost and rightmost sets of 4 bits separately, and use the table of hexadecimal digits in Figure 1.10 to work out the hexadecimal code for each.

Leftmost 4-bit binary integer				Hex code
$8=2^3$	$4=2^2$	$2=2^1$	1	
1	1	0	0	C

Rightmost 4-bit binary integer				Hex code
$8=2^3$	$4=2^2$	$2=2^1$	1	
1	1	0	1	D

1100 (binary) = 12 (denary)
= C (hexadecimal)

1101 (binary) = 13 (denary)
= D (hexadecimal)

So the hexadecimal code for 11001101 is CD.

Check your understanding – Working out hexadecimal codes

Write down the hexadecimal shorthand codes for each of these binary patterns

1 10011100
2 00111101
3 11100011
4 01010101
5 11110000

How do I convert hexadecimal codes to binary patterns?

We will look again at one of the hexadecimal codes in the settings for the sound card: CC3F. It has 4 hexadecimal digits, each of which is shorthand for 4 bits, so the bit pattern for the whole code will have 16 bits.

We will take each one in turn:

C (hexadecimal)   = 12 (denary)   = 1100 (binary)

C (hexadecimal)   = 12 (denary)   = 1100 (binary)

3 (hexadecimal)   = 3 (denary)   = 0011 (binary)

F (hexadecimal)   = 15 (denary)   = 1111 (binary)

So:

CC3F (hexadecimal)   = 1100 1100 0011 1111 (binary)

Check your understanding – Converting hexadecimal codes to binary patterns

Write down the binary patterns that correspond to each of these hexadecimal codes

1 6A
2 D1
3 0B
4 56
5 FF

CPU instruction set

What is in the CPU?

The CPU is itself made up of two units:

- The *Control Unit* fetches the next program instruction from main memory and then carries it out.
- The *Arithmetic and Logic Unit* (ALU) manipulates binary patterns using the arithmetic and logical operators that are described later.

Since the task of the CPU is to run programs, we need to look at how these programs are created.

What is a program?

Here are some program instructions written in the programming language Visual Basic. You do not have to understand them, but just notice that they are made up of words and abbreviations that look a bit like ordinary English.

```
Function IsLoaded(ByVal strFormName As String) As Integer
  Const conObjStateClosed = 0
  Const conDesignView = 0
  If SysCmd(acSysCmdGetObjectState, acForm, strFormName) <>
      conObjStateClosed Then
    If Forms(strFormName).CurrentView <> conDesignView Then
      IsLoaded = True
    End If
  End If
End Function
```

Programs in Visual Basic (or any other programming language) have to be converted into the code that the CPU uses, known as **machine code**. This conversion is done by a piece of software known as a *compiler*.

What does it mean?

Machine code – In machine code, binary patterns represent each of the instructions in a program. When a computer runs a program it is carrying out the machine code instructions. Machine code instructions are the actual instructions that control the computer. Machine code instructions are, like all other data, stored in binary patterns.

How does the CPU run a program?

The machine code instructions that make up a program have to be in the computer's main memory (RAM) in order for them to become active.

Programs are normally stored on backing store, usually on a hard disk. When a user, or the system, needs to run a program it has to be 'loaded' (or transferred) from backing store into main memory.

Then the first instruction in the program is fetched (transferred) from main memory to the Control Unit of the CPU. The Control Unit executes (carries out) the instruction, and probably uses the ALU to do this. When the instruction has been executed the next instruction is fetched from main memory. This is known as the *fetch–execute cycle*.

The CPU has a number of **registers** where data can be stored temporarily whilst a program is running.

What does it mean?

Register – a register is a small memory, which may hold only 1 byte or a few bytes of data. It is used to store data temporarily whilst a program is running. There are several registers in the CPU.

What are the registers in the CPU?

The main registers are:

- *Sequence Control Register (SCR)* – this is also known as the program counter. It holds the address in main memory where the next program instruction can be found.
- *Instruction Register (IR)* – this holds the program instruction that the CPU is executing at present.
- *Memory Address Register (MAR)* – this holds the address of a location in main memory. The CPU puts an address in the MAR when it wants to transfer data from the main memory to another part of the system.
- *Memory Buffer Register (MBR)* – this holds the data that is to be transferred to or from the main memory.

Main memory has direct access to the MAR and MBR and responds to whatever is placed in them by the CPU.

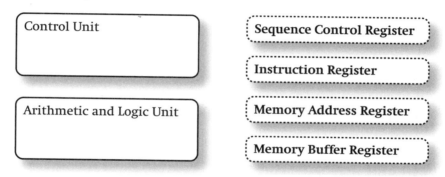

Figure 1.11 The elements that make up the Central Processing Unit

What is the CPU instruction set?

The set of machine code instructions that can be used by a particular CPU is known as the CPU instruction set.

The CPU instruction set will contain instructions to carry out:

- transfer operations
- input or output operations
- processing operations.

A machine code program will be made of thousands or millions of instructions selected from the CPU instruction set.

How can CPU instructions transfer data?

The CPU has to transfer data within the CPU itself and between the CPU and main memory.

All data is stored as binary patterns, so there have to be places where the data can be stored.

- In the CPU, data is stored in registers. Each register holds 1 or more bytes.
- In main memory, data is stored in one of the millions of storage places, known as locations. Each location has its own memory **address**.

The CPU can transfer data:

- from one register in the CPU to another

- from a register in the CPU to an address in main memory
- from an address in main memory to a register in the CPU.

Although we talk about transferring data, the data itself is actually copied from one location to another, and is not deleted. If new data is transferred to a location then at that point it overwrites the old data.

Data is transferred within the CPU and from the CPU to main memory along communications channels called *buses*. In practice, data, in the form of binary patterns, may be sent down one of three buses:

- The *data bus* carries all kinds of data from input devices, to output devices, and to and from memory.
- The *address bus* runs between the registers in the CPU and locations in memory. It carries the number which corresponds to an address where data is stored in memory.
- The *control bus* carries control signals from the CPU to the other components, telling them whether to read or write data.

What does it mean?

Address – main memory is made up of a large number of locations where binary patterns can be stored. Each location is allocated a number which acts as its address. This means that the data at each location can be accessed directly, if the address is known.

How can CPU instructions handle input and output operations?

The CPU itself cannot communicate directly with the real world. A computer system has to include devices that will allow data to be input into the system, and other devices which will do something useful with the data that is output from the CPU.

For example, the keyboard and mouse are input devices, and they send data to the CPU whenever they are used. The monitor and printer are output devices which take output data from the CPU and convert it into screen or printed displays.

The CPU works at a vastly faster rate than input and output devices. So if a machine code instruction is to send some data to an output device like a printer, the CPU does not halt all activity whilst this is going on. Instead it sends a control signal (a binary pattern) to the printer, which effectively asks it whether it is ready to receive data. The CPU then carries on with other instructions until the printer sends a control signal in response. The control signal from the printer is a sign to the CPU that it can now stop what it is doing and transfer the data to the printer.

What kind of processing operations can the CPU instructions carry out?

The CPU can carry out two kinds of processing operations. Both are carried out in the Arithmetic and Logic Unit (ALU). These are:

- *Arithmetic operations* – these include the basic operation of adding two numbers together (in their binary format). You might imagine that the ALU also needs operations for subtracting, multiplying and dividing numbers, but in fact it can manage with just an addition operation, together with another operation called 'a logical shift'.

■ *Logical operations* – these include operations known as AND, OR and NOT. Logical operations allow the ALU to combine binary patterns in a number of different ways.

In practice, many of these operations can be combined to carry out more complex tasks.

How does the ALU add numbers?

When young children learn to add numbers, they have to remember number bonds – simple additions with single digits, such as 7 + 9 = 16. They use all the number bonds when adding larger numbers, working from right to left along the columns, and carrying digits to the next column when necessary.

	3	4	7	1
+	2	3	9	8
	5	8	6	9

Carry: 1

In the shaded column, three digits have to be added. This can be done by adding two digits together then adding the third digit to the result.

Exactly the same process is used with binary integers.

When two binary integers are added together, the ALU has to use four number bonds:

0 + 0 = 0

0 + 1 = 1

1 + 0 = 1

1 + 1 = 10 .... because 10 (binary) = 2 (denary)

This last number bond creates a carry to the next column, as in this example:

	0	0	1	1
+	1	0	1	0
	1	1	0	1

Carry: 1

Sometimes when the carry bit is added to the other two bits, the sum is 11 (binary), as in this example:

	1	0	1	1
+	0	0	1	1
	1	1	1	0

Carry   1   1

Check your understanding – Adding binary integers

Add together these pairs of binary integers

1 1010 + 0100

2 0011 + 0010

3 0110 + 0101

4 1011 + 0011

What can the ALU do with logical operations?

AND

The logical operation AND combines bits using these rules:

0 AND 0 = 0

0 AND 1 = 0

1 AND 0 = 0

1 AND 1 = 1

You can see that the result is 1 only when both the first bit is 1 *and* the second bit is 1. The AND operation can be used to change one of the digits to zero in a number stored in BCD format:

	1	0	0	1	0	1	1	1	97
AND	1	1	1	1	0	0	0	0	Mask
	1	0	0	1	0	0	0	0	90

A *mask* is a binary pattern that is used in a logical operation to achieve an effect.

OR

The logical operation OR combines bits using these rules:

0 OR 0 = 0

0 OR 1 = 1

1 OR 0 = 1

1 OR 1 = 1

You can see that the result is 1 when the first bit is 1 *or* the second bit is 1. This includes the case when both are 1.

The OR operation can be used to switch a character from upper case to lower case. The character code for 'B' is 01000010, and the character code for 'b' is 01100010, so:

	0	1	0	0	0	0	1	0	B
OR	0	0	1	0	0	0	0	0	Mask
	0	1	1	0	0	0	1	0	b

Can you work out what operation is needed to switch a lower-case character to upper case?

NOT

The AND and OR operations each work on 2 bits, whereas the logical operation NOT works on just 1 bit:

NOT 0 = 1

NOT 1 = 0

So the NOT operation simply swaps (or inverts) the value of a bit.

The NOT operation can, for instance, be used to change a colour to its inverse. High resolution colours use 3 bytes (24 bits) to store the code for each colour. Each byte holds a binary pattern that represents the code for the Red, Green or Blue tones that make up the colour. For example, the code for cornflower blue is 01100100 10010101 11101101.

	Red	Green	Blue	
NOT	0 1 1 0 0 1 0 0	1 0 0 1 0 1 0 1	1 1 1 0 1 1 0 1	Cornflower blue
	1 0 0 1 1 0 1 1	0 1 1 0 1 0 1 0	0 0 0 1 0 0 1 0	Mustard

In the above you can see that when NOT is applied to all the bits, the result is the code for a mustard colour. This is the inverse colour for cornflower blue. As you might guess, black is the inverse of white. Other inverses are fuschia/lime, aqua/red, blue/yellow.

Further research – Colour inverses

Try changing the colour of text in a document to any colour you choose. Then highlight the text with your mouse, and you should see the colour change to its inverse.

Have you noticed other circumstances in which a colour changes to its inverse on a computer screen?

Basic instruction format

There are several different types of CPU on the market, and each type has its instruction set. Although CPU instruction sets do differ, they all use a similar format for the instructions.

Each machine code instruction consists of two types of data:

- operation code (opcode)
- operand.

What is an opcode?

An opcode states what must be carried out. All machine code instructions have exactly one opcode. For example, an opcode could instruct the CPU to store a value in memory, or to add one number to another.

What is an operand?

There may be one operand, several operands, or no operands at all in a machine code instruction. An operand is the information that the opcode has to work on. It may be a number or a character (stored in its binary pattern, of course).

In many cases, the operand is an address in memory. The opcode will instruct the CPU to find the data at that address in memory, and then use that data.

Test your knowledge

1 List input and output devices that might be found in a typical computer configuration.
2 What is the difference between a backing store device and storage media? Give examples of each.
3 Why does a computer system need both main memory and backing store?
4 Explain these computing terms:
- bit
- byte

▶

◀

- kilobyte
- megabyte
- gigabyte.

5. Why is ASCII important?
6. What are these? Give examples of each.
   - decimal number
   - denary integer
   - binary integer
   - Binary Coded Decimal
   - hexadecimal code.
7. List the main components of the CPU and explain briefly what each does.

1.2 Functions of software

Introduction to software

What is the role of software?

In the previous section we saw how a computer stores and carries out programs. Programs are initially written in a programming language, like Visual Basic. But the program has to be converted into machine code instructions before it can be used by the computer system. The machine code instructions will be selected from the CPU instruction set.

Software is a general term used for programs. Hardware refers to the physical components of a computer system, but on its own it can do nothing. Software is needed to control the hardware and to turn it into a useful machine.

Software falls into two categories:

- *Systems software* – this controls a computer system.
- *Applications software* – this carries out specific tasks for an organisation or for an individual user.

Systems software must be in place on a computer before applications software can be used.

Further research – Check out your operating system

If you are running Windows® on your own desktop computer at home you can look at the Windows folder on the C: drive. In it you will find a very large number of programs, which together control the computer system.

If you want to make any changes to the system you should go to the Control Panel (select Settings from the Start Menu). You will not be able to change the core functions of the operating system. But you could, if you like, modify aspects of the display, add or remove fonts, install new software, install new hardware drivers, change how the mouse responds, defragment a drive, etc.

▶

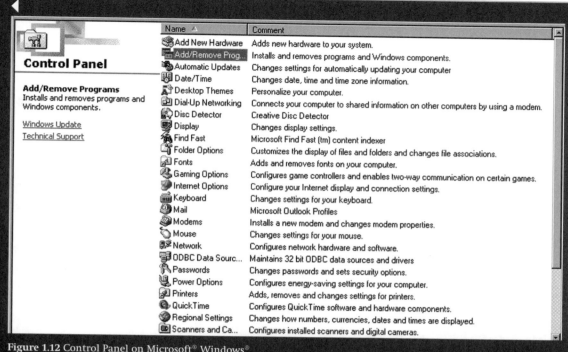

Figure 1.12 Control Panel on Microsoft® Windows®

Windows® was originally the name of the graphical user interface that Microsoft® built on top of its original operating system MS-DOS. But today it is difficult to separate the core operating system's components from the user interface which communicates with it, and current versions of Windows® do not need DOS at all.

Systems software

What is systems software?

Systems software includes the operating system, together with add-on programs known as system utilities. The end user is not usually aware of the systems software. In comparison, the technical users in an organisation, such as systems administrators, spend most of their time working directly with the systems software.

The main function of systems software is to manage the resources of the computer system. As we saw earlier the CPU controls the use that the computer system makes of resources, such as memory, input devices, output devices and backing store. These can be controlled only through the instructions in the operating system.

Systems software often works in the background whilst a user is doing something useful with applications software. For example, when you are word processing a document and you send it to the printer, you are not aware of all the processes that the systems software has to go through to make it happen. The applications software works directly with the systems software, so that the user does not have to worry about it.

What is an operating system?

The core of the systems software is the operating system. You will probably be familiar with a version of Microsoft® Windows®, which is an operating system that is widely used on desktop computers. However there are several others that you may also have heard of, such as the Apple Mac OS.

More complex operating systems are used for network systems, such as Windows® .NET, OS/2, Unix and Linux.

The operating system is never a single program but a collection of programs, each of which carries out a specific task. Extra programs can often be added to the main operating system. For example, when a new printer is added to a system, the relevant printer driver has to be installed to enable the operating system to communicate with the device.

Check your understanding – Managing hardware efficiently

If the operating system has been configured correctly, the hardware resources will be used smoothly so that the user will not really be aware of what the operating system is doing.

Here is an example:

When a user is viewing a complex page from the Internet, the user does not have to wait until it is all downloaded before he or she can do anything else. The operating system communicates with the modem in short spurts, leaving time in between for the user to do other things.

A modem (or any other input device) that wants to send data to the CPU first sends a signal, called an *interrupt*, to the CPU. The operating system determines when the interrupt will be handled, then stops whatever else it is doing to transfer the data.

Can you find other examples of good hardware resource management?

What does the operating system do?

The operating system carries out these tasks as needed:

- allows the user to select and launch programs, as well as launching some programs automatically
- allocates space in memory to programs
- loads programs, by transferring them from backing store into memory
- runs programs, by transferring instructions one at a time from memory to the CPU, then executing them
- manages backing store, by creating, opening, moving, deleting and renaming files
- manages input and output devices, by controlling the data that flows between them and the CPU
- allows the user to configure the system, that is, make changes to the way in which the operating system works.

The operating system is designed to make the computer system as efficient as possible.

Further research – Improving performance

The user is able to make certain changes to the way the operating system functions – these may or may not improve the performance of the system.

For example, you may notice that your operating system has become quite slow, especially when it is saving or loading files. One option is to defragment the disk – this rearranges all the files so that they make the best use of the space. This only really improves performance if the disk is more than 75 per cent full.

Another option is to change the virtual memory settings in Windows®. Virtual memory allows the system to load only part of a program into memory when it is running. You can see that although the user may want to make changes, the advice given is to leave it to someone with good technical knowledge, as the changes could actually make the system perform more slowly.

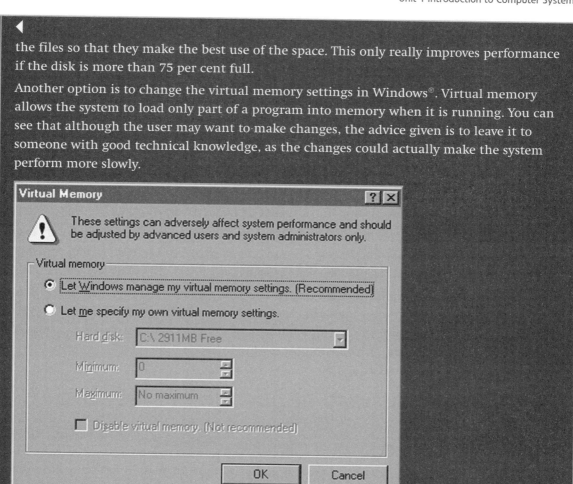

Figure 1.13 Virtual memory settings in Microsoft® Windows®

Applications software

What is applications software?

A computer system can do nothing at all without systems software. But for a computer system to be useful it must also have applications software. Examples of applications software include a hospital patient records system, a desktop publishing package, an arcade game or an Internet browser.

Software may be bought ready-made, or may be designed specifically for one organisation. Applications software is used by an end user, who may be very experienced at using it, but will probably not have any specific technical knowledge about the operating system.

What can applications software be used for?

Applications software can be used for many purposes. Here are a few general categories that might be used in an organisation:

■ To carry out business transactions, such as dealing with customer orders for a mail order company, sending out mobile phone bills, booking facilities in a health club or managing bank accounts. (A transaction is a single action such as placing an order, making a phone call, making a booking or withdrawing cash.)

- To create business documents, such as letters and reports.
- To handle communications, such as access to the Internet and internal e-mail.
- To manage finances.
- To present information to an audience, whether in printed or electronic form.
- To create and manipulate images.
- To manage projects.
- To design products.

Applications software is also used outside the business environment for many purposes, such as for playing games, recording music, genealogy, and a host of other leisure pursuits.

Sometimes an organisation will have applications software developed specifically to meet its own needs. This is known as *bespoke software*. For example, the system used by air traffic controllers is a special, one-off, bespoke system.

In many cases an organisation will find that *general-purpose applications software* is already available to buy, and that it meets its needs perfectly well. For example, virtually everyone uses one of the standard word processing packages, and it would be very surprising if an organisation developed its own word processing software.

General-purpose applications software

What is general-purpose applications software?

General-purpose applications software is software that can be used for many different tasks. Anyone can buy general-purpose software, so it is designed to meet the needs of a wide range of users.

General-purpose applications software is ready-made, and can be installed and used immediately. It is normally sold as a complete **software package** and can be bought through a high street store, from an Internet retailer or through a mail order software supplier. It is often supplied on an optical medium, such as a CD or DVD-ROM, or it can be downloaded from the Internet.

What does it mean?

Software package – a software (or applications) package is a collection of programs, files and manuals that are purchased together as a piece of applications software.

Software packages are available for:

- word processing
- spreadsheets
- database management
- drawing and painting
- communications (e-mail and Internet browsers)
- presentation graphics
- web design
- desktop publishing.

Some software packages are used for more specialist purposes. These include applications software for:

- project management
- computer aided design (CAD)
- accounting.

See Unit 2 for more information about all these types of applications software.

Check your understanding – General-purpose applications packages

Make a list of all the general-purpose applications packages that you have access to at your centre.

Are there others that you would like to use?

Bespoke software

What is bespoke software?

Bespoke software is custom made to meet the needs of a single organisation. It is one-off, so no one else will have the same software.

A large business like a bank may employ its own software developers who will devote thousands of person-hours to produce a substantial piece of bespoke software, such as a system for handling all the transactions at its automatic teller machines (ATMs, or cash machines).

A smaller organisation may use an outside consultant to develop bespoke software, if they cannot find anything ready made that is suitable.

What are the advantages of using bespoke instead of general–purpose applications software?

There are quite a few advantages in using bespoke applications software:

- Bespoke software should meet the precise needs of the organisation. This is important if the needs are unique.
- Bespoke software will carry out exactly the tasks that the organisation wants. It will cover everything that it asks for, but will not include unnecessary functions.
- The user interface for bespoke software will be designed, in collaboration with the organisation, to meet its preferences.
- The developer of bespoke software will normally be available to provide support when it is new and also as problems arise later.

There are also some disadvantages in using bespoke applications software:

- Bespoke applications software is expensive, as one organisation has to pay all the costs.
- The organisation will have to wait for the software to be developed.
- The organisation may find that the final software is not up to expectations.

What are the advantages of using general–purpose instead of bespoke applications software?

There are also many advantages in using general-purpose packages, and the organisation may have to weigh one against the other:

- General-purpose software is quite substantially cheaper than bespoke software.
- General-purpose software will be available to use immediately.
- Users may already be familiar with the software or with similar packages.
- General-purpose software will have been tested thoroughly by other users, and should be robust.
- The organisation will be able to view and check out the software before it purchases it.
- There will usually be extensive and cheap support available from the software developers, in the form of manuals, phone help desks and websites.

The main disadvantages relate to the tasks that it performs:

- General-purpose software may not carry out all the functions that the organisation needs.
- General-purpose software may include a number of unnecessary functions which might distract the users.
- The user interface may not suit all the users.

Further research – Bespoke applications packages

Find out whether your centre uses any bespoke packages. If there are any, then they will probably be used by office staff rather than by students.

Software configuration

What is software configuration?

Software can often be configured to suit an individual user. Configuration changes can be made both to the appearance of the user interface and also to the way in which it operates. Configuration allows the user to personalise the software so that it matches his or her own way of working. The configuration choices the user makes are often known as *preferences*.

Both system software and applications software can be configured. The information about the user's preferences is stored in a configuration file.

Further research – Configuration files in Windows®

You may not be allowed to do this exercise on a student network at your centre, but may be able to use a standalone computer, or to use your home computer.

Use the search facility on the computer to find all the files containing 'config'. You should find a number that are clearly related to applications that you use.

Older versions of the operating system Windows® have a file called config.sys. This file was used as the initial configuration when it booted up.

Later versions of Windows® store configuration data in a configuration file called the registry. The registry is a database which holds information about which files are to be loaded at startup, and identifies the drivers for devices like printers. It also contains data about all the file types that are used and about the layout of the desktop.

Next, search for files with .ini as the filename extension (the second part of the filename). These initialisation files are also configuration files for applications software. Figure 1.14 shows some of the .ini files that you might find.

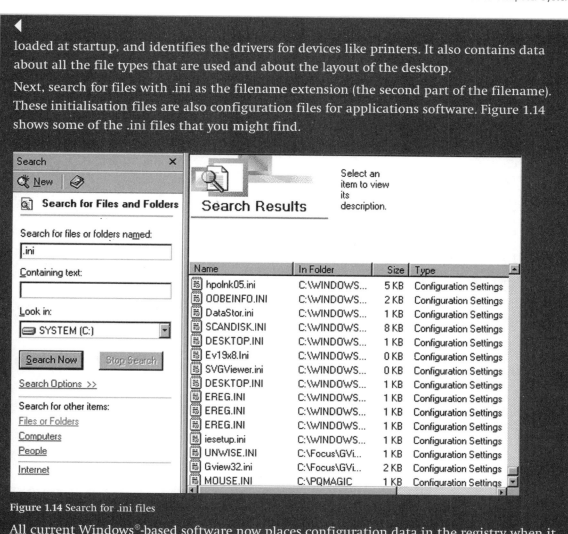

Figure 1.14 Search for .ini files

All current Windows®-based software now places configuration data in the registry when it is installed. Any .ini files that you find are probably for old software packages or for non-standard applications.

How can I configure the operating system?

Users can make many changes to the configuration of their own standalone computer systems. But when a desktop computer is linked into a network, the network administrator may limit the changes that can be made. In this section we will assume that you have full access to all the configuration options on a computer.

All the examples refer to Windows®, but you should find similar options available to you if you use another operating system. Different versions of Windows® do vary in the way they present options to users, so the illustrations may not exactly match what you can see on your computer system.

The safest way to configure the operating system is to use the Control Panel, which can be found by selecting Settings in the Start menu. The Control Panel contains a number of programs which allow you to configure different aspects of the system. You are warned not to make any changes unless you are sure you want to do them.

Check your understanding – Using the Control Panel in Windows®

Try these out in the Control Panel in Windows®.

1. Select 'Display'. This allows you to:

■ select a background for the desktop – known as a wallpaper – or create a pattern of your own.

■ select and configure a screen saver, from the ones available.

■ choose colours, fonts and icons to be used in each window.

■ place a web page on the desktop instead of wallpaper (only advisable if you have broadband access to the Internet).

■ Select the screen resolution – this is the number of pixels (dots of colour) that make up each screen. Larger screens can comfortably display more than smaller ones. But users may also prefer to have more or less information displayed at one time, or may find the text in one setting easier to read. Most people use the settings 800 by 600, or 1024 by 768.

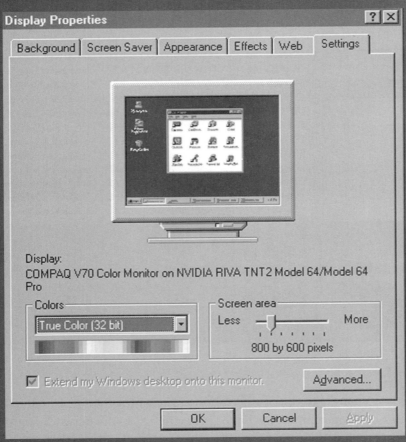

Figure 1.15 Display properties in Windows®

2. Select 'Desktop Themes' in the Control Panel. This extends the Display options and lets you:

■ select backgrounds, screen savers, fonts, colours and icons that look good together

■ assign sounds to events

■ select a range of personalised pointers.

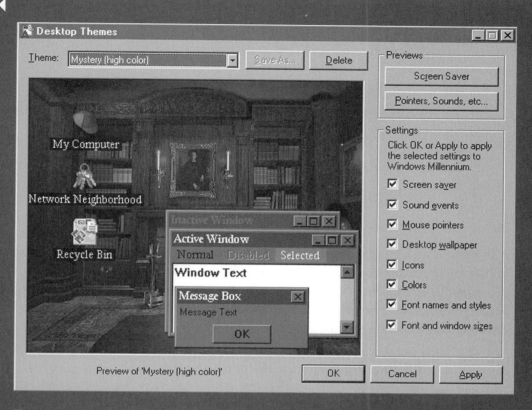

Figure 1.16 Mystery – a desktop theme in Windows®

3. Select 'Date/Time' from the Control Panel to:
   - adjust the date and time that is displayed on screen
   - change the time directly to another time zone.

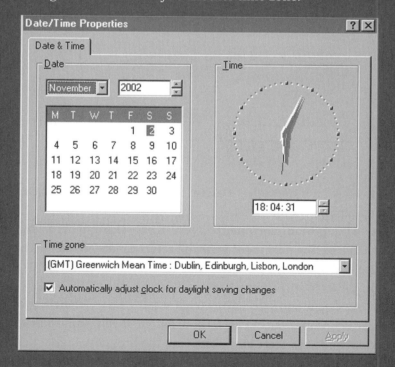

Figure 1.17 Setting the date, time and time zone in Windows®

How can I change the appearance of the user interface from the desktop?

You can make a limited number of configuration changes directly from the desktop. Here are some ideas:

■ You can move the icons around on the desktop.

■ You can drag the Taskbar (at the bottom of the screen) and any of the toolbars to the top or sides of the desktop.

■ You can go directly from the desktop to many of the Control Panel options. For example, if you double click on the time (in the bottom right corner) the Date/Time properties box will open.

How can I manipulate shortcuts?

A shortcut is an icon that allows you to go directly to a file without having to search through all the folders in 'My Computer' to find it. You can create a shortcut to a program, to a document or to a folder. If you click on a shortcut it will carry out the most appropriate action – a program shortcut will launch the software, a document shortcut will open the document, and a folder shortcut will display the contents of the folder.

You will find a number of shortcuts on the desktop. A large icon for a shortcut, like this one, displays a small bent arrow to indicate that it is a shortcut.

Figure 1.18 A shortcut icon

When you select **Programs** in the main Start menu, what you actually see are shortcuts to the programs, like the Calculator icon, for example.

Figure 1.19 Shortcuts in the Start menus

You can:

■ *delete a shortcut* – right click on it and select **Delete**. This will not delete the actual software or document, but only remove the shortcut.

■ *create a new shortcut* to an important document – open the My Documents folder and locate the document. Right click on the document icon and select Create Shortcut. The shortcut icon will appear in the folder. You can now drag this to wherever you would like it to be, including the desktop.

■ *copy a shortcut* – right click on it and select **Copy** (Figure 1.20). Go to wherever you want to place the shortcut, right click and select **Paste**. For example, if you want to have a program shortcut on the desktop, go to the Start menu and find the program. Right click and select **Copy**. You can then right click on the desktop and paste the shortcut in place.

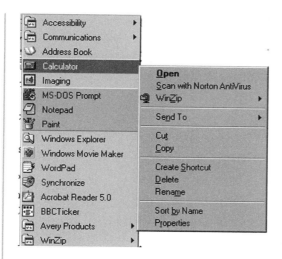

Figure 1.20
Right click on a program in the Program menu, then select **Copy**

Using either dragging or copying and pasting, you can place a shortcut:

- in any folder
- on the desktop (for example, you can copy a program shortcut from the Program menu to the desktop)
- in the Start menu – this is another way of making important files or programs easily accessible (just drag the icon on to the Start button itself)
- in the Quick Launch toolbar on the Taskbar (see Figure 1.22) – drag the shortcut on to the toolbar.

How can I customise the Taskbar?

The Taskbar is the area at the bottom of the screen. It displays a shortcut to each of the documents or software that you have opened – these are the tasks – so you can switch between them. You can make a number of changes to the Taskbar.

- In the Control Panel, select 'Taskbar and Start Menu' to make some changes to its behaviour.

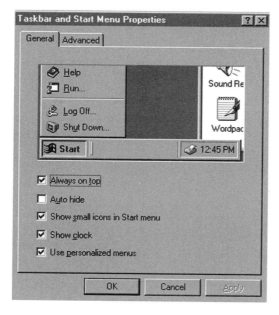

Figure 1.21 The Taskbar and Start Menu properties

■ You can add extra features to the Taskbar. Right click on a blank area of the Taskbar, and then select **Toolbars**. Select **Quick Launch** (if it not already ticked). This useful toolbar holds shortcuts to programs that are frequently used. You can delete some of the shortcuts and add others of your own if you like.

Figure 1.22 The Quick Launch toolbar in the Taskbar

■ If you are using a large screen you may want to add other toolbars to the Taskbar. You can enlarge it by dragging it upwards. Right click and select **Toolbars** to choose other standard toolbars or to create your own. Note that the Links toolbar contains the Internet links that you may have added to the Links folder in Favourites.

Figure 1.23 Good use of the Taskbar

Check your understanding – Configuring the desktop

Can you suggest some improvements that could be made to the desktop display on the computer system you use at your centre? Do you know how to make the changes?

How can I configure general-purpose applications software?

Many business-applications software packages are built to the Windows® standard. These include Microsoft® software as well as software produced by other companies. That means that many of the configuration options you select in Windows® will also affect the applications. For example, your choice of colours, fonts, etc. that you make in Display and Desktop Themes will also be active in the applications.

Some applications (such as most games, as well as some specialist software) are not built to the Windows® standards. These may or may not allow you to change how they appear.

All the examples here will relate to widely used Microsoft® software, but you might like to check how much applies to other applications.

How can I change toolbars in applications software?

A toolbar contains a set of icons representing options that the user can choose from. One or more toolbars often appear at the top of the window. Toolbars that 'float' anywhere on the screen are known as *toolboxes*.

Figure 1.24 Typical toolbars in Microsoft® Word

Here are some changes that you can make to toolbars or toolboxes:

■ You can move a toolbar, or detach it from the top of the window and change it into a toolbox. Click on the small bar at the left edge of the toolbar and drag it to wherever you want it to go. Move it back to the top of the window to turn it back to a toolbar.

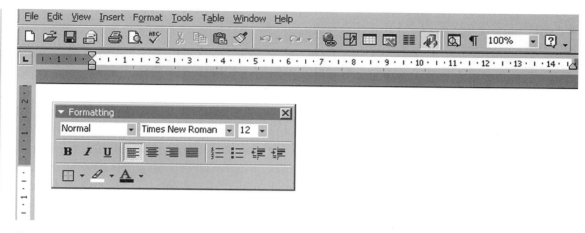

Figure 1.25 The Formatting toolbar is now a floating toolbox

- You can add extra toolbars from the selection that are offered. Right click anywhere on one of the toolbars, then select the toolbars you are likely to need. Do not overload the screen or there will be little space left for the document. Just choose the toolbars that will help you with your work.

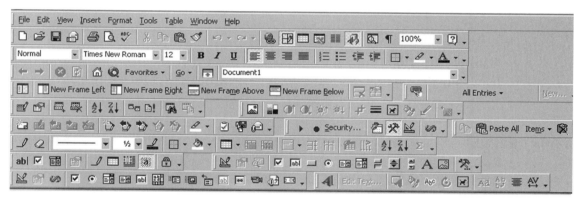

Figure 1.26 Displaying all the toolbars in Microsoft® Word makes the screen very cluttered

- You can change the appearance of the icons on the toolbars. Right click on a toolbar and select Customize. Click on the Options tab for some useful variations.

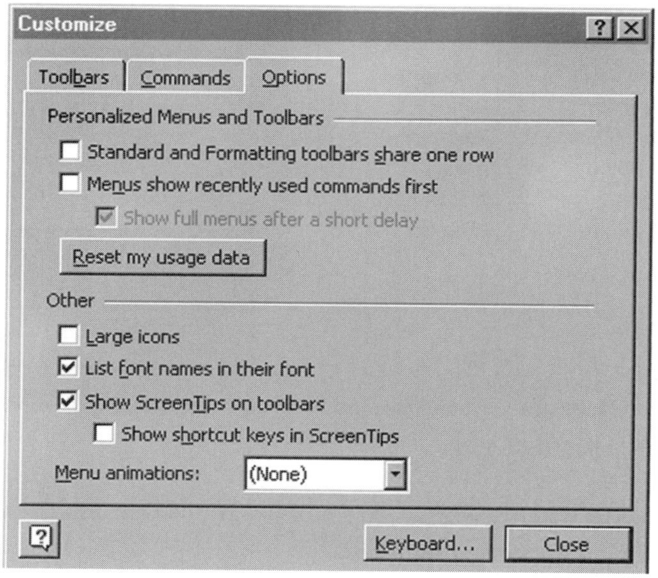

Figure 1.27 Customising the appearance of toolbars

How can I create templates?

Most people who use standard applications at work find that they produce similar documents over and over again. For example, someone may write a monthly newsletter, and use the same layout each month, just varying the content. Also most organisations have a corporate style, that is, a set of rules about what fonts and colours to use and how the logo is to be displayed.

A **template** is a document that has all these features built in, so that it can be used every time a new document of that type is created.

?

What does it mean?

Template – is a document written in a software package that can be used over and over again for a variety of purposes. Typical examples are headed letter stationery or memo formats.

Here are a number of ways of using them:

■ Many packages have built-in templates that you can make use of. Try some of them out by launching the applications software or by selecting **New** from the **File** menu.

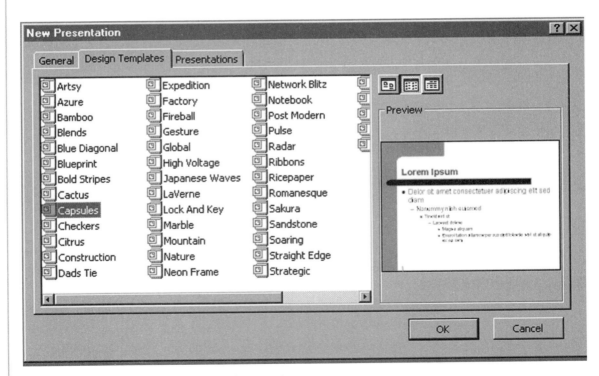

Figure 1.28 Templates provided in Microsoft® PowerPoint

■ Some templates are created by *wizards*, which are small programs that ask the user for information before creating a customised template.

Figure 1.29 The Fax wizard in Microsoft® Word

■ You can create your own templates in many software packages. Open a new document (you can use an existing template as the basis for your own template or you can start with a blank document).

Add all the features that you want in your template. Depending on the purpose of the document, you might want to add a heading, a logo, headers and footers, address and date, columns, etc. You can also add styles to the style list.

You can also add or remove toolbars and save your configuration in the template.

Make sure that you do save it all as a template, then it will appear with the other templates when you create a new document. Usually you do this by selecting **Save As**, then choosing **Template** in the Save as Type textbox.

Case study – Using and creating styles in Microsoft® Word

When you create a document you normally select from the wide range of fonts, font sizes, font styles (bold, italic, underline) and effects (shadow, outline, etc.), font colours and alignment options (centre, left, right, justified). Each combination of these options is known as a *style*.

If you use more than one style in a document then it is irritating to have to recreate a style each time you need it. There are several ways of speeding up this process. You can then add styles to a template for future use.

1. To use the Style list

■ Key in some text and then highlight some or all of it.

■ Click on the down arrow on the Style list box, which is at the left end of the Formatting toolbar (next to the list of fonts).

- Select the style you want to apply to the text.

Figure 1.30 The default style list

2. To add a style to the Style list

- Key in some text and then apply your own choice of font, size, colour, etc.
- Highlight some or all of this text. Click in the Style box and then key in a name for the style you have created. Press return (important!).
- Your new style has been added to the Style list, and can be used anywhere in the document.

Figure 1.31 A new style added to the style list

How can I configure how the applications software operates?

Most software packages offer you a number of other configuration options, usually by selecting **Preferences** or **Options**.

For example, the Internet Options dialogue box in Internet Explorer (found in the Tools menu) lets you select your Home page – see Figure 1.32. This is the page that is opened when the browser is launched. Most users do not realise that they can change this. The Home page can be any page on the Internet, or a webpage that you have created and stored on the hard disk.

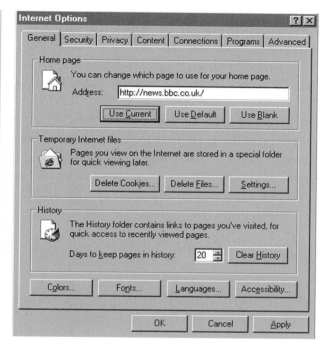

Figure 1.32 The Internet Options box in Internet Explorer

Below is the Options dialogue from Microsoft® Excel. The General tab allows you to identify the default file location. This is the folder where it will initially look for files and save files. You can change this to another folder. You can also specify the standard font to be used on spreadsheets, and how many sheets will be provided in a new workbook.

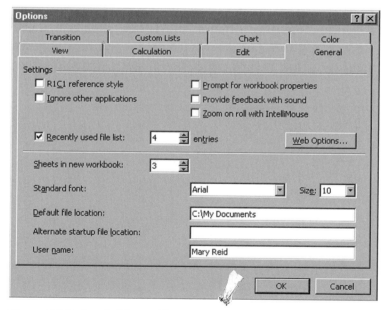

Figure 1.33 Options in Microsoft® Excel

Test your knowledge

1 What is the difference between systems software and applications software?
2 What is an operating system?
3 Why might a business decide to pay for bespoke software rather than purchase a general-purpose package?
4 Why do users like to configure the desktop display on their computers?
5 New versions of operating systems are launched from time to time, but installing them on a large network could be expensive. Can you think of some reasons why an organisation might consider it a good idea to spend money on a new version of an operating system?
6 What are:
   ■ toolbars and toolboxes
   ■ templates
   ■ style lists?

1.3 Hardware specifications

Introduction to hardware

What are the main hardware components in a computer system?

In section 1.1 we looked at logical computer configuration. We saw that a computer system is made up of a number of devices. In this section we will look at the **technical specification** of some of these devices in some detail and we will decide how to put a system together to meet a user's needs.

We saw that the main components that make up a computer system are:

■ Central Processing Unit (CPU/processor)
■ main memory
■ input devices
■ output devices
■ backing store devices
■ storage media
■ connections.

Of these, the input, output and backing store devices are often known as *peripheral devices*, or just peripherals.

What does it mean?

Technical specification – the technical specification of a device in a computer system is a list of its properties. It usually refers to the capacity and/or performance of the device.

What should I consider when choosing a processor?

The majority of desktop and laptop computers have very similar processors installed. They currently fall into three groups:

- Intel Pentium series (Pentium 3, Pentium 4 etc.) and Intel Celeron series
- equivalent processors, such as the AMD Athlon and Duron series
- Apple G series (G3, G4, etc.).

If you buy an Apple system then it will have an Apple processor. On the other hand the Intel Pentium and equivalent processors are virtually interchangeable with each other, and are used by many different computer manufacturers, although they do differ in their performance.

The speed of a processor is measured in hertz, where 1 hertz = 1 cycle per second. This refers to the fetch–execute cycle, which is the process of copying one program instruction from main memory to the Control Unit, then executing the instruction. Today's processors can carry out many millions of cycles per second, so the processor speed is measured in megahertz (MHz) or gigahertz (GHz).

What does it mean?

Performance – performance is a way of describing how well a device in a computer system does its job. This often relates to the speed at which it works.

The speed of the processor is not the only measure of a processor's **performance**. Some processors with slower cycle times are constructed to handle instructions more efficiently, so may actually work through programs faster than processors with higher speeds.

What should I consider when choosing main memory?

Main memory is made up of RAM semiconductor chips. RAM means Random Access Memory, which indicates that all data stored in memory can be accessed equally quickly.

The main property of RAM is its **capacity**, which is measured in Mb or Gb. This is the number of bytes that can be stored in memory whilst the computer system is switched on.

In order for a program to run it must first of all be copied from backing store to main memory. As it runs it creates additional data files; for example, when you load word processing software into memory you then create a document which contains further data. Documents and other data also have to be stored in main memory.

Several programs and their data files can be held in different parts of main memory at the same time. So the capacity of main memory determines how many programs can be loaded, and how many documents you can create.

If you try to load too many programs, or work on too many documents at the same time, you will get a system message telling you that the system is running out of resources. If this happens frequently, then you can add extra RAM to a system, or replace existing RAM chips with larger ones.

You can find out the capacity of the main memory in your system – if you are using Windows® select 'System' in the Control Panel menu.

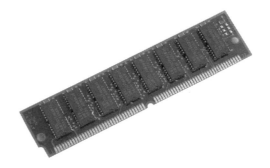

Figure 1.34 A RAM chip

What should I consider when choosing a screen?

The main output device for a computer system is the screen, or monitor. Screens are measured in two ways:

- *Size*: the length along a diagonal of the display area.
- *Resolution*: the number of pixels (colour dots) that it can display horizontally and vertically.

Generally speaking the larger screens give higher resolution and cost more.

There are two main types of screen:

- *CRT monitor* – a Cathode Ray Tube monitor is the traditional type of monitor that is still widely used.
- *LCD screen* – a Liquid Crystal Display gives a completely flat screen and is commonly used for laptops and hand-held systems. LCD monitors can also be used with desktop systems.

LCD screens use far less power than CRT ones, but they do need back lighting. The display cannot be easily seen from an angle. At the moment, LCD screens are considerably more expensive than CRT screens.

Generally LCD screens cost more than CRT screens, and larger screens cost more than smaller ones.

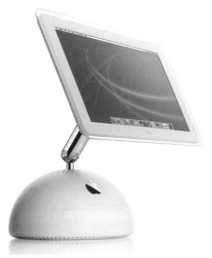

Figure 1.35 An LCD monitor

The quality of the pictures on a screen depend to a certain extent on the resolution of the screen. But of far greater importance is the graphics card that has been installed. A graphics card is, in fact, a second processor that carries out all the calculations needed to display high-quality graphics. It enables the user to change the resolution of the screen (up to the maximum allowed by the screen itself), and the number of colours that can be displayed. The graphics card also handles video and 3D animations fast enough for them to appear realistic.

Further research – Typical technical specifications

These were typical specifications at the time of writing (early 2003). Chose a computer magazine and check these against systems currently on sale.

Device	Capacity	Speed
Processor (CPU)		700Mhz to 3Ghz
RAM	256Mb to 512Mb	
Hard disk drive	10Gb to 80Gb	
Floppy disk drive	1.44Mb	
CD-ROM drive	650Mb	Data transfer speed = 24x to 52x *
CD-RW drive	650Mb	Data transfer speed = 24x to 52x *
DVD drive	4.7Gb to 17Gb	Data transfer speed = 8x to 16x *
Tape drive	8Gb to 40Gb	Data transfer speed = 3 to 12 Mbytes per second, equivalent to 20x to 80x

*The speeds shown are for reading data; writing data is a slower process.

Screen	Size (diagonal)	Resolution
CRT monitor	15" to 21"	1024 × 768 to 2108 × 1536
LCD monitor	12" to 21"	1024 × 768 to 1600 × 1024

Figure 1.36 Technical specifications

What should I consider when choosing a printer?

The most common types of printers used today are:

- *Inkjet printers* – these squeeze tiny bubbles of ink onto the paper to form the characters and images. The quality of the output is measured in dots per inch – more dots per inch give better pictures, but take longer to print. They can print onto a variety of papers, including glossy photo paper. The ink is stored in ink cartridges. Four colours are used – black, cyan, magenta and yellow.

- *Laser printers* – these use the same technology as photocopiers. The laser places an electrostatic charge on a drum to match the image. Toner powder is attracted to the charged areas on the drum, and the image is printed when the paper is pressed against the drum and briefly heated. Colour laser printers use the same colours as inkjet printers, but the paper has to be charged and printed four times, once for each colour.

Laser printers produce high-quality output but cost more than inkjet printers. Colour laser printers are considerably more expensive than black laser printers. Laser printers are generally faster than inkjet printers.

Figure 1.37 A laser printer

When comparing the price of printers it is important to remember the cost of the ink cartridges or toners, and to calculate how often these will have to be replaced.

What should I consider when choosing backing store devices and storage media?

Data is stored on storage media, such as disks and tapes. Main memory holds only the programs and other files that the computer is actually using, and only for as long as it needs them. So all programs and data files have to be stored on a medium so that they can be loaded into memory when needed.

Storage media may be:

- *Read Only Memory (ROM)* – the data is stored permanently and cannot be erased, and no new data can be added. The most common type are CD-ROMs.
- *Recordable (R)* – data is stored permanently and cannot be erased. But new data can be added until it is full up. This is also known as WORM (Write Once, Read Many) technology.
- *Read and write (RW)* – the data can be erased and new data can be added.

Two technologies are used for storing the data:

- *Magnetic* – tiny spots on the surface are set up as individual magnets. The magnetic field of each spot is aligned in one of two directions, which represent the binary values 0 or 1. Magnetic storage is used on tapes and floppy disks.
- *Optical* – tiny pits on the surface represent a binary value 1, whilst flat areas represent 0. The light from a laser reflects cleanly from a flat area but is scattered by a pit. Optical storage is used on CDs.

Here are the main types of storage media:

- *Hard disks* are magnetic, read and write media. They can have a high capacity and are used as the main backing store for virtually all computer systems.

- *Floppy disks (diskettes)* are small, magnetic, read and write media. They can only hold 1.44Mb of data each. Because of their limited capacity they are not used very frequently today.
- *CD-ROM* denotes read-only, optical disks. They can hold up to 650Mb.
- *CD-R* denotes CDs that are recordable. Recording on a CD-R is often referred to as 'burning'.
- *CD-RW* denotes CDs that can also be erased and written to.
- *DVDs* (Digital Versatile Disks) are high-capacity CDs that can be used for a wide range of digital data, including video. They come in plain DVD (i.e. ROM), DVD-R and DVD-RW (also known as RAM) formats.
- *Tapes* are magnetic media mainly used for security purposes. The complete contents of a hard disk may be copied to tape daily, and the tapes stored carefully in case the hard disk is damaged or corrupted. Digital Audio Tapes (DATs) are commonly used, although other formats are available.

Backing store devices are used to read and write data onto storage media (disks and tapes). They are normally known as *drives*. Some drives are designed so that the storage media cannot be removed, whilst others are removable.

- Most drives work with *removable media*. Removable media can be used to transfer data from one computer system to another. New software is often presented on a removable medium, so that users can install it on their own systems. Removable media include floppy disks, CDs and DVDs of all types, and tapes.
- The disks used in hard disk drives (HDDs) are *fixed media* and cannot usually be removed. Hard disks are able to work fast because the individual disks are held in a sealed, dust-free casing. This means that the head that reads and writes the data can be positioned very close to the surface of the disk, without actually touching it. Sometimes hard drives are referred to as internal drives, simply to emphasise the fact that they are placed inside the main tower or desktop unit.

It is useful to compare the speeds of the drives, but this is not as easy as it sounds because of the different technologies used. The speeds of CD and DVD drives can be directly compared with each other. The first CD drives that were produced read the data at 150Kb per second. Today the speed is given as a multiple of the original speed. So, for example, a CD with a speed of 52× reads data fifty-two times faster than 150Kb per second, that is, at 7.8Mb per second.

Further research – Finding out the capacity of storage media on a computer system

You can find out the capacity of the storage media on a computer system that you are using by opening My Computer from the desktop. You will see a list of all the drives. Right click on each in turn to read the properties of the storage medium that is in place.

In Figure 1.38 the hard disk in drive D has a capacity of 27.9Gb, of which 4.09Gb has been used.

▶

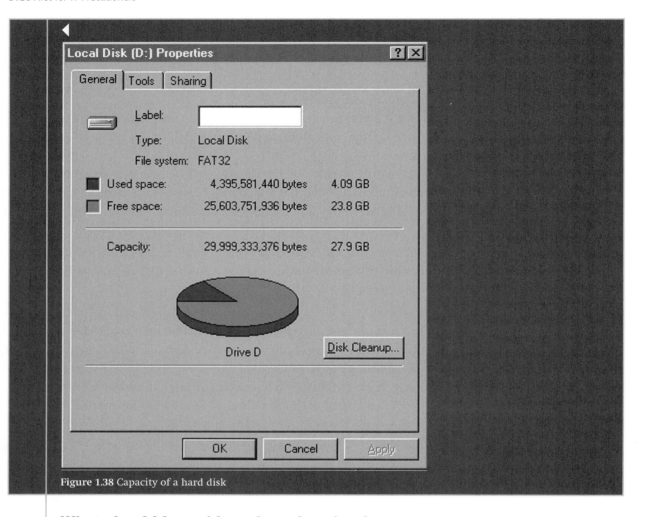

Figure 1.38 Capacity of a hard disk

What should I consider when choosing how to connect a system together?

The various devices that make up a computer system have to be connected to each other. Computers themselves are then connected into networks.

These connections use various types of data transfer. Whatever the method, each consists of:

- A *method* of transferring the binary data. This could be through a cable, made of copper or optical fibres. Alternatively the method could use radio, infrared or microwave signals.
- An *interface*. This consists of a *port*, which is a socket where cables can be plugged in or signals picked up, plus built-in software that controls it.

There are a number of types of connection, including these:

- *Serial connections* use cables that transfer binary patterns in a steady stream from one component to another.
- *Parallel connections* transfer many bits at the same time along a set of parallel wires. If 1 byte (8 bits) is transferred along a parallel cable, each bit will travel along a different wire, so the result will be about eight times faster than using a serial cable. Parallel connections are only used over short distances.

  Some parallel cables are easily recognised by their flat ridged structure. Not all parallel cables look like this, and most bundle the wires together inside an outer casing so that they look much the same as serial cables.

Figure 1.39 A Flat (ribbon) parallel cable.

In the past each device in a computer system had its own direct connection to the CPU.

■ Many devices such as the keyboard and monitor use serial connections. The standard serial interface to connect the CPU to its peripherals is RS232.

■ A parallel connection is often used to connect a printer to the CPU. These usually work with the standard Centronix interface.

Today it is more common for several devices to be linked together in a 'daisy chain'. They then share a single port. Examples include:

■ *Universal Serial Bus* (USB) is a fast serial interface that can replace both serial and parallel ports and can be used with most peripherals, especially the slower ones.

■ *Firewire* is a very fast serial interface that is gaining in popularity.

■ One common fast parallel interface is known as the *Small Computer Systems Interface* (SCSI, pronounced 'skuzzy'). It is used to connect printers and hard disk drives to the CPU through a single SCSI port.

■ *Enhanced Industry Device Electronics* (EIDE) parallel interface is an alternative to SCSI and is widely used with disk drives.

Computers can be connected together to give a *Local Area Network* (LAN). The connections between them can also be of several types:

■ Most of the connections in a LAN use serial cables. The most common standard is *Ethernet*, which is thousands of times faster than RS232.

■ There is a growing use of wireless connections to connect small networks. These use radio signals to carry the data communications, instead of cables. That means that computers can be moved around (within a limited area) and still remain connected to the network.

Computers also connect to the Internet. The Internet is an example of a *Wide Area Network* (WAN). WANs use a variety of connection methods; some make use of public networks. The connection between a computer and the Internet is one of two main types:

■ A connection can be made through a *dialup modem*. The modem has a serial connection to the CPU, which then sends the signal along an ordinary telephone line. Modems usually transfer data at a speed of up to 56,000 bits per second.

■ A *broadband connection* is one that can carry more data than using the traditional dialup method. Broadband connections can carry data at speeds from 512,000 bits per second right up to 600 million bits per second. The most common methods are

    ■ ISDN (Integrated Services Digital Network), which uses a dedicated digital network

    ■ ADSL (Asynchronous Digital Subscriber Line), which works over ordinary BT telephone lines

    ■ *cable* connections provided by the Cable TV companies.

Check your understanding – Specifications of current systems

Find an advertisement or review for a computer system that is on sale at the moment. Analyse and explain the technical specification.

How do I select hardware to meet a user's requirements?

When a user asks for advice in selecting a new system, it is important to understand the user's individual needs. The requirements could include:

- what he or she wants to use the computer for, e.g. to send e-mails, create newsletters, play games, etc.
- the maximum cost
- any specific needs, e.g. disabilities.

These should allow you to identify the *minimum* specification for a computer system.

In practice, it is always a good idea to go beyond the minimum specification. This is because:

- new software and hardware come onto the market all the time, and the person does not want to find it impossible to use them
- once a user has started using a system he or she will discover its capabilities and want to do new tasks with it.

Case study – Systems to suit users' requirements

1 *Problem*: George is the Secretary of a Residents' Association. He wants to buy a standalone computer so that he can write agendas for meetings and letters.

Solution: George needs, as a minimum, an entry-level system with the simplest processor on the market, with basic RAM and hard drive capacity. He would need a CD or DVD drive in order to install the word processing software that he chooses. Once he starts using the computer he will probably become a little more ambitious and want to produce newsletters and other printed material. He might want to spend a little more on a good-quality colour inkjet printer.

2 *Problem*: Margaret is elderly and wants to use the Internet to search the Web and send e-mails to her family.

Solution: Margaret's computer system could be similar to George's with the addition of a modem or broadband connection. She would also benefit from a good-quality graphics card, and a higher resolution screen. Although she may not think of using the computer for other purposes, in the future she may find that she wants to switch to the Internet whilst using other software. More RAM would be a good idea.

3 *Problem*: Asad maintains a database for a small company that tracks down and sells old comic books. The database has grown quite large as it holds details of many comic books over a long period and where they can be found.

Solution: Database software tends to use quite a lot of memory, so Asad needs a moderately fast processor with sufficient RAM and hard disk capacity. He will probably want to print out lists, so will need a fast printer. He may not need colour printing, so a basic laser printer will probably be suitable.

▶

4. *Problem*: Elisha is a garden designer. She uses specialist software to create 3D drawings of her designs so that she can see what they look like from all angles. She also prints these off to give to her customers.

Solution: Elisha needs a high-quality graphics card with a high-resolution screen. To support the heavy use of graphics she also requires the fastest processor she can afford, a substantial amount of RAM and extensive hard disk space. If the graphics are to be printed then she will have to find a printer that produces a suitable quality of output, probably in colour.

Can you draw up a shopping list for each of these users? You will have to look through computer magazines and websites to find the best solutions.

Updating hardware

Why does hardware have to be updated?

Computers are replaced or upgraded quite frequently. At one time the only way a user could improve his or her computing power was by throwing away the old computer and buying a completely new one. That is no longer the case, and most computer systems can be improved by just replacing parts of it.

Software is improving all the time, but more complex software can be run only on more advanced hardware. A user may find that new software works properly only if the system has some or all of these:

- a faster processor
- more RAM
- more space on the hard disk
- a more efficient graphics card
- a larger screen
- a faster Internet connection
- a better quality printer.

In fact, software developers are always pushing the hardware to its extremes, and that in turn creates more demand for better hardware.

At the same time, hardware manufacturers are developing better technologies to match the demand.

Case study – Moore's Law

In 1965 Gordon Moore, the founder of Intel, said that the power of computers doubles roughly every eighteen months. He was originally talking about the number of components that could be fitted onto an integrated circuit – the kind of chip that is used to build processors and RAM memory. This rule still seems to be true today, however we interpret it.

This table shows how the speed of Intel Pentium processors has increased from 1993 to 2002. The speed given is the fastest on the market for that particular year.

1993	Pentium	66Mhz
1994	Pentium	120Mhz
1995	Pentium Pro	150Mhz
1996	Pentium Pro	200Mhz
1997	Pentium 2	300Mhz
1998	Pentium 2	400Mhz
1999	Pentium 3	733Mhz
2000	Pentium 3	1Ghz
2001	Pentium 4	2Ghz
2002	Pentium 4	2.8Ghz

Figure 1.40 Speed of Intel processors

Plot these values on a graph. Do they seem to be obeying Moore's Law?

How can hardware be updated?

The hardware that makes up a computer system can be updated by:

- upgrading some of the components
- replacing some of the components
- adding new components
- replacing the complete system.

A user should always check whether better performance can be achieved by replacing some of the components before committing to a complete new system.

These components can be upgraded:

- *RAM* – if the system is slowing down, or crashing when too many programs or documents are loaded, then the main memory may be too small. Extra RAM memory will improve performance.
- *Hard disk* – if a hard disk is more than 75 per cent full, it will tend to slow down when saving and loading files. Defragmenting the disk may help temporarily, but the permanent solution is to replace an existing disk, or add another one. If a disk is replaced then its contents will have to be copied to the new disk. It is usually simpler to add another disk.

These components can be replaced:

- *Processor* – the processor can be changed for a more recent, and therefore faster, processor.
- *Printer* – the output from a printer can sometimes be improved dramatically by replacing the printer with one that works at a higher resolution, or by switching from inkjet to laser. A new printer may also speed up printing, and allow the user to work with a variety of papers.
- *Screen* – a larger, higher resolution screen may make it easier for the user to work with several documents or programs at the same time.
- *Dialup modem* – switching to broadband will speed up Internet access and provide 24-hour connectivity.

These new components can be added to the system if they are not already in place:

- *CD-RW or DVD-RW drives* – these can be installed in addition to an existing CD-ROM drive. These will allow users to burn their own disks, so that they can transport files to other computers
- *External drives* – there are a number of alternative external drives on the market and these can be used for backing up the system, or for transporting files.

The user may choose to replace the complete system with:

- *Desktop computer* – if the current computer system is very old and becoming unreliable, it may be best to replace it with a new system. The user should always identify his or her minimum needs, then project ahead to allow for future demands on the system. The user should ensure that the system can be easily updated.
- *Laptop computer* – a laptop allows users to take their work with them. It is useful if they want to work away from their usual place of work, or if they need to make presentations to clients.

Test your knowledge

1 What is a technical specification?
2 How do we measure the capacity and the performance of a hard disk drive?
3 What are the two types of screen (CRT monitor and LCD) best suited for?
4 What is the difference between fixed and removable storage media? Why might both be needed in a computer system?
5 Give some examples of where serial and parallel connections could be used in a computer system.
6 Why might a user decide to upgrade a standalone system by adding extra RAM?

1.4 User interaction with computer systems

What is user interaction?

Whenever you use a computer you interact with it through a **user interface**. This is true of both applications and system software.

- *Applications software* – all the software applications that you use, from games to finance packages, are interactive. They give information to the user and they require input from the user.
- *Systems software* – some of the software that is loaded on your computer works invisibly in the background and you rarely need to communicate with it; this is true of some of the core components of the operating system. However you still need to interact with many components of the system, so all operating systems have some kind of user interface.

What does it mean?

User interface – a user interface is the point of contact between a user and the software. It consists of a visual display on the screen, which may be controlled using both the keyboard and a mouse or other device. Some user interfaces incorporate sound as well.

What is a graphical user interface (GUI)?

Graphical user interfaces are used for both applications software and systems software.

Figure 1.41 is an example of a GUI for desktop publishing software.

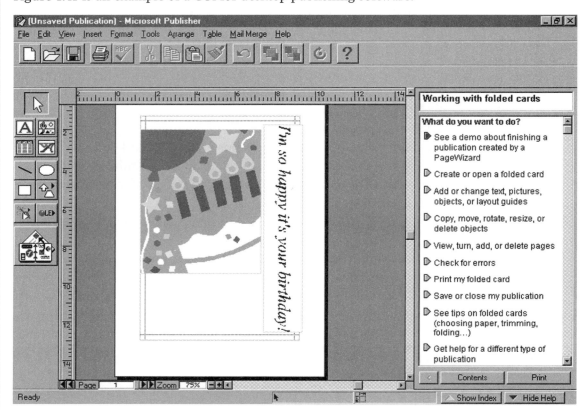

Figure 1.41 A graphical user interface

Many software applications have user interfaces that are similar to this one. It allows the user to carry out a large number of actions, such as printing the document, zooming into the document, selecting drawing tools, viewing help pages, etc. The graphical components help the user to make sense of the options in what would otherwise be a very crowded display.

GUIs are also used for operating systems, and you will probably be familiar with Microsoft® Windows®.

Figure 1.42 The graphical user interface for Microsoft® Windows®

? What does it mean?

Graphical user interface (GUI) – a graphical user interface incorporates graphics into the visual display. The graphics are not simply used as decoration but are used to replace text and to convey meaning to the user.

Operating systems

How does the user interact with the operating system?

The user can interact with the operating system in two distinct ways:

- through a command line interface, such as MS-DOS
- through a GUI, such as Microsoft® Windows®.

Before GUIs were introduced all interaction was through a command line interface.

Further research – MS-DOS command line interface

If you are using a version of Microsoft® Windows® you can switch into a command line interface, and find out what computing was like years ago.

If you select **Programs** in the Start menu you should find MS-DOS Prompt. Click on this and this window will open:

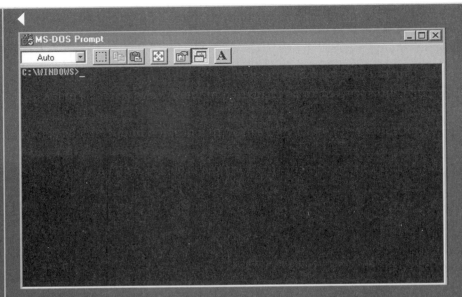

Figure 1.43 The MS-DOS window

There are a few icons at the top of the window, but you have to imagine that they do not exist. Once you move into the main black screen you will find yourself in a world in which the mouse does not work, and there are no icons or drop down menus. To make anything happen at all you will have to enter some commands from the keyboard.

Before you start you need to know that folders are referred to as *directories*. A directory inside another one is called a *subdirectory*. You will notice that you are in the Windows® directory on the C drive.

Try keying in these commands:

■ **DIR** – this is short for Directory, and is the command to list all the files in the current directory. The screen will scroll rapidly as the details of all the files and subdirectories are displayed. At the end of the list the system will state how many files and subdirectories there are in the Windows® directory.

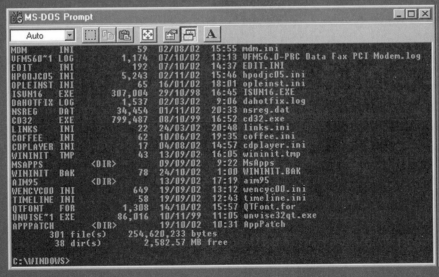

Figure 1.44 A directory listing in MS-DOS

- **DIR /P** – this will slow down the display and allow you to read the information one screen at a time.
- **CD HELP** – CD stands for Change Directory. You may have noticed a subdirectory called HELP. This command opens that directory. Use DIR /P to see its contents.
- **CD ..** – this changes the directory to the *root directory*, which is the main directory for the C drive itself.
- Most of the files are datafiles rather than programs. The filenames for programs end with .exe. To run (execute) a program you have to find it in a directory and then key in the first part of the filename.
- **EXIT** – to leave MS-DOS.

Can you work out how you could carry out all these commands in Windows®?

How have the user interfaces for operating systems developed?

Years ago computer systems were all managed by computer professionals, known as administrators. They would configure and control the operating system on a large and expensive 'mainframe' computer. The administrators were trained to use a command line interface and had no problems in remembering the commands.

In comparison, the end users just interacted with the applications software that they could use on their terminals, which were connected to the mainframe. Similar systems are still in use today in shops, where a sales assistant uses a Point of Sales (POS) terminal – the correct name for a cash desk – and does not have to worry at all about the operating system that supports it.

The first desktop computers were introduced in the 1970s and became common in offices and homes in the 1980s. New computer owners found that they were in charge of a complete computer system. Each user had to act as both an administrator and an end user of applications software. So ordinary users had to learn to use the operating system for their computers, which meant that they had to use a command line interface.

The command line interface allowed users to carry out some straightforward system administration for themselves, such as moving, deleting and copying files, managing directories, installing software, installing hardware, selecting and launching applications software.

But the command line interface made many people think that it was difficult to use a computer. It made sense for the computer industry to develop an interface to the operating system that would be easy for a non-professional to use.

When were GUIs first developed for operating systems?

The concept of a graphical user interface was first developed in 1973 by Xerox, for its research Alto computer. It was designed to help a non-technical user work effectively with the operating system. The GUI had a three-button mouse, a black and white bit-mapped display, and windows. This was quite remarkable at the time as all other visual display units could only present text and used command line interfaces. By 1981 they had added clickable icons, dialogue boxes and a high-resolution screen (Figure 1.45).

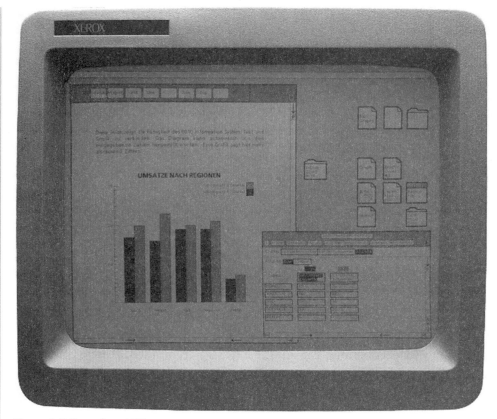

Figure 1.45 Xerox Star, 1981

Two years later Apple introduced the Lisa, which was the first desktop computer system with a GUI. This featured pull-down menus, menu bars and overlapping windows. The Lisa was followed by the Macintosh series (Figure 1.46).

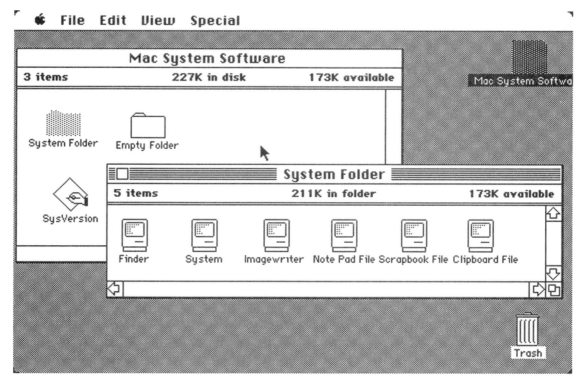

Figure 1.46 Apple Macintosh, 1984

In 1985 Microsoft® launched its Windows® interface. This had windows which could not be overlapped, but it introduced the task bar at the bottom of the screen (Figure 1.47).

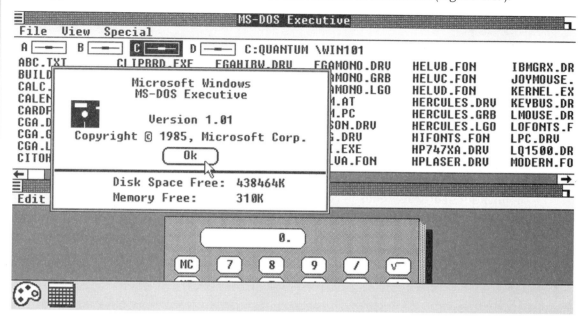

Figure 1.47 Microsoft® Windows®, 1985

Later versions of Windows® introduced many new features and it is interesting to see how much it has changed (Figure 1.48).

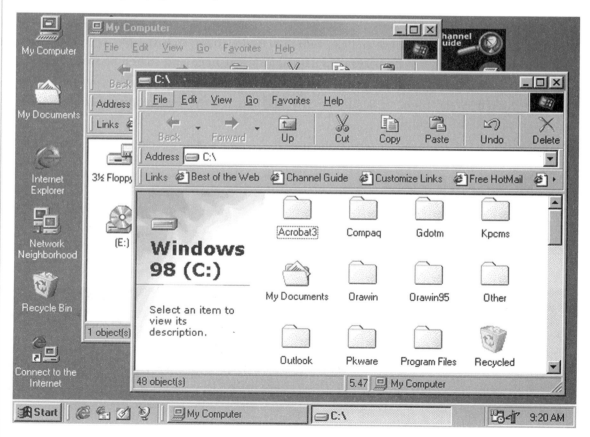

Figure 1.48 Microsoft® Windows®, 1998

Why are GUIs used with applications software?

All the examples so far have been of GUIs for operating systems. As more and more people used desktop computers at work and at home, it was very important that the manufacturers offered systems that people could use without technical assistance.

However software applications were also developed using GUIs. All applications for Apple Macintosh computers were forced to conform with the Apple GUI right from the start. There was more freedom to experiment on the Windows® platform, although Microsoft® products were all developed with the same look and feel as Windows®.

Today there are very many software packages on the market, produced by many different companies. Although software developers can create their own distinctive GUIs, they know that they will be able to sell more if the software is easy to learn. So most business applications software tends to conform to a fairly standard presentation, largely based on the style of Microsoft® Windows®.

Today end users expect all software to be **user friendly**. They want to spend their time using the computer to do the tasks they have planned; they do not want to waste any more time than necessary in learning how to use it.

What does it mean?

User friendly – an interface is user friendly if the intended user can use it easily.

How do GUIs support multi-tasking?

Modern GUIs usually support **multi-tasking**. That means that the user can launch more than one application at a time and can switch between them. For example, you may start writing a document in a word processor, then open a spreadsheet, and switch between the two.

The GUI for an operating system makes it easy to identify which software is launched and to switch between them. In Windows® the Taskbar, and the facility to *minimise* windows, both support multi-tasking.

Multi-tasking is made easier for the user if the applications packages have similar GUIs.

What does it mean?

Multi-tasking – the ability to hold several programs and data files in memory simultaneously, so that the user can switch between one task and another.

Check your understanding – Multi-tasking

In Windows® the Taskbar displays shortcuts to all the documents that are currently open. Each of these represents a different task. All of these documents, and the applications software they are using, are being held in memory at the same time.

Windows® supports multi-tasking, so the user can switch between one task and another.

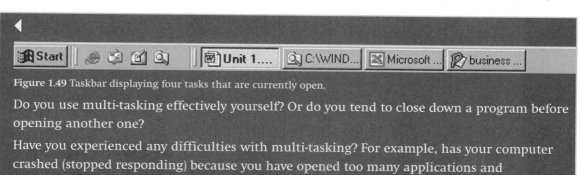

Figure 1.49 Taskbar displaying four tasks that are currently open.

Do you use multi-tasking effectively yourself? Or do you tend to close down a program before opening another one?

Have you experienced any difficulties with multi-tasking? For example, has your computer crashed (stopped responding) because you have opened too many applications and documents?

User categories

What kind of users are there?

Computer users fall into three broad categories:

- *end users* who use applications software
- *technical users*, such as administrators, who work with operating systems
- *software developers*, such as programmers, who create programs.

All three types are users of the computer systems, although they all interact with computers in different ways. In a work environment, users will not usually stray from one category to another. Most of the users in an organisation will be end users, and they will not be expected to do any programming or to carry out any technical tasks.

Today many people own computers for their own personal use, and they have to act both as end users and as administrators. However, they would not normally act as software developers.

What is an end user?

Whenever a person uses applications software he or she is working as an end user. Today we do not expect end users to have any technical skills in managing their computer systems. Instead they should be able to concentrate on their business tasks, using a computer as a tool.

How do end users interact with the operating system?

An end user is rather like a car driver. The normal driver does not need to understand car mechanics in order to use the car successfully. But the driver does have to do some simple maintenance tasks, like filling it with petrol, checking and topping up water and oil, and pumping air into tyres.

In the same way the end user may have to do some simple maintenance with the 'engine' of the computer – the operating system. They can:

- launch applications software
- set up new directories
- move or delete files
- configure the display.

End users almost always use GUIs to carry out these tasks.

Check your understanding – End users and maintenance

Use the GUI-based operating system that you are familiar with and show how the GUI helps you to carry out maintenance tasks. Think how this might compare with a command line interface.

What is a technical user?

The technical users look after all the computer systems in an organisation. Most companies run a network, so the technical staff will be responsible for managing the network as well as all the individual desktop computers linked to it. In order to do this they carry out a number of tasks.

- They *maintain the computer systems*. This includes configuring the operating system, setting up user accounts, ensuring that data is backed up, preventing unauthorised access and viruses, maintaining supplies for peripherals (e.g. printer paper), and dealing with day-to-day problems with hardware and software.
- They *plan and carry out changes*, by installing new hardware and software, and planning major upgrades.
- They *support end users*, often by providing a helpdesk for end users.

A number of job titles are used when referring to the technical staff who maintain computer systems:

- A *network manager* (or system manager) is in charge of the network and its administration, and will plan and manage any large upgrade projects.
- An *administrator* (or systems administrator, or network administrator) is a computer professional who works directly with the network operating system to ensure that the network functions as intended.
- A *technician* carries out the day-to-day maintenance tasks with hardware and software. He or she may check and configure individual desktop computers, install new hardware and software, check the connections, and provide help to users.

In a small organisation one person may carry out all three roles.

How do technical users interact with the operating system?

Technical users work directly with operating systems. This will normally mean configuring the network operating system as well as the operating systems running on each of the computers that make up the network.

In this unit we have been concentrating on operating systems for single desktop computers. If you study Unit 15 you will learn more about network operating systems.

Many network operating systems use GUIs, but technical users often like to use the command line interface instead. Many find that it is quicker to enter a command than to search through a menu for an option.

One of the jobs of an administrator is to set up and maintain 'user accounts' on the network. Each user in the organisation will be allocated a personal user identification (ID), and a password associated with it. For security reasons the user will be able to change the password.

The administrator will assign 'access privileges' to each user, so that the user will be able to access only certain files on the network. This means that each user will be barred from using some of the applications software and will be able to use only the datafiles that he or she has created or agreed to share with others. In particular, most users will not be able to make any configuration changes to the network operating system, or even to read most operating system files.

The technical staff will be the users with the highest level of access privileges. They will be able to read and change many aspects of the system. Administrators become very skilled at managing and troubleshooting network operating systems.

What is a software developer?

A software developer designs and creates new software by writing programs in a programming language. Applications programmers write applications software and systems programmers write systems software.

You will learn more about programming if you study Units 5 and 20.

How do software developers interact with the operating system?

All programs have to interact with the operating system, so the people who write the programs do have to understand how the system works. In particular, they often need to know the command line instructions in some detail, as these may have to be incorporated into their programs.

Test your knowledge

1 What is
- a user interface
- a graphical user interface
- a command line interface?

2 Why do we need good user interfaces for
- operating systems
- applications packages?

3 What features are available in the GUI for a current operating system that were not to be found in earlier versions?

4 What do we mean by multi-tasking? How can multi-tasking help the end user?

5 What tasks are done using the operating system by:
- end users
- programmers
- technical staff?

 Assessment tasks

This section describes what you must do to obtain a Merit grade for this unit.

A Distinction grade may be awarded if your work demonstrates a deeper understanding of the topics and is of a higher quality. The highlighted sentences indicate the quality of work expected at Distinction level.

How do I provide assessment evidence?

Your evidence will either be all in the form of a written report, or may be a mixture of the following:

- written reports
- answers to set questions
- printouts from software packages.

You could also present some of the material in a presentation, in which case you could include witness statements as well as printouts.

All your evidence should be presented in one folder, which should have a front cover and a contents page. You should divide the evidence into four sections corresponding to the four learning outcomes.

Task 1

Learning outcome 1 – Demonstrate an understanding of basic computer principles

1 Write notes to show that you understand:
   - how binary patterns are stored and transmitted in a computer system
   - how binary patterns can represent different types of data, including numbers and characters.
2 Carry out some calculations (provided by your tutor) to show that you can:
   - convert binary patterns to integer denary numbers and vice versa
   - convert binary patterns to hexadecimal numbers and vice versa
   - convert integer denary numbers to BCD and vice versa
   - convert denary numbers to hexadecimal numbers and vice versa.
3 Draw and label a block diagram showing the components of a basic computer system. Add labelled arrows to show the data flows between the components. Hint: do not simply copy this out of this book!
4 Think about any common use of a computer system, such as using a graphics package to design a logo. Using this as an example, explain the role of each component in your diagram. You need to think about what each component is used for during this activity.

To obtain a Distinction grade, you should make sure that you show in your diagram the components that make up the CPU and that you explain what they do.

Task 2

Learning outcome 2 – Demonstrate an understanding of the functions of software

1 State the general role of software in a computer system.
2 Using examples, explain the role of an operating system.
3 Using examples, explain the role of applications software.
4 Write down a list of general-purpose software packages that you are familiar with. For each one, describe its type (spreadsheet, word processing, etc.) and its purpose. You may like to present this information in a table.
5 Explain the advantages and disadvantages of using general-purpose rather than bespoke software.

Task 3

Learning outcome 3 – Interpret computer hardware specifications

To carry out this task you need the technical specification for a computer system. You may be able to find one in the sales literature of a computer supplier, but do make sure that it has enough detail. Alternatively, you should find a full technical specification in the documentation supplied with a new computer system.

Write a guide that explains the technical specification of a computer system. You should write the guide with the needs of an ordinary, non-technical user in mind.

> To obtain a Distinction grade, you should also list a range of software applications, and for each one you should select and justify the technical specification of a computer system that could run it. Make sure you select a wide range of software that requires different computer power and capacity.

Task 4

Learning outcome 4 – Describe how various categories of user may interact with computer systems

1 Explain the difference between a command line interface and a graphical user interface for an operating system.
2 List some maintenance tasks that a user would do by using the operating system. For each one, explain the advantage of using a GUI approach.
3 You have to configure the appearance and operation of a general-purpose software package to meet particular user needs. To do this:
   - Identify the user that you are working for. This could be a specific person that you know, or could be a type of user, such as students taking this course.
   - Identify the software package that you will be configuring.

■ Configure the package to meet the user's needs. You should pay attention to the layout and appearance of the user interface. You should also configure any preferences and other options that affect how the software operates.

4 Explain why users might need to update their hardware and operating systems. You should refer to the software packages that users might want to use, and explain why they might affect the choice of hardware and operating system.

5 Select two or three different categories of user. For each one, write down a list of tasks that he or she might do that would involve working with the operating system.

To obtain a Distinction grade, you should expand your answers to show that you can:

6 In (1) and (2) above, describe the development of operating systems from MS-DOS through to today. Explain how computer usage has been improved and extended, using a range of software applications as examples.

7 In (3) above, also configure the desktop of a GUI operating system to meet the user's needs. This should include application shortcuts.

UNIT 2: USES OF INFORMATION TECHNOLOGY

Success in this unit

What are the learning outcomes?

To achieve this unit you must:

- describe the development of information and communication technology
- use a range of general and specialist software applications
- present information on legislation, health and safety, and security
- evaluate the uses of software applications.

How is this unit assessed?

This unit is internally assessed. You must provide evidence in the form of a variety of documents that show that you meet the learning outcomes.

How do I provide assessment evidence?

Your evidence will probably be a mixture of the following:

- written reports
- printouts from software packages
- witness statements
- observation sheets.

All your evidence should be presented in one folder, which should have a front cover and a contents page. The section headed *Assessment tasks* towards the end of this unit gives you more detailed advice about how to prepare for the assessment.

Introduction

About this unit

In this unit you will be finding out how **Information and Communication Technology (ICT)** is used in industry and commerce. You will learn how computers and other technologies have affected the way businesses are run, and how ICT has encouraged the development of completely new industries.

This unit is not about how people use ICT at home. So you will not, for example, be looking at software that is sold solely for home or educational use, such as games or learning packages.

? **What does it mean?**

IT and ICT – the terms Information Technology (IT) and Information and Communication Technology (ICT) are widely used and mean much the same. Both refer to the use of modern electronic (digital) technologies to store and communicate information. They cover all the hardware and software that make up computer systems, and include a wide range of computer networks, including the Internet.

Will I use software packages?

Yes. In order to understand how ICT is used it is essential that you learn to use all the basic packages that are used in industry and commerce. You should also experience a number of specialist packages; some of these you will be able to use directly and some you will have to observe in use by others.

If you have taken IT courses in the past you will probably be familiar with some of the material. However there is always more to learn, so you should make sure that you have really mastered all the techniques described in this unit.

Before you start, you should check which business applications are available on the systems at your centre. Although you may want to use additional software on a computer at home, your assessor will want to monitor your work, so you need to discuss how this can be achieved.

2.1 The development of Information and Communication Technology

Development of computers

How did computers begin?

The first fully programmable electronic computers were built just after the Second World War in Britain and the United States. They were very large and expensive machines, often filling complete rooms and requiring constant maintenance by a team of technical staff.

During the war early computers had been used to decode encrypted military messages. Afterwards engineers used them to carry out complex mathematical calculations. It was not long before computer designers realised that they could also be used to store other kinds of information. Once each letter of the alphabet had been given a standard computer code it became possible to store any form of text.

Since then computers have been used to store data about the pixels (dots of colour) that make up pictures and also data about small samples of sound. Today there is very little information about the real world that cannot be represented as a computer code.

All computers can be programmed. A program is a series of instructions to the central processing unit of a computer which enable it to input data and then to manipulate and generate useful output. One consequence of the growth of computers has been the creation of a whole new industry devoted to the development of software.

How have computers developed?

At first computers were found only in universities and other research establishments. In the 1950s some far-seeing commercial companies had begun to see how they could be used to speed up laborious clerical tasks. However computers remained very large, expensive and beyond the reach of most companies until the invention of the microchip in the 1960s. Computer engineers were able to imprint thousands of circuits on to a small sliver of a glassy substance called silicon, and this meant that computers could be reduced dramatically in size. Smaller affordable computers that could fit on a desk became known as *desktop computers*.

Many millions of desktop computers were sold worldwide during the 1980s. In many organisations these were networked together to form powerful systems, which were managed by technical staff. However in many small businesses a few **standalone computers** were bought for the use of non-technical administrative staff, who were sometimes defeated by the complexity of the operating systems. The development of systems to support such users resulted in the graphical, intuitive user interfaces (such as Windows®) which we are familiar with today.

What does it mean?

Standalone computer – a standalone computer is one that is not connected permanently to other computers in a local area network.

What about the 'communications' in ICT?

Most computers used in businesses today are linked to other computers in a network. Desktop computers are usually part of a local area network (LAN), which enables them to share the use of software and databases, and to communicate with each other through internal e-mail. Computers on a LAN can also share hardware devices such as printers.

Computers on a local area network may also have a **communications** link through to the Internet, which is a massive worldwide network. Standalone computers can be linked into the Internet using a temporary connection through a phone line. Even portable hand-held and laptop computers use the Internet via a mobile or landline phone.

What does it mean?

Communications – communications (in ICT) refers to the signals that are sent from one computer to another in a network.

Further research – Developments in ICT

Use books, newspapers and the Internet to find out about how ICT has developed, especially in the last ten years.

Speak to people who have been using IT in their work for ten years or more and ask them about the changes they have experienced. You should ask about changes in both the hardware and the software.

Contribution of ICT to industry and commerce

What are industry and commerce?

This may seem like an obvious question, but you do need to be clear about a number of words and phrases that we will be using.

A **business** is any organisation that provides goods or services to customers. We use it in the broadest possible way, so that covers all kinds of industry as well as commerce.

What does it mean?

Business – a business is any organisation that provides goods or services to customers.

Products are the goods or services provided by businesses. The term 'goods' usually refers to physical objects, such as clothes, electronic devices or even complete buildings. 'Services' on the other hand are not objects that can be picked up and taken away, but they include the offerings of businesses like banks, travel agents and hairdressers.

? **What does it mean?**

Product – products are goods or services.

Industry usually refers to businesses that actually produce the goods or services that are then sold to customers.

? **What does it mean?**

Industry – an industry is a business that makes goods or services.

A *manufacturing industry* is a business that makes and assembles physical goods from raw materials. A factory is often used to manufacture goods; for example, when cars are assembled from components in a factory they form part of the motor industry. Some industries do not use traditional factories to make their products; for example, farming can be considered a manufacturing industry as it produces food products.

A *service industry* is one that creates services that can be sold to customers. It is as much an industry as a manufacturing industry, even though it will not use a factory. For example, an tour operator may put together a holiday package, which will include flights, hotel accommodation, meals and excursions. The package is a service that can be sold to customers, like any other product. Similarly, an insurance company will create a travel insurance policy and will then offer this product to travel agents to sell to their customers.

When we use the term '*commerce*' we usually mean businesses that buy and sell goods and services. This includes all kinds of shops, as well as large companies that import and export goods. It also includes all the places where a customer can buy a service.

Some organisations, such as music businesses, have both industrial and commercial sections. The industrial section will create and record music, whilst the commercial section will run shops where the music is sold. These are often run as separate companies within the one organisation.

How is ICT used in industry and commerce today?

Industrial and commercial businesses all have to carry out many procedures. Many of them can be done more efficiently using ICT.

In industry:

- keeping records of materials held in stock that will be used to make products
- keeping records of products that have been manufactured
- scheduling production
- warehouse control
- designing products and methods of production.

In commerce:

- keeping records of products in stock or services ordered
- customer records
- sales
- handling complaints – customer relations.

In both industry and commerce:

- general word processing of letters, reports, agendas, etc.
- accounts
- budgeting
- marketing – preparing leaflets and advertisements
- payroll
- staff records
- staff rotas.

What are the benefits of ICT to industry and commerce?

Industry and commerce provide goods and services to customers. All businesses have to pay for staff, for the costs of the buildings they use, and for all the expenses involved in running a business, including ICT. Industries must also buy in the raw materials and components from which they make products, and also the machinery used in manufacturing. A business can survive only if it manages to sell its products or services so that it raises sufficient income to cover all the costs and to make a profit. ICT is useful to a business only if it makes it more successful.

So a business may decide to invest in ICT for one or more of these reasons:

- ICT can help a manufacturing industry *to increase the number of products* it makes. By investing in new computer-controlled machines, a business may be able to produce more products in the same time and with the same number of staff. Of course, this will be profitable only if they then sell enough products to more than cover the cost of the new technology.
- ICT can help a commercial business *to provide better services to customers*. For example, an insurance broker offers advice to people who need insurance for their car or house, or for any other purpose. They will probably use an extensive database of all the types of insurance offered by many insurance companies. This will help them to find the best deal for their clients.
- ICT can enable a business *to carry out its administrative tasks more efficiently*. This could mean, for example, that orders could be processed quicker and that mistakes (and complaints) could be avoided. As a result fewer staff might be needed to do the same amount of work, so the costs could be brought down. Alternatively, the staff time that has been freed up can be used to increase the business.

How are working patterns affected by ICT?

The use of ICT has changed the way in which people work and the skills they need.

- *IT skills* – most employees today need to be able to use IT. Older staff in many organisations have had to learn completely new skills, and some find this difficult. IT was introduced into the National Curriculum so that all young people now enter the world of work with basic IT skills.
- *Life Long Learning* – the growth of computer technology means that most people will have to carry on learning new skills throughout their working life. As a result, businesses have had to provide more training than they did in the past, and the concept of 'Life Long Learning' has become commonplace.
- *Growth of service industries* – service industries have grown considerably in the UK, as it is

much easier to provide the office accommodation and ICT, than to build a factory. More people now work in an office than in a factory, so the nature of work has changed.

- *Teleworking and flexitime* – many employees do not always have to be present in the office, for fixed hours from 9am to 5pm. Some work can be done at home or in a local business centre, using portable computers with communications links into the organisation's network. This is known as *homeworking* or *teleworking*. The use of e-mail means that messages can be left for colleagues who can deal with them when convenient, so employees can work flexible hours (flexitime) to fit in with family and other commitments.

- *Time-displaced communications* – communications around the world can be made simple through e-mail. In the past someone in the UK might have made a phone call in the middle of the night to a catch a colleague at work in Japan. Today an e-mail can be sent one afternoon and the reply read the next morning.

- *Virtual conferencing* – people do not always have to be in the same room in order to hold a meeting. Telephone or Internet conferencing can be used, allowing people to speak to each other, or post comments in real time in a chat room.

Further research – Using ICT at work

Ask people you know how their work has been affected by the use of ICT, especially over the last ten years or so.

Test your knowledge

1 What do these mean?
- business
- industry
- commerce
- product
- goods
- services
- service industry.

2 How can ICT enable a manufacturing industry to become more successful?

3 What services are available now that could not have been offered without ICT?

4 What do these terms mean?
- Life Long Learning
- flexitime
- teleworking
- time-displaced communications
- virtual conferencing.

2.2 General and specialist software applications

What is a software application?

Software is a general term that covers all kinds of computer programs. As you saw in Unit 1, software is usually categorised as systems software or applications software. Systems software is another name for the operating system and other programs that support it. Applications software covers all the software that enables users to do useful things with a computer, from word processors to games.

A piece of applications software is normally referred to as a *software application*.

What is the difference between general and specialist software applications?

A software application can be designed for a wide range of uses, or it can be designed for specialist use.

A word processing package is used by all kinds of people for all sorts of reasons, so we refer to it as a *general software application*.

In comparison, you may have seen a kitchen planner using a *specialist software application* to design a new kitchen and to plan the layout of kitchen units. The software used is created specifically for this purpose, and cannot be used for any other task, such as designing a garden.

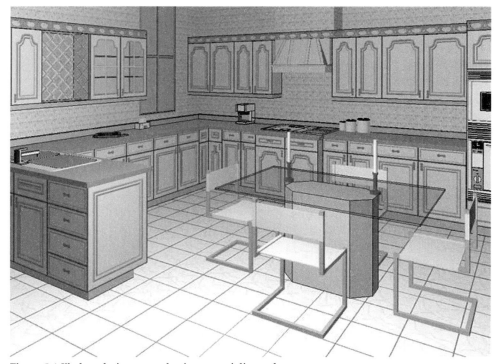

Figure 2.1 Kitchen design created using a specialist package

What is a software package?

An application or *software package* is, as the name implies, an extensive collection of programs which form one software application. This description applies to most general and specialist software applications these days.

A software package will be marketed like any other product under its own trade name. You will be familiar with a number of software packages such as Microsoft® Word, Adobe® Paintshop and Macromedia® Dreamweaver.

The term 'package' implies that the end user will be able to choose which components of the package he or she wants to install. Users would also expect to receive full documentation so that they could use the package straightaway. The documentation may be in the form of a printed manual, but is more likely to be provided in electronic form.

What are files?

When you use a software package you can usually generate a file which you then save on backing storage. You are invited to give the file a name. The software will then add a **file name extension**, which identifies the type of file.

Files produced by a word processor or desktop publishing software are usually called *documents*. Other files can be referred to as *data files*, *image files*, *sound files*, etc.

? What does it mean?

File name extension – a file name extension is a set of characters added to the file name to identify the type of file it is. Here are some examples:

File name extension	File type
.doc	Microsoft® Word file
.htm or .html	Webpage written in HTML
.bmp	Bitmapped image, produced by painting packages such as Microsoft® Paint
.txt	Text file that uses only ASCII characters
.pub	Microsoft® Publisher file

Figure 2.2 File name extensions

General software applications

What are general software applications?

Many types of general application packages are available today. They are designed for non-technical people to help them to carry out common tasks. This makes it possible for computers to be used for very many straightforward purposes every day in all kinds of businesses.

In this section we will be looking at software packages for these types of general software applications:

- word processing
- desktop publishing
- database
- spreadsheet
- graphics
- presentation
- communications.

How can I learn to use general software applications packages?

You should spend some time familiarising yourself with a software package for each of the types of application listed in this section.

If you need some support to do this, then in Unit 8 we will also look in more detail at some of the facilities in Microsoft® PowerPoint. Unit 7 includes a tutorial in Microsoft® Access.

Apart from those, this book will not be giving you detailed guidance on how to use standard business applications. The activities in this section will hopefully encourage you to pick up some new techniques. Do not be afraid to experiment.

If you do need help in learning to use a package, you may be able to use a tutorial built in to the help facility, you may use one of the many books that introduce you to specific packages, or you may find useful tutorials on the Internet.

What are word processing packages used for?

Word processing software is the most commonly used type of package in business. Before word processing facilities became widely available, documents were first hand-written and then typed up on a typewriter. It was very difficult to correct errors once they had been typed, so sometimes a document had to be typed several times before it was correct. Sometimes a document would be dictated by a manager to a secretary who would jot it down in shorthand, before returning to a typewriter to type it up. Typing and shorthand writing were skilled tasks and specialist staff were employed to do them.

Today, many employees use word processors to prepare their own documents. They can create standard documents, such as letters, which they can use more than once, with only minor changes.

Word processors have reduced the time taken to produce standard documents and have reduced staff costs. Many employees outline and then develop a document directly on the computer.

Word processing packages, such as Corel® WordPerfect, Lotus® Word-Pro or Microsoft® Word, can be used to produce:

- letters
- reports
- memos
- articles
- orders and invoices
- notices

- leaflets
- newsletters
- books.

Word processing packages also offer additional features which can be used to create:

- e-mail messages
- webpages
- mailing labels
- mail-merge letters.

Check your understanding – Copying, cutting and moving text in Microsoft® Word

1 How many methods can you use to copy and paste text in Microsoft® Word?
2 What is the Clipboard?
3 What is the difference between copying, cutting and deleting text?
4 Do you know how to move text using drag and drop?

Did your answers to these questions match the ones below?

1 You can copy text by highlighting the words, then:
  - clicking on the Copy icon in the toolbar
  - selecting **View** from the main menu then **Copy**
  - using CTRL+C – to do this, hold down the key marked Ctrl (for 'control') and then key in C (this is known as a hotkey combination)
  - right-clicking on the text and selecting **Copy**.
  Similarly, you can paste text using any one of the four methods. Choose the method that best suits your way of working.
  Can all these methods be used in other packages?
2 When you copy text it is stored in a temporary area of memory called the Clipboard. When you paste text, the last item that was placed on the Clipboard is used. You can, in fact, store more than one item on the Clipboard. To view the Clipboard in Word, select **View**, then **Toolbars**, then **Clipboard**. You can then paste an earlier item by double-clicking on it.
3 When you:
  - copy text it is placed on the Clipboard
  - cut text it is removed from the document and a copy is placed on the Clipboard, so you can paste it elsewhere
  - delete text it is removed from the document and it is not copied to the Clipboard.
4 You can move text to another position in a document by cutting and pasting it. But you can also move it in one step by dragging and dropping. To do this, highlight the text, then click on it again and hold the left mouse button down whilst you move it to its new position.

How are desktop publishing packages used in business?

Desktop publishing software was originally designed for newspapers and magazines. Before the software was available, editors would assemble stories provided by journalists and literally cut out and paste the stories on to a board. They would then add photographs, illustrations, headings and lines.

Desktop publishing offers the same facilities, but in electronic format. Individual contributors can send their word-processed stories to the editor's system, who can then import them into the page layout. Stories, headings and images can be easily edited and moved around to fit the space.

Once a page is ready it can either be printed, or be sent, still in electronic form, to produce a plate for large-scale printing.

Desktop publishing software packages can usually combine material created in a number of other formats and using many different packages. On a smaller scale, a desktop publishing package makes it easy to arrange text and images on a page for a notice, for a leaflet, or for some other kind of publicity.

Desktop publishing software, such as Adobe® PageMaker or Microsoft® Publisher, can be used in business to create:

- newsletters
- notices
- leaflets
- publicity materials
- invitations.

Check your understanding – Formatting text in Microsoft® software

Application packages allow you to change the appearance of text in many ways – this is known as *formatting*. Most Microsoft® packages allow you to format the text using a Formatting toolbar. Packages produced by other companies offer very similar facilities.

You highlight the text you want to format, then select from a wide range of formatting options. The format options can be selected using any one of these methods:

- clicking on icons in the Format toolbar

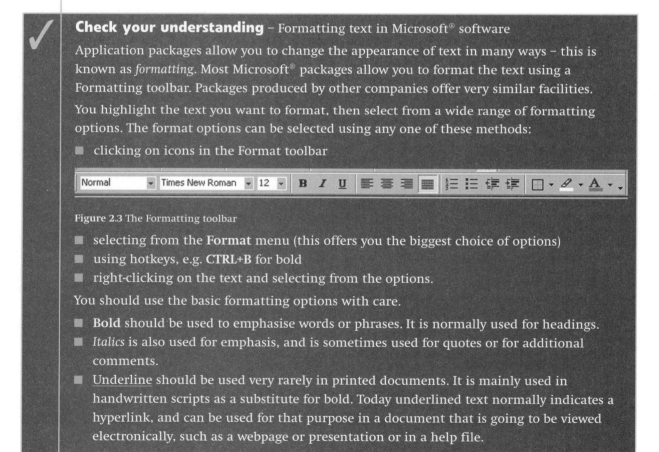

Figure 2.3 The Formatting toolbar

- selecting from the **Format** menu (this offers you the biggest choice of options)
- using hotkeys, e.g. **CTRL+B** for bold
- right-clicking on the text and selecting from the options.

You should use the basic formatting options with care.

- **Bold** should be used to emphasise words or phrases. It is normally used for headings.
- *Italics* is also used for emphasis, and is sometimes used for quotes or for additional comments.
- Underline should be used very rarely in printed documents. It is mainly used in handwritten scripts as a substitute for bold. Today underlined text normally indicates a hyperlink, and can be used for that purpose in a document that is going to be viewed electronically, such as a webpage or presentation or in a help file.

What is a database management system?

Database management systems structure and organise the data used in a database. You can read more about databases in Unit 7.

A database management system, such as Lotus® Approach or Microsoft® Access, can be used in business to store data about:

- stock in a shop or factory
- orders from customers
- orders sent to suppliers
- case notes (for doctors, social workers etc.)
- personnel (employees)
- mailing lists
- logsheets.

What can a spreadsheet package be used for?

Spreadsheet applications were the first business software packages to appear, after word processors, for desktop computers. A worksheet is laid out as a very large table consisting of many cells. Each cell can hold a value or a formula. A formula can carry out calculations based on values held in other cells. Each cell can also be formatted to hold data of a specific type, such as a number, a date or simple text.

Spreadsheets also include graphing and charting functions, which will generate all kinds of charts using data held in the cells. A spreadsheet can be interactive, allowing the user to enter 'what if?' queries. Many users have discovered that spreadsheets can also be used to print forms and other documents that need cells or tables.

A spreadsheet package, such as Lotus® 1–2–3 or Microsoft® Excel, can be used in business for:

- accounts
- budgets
- scientific calculations
- statistical analysis
- simple databases
- interactive 'what if?' calculations
- form designs.

Check your understanding – Formatting data in Microsoft® Excel

You can format numbers so that they appear with a fixed number of decimal places.

- On an Excel spreadsheet, enter a column of numbers like this:

	A
1	3.9
2	240
3	4.389
4	42.01
5	97

Figure 2.4 Numbers entered in Excel

It is difficult to compare the numbers because the decimal points do not appear under each other.

■ Highlight the column, select **Cells** from the **Format** menu, then click on the **Number** tab. Select *Number* in the Category box, and *1* in the Decimal places box.

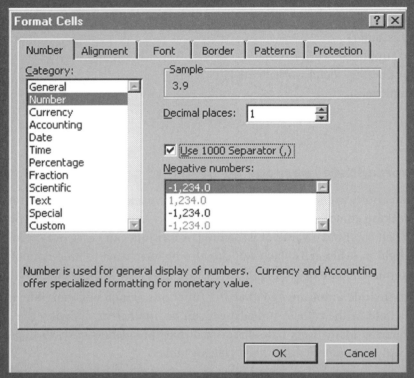

Figure 2.5 The Formatting Cells dialogue box in Excel

The column of numbers will now look like this:

	A
1	3.9
2	240.0
3	4.4
4	42.0
5	97.0
6	

Figure 2.6 Formatted numbers

Note that the integer 240 has been given a decimal place, and that other numbers have been rounded.

■ For money, select **Currency** in the dialogue, then select two decimal places and the £ sign. Of course, you can use other currency signs instead.

	A
1	£3.90
2	£240.00
3	£4.39
4	£42.01
5	£97.00
6	

Figure 2.7 The same figures formatted as currency

✓ Check your understanding – Sorting data in Microsoft® Excel

In Excel, enter a set of numbers into a column, click on one of the cells, select **Data** from the main menu, then **Sort**. Decide whether to sort the data in ascending order (from 1 to 999) or descending order (from 999 to 1). You can use exactly the same technique for sorting text alphabetically, for instance, a list of names.

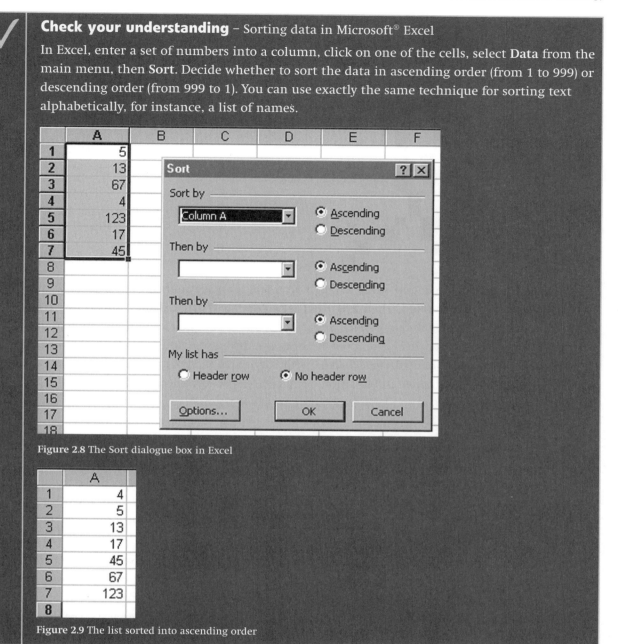

Figure 2.8 The Sort dialogue box in Excel

Figure 2.9 The list sorted into ascending order

How can a package be used to create graphics?

The term *graphics* covers all kind of images stored in digital form. They include photos that have been scanned in or downloaded from a digital camera, or images 'painted' or 'drawn' using graphical software. Clip art is used to describe pre-drawn images that you can use freely in your documents.

Images are stored in two basic formats – bitmap or vector.

- A *bitmap* image is made up of thousands of tiny cells of colour known as *pixels*. If you zoom in on a bitmap image you can see clearly that it is made up of lots of individual square dots (Figure 2.10).

Figure 2.10 Enlarged bitmap image showing the individual pixels

Each pixel has a colour value which is stored as a binary code. If the value for each pixel is stored in 1 byte (8 bits) then 256 different colours will be available – this is just about adequate for line drawings such as cartoons, but is not good enough for photographs. Two bytes (16 bits) per pixel gives over 64 thousand different colours and this is known as High Colour. True Colour can be achieved with 3 bytes (24 bits) per pixel and this gives a choice of millions of colours; in fact, more than can be distinguished by the human eye.

Software packages for creating bitmaps are often known as painting applications. They offer many different pens and brush shapes that can be used for drawing images.

Photographs are stored as bitmaps and they can be edited in painting packages, but specialist photo editing packages are usually used for this purpose.

A *vector* image consists of one or more separate objects, such as lines, circles and other shapes. Each object can be manipulated individually without disturbing the others. For example, a rectangle can be drawn, and then it can be moved around the page, enlarged or reduced in size, filled with a colour, or deleted.

When a vector image is saved, what is actually stored is information about the properties of each of the objects. The properties for each object will specify the shape, position, colour, etc. So a more complex image with lots of objects will require more information than a simpler image. It will therefore need more storage space. Generally speaking, a vector image takes up less memory than a bitmap.

Software packages for creating vector images are often known as *drawing packages*.

It is possible to convert a vector image to a bitmap, by a process known as 'rasterizing'.

Bitmap graphical packages, such as Adobe® Paintshop, Microsoft® Paint and Microsoft® Photo Editor, can be used in business to:

- create 'paintings' and other images
- create and edit photographs.

Vector graphical packages, such as Adobe® Illustrator, Corel® Draw, Macromedia® Freehand and the drawing tool integrated into Microsoft® Office products, can be used to:

- create technical drawings, such as maps and product designs
- create cartoons and other line drawings.

Spreadsheet packages usually have a wizard for creating charts and graphs, which are vector images.

✓ Check your understanding – Creating bitmap and vector images

We will use the Drawing application that is built in to Microsoft® Word as an example of a vector graphics package. In comparison, Microsoft® Paint allows you to create and edit bitmapped images.

An image is a document in its own right and can be saved as a separate file. Bitmapped images often have the file extension .bmp, so for example, a picture you create in Paint may be saved as mypicture.bmp.

- *Bitmapped images* – you can create simple bitmapped images in Microsoft® Paint, or in a number of other more sophisticated painting packages. Paint offers you a number of tools – brushes, pens, and spray cans – as well as lines and freeform shapes. A new colour can be applied to an area with the Fill tool. Once lines and colours have been placed on the image they are fixed and can be removed only by painting over with another colour.

Figure 2.11 The toolbox in Microsoft® Paint

- *Vector images* – you can create vector images by using the Drawing tool in Microsoft® Word. In the **Insert** menu, select **Picture**, then **New Drawing**. A drawing area appears on the page and the Draw toolbar appears.

Figure 2.12 The Draw toolbar built in to Word.

A vector image is made up of one or more individual objects, such as lines, rectangles and textboxes. Try using the **Rectangle**, **Oval**, **Line**, **Arrow** and **Autoshape** buttons. You can change the line and fill colours, and the style of lines and borders, by clicking on an object then using the buttons to the right end of the toolbar.

When you click outside the drawing area the toolbar disappears and the drawing becomes part of the document. However you only have to double-click on the drawing for the drawing tools to appear again. This means that you can edit the drawing at any time.

Figure 2.13 Doodles produced using the Drawing tool

How can presentation packages be used?

Presentation packages, sometimes known as presentation graphics, are used to provide the illustrations for talks and lectures. They offer many useful templates which can be customised by the addition of your own text and images.

Presentation packages, such as Microsoft® PowerPoint and Lotus® Freelance, can be used to:

■ create slides that can be printed on to transparencies
■ create a slideshow that can be projected directly from the computer on to a screen
■ print notes for the speaker and the audience.

? What does it mean?

Presentation – a presentation is an illustrated talk given in a business context.

What are communications applications?

All organisations today use communications software for access to the Internet and often for internal e-mailing as well.

■ A *browser* is a package that displays pages that have been created in web format. Although they are generally used for viewing webpages on the Internet, they can also be used to view pages that can be seen only within the organisation. An intranet (note the 'a') is a set of webpages which are stored on the internal networks of an organisation, so cannot be viewed from the Internet. They can be used to share information across an organisation. The most commonly used browsers are Microsoft® Internet Explorer and Netscape® Navigator.
■ An *e-mail client* is a package that allows the user to read, create and store e-mail messages. By connecting to a network it also handles the communications, either within the organisation's own networks, or externally through the Internet.
Microsoft® Outlook includes an e-mail client along with a number of scheduling tools. Outlook Express is a simpler version which handles only e-mails.

Specialist software applications

What are specialist software applications?

A specialist software application concentrates on one particular task. It is often possible to carry out the task using a general software application, but the specialist software should not only make the task easier, but will also offer extra facilities.

For example, earlier we saw a kitchen design package (page 74). Kitchen designers could use any design package, but the specialist package includes images of standard kitchen units, all drawn to scale. Individual manufacturers have their own versions of packages which will include images of all the units they make, and will also list the costs of all the chosen units. Many of these packages can also generate a picture of the final kitchen, seen from any angle.

You will not see specialist packages advertised as widely as general packages. Instead, they will be marketed directly to the businesses that are likely to want to use them. But if you search on the Internet you should be able to find examples of packages for these types of application:

- Computer Aided Design (CAD)
- Computer Aided Manufacture (CAM)
- design for particular needs
- finance
- project planning
- diaries and appointments.

How can I learn to use specialist software applications packages?

You should learn to use at least one specialist software package. This could be selected from the types listed above, or you may be able to use a different type.

You should also be familiar with a number of other packages, even if you cannot use them directly. You may have the opportunity to watch someone using a specialist package and to ask questions about it. Or you may have to carry out some research by searching on the Internet to find out what is available.

This book will not be providing you with instructions on how to use specialist packages, as there are so many different ones on the market.

What are CAD packages used for?

General vector drawing packages can be used for many tasks, but they do not usually have all the facilities that an engineer or product designer might need. Computer Aided Design (CAD) software includes thousands of pre-drawn standard objects.

CAD packages usually allow the user to zoom in and out, and to pan round an object. Or the object itself can be rotated. Objects can be shown as plans (seen from above), as elevations (seen from the sides) or as 3D images. Sometimes an object is developed as a wireframe and then a surface is added to make it appear realistic.

Each element of a vector drawing is a separate object, and many CAD packages exploit this by allowing the user to add extra data about each object. So, for example, information about the cost of the materials used for each component can be entered and then the package can automatically calculate the total cost of the whole product.

CAD packages, such as AutoCAD® by Autodesk®, are used to design:

- products to be manufactured, such as furniture and cars
- large structures such as bridges and motorways
- integrated circuits (the electronic circuits built on to silicon chips)
- maps.

Case study – English Heritage

English Heritage looks after the world's first cast-iron bridge, which was built in 1779 in Coalbrookdale. In order to keep it in good repair they needed to understand how it was constructed. The only information they had about how it was built was a painting of it under construction. So English Heritage used AutoCAD to create engineering drawings of the bridge.

Figure 2.14 Part of the structure of the bridge drawn in AutoCAD

Use the Internet to find other examples of drawings created in AutoCAD or other CAD packages. If you know someone who uses a CAD package at work then you could ask to view some finished drawings.

How are CAM packages used?

Computer Aided Manufacture (CAM) packages actually control machines that make products. In practice, they often create a cast (or mould). The mould is then filled with material, such as molten aluminium or plastic, and left to set. The object is removed from the mould, and checked carefully. This first casting is known as a *prototype*, and it is often made in a different, and cheaper, material from the final product.

Changes may be made to the design before the final cast is made. The cast can then be used to produce many copies of the product.

CAM packages always include CAD design tools, so are often known as CAD/CAM software. There are many CAD/CAM packages on the market, many of them specialising in particular industries. You may come across SURFCAM by Surfware®, EdgeCAM by Pathtrace®, or software by Delcom®. You may also get a chance to use a CAM simulator package – this is software written for educational use which you can experiment with without actually creating a cast.

CAD/CAM can be used to produce:

- consumer products, from sports shoes to dinner plates
- packaging
- components for cars, aircraft and boats
- tools for use by engineers and surgeons.

Case study – Jaguar badge

The famous lion's head badge mounted on Jaguar cars was remodelled using a CAM process. First a line drawing was done using a package called ArtCAM®.

Figure 2.15 The original line drawing created in ArtCAM®

Then a 3D image of the badge was produced. The company was able to visualise the final badge and suggest minor changes.

Figure 2.16 The 3D image produced by the software from the drawing

Once the design had been agreed, the data was sent to the milling machine which ground out a stamp.

Figure 2.17 The milling machine creates the stamp from the design.

source: www.delcam.com for all images

Finally, the stamp was used many times to press the design on to aluminium sheets which had already been printed with the colours.

Figure 2.18 The final badge with the embossed lion's head.

Which common household objects might have been designed by CAM?

What kinds of specialist design packages are available?

A CAD package is very versatile, and can be used for many different projects. However, if a designer is concentrating on a particular kind of project, he or she may be able to purchase a package that has been specifically created to meet the needs. Design packages are available for designing a huge variety of things, including kitchens, gardens, architecture, electrical circuits, etc.

These design packages will include a set of objects such as kitchen units, plants and electrical components. Users can often view the designs from different angles. For example, the kitchen shown in Figure 2.19 is designed on a plan, but can also be viewed as a 3D image (Figure 2.20).

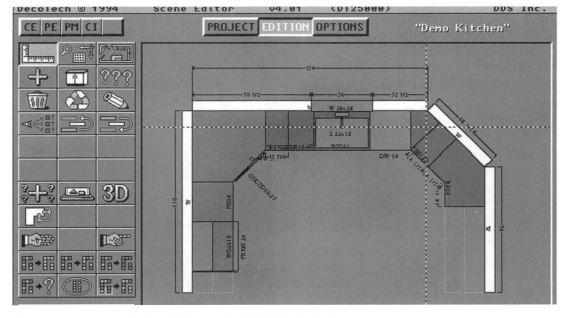

Figure 2.19 Creating a plan for a kitchen in DecoTech™ Professional

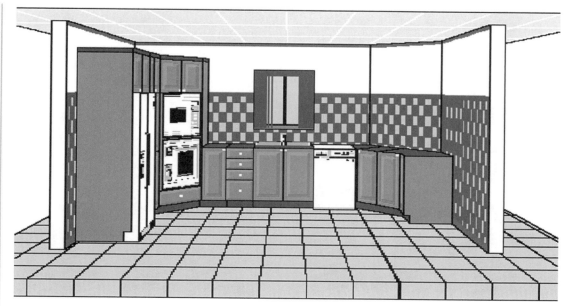

Figure 2.20 3D image of the kitchen in the plan

Software is also used by architects when designing buildings. In the example shown in Figure 2.21, the architect can view the plan and the 3D image at the same time.

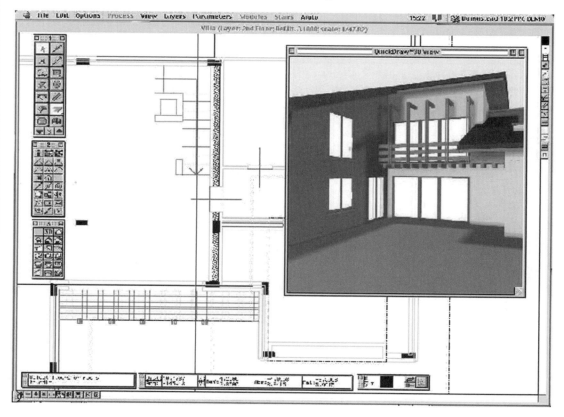

Figure 2.21 Architectural design in Domus.Cad

Source: www.interstudio.net

Software can be used to design electronic and electrical circuits of all kinds, as in Figure 2.22. Specialist software will often let the user simulate a real circuit by showing what would happen if the power was switched on.

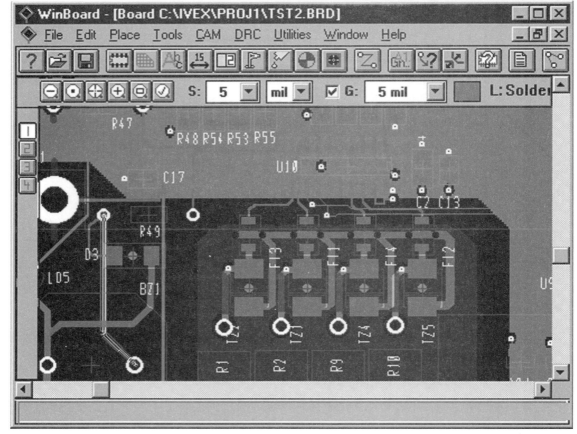

Figure 2.22 A design for a printed circuit board created in WinBoard
Source: www.ivex.com

Further research – Animation

Look closely at the animated objects, such as people and cars, in computer games. They will have been drawn using a specialised vector drawing package, rather like a CAD package. Each object will be composed of many smaller objects, each of which will have a lot of data associated with it. These objects will have been drawn as wireframes, with surface textures added.

You will have seen the same techniques at work in film animation. Again, very specialised software is used for animation, but it is widely used for live action films as well as cartoons.

Share your observations with fellow students.

How are software packages used for financial purposes?

A great many accounting tasks can be carried out using a spreadsheet package. For these to be most useful, the user has to spend some time setting up templates to match his or her needs. Another approach is to purchase a specialist financial package.

Financial packages, such as those produced by Sage®, can be used for:

- keeping business accounts
- financial forecasting – budgeting for the future
- payroll – paying employees
- costing jobs – working out how much to charge for a service
- Internet trading.

You may have used Microsoft® Money – this is a financial package for home use, and is not suitable for business purposes.

How are project planning packages used?

In business a project is a task that takes days or months to complete. For example, a building project would start with the specification and design of a new building and carry on through until the building is complete. Such projects are very complex and involve a lot of people and materials, all of which have to be scheduled so that the project runs smoothly.

Software projects are very similar, especially the large ones where many people work together to create a new software application.

Project planning software helps the project manager to plan the whole project from beginning to end. The manager will want to make best use of the employees so that they are kept busy all the time and are not idly waiting for another part of the project to be completed. The manager also needs to ensure that any materials needed are ready in time. The software usually allows the user to draw diagrams which show how the project should progress.

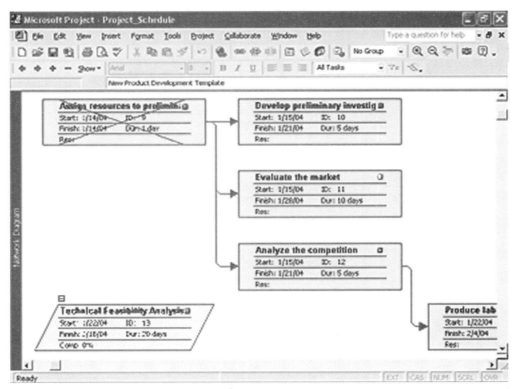

Figure 2.23 Planning a project with Microsoft® Project

Project planning packages, such Microsoft® Project, let the user:

- list and schedule all the tasks
- make changes to the schedule if necessary
- produce reports
- keep account of how long individual employees have worked on the project.

What packages can be used for diaries and appointments?

Many organisations provide diary (or calendar) software so that employees can keep records of their appointments and meetings at work. These are often made available to colleagues through the network so that they can check each other's diaries and plan meetings when all the people involved are free.

In addition, many people use a palmtop computer to store their appointments in an electronic diary. These can often be synchronised with the software held on a network at work. This means that each person can carry the data around, and be reminded of appointments when away from his or her desk.

Diary packages, such as Microsoft® Outlook, usually offer:

- daily personal appointments
- reminders
- address book.

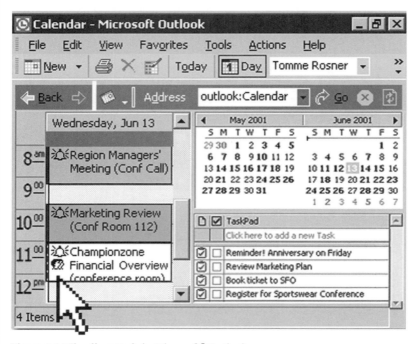

Figure 2.24 The diary tools in Microsoft® Outlook

Some businesses, such as hairdressers, and doctors' surgeries, make appointments with clients, whilst leisure centres allow members to book facilities. There are a number of specialist software packages which can help them with these processes (e.g. Figure 2.25).

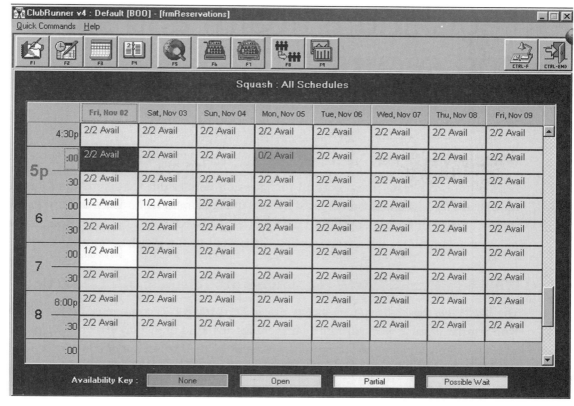

Figure 2.25 Leisure centre bookings scheduled in Clubrunner®

Test your knowledge

1 Name six types of business document that could be prepared using a word processing package.
2 What types of documents are easier to create with a desktop publishing package than with a word processor?
3 Data in a cell in a spreadsheet can be formatted in many ways. Name as many different formats as you can and give examples of each.
4 Explain the differences between a bitmap and vector image.
5 Specialist design packages are available for designing kitchens, buildings and circuits. Can you suggest some other areas that could benefit from design packages?
6 Describe three types of project that can be planned with a project-planning package.

2.3 Legislation, health and safety, and security

Legislation

What is legislation?

Legislation is the term that covers all the laws and regulations that apply to us. In the UK we may be affected by legislation created by Acts of Parliament (from Westminster) or by regulations arising from European Community (EC) directives or by legislation enacted by regional assemblies, such as the Scottish Parliament or the Welsh Assembly.

What health and safety regulations are relevant in an IT setting?

The *Health and Safety (Display Screen Equipment) Regulations 1993* cover work done by employees who regularly use a 'workstation' that includes any kind of display screen. A display screen could be a normal computer monitor or it could be the flat screen of a laptop or hand-held system or even the screen at a point-of-sale terminal in a shop. The regulations are designed to protect the health and safety of employees.

Under the regulations employers have to:

- *Analyse workstations, and assess and reduce risks* – this means that they must look at the complete workstation, including all the furniture. They have to take into account any special needs of individual staff.
- *Ensure workstations meet minimum standards* – the regulations list the standards that have to be met by keyboards, desks, chairs, lighting and screens.
- *Plan work so there are breaks or changes in activities* – it is up to the employer to negotiate these breaks with employees, but short, frequent breaks are better than longer, less frequent ones.
- *On request arrange eye tests, and provide spectacles if special ones are needed.*
- *Provide health and safety training and information.*

Figure 2.26 An employee working at a work station

What is the Data Protection Act and how does it affect me?

The *Data Protection Act 1998* applies to personal data only. Personal data is information about individual living persons. It does not cover information about people who are dead, or information about groups of people where it is impossible to identify individuals.

In the Act a *data controller* is someone who is responsible for storing personal data. A *data subject* is a person that the data refers to. The data controller is obliged to protect the data in a number of ways, but all the data subjects have rights to view the data about themselves.

There are eight data protection principles. Personal data must:

1 be processed fairly and lawfully
2 be obtained and processed for limited purposes
3 be adequate, relevant and not excessive
4 be accurate
5 not be kept longer than necessary
6 be processed in accordance with the data subject's rights
7 be secure
8 not be transferred to countries outside Europe without adequate protection.

Principle 2 means that data must normally be obtained with the consent of the data subject. Principle 6 ensures that data subjects have the right to be given a copy of the data about them.

An earlier Act related only to data stored on a computer system, but the 1998 Act covers all personal data, including documents stored in a filing cabinet or lists written on paper.

The Information Commissioner is responsible for regulating data controllers. Every organisation or individual who processes personal data must complete a form, explaining how they intend to collect, store and use personal data. This is then sent to the Commissioner for approval.

There are some exceptions. The Data Protection Act does not apply to data held for 'personal, family or household purposes', so you do not have to worry about declaring your personal address book or mobile phone. Also data collected for national security, for the investigation of crime and for taxation purposes does not have to be declared to the Commissioner.

What is copyright and how does it apply to software?

When someone writes a book, composes music or creates a work of art, he or she (or his or her employer) normally owns the copyright to that work. This means that no one else may print, copy, perform or film the work without permission. In Britain, normally copyright extends for 50 years after the creator's death, and the rights extend to the creator's heirs.

This means that you should obtain permission from the copyright holder before photocopying books, copying music or videos, performing plays or reproducing photos, etc. and you may have to pay for a licence to do so. Sometimes blanket permission is given, for example, to make limited copies of books for educational use.

For many years is was not clear whether software developers could claim copyright for their work. *The Copyright, Designs and Patents Act 1988* made it clear that software should be treated in the same way as books and articles.

When you buy software most of the price covers the cost of the licence for its use. This usually gives you permission to make one copy for your own use, plus any necessary back-up copies.

If you worked on your own as a software developer and you created some software that people wanted to obtain, you would expect to make some money from selling it. You would have the copyright to the software, and you would be very unhappy if someone else were to copy it and then sell it.

Software piracy costs the IT industry millions of pounds each year in lost sales. This means that software companies have to put up the price of their products and the customer has to pay more. You may be aware that a similar problem exists in the music industry.

The Copyright, Designs and Patents Act 1988 makes software piracy illegal.

?

What does it mean?

Software piracy – software piracy refers to the illegal copying and selling of software.

What is the Computer Misuse Act?

The *Computer Misuse Act 1990* was designed to deal with unauthorised access to computer systems, or '**hacking**'. Sometimes hackers gain unauthorised access simply out of bravado, but in many cases they have criminal intentions, as they wish to either shut down systems or to steal or alter information.

?

What does it mean?

Hacking – hacking is the actions of people who gain access to computer systems when they have no right to do so.
The technical term for hacking is 'unauthorised access', and the Computer Misuse Act is the law in the UK that deals with this offence.

Three kinds of offence were made illegal by the Act, and they are, in ascending order of seriousness:

1 *Unauthorised access to computer material* – an employee who uses a computer at work will be given permission (be authorised) to use certain software and to work with particular data in a database. Normally the systems administrator will set up access privileges on the network. These will ensure that when employees log on with their own user IDs and passwords they will be able to use and see only those parts of the system that they are allowed to use.

If an employee logs on with someone else's user ID (without permission) then he or she would be gaining unlawful access. Also, if the person finds loopholes in a system and uses them to access parts of the system that he or she is not allowed to visit, then that too counts as an illegal activity.

People who accidentally gain access to a system are not guilty of an offence, although they would be if they continued to explore the system after realising what had happened.

Notice that gaining access as an experiment or 'for a laugh' is still a criminal act.

The law does not just apply to employees, but to anyone who uses a computer and to any computer system.

Examples of offences under this section include logging on to a system with someone else's user name and password, or altering, deleting, copying or simply reading programs or data when not authorised to do so.

2 *Unauthorised access with intent to commit or facilitate commission of further offences* – if someone gains unauthorised access to a computer system and does so in order to commit a crime, then he or she is guilty of a more serious offence. For example, a person might try to transfer money illegally from one account to another, or might want to find out incriminating information that could be used to blackmail someone.

3 *Unauthorised modification of computer material* – if a person deliberately alters or deletes information held on a computer system without the authority to do so, then he or she is acting illegally. This part of the Computer Misuse Act is also designed to catch people who introduce **viruses** to systems.

What does it mean?

Virus – a virus is a small computer program that can cause damage to a computer system. Viruses usually spread by being attached to programs or documents, which are then distributed on disk or by e-mail.

Case study – How does the Computer Misuse Act affect me?

The Computer Misuse Act will affect you only if you deliberately try to gain access to a computer system, or to change computer data, when you do not have permission to do so. If you do any of these things by accident, then you should not be in trouble.

To cover yourself, if you do delete some data by accident at work, you should admit this straightaway to your manager, explaining that it was a mistake. Similarly, if you find that you have been given access to parts of the system that you should not visit then you should report that to the network administrator straightaway.

Also, if you discover that you have passed on a virus then you should apologise and warn the people who received it. But do remember that someone is guilty of committing an offence only if he or she does so with intention, so you need not worry that you may be prosecuted if you pass on a virus accidentally.

Have you received any information or warnings about the Computer Misuse Act at your centre? If not, you could offer to create a summary of the Act and its implications for students, and this could then be used as part of your assessment evidence.

Security

You have just been reading about a number of laws that apply to IT systems. In all cases, the important thing is to ensure that the software and data are protected.

The Computer Misuse Act deals with unauthorised access to IT systems, and the law is needed because people do try to use computers when they have no right to do so. This section looks at some of the ways in which organisations can protect their systems from illegal access.

What is security?

IT systems have to be protected from unauthorised access. Someone may access a system illegally in order to read sensitive information, and even though this may not cause any damage to the system it may create all kinds of problems for the organisation. Worse still, the person may actually change data or even delete it.

The main aims of security are to:

- maintain the system as intended
- protect the system from unauthorised changes being made to the software or data
- protect the system from both accidental and deliberate illegal access
- detect successful and unsuccessful attempts at illegal access
- provide a means of recovery if things go wrong.

How are IT systems at risk?

IT systems can be kept secure only if the people who look after them remember to do certain tasks on a regular basis. It is very important for people who use computers to consider all the ways in which their computer systems could be at risk.

Risks tend to fall into two categories – physical risks and software risks.

What are the physical risks to IT systems?

Unauthorised access to IT systems can happen as a result of:

- people gaining entry to buildings and rooms
- theft of hardware, disks and documents
- tapping into networks.

Unauthorised access is normally deliberate, but if the security in a building is not good enough, someone may innocently wander into a forbidden area.

What physical security procedures can be used?

Physical security procedures are tasks that protect the hardware, network connections, disks, and the rooms they are kept in, from being used improperly, either deliberately or by accident.

IT systems can be protected by:

- security guards, locks and intruder alarm systems
- keeping all disks in locked boxes and drawers
- placing servers in a part of the building that cannot be reached easily from outside (for example, not on the ground floor).

What are the software risks to IT systems?

Data or software should be altered or deleted only by someone who is allowed to do so. However, just reading data can also cause damage to an organisation, even if it is not deleted or altered in any way.

The main risks from unauthorised access are that:

- software or data is deleted
- software or data is altered
- confidential data is read or copied
- information is passed on to another person who is not allowed to read it
- software is used by someone who is not allowed to use it.

Most cases of unauthorised access are carried out by people deliberately.

Remember that the third offence under the Computer Misuse Act was the unauthorised modification of computer material. This offence can also be committed by someone who deliberately introduces a virus to an IT system. Unfortunately, many computer viruses are spread automatically, so systems have to be protected from the damage they can cause.

How can security procedures protect software?

The technical staff in an organisation can use software security procedures to prevent any software risks.

- Network administrators set *access privileges* for users. Users are given their own *User Identity (User ID)* and *password*, which they key in when they log on. The administrators then allocate the right level of access to each of the users, depending on the work that they do. This means that each user will be authorised to use certain software and will be allowed to view certain data. If the user attempts to gain access to anything else, then he or she will be breaking the law under the Computer Misuse Act.
- Important software files can be *encrypted*. Encryption is the correct term for secret code. To encrypt a file the system needs an algorithm (a set of rules) and a key (a special number). Encryption uses the algorithm and key to convert each byte or character of the original file into a different byte or character, and the encrypted file is saved. Another key is usually needed to decrypt the file back to its original state. It is virtually impossible for anyone to decrypt the file unless they know the algorithm and key to use.
- Computer viruses can cause a lot of damage to software, by deleting and altering programs and data. They can be spread from one computer to another through a network system, or on disks. Most viruses today are spread through e-mail. The best way to prevent virus damage is to install *virus protection software* on networks or on standalone computer systems. Virus protection software works with a virus data file, which contains information about all known viruses. The software uses the data file to check whether programs or data have been infected. It can be configured to check every new file that is placed on the system, including all e-mails, and it will also spot any unexpected changes to the system. A full virus check can be run periodically to check that nothing has slipped through. Since new viruses are being released all the time it is very important regularly to update the virus data files that enable the software to detect and identify the viruses.

How can an ICT system recover when things go wrong?

The main aim of security is to maintain the system – hardware and software – as intended. So if things do go wrong it is important to be able to re-create the system that existed before the damage was done.

Hardware can often be replaced by suppliers and the cost covered by insurance. It is far more difficult to replace the software and data. However, if proper **backup** procedures have been followed then the software and data can be copied from the backups and the system can revert to how it was before.

What does it mean?

Backup – a backup is a copy of software and data that is kept in case the original becomes damaged.

What software security procedures can be used to recover an ICT system?

Every single file on an ICT system should be copied and the copy kept on a disk or tape of some sort. This copy is known as a **backup**, and it can be used if the original is damaged.

When you use a word processor you will probably find that you can set it up so that it always saves a backup copy of each document. This can be very useful if you save something then realise that you have made a mistake and want to go back to a previous version. But as the backup is usually saved on the same disk as the original file, it is not much help if the disk itself is damaged.

An end user on a standalone computer is much wiser to save a backup copy of a file on to another disk as a security measure. On a network there is no need for individual users to create backups, as all the files will be backed up regularly. This is an automatic process during which all the files on the system will be copied on to a removable disk or digital tape. In most organisations this will happen in the middle of the night when no one is at work on the system. The disk or tape will then be removed by a network administrator in the morning and locked in a safe.

Test your knowledge

1   What must employers do to comply with the Health and Safety (Display Screen Equipment) Regulations 1993?
2   What are the main points of the Data Protection Act?
3   What is unauthorised access to a computer system and how can it be prevented?
4   List three physical risks to computer systems. In each case, explain how systems can be protected from these risks.
5   Explain what role these play in the security of computer systems:
    ▪ user ID and password
    ▪ encryption
    ▪ virus protection.
6   Explain how backups can be used to recover a system after a major disaster like a fire.

2.4 Evaluate the uses of software applications

How can I evaluate a software package?

When you **evaluate** a software package you should first discover what its purpose is. This should be stated in advertising material, as no one should purchase software without knowing what can be achieved with it.

The purpose may be to provide basic software suitable for beginners. Or it may be to provide a full package offering all the features that a professional would need. You cannot complain that software cannot be used to carry out more complex tasks if it was designed for people with non-specialist needs.

You should ask yourself these questions:

- *What is its purpose?* The package could be for general or specialist use and it could be designed for beginners or for more advanced users.
- *What is it used for in industry and commerce?* The package will be used for a variety of tasks and for solving many different problems.
- *Why it is suitable for those uses?* You should decide whether a package is the best one for a particular use, and what features of the package make it suitable.
- *How easy is it to use?* The answer to this question will depend on the skills of the user, so perhaps it should be asked again as 'How easily can the intended user use it?' Section 1.4 in Unit 1 considered categories of users and how the user interface helped them to use software. A user-friendly interface is easy for the intended user to use.
- *How effective is it?* You should identify the good and bad points and how it can be improved.

What does it mean?

Evaluate – a product, such as a software package, is evaluated by assessing how effective it is in use.

Uses of general software applications

What are the main uses for general software applications in industry and commerce?

General software packages are designed to simplify basic office tasks, such as:

- *Presenting information* – information can be presented in text, in diagrams, in pictures, in charts, and even in sound. The style of presentation is often important.
- *Numerical modelling* – numerical data can be analysed, calculated and presented.
- *Communications* – messages can be sent from one person to another electronically.
- *Software application development* – new applications can be developed.

Which applications are suitable for the presentation of information?

Many packages can be used to present information, and it is important to select one that is suitable for the task. Information can be presented in a printed form or on screen. Remember that there is often a lot of overlap between the features of different packages.

These types of application can all be used to present information:

- word processing
- desktop publishing
- spreadsheet
- database
- presentation graphics
- painting packages (for bitmapped graphics)
- photo editing

- drawing packages (for vector graphics)
- Internet browser
- web design.

Several of these can be used together; for example, a graphic could be created in a drawing package then pasted into a document prepared with desktop publishing software.

The table below shows some of the many things that can be done in these packages.

	Word processing	Desktop publishing	Spreadsheet	Database	Presentation graphics	Painting	Photo editing	Drawing	Internet browser	Web design
Create and edit text	✓	✓	✓	✓	✓	?	?	✓		✓
Text styles	✓	✓	✓	✓	✓					✓
Create graphics	?	?	?	?	?	✓	?	✓		?
Edit graphics						✓	✓	✓		
Create charts and graphs			✓	?				?		
Create tables	✓	?	✓	✓	✓					✓
Present on screen	?	?	✓	✓	✓				✓	✓
Print document	✓	✓	✓	✓	✓	✓	✓	✓		
Search for data	?	?	✓	✓					✓	
Sort data			✓	✓						

Figure 2.27 Software applications for presenting information

Check your understanding – Word processing versus desktop publishing

Can you do all of these in both word processing and desktop publishing packages?

1 set up four columns of text across a page
2 create a three-fold leaflet from a template

Figure 2.28 A three-fold leaflet as illustrated in Microsoft® Publisher

3 create a business card that can be printed on standard business card stationary
4 wrap text around a graphic

Figure 2.29 Text wrapping around an irregular graphic

5   use a thesaurus to check words
6   set up a style list
7   check two pages on screen at the same time
8   add a hyperlink.

You can do some of these tasks equally easily in both types of package. But you will find that some tasks are much easier to carry out in one of the packages.

Which applications are suitable for numerical modelling?

Numerical modelling uses numbers to represent problems in the real world. The accounts of a company are one way of understanding how the business is going, providing a numerical model of its finances.

Numerical modelling comes into its own when it is used for 'what if?' queries. For example, the Finance Director may draw up a budget for the coming year. Some of the figures will be known in advance, some can be estimated quite accurately, whilst others can be guessed only roughly. A 'what if?' scenario can be used to try out different guesses and to see what effect these will have on the budget. For example, if the business imports products from overseas then the Director would be interested in how the rates of exchange could affect the business.

Numerical modelling is not just used for financial purposes. Some kinds of organisation want to be able to predict the future demand for their services. For example, a car insurance company needs to have a good idea about the number of claims its customers will make in the future. If it underestimates the claims then it may not have enough funds to meet them all. A numerical model will be used to come up with the best possible estimate.

Spreadsheets were originally designed for just this type of activity. Today, however, many database management systems can be configured to perform numerical modelling as well.

Which applications are suitable for communications?

People working in industry and commerce need to communicate with each other. They communicate with:

- other people in the same organisation
- people in other organisations
- the general public.

The main means of communication are:

- face-to-face conversation
- printed documents
- telephone
- electronic.

ICT can be used to support most means of communication, but is particularly important for the last type.

Electronic communications include:

- internal e-mail through the organisation's local area networks
- external e-mail through the Internet
- intranet – web-style pages that can be viewed only within the organisation
- webpages on the Internet.

The main software applications for these uses are Internet browsers, e-mail clients and web design packages, but some of them can be carried out in other packages.

	E-mail client	Internet browser	Web design	Word processing	Presentation graphics	Desktop publishing
Create e-mails	✓			✓		
Manage e-mails	✓					
Create and edit webpage			✓	?	?	?
Display webpage		✓				

Figure 2.30 Software applications for communications

What applications are suitable for software development?

So far, this unit has not looked at how software applications are developed. Software developers themselves use specialist software to enable them to design and write the applications that end users use. They can use one of two types of software:

- *Programming environment* – programs are written in a programming language. You may have heard of a number of these, including Visual Basic, C++ and Java. A programming environment is complex software that has two main components – an editor and a compiler. The editor is a bit like a word processor, in which the programmer can write a program in the programming language. The compiler then converts the program into machine code instructions.
- *Application generator* – programming is a time-consuming process, and application generators can speed this up. In an application generator, the application developer can simply select standard modules (small programs) and put them together to form the application, without knowing much programming. A professional developer may also adapt the modules and add further programming.

You may not have realised that you have probably already used an application generator. Generally speaking, the ability to create new applications is added to a general software application. The main software applications in Microsoft® Office (Word, Excel, Access, PowerPoint) are all application generators, as are some Lotus® applications.

If you take the specialist units in Software Development, then you will learn how to design software applications and write the programs.

Further research – Using Microsoft® software as application generators

Launch Access and use one of the database wizards to create a standard database. This database, with all its forms and reports, is a software application in its own right.

The wizard put the application together for you, and generated all the program code. You can view the program by selecting **Tools**, then **Macro**, then **Visual Basic Editor**. This opens up the programming environment that is built in to Access.

To view some of the program code, click on the folders and files in the Project pane.

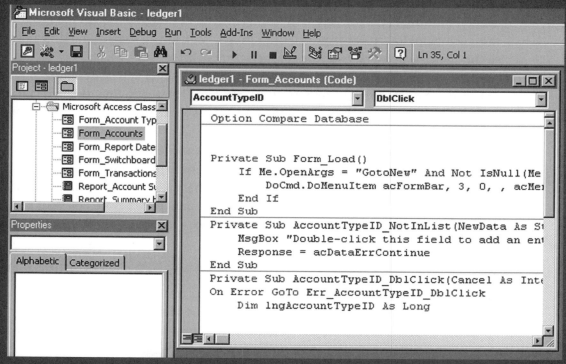

Figure 2.31 Program code in Microsoft® Access

Switch back to the usual view of Access by clicking on the icon at the left end of the main toolbar.

You can also view the Visual Basic environment in other software. In Word, Excel or PowerPoint, select **Tools**, then **Macro**, then **Visual Basic Editor**. There will be little to see at this stage, but an application developer could use this to create a customised application for a client.

Use of specialist application packages

What are the main uses for specialist software applications in industry and commerce?

Specialist software applications are normally used when the general applications do not have all the features that the user wants. For simple uses often a general application will do, but specialist applications are the best choice for professionals.

In this section we will compare the use of general and specialist applications.

What are the advantages of using specialist software applications?

Specialist software applications are chosen for these reasons:

- *Specialist packages can be used to carry out more complex tasks* – in some cases, the tasks simply cannot be done in a general package. Engineers and other designers have the choice of general drawing packages, standard CAD packages, or design packages for specific types of use, such as architectural drawing. They are very unlikely to use general drawing packages, so the choice is between two types of specialist packages.
- *Specialist packages produce better quality output* – the printouts will be designed to meet the industry standards and will conform to all the technical requirements. Financial software will produce standard pay-slips and the formats required for tax returns and annual reports.
- *Specialist packages are written for professionals* – they assume that the user has a good understanding of the area of work and does not need explanations every step of the way. A project-planning package will be used by project managers, who will already be using standard techniques and diagrams when planning projects. They do not need explanations about these techniques; what they value are software tools that make the process easier.

What are the disadvantages of using specialist software applications?

- *Specialist packages are more expensive than general packages* – general packages have a much bigger market than specialist ones, so can be sold at a lower price.
- *Specialist packages take longer to learn* – because of their complexity, users may have to undergo expensive training before they can use the packages effectively.
- *Specialist packages may not be widely known* – there are several packages aimed at each specialist area. An employee may learn to use one package and then move to another company where a different package is used.

Test your knowledge

1 What should be considered when evaluating a software package?
2 For each of these tasks, select one software package that could be used and evaluate its effectiveness.
   - Preparing a poster to advertise a social event in a company.
   - Writing a report that analyses the responses to a customer survey – including tables and graphs.

▶

◀

- ▪ Attractively presenting on-screen information that has been retrieved from a database.
- ▪ Telling the general public about a new product.
- ▪ Creating a new application to handle personnel records in a company.

3 What are the main differences between a programming environment and an application generator?

4 A college library wants to purchase software to manage its book catalogue and to handle book loans. What would be the advantages and disadvantages of using specialist software for this purpose?

 Assessment tasks

This section describes what you must do to obtain a Merit grade for this unit.

A Distinction grade may be awarded if your work demonstrates a deeper understanding of the topics and is of a higher quality. The highlighted sentences indicate the kind of work expected at Distinction level.

How do I provide assessment evidence?

Your evidence will either be all in the form of a written report, or may be a mixture of the following:

- written reports
- research notes
- printouts from software packages
- material used in a presentation
- witness statements
- observation sheets.

All your evidence should be presented in one folder, which should have a front cover and a contents page. You should divide the evidence into four sections corresponding to the four tasks.

For this assessment you have to provide information about the development of ICT (Task 1), about legislation and related issues (Task 3), and about software applications that you have evaluated (Task 4). You can prepare and present this information using a variety of general applications. For example, you could use:

- a word processing package to write a report about the history of ICT
- desktop publishing to create a leaflet explaining the Data Protection Act
- presentation graphics to make a presentation of your research into security
- a graphics package to prepare illustrations for any of these
- a spreadsheet package to create graphs and charts
- an Internet browser to carry out research.

Each of these could then count towards Task 2.

Task 1

Learning outcome 1 – Describe the development of information and communication technology

Carry out some research into the history and development of ICT, especially over the last ten years. Present your findings and make sure that you include how:

- ICT has developed
- ICT is used today in industry and commerce, with examples
- industry and commerce have been changed by the use of ICT, referring to some real-life examples.

To obtain a Distinction grade, you should also identify several (at least three) major effects of ICT on industry and commerce.

Task 2

Learning outcome 2 – Use a range of general and specialist software applications

1 You should use at least three different general software packages to solve problems. Since you will be using packages for Tasks 1, 3 and 4, it would be sensible to include these in your evidence. You may also tackle other problems of your own choosing, and can include work prepared for other units.

In some cases you will use more than one package to solve a problem. For example, you might use an Internet browser to search for statistical data, which you then enter in a spreadsheet. Graphs produced from the spreadsheet could then be included in a word processed report.

The output should demonstrate that you can:
- enter, edit and delete data
- sort data
- search data
- format data
- produce graphs and charts
- create other images.

You may want to include witness statements, especially for a presentation, but obtain printouts if at all possible.

For this task, provide a list of all the documents and describe what each demonstrates.

If you include the work for Task 1, 3 or 4 then there is no need to print them out again for Task 2, but simply refer to them.

2 Select a problem that could be solved using either a general or specialist package. This could, for example, be a design that could be created in a drawing package or using specialist design software. Use each package to solve the same problem and provide evidence of the output.

3 Compare the differences between the two packages used in 2.

To obtain a Distinction grade, you should use a variety of software packages to solve a number of general and specialist problems, and this should include at least two specialist packages.

Task 3

Learning outcome 3 – Present information on legislation, health and safety, and security

1 Write an account of at least *two* pieces of legislation that relate to IT, including the Data Protection Act.

2 Describe at least *four* examples of security procedures that can be designed to prevent illegal access to software applications or data.

To obtain a Distinction grade, explain the implications of legislation and data security for people who work with ICT. Make sure that you consider the implications for technical staff as well as end users.

Task 4

Learning outcome 4 – Evaluate the uses of software applications

Evaluate *three* different types of specialist application software, and explain for each:

- its purpose
- what it is used for in industry and commerce
- why it is suitable for those uses.

You may choose some applications which you cannot use directly yourself, for example, a sales application in a shop. In that case you could carry out your research through observations, discussions with end users, Internet searches and reading.

To obtain a Distinction grade, evaluate in some depth at least six software applications. At least three of these should be specialist applications. In addition to the points above, include for each:

- how easy it is to use (given the expected skills of the user)
- how effective it is.

Use the correct technical language about the software.

UNIT 3: INFORMATION SYSTEMS

Success in this unit

What are the learning outcomes?

To achieve this unit you must:

- describe organisational structures and characteristics
- describe roles of IT practitioners
- explain why organisations use IT
- explain the importance of data safety and security.

How is this unit assessed?

This unit is internally assessed. You must provide evidence in the form of a variety of documents that show that you meet the learning outcomes.

How do I provide assessment evidence?

Your evidence will probably be a mixture of the following:

- written reports
- printouts from software packages
- material used in a presentation
- witness statements
- observation sheets.

All your evidence should be presented in one folder, which should have a front cover and a contents page. The section headed *Assessment tasks* towards the end of this unit gives you more detailed advice about how to prepare for the assessment.

Introduction

About this unit

In this unit you will learn about how IT is used to store and process the information that is used by organisations.

In order to understand what information is needed, you will also have to understand the different kinds of organisations that exist and how they work. That is why the unit begins with a section exploring different kinds of organisational structures.

In Unit 2 you learnt about commercial and industrial businesses, and about the goods and services that they provide. In this unit you will learn more about different types of business and how they are usually structured. You will learn about the role that IT plays in these businesses and how it can make them more successful. You will also find out about career opportunities in IT, and some of the responsibilities that IT staff have in relation to information.

What is an information system?

ICT is used for all kinds of purposes which include controlling robots and other machinery, manufacturing products and playing games. By far the greatest use of computers is made by businesses around the world to handle all the information that they use every day.

An information system is the hardware and software used primarily to process the information used in a business.

3.1 Organisational structures and characteristics

What is an organisation?

People like to meet in groups to do things together. Some of these groups are informal, such as friendship groups. But in other cases, activities become a little more structured and an organisation, such as a club, is formed. In an organisation people take on specific roles and jobs. An organisation has a structure.

What is a business organisation?

We need to remind ourselves that a business provides goods or services for customers.

Some businesses are very small. For example, many skilled people, such as electricians and aromatherapists, work alone. These are the simplest business organisations.

Other businesses consist of just a handful of people who each take on different aspects of the work. Yet others may employ many thousands; each employee will have a clearly defined role within the organisation. Larger organisations need more complex structures than smaller ones.

Characteristics of an organisation

What is the purpose of an organisation?

Each organisation has its own specific purpose, or aim, and will have been set up with certain purposes in mind. For example, a charity that finds homes for unwanted pets has a very clear purpose. All its fundraising and other activities will be done with the aim of re-housing animals.

The main aim of a supermarket chain will be to make profits for the company. It may also have other aims as well; for example, it may aim to provide goods for certain community groups with specific dietary needs, such as Muslims or vegetarians.

Many organisations today write a sentence or two to explain their aims and call it a 'mission statement'.

MISSION STATEMENT

" To become the **world's leading** independent centre of **excellence** in **academic research** on the **impact** of the **Internet** on **society**, and in **informing policy** and **generating debate**. "

Reproduced with permission of Oxford Internet Institute

Figure 3.1 The mission statement of the Oxford Internet Institute

What is the identity of an organisation?

An organisation will also have a distinct identity. This may be obvious from its name. For example, you would expect the Middletown Bee-keepers Club to have members from one town, with a common interest in bee-keeping. The name also tells you that it operates as a club where people meet to share ideas rather than as a business.

How is an organisation accountable?

All organisations are accountable in some way. That means that they have to explain what they are doing to other people – maybe to shareholders, or to members, or to a Board of Directors. Large public organisations, such as hospitals and local authorities, are accountable to the general public.

Why do organisations have leaders?

Organisations with more than a few people need leadership. The person in charge may be known as a manager, chairperson, president or leader, but in all cases this person will take the ultimate responsibility for what happens. Leaders need to be good at planning for the future and also good at getting other people to work with them.

> **Check your understanding** – Mission statements
>
> Select an organisation that you are involved with. It could be the college where you are studying, or your employer, or a club that you belong to.
>
> Find out:
>
> - whether it has a mission statement and, if so, what it is
> - what its distinct identity is
> - who it is accountable to
> - who its leaders are and what their official positions are called.

Types of organisation

Are there different types of business organisation?

Business organisations do vary in size, but the major difference between one type of business and another lies in their accountability.

Some common types of business organisation are:

- sole trader
- partnership
- private limited company
- public limited company
- multi-national company
- public service organisation
- commercial organisation.

What is a sole trader?

A sole trader is a person who runs his or her own business and does not employ anyone else. Examples might include a physiotherapist who owns a private practice, a plumber, an accountant working alone, or a potter producing craft goods.

Figure 3.2 A sole trader works alone

What is a partnership?

If two or more people form a small business they usually have a partnership agreement. This is a legal document in which they agree to share equally in the profits of the business.

Figure 3.3 A business partnership

What is a company?

People working as sole traders and/or in partnerships have one major problem in common. They are all responsible for any debts that their businesses have. If they are not paid for goods or services that they have supplied to a customer, then they can, of course, go through the courts to reclaim the money owed to them. However, in some cases it can take a very long time to get it back and that can have a serious impact on the business.

Partners and sole traders may also find themselves sued by other people if they are unable to meet contracts, sometimes through no fault of their own. They can also be in difficulty if important equipment, such as vehicles or tools, are stolen or damaged. Worse still, if one partner disappears the remaining partners are responsible for all the debts.

One solution to these problems is to form a company by registering the business with the Registrar of Companies at Companies House. A company is a 'person' in its own right, and can own property or sue others in the courts. The people who are involved in setting up the company are the owners of the company.

There are two main types of company:

■ private limited company
■ public limited company.

The term 'limited' means that each owner is responsible only for a limited proportion of the debts that the company may have.

What is a limited company?

Usually all the owners of a company have *shares* in the company. A share entitles the owner to part of the profits of the company. The annual payment of profits to each shareholder is known as a *dividend*.

The amount of shares owned by someone also determines the maximum amount that the owner would lose if the company closed down. So if someone owns shares to the value of £10,000, he or she would be responsible only for debts up to that amount.

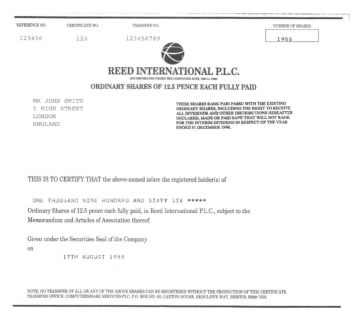

Figure 3.4 A share certificate

When a company is first set up, the owners pay money to the company and get shares in return. The owners have *invested* money in the company, so it is in their interest to make sure that the company is financially successful. If the company does well then the investment is safe, and they can expect to get a share of the profits as well. However, if the company does badly then the owners will not receive any profits, and if eventually it has to close down then the owners will lose the money that they invested at the start.

A limited company is accountable to its shareholders.

What is the difference between a private limited company and a public limited company?

The shares in a private limited company may not be offered for sale to the general public. This means that the original owners of the company can keep control of the business.

A public limited company has the letters 'plc' after its name. This kind of company can sell its shares to the public, usually through the Stock Exchange. Many people can buy shares in these businesses, hoping that they will receive good dividends each year. The prices of shares do go up and down depending on how successful a company appears to be.

What is a multi-national company?

A multi-national company is one that has branches in many countries in the world. It may buy raw materials from one country, which are then sent to factories that produce goods in another country. The final products may be sold to customers in other parts of the world. This means that the company can chose the cheapest suppliers of raw materials from anywhere in the world. They can then set up factories in the countries where labour is cheap, but they can market their products anywhere. This should mean that customers get good value, but in practice it can mean that workers in poorer countries are exploited.

Some of the largest multi-national companies, such as Microsoft®, have more money than many small countries themselves, and have a significant impact on the world economy.

What is the difference between a public service and a commercial organisation?

You may be surprised to learn that schools and colleges are businesses. They provide educational services to their 'customers', that is, their students.

Independent schools charge fees for the services they give, and these fees are paid by the customers (or more usually by their parents). However, most students do not pay for their schooling because the costs are met from public funds, which come from Government. Of course, Government funding is raised through income tax and other taxes, so parents and other members of the public do pay for schools indirectly.

Organisations which provide services that are paid for out of public funds are known as public service organisations. They are directly accountable to the public and to Government. A commercial organisation, on the other hand, raises all its income directly from its customers.

Further research – Types of business organisations

Do some research to find out about a number of organisations. Include examples of each of these types:

- sole trader
- partnership
- private limited company
- public limited company
- multi-national company.

You can find examples in your home area, and also by searching on the Internet. Keep notes on all your research. Make sure that amongst the organisations you have included at least one public service organisation and at least one commercial organisation.

Structure of an organisation

How are organisations structured?

The leader of any organisation makes decisions, but in a large organisation it is impossible for one person to take all the decisions, so the work is divided up into several areas of responsibility. These areas are sometimes referred to as *business functions*. For example, a garden centre will have personnel, finance, sales and horticultural staff, and each section will be led by a manager.

What does a manager do?

A manager is a leader who is responsible for the work of a number of employees. He or she has to decide:

- what tasks should be done, by whom and in what order
- how money is to be spent
- what targets to aim for
- how to deal with emergencies and other problems
- which staff to employ.

What is a hierarchy?

Larger organisations have managers at several levels. In the Army, for example, there are many levels of responsibility, from the Field Marshall at the top, down through Colonels and Captains to the Sergeants and Corporals. All except the private soldiers are managers of one kind or another.

Many industries and commercial organisations have a number of levels of responsibility, though few have as many levels as the armed forces. At the top, the most senior manager is often known as the Managing Director, or the Chief Executive. Below that come the *senior managers* who lead large departments. They in turn are responsible for the work of *middle managers* who will manage sections or branches within the main departments. The actual work of the individual employees is usually the responsibility of *junior managers*, who may be known as supervisors or team leaders.

A *hierarchy* is a structure with several levels in which each person is responsible for the work of all the people below. This is best shown through a diagram known as an organisation chart.

How do you draw an organisation chart?

An organisation chart shows the managers and their staff in boxes arranged as a simple 'tree' diagram. The most senior people will be at the top of the chart; the lines below them lead to the people who work for them (e.g. Figure 3.5).

In an organisation chart you can always work out who someone's **line manager** is because it is the person just above him or her in the diagram.

? **What does it mean?**

Line manager – a person's line manager is the individual's immediate boss.

Kingsmond Creatives

Figure 3.5 Part of an organisation chart for a company

Check your understanding – Draw an organisation chart

Microsoft® PowerPoint has a very useful tool that will help you to draw an organisation chart.

■ Launch PowerPoint and select **Blank Presentation**.
■ The next window asks you to choose an Autolayout. Select the one that looks like an organisation chart. This will create a new slide.
■ As directed, double-click on the image to create a chart – this takes you into the organisation chart window.

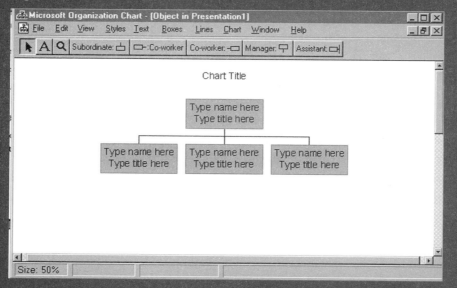

Figure 3.6 Organisation chart window in Microsoft® PowerPoint

■ Click on each box in turn to add the name and job title of each person.
■ To add a new person, click on the **Subordinate** button, and then click on the box containing the details of that person's line manager.
■ Click on the new box to add the name and job title.

It is usually easiest to draw an organisation chart from the top down.

Who makes the decisions?

In one sense all the people who work for a business have to make decisions throughout the day. The hierarchy within an organisation decides who makes which decisions. Here are some examples in a chain of fast food outlets:

- The individual worker serving customers decides when more chips should be cooked.
- The supervisor (junior manager) sorts out staffing rotas.
- The branch manager (middle manager) recruits new staff or sacks employees.
- The regional manager (senior manager) sets targets for each fast food outlet to meet.
- The managing director decides where new outlets are to be opened.

Figure 3.7 People working at a fast food outlet

What does a director do?

All registered companies must have one or more directors. The directors have to make an Annual Report to the shareholders and send the accounts to the Registrar of Companies. All the directors of a company form the *Board of Directors* and they are ultimately responsible for everything that happens to the company.

Some directors may work full-time for the company, and they are known as *executive directors*. An executive director will normally be one of the senior managers in the company.

The *Managing Director* (or Chief Executive) is an executive director who has overall responsibility for the management of the company.

Some companies have *non-executive directors* who do not work full-time for the company. They may be major shareholders (in the case of a private company), or they may be people who have expert knowledge that the company wants to use from time to time.

What is a shareholder?

Anyone who owns shares in a company is a shareholder. Shareholders are the owners of the company. In the case of a private company there will be a small group of shareholders who will know each other and will all be trying to make the company succeed. In comparison, there could be many thousands of shareholders in a public company, and most of them will not be involved in the day-to-day affairs of the company.

All shareholders are entitled to attend the Annual General Meeting of the company and to see the Annual Report.

Further research – Study organisations further

Select two of the organisations you looked at earlier, and study them in more depth. If possible, choose ones where you can talk to a number of employees. Failing that, make sure that you can get hold of a lot of public information on the organisations.

Read through Task 1 under the *Assessment tasks* at the end of this chapter and check that you are going to be able to find out the answers to all the questions.

Test your knowledge

1 What do these terms mean?
  - sole trader
  - business partner
  - limited company
  - shares
  - private limited company
  - public limited company
  - shareholder
  - multi-national company
  - public service organisation
  - director.
2 Explain the differences between senior, middle and junior managers.
3 How can you work out the hierarchy in an organisation from an organisation chart?

3.2 Roles of IT practitioners

Roles in IT

In this section we will be looking in more detail at some of the roles of IT practitioners. It is important to remember that they exist only in order to help organisations do their main work of providing goods and services.

What is an IT practitioner?

Most employees these days use IT in some form or another as part of their work. As we saw in Unit 1, computer users fall into three broad categories:

- *end users* who use applications software
- *technical users*, such as administrators, who work with operating systems

■ *software developers*, such as programmers, who create programs.

Most people who use IT at work are end users, which means that they use computers and data communications as tools within their normal work.

End users can use IT successfully only because of the many IT specialists who have developed the hardware and software, who manage the data and networks, and who help them to use it. These specialists – the technical users and the software developers – are known as *IT practitioners*.

There is also a small number of end users who are IT specialists and can also rightly be called IT practitioners as well.

IT practitioners who maintain data systems (end users)

■ A *data entry clerk* does in fact need rather more technical skills than most, so is classed as an IT practitioner. He or she keys in data that has usually been written down on a document or form of some kind. This work has to be done quickly and accurately.

■ The database in an organisation will contain all the information that it needs. The *database administrator's* job is to make sure that the data is collected, entered and stored correctly, and that information is produced accurately for end users.

IT practitioners who look after computer systems (technical users)

■ A *network engineer* designs and sets up computer networks for customers. He or she also updates networks when needed and solves any major problems.

■ A *network (or system) manager* is responsible for all the network administrators and technicians in a large organisation. The manager will plan any upgrades to the system.

■ Computer networks have to be managed on a day-to-day basis, and this work is done by a *network (or system) administrator*. Most of the work is concerned with making sure that end users have access to the right software and to maintaining data security.

■ A *technician* usually looks after the day-to-day maintenance tasks with hardware and software in a computer system. He or she will be responsible for ensuring that all the computers, printers and other devices function correctly and that the data communications links work.

■ When an end user needs help with IT software and hardware, he or she will usually contact *user support staff*, who run the 'help desk'.

Further research – IT practitioners

Try to meet as many IT practitioners as you can, and ask them about their work.

Select two kinds of jobs that exist in IT and find out as much as you can about them. If at all possible, talk to people who hold the jobs.

Try to decide which of the jobs appeal to you as a possible future career.

IT practitioners who develop new systems (software developers)

■ A *systems analyst* looks at the ways in which information is handled in an organisation and then works on designing a better system. Analysts often work with teams of computer engineers, software engineers and programmers to develop new information systems.

- A *programmer* takes the design for a new piece of software and then writes the computer program. Programmers can use a number of programming languages such as Visual Basic, Java or C++.
- An *application developer* will use an application generator to create a new application. Application generators, such as Microsoft® Access, allow the developer to create an application very quickly, using a number of tools such as a form or report designer. These tools generate the program code directly. The developer can then add further features to the basic application by adapting and extending the program code.
- Webpages are designed and programmed by a *web designer*. The designer uses Hypertext Mark-up Language (HTML) together with other specialist languages. Many sites are also linked directly to a database.

Further research – Jobs in IT

Look through advertisements for jobs in the IT industry. You may find these in local newspapers and in local employment agencies. National newspapers often cover IT jobs on a particular day of the week. There are also some specialist papers and magazines, such as *Computer Weekly*, which carry a large number of job advertisements. You can also find a number of employment agencies on the Internet that specialise in IT work.

Note down the kinds of jobs you have found and what the post holders will be expected to do.

Test your knowledge

1 What do we mean by an IT practitioner?
2 What is the difference between the work done by a systems analyst and a programmer?
3 What do network managers and network administrators do?
4 How does the work of a database administrator differ from that of a systems administrator?

3.3 Why organisations use IT

Organisations and IT

It is very unusual to find a business organisation that does not use IT these days. Most sole traders have a PC, and all large organisations use computer networks.

Fifty years ago no more than a handful of large businesses would have bought computer technology, and this was at very great cost. Now that computer systems are very powerful and relatively cheap, everyone can use them.

But why do business organisations use IT? The main reasons are to:

- improve **efficiency**
- increase productivity

- make the business more competitive
- support decision making
- improve and extend communication
- improve the company image.

What does it mean?

Efficiency – efficiency compares the outputs of an organisation with the inputs to it. An efficient organisation is one that gets the most out of the work, money and materials that it puts into it.

More about efficiency

The main input to any business organisation is the hours worked by the employees, but there are other inputs, such as the raw materials used to make products and the money that is invested in office space and equipment. The outputs of a business are the goods and services that it provides. A highly efficient business organisation is one which gets the maximum outputs for the minimum inputs.

For example, a clothes manufacturer uses large amounts of fabric, and quite a lot of this is wasted. Some of the fabric is always left over between the pieces that are cut to make garments. Perhaps the garments (the output) could be made from a shorter length of fabric (the input) if the pieces were positioned differently. This could make the business more efficient as it would be getting the maximum output from the minimum input.

The business becomes more efficient if any change in practice means that the ratio of outputs to inputs is improved. Another way to describe this is to say that the amount of wasted work, money or materials is reduced.

How can IT improve efficiency?

How can the use of technology help a business to get the most out of the work, money or materials that are input?

- An organisation can get the most out of the *work* done by employees by increasing **productivity**. This is covered in the next section.
- IT can often be used to work out how to get the most out of the raw *materials* it uses. The production engineers at the clothes factory may find that it is quite difficult to work out how to position the patterns on the cloth, and will probably use Computer Aided Design (CAD) software to work out the best solution.
- The business will invest *money* in the buildings that it uses and in the equipment that it needs for manufacturing or in the offices. How can IT help the business to get the most out of these investments?

What does it mean?

Productivity – productivity measures the amount of goods or services produced by workers in a given time.

Case study – Getting the most out of an investment

The directors of an insurance company wanted to make the company more efficient so they could make a greater profit for their shareholders.

They realised that one major input was the money that had to be invested in the Head Office, which was located in a prime position in London. They asked whether they needed to keep the Head Office in London and whether they could move to a town where they could rent offices much more cheaply.

The original reason for being in London was so they could be physically close to the banks and to the large companies for whom they provided insurance. With modern ICT they could keep in contact without necessarily being close by. So they moved the Head Office to Milton Keynes. Of course, the IT equipment itself had to be paid for, but they believed that this move would make them more efficient.

Do you think they were wise to make the move? Can you see any drawbacks to this plan?

More about productivity

Suppose a group of workers in a television factory normally produces 1,000 televisions in one week. If the same group manages to produce 1,150 televisions in the next week, then we would probably say that productivity has gone up. However, it would only be an increase in productivity if the same hours were worked both weeks.

Suppose in the third week, the workers still produce 1,150 televisions. But this week, one of the workers is on holiday. Has productivity increased or stayed the same? In fact, the workers are more productive because the number of televisions produced for each hour worked has actually gone up. If they all carry on making televisions at the same rate, then when the absent worker returns the actual number produced in a week should go up again.

It is easy to measure productivity when goods are being manufactured. But how can we measure the productivity of office workers? Although they do not produce goods they do have to complete a range of tasks. We could count how many letters they write, how many complaints they deal with or how many orders they handle. Or we could try to work out the financial value of their work, such as the value of the sales that they make. So, if an office worker gets through more tasks during a period of time, or makes more profit for the company, then that person's productivity has increased.

Remember that an efficient organisation is one that gets the most out of the work, money or materials. So improved productivity will help to make an organisation more efficient.

What effect can IT have on productivity?

Long before computers were widely used in business, the process of writing a letter or report was quite complicated. A manager might dictate a letter to a typist who would write it down in shorthand, and then type it on a typewriter. The letter would then go back to the manager, who would check it. If any mistakes were found the letter would have to be typed again from the beginning.

Figure 3.8 A manager dictating to a shorthand typist

Today, the manager will probably draft the letter straight on a PC, making corrections as needed. This will then be passed electronically to an administrator who will print it out on headed stationary. The process is much quicker and takes far less of the administrator's time.

Figure 3.9 Much more efficient!

Many organisations have recognised that people who were formerly employed as typists can be used much more productively. In many cases they are now employed as office administrators or personal assistants, with a far wider range of responsibilities than before.

Office administrators will frequently create standard letters on their computers, just varying the wording to suit a particular circumstance. This means that they can deal with more customers in a given time and be more productive.

IT can increase productivity in a factory quite dramatically. Cars are now made using many robotic tools. These automate the manufacturing processes and can be managed by far fewer employees than before.

Increased productivity through the use of IT can mean that the same numbers of employees do more work between them, or it may mean that fewer employees are needed to do the same amount of work.

How can IT help an organisation to be more competitive?

If two businesses are both trying to supply similar goods or services to the same group of people (or market) then they are competitors. For example, McDonald's and Burger King are competitors in the fast food market.

A business will have to work harder to sell its products if it has a competitor. In order to succeed it will have to become more **competitive**. This means that it will have to examine many aspects of the business and compare them with its rival. To be more competitive, the company will have to compare, amongst other things, the range and quality of the goods or services that it provides and the prices it charges.

A business can become more competitive if it:

- increases efficiency
- increases productivity
- introduces new products (goods or services).

We have already seen how IT can support the first two.

IT can also enable a business to offer completely new services, which could not be offered without it. For example, back in the 1980s many banks introduced Automatic Teller Machines (cash machines) that allowed customers to withdraw cash outside bank opening hours. As a result, many more people opened bank accounts. More recently, Internet banking has provided an even more flexible service for bank customers.

What does it mean?

Competitive – two businesses are competitive if they are both trying to sell goods or services to the same market.

Case study – McDonald's and Burger King

How can the two fast food giants compete? Suppose McDonald's decides to charge less than Burger King for its burgers. Now this could be achieved by using cheaper ingredients, but there is always the danger that the customer will not like the burgers as much. Or McDonald's could simply become more efficient in the ways described earlier by clever use of IT.

On the other hand, McDonald's could become more competitive by keeping the prices the same as at Burger King but increasing the quality of the food. It could add extra ingredients, or make larger portions. Although the ingredients would be more expensive, it could save by making its staff more productive.

Or, McDonald's could introduce new types of meals, and hope to attract more customers because of the wider range of products.

Whichever it chooses to do it will have to publicise the improvements, and the cost of advertising has to be taken into account.

In comparison, how can the large software suppliers, like Microsoft® and Lotus®, make themselves more competitive?

In what ways can IT support decision-making?

Managers have to make many decisions. They have to organise the work for their staff and decide what tasks or projects should be done next. They must assess the performance of their sections or departments in the past and then plan for the future.

Good decisions can be made only if the manager has the right information. The information must be accurate, relevant, up to date and easy to understand. Information systems store a great deal of data about an organisation. This can be useful to a manager only if it is summarised and output as useful information.

For example, a chocolate processing factory stores large amounts of data about the ingredients for individual products, about the time taken to make each product, and about the demand for them. Some of the products, such as Easter eggs and chocolate tree decorations, are seasonal. Each year the sales manager has to decide how many Easter eggs should be made, and which types. The production manager decides when they can be fitted into the production run and makes sure that the ingredients are ordered in time. Both managers need good information – about sales in previous years, about what their competitors produced, and about the prices of ingredients on the world market.

Good IT systems, such as databases, can store all the data. They can also produce reports of all the information needed by the managers. These are known as *Management Information Systems*.

How can IT improve communication?

People communicate with each other in a variety of ways, including:

- face to face
- written documents – letter, report, memo
- telephone
- e-mail
- fax.

Each method has advantages and disadvantages. Most organisations use a mixture of them all, but almost all of them can be improved by the use of IT.

- *Written documents* are much more legible when printed than when handwritten. Word processing software has transformed the way in which we produce documents today. Documents can be checked for grammar and spelling, and attractive layouts can be used.
- *Telephone systems* are much more reliable, and give much clearer sound, when they are digitally controlled. Modern networks within organisations can use the same digital cables to carry both computer data and voice. These systems can then use effective voice-mail and queuing systems for callers.
- *E-mail* is fast becoming the preferred method of communication for a great many employees, and of course, this is entirely dependent on good IT communication networks. The main advantages of e-mail are the speed of delivery and the fact that the person receiving an e-mail can read it and deal with it at a time that is convenient to them. The informality of e-mail also means that people can often write an e-mail very rapidly.
- *Fax* (facsimile documents) is gradually being replaced by e-mail, but is still useful for transferring handwritten or drawn material electronically. However, if high-quality is required it is better to scan a document and then send it as an e-mail attachment.

How can IT be used to improve the company image?

The image of a company is the mental picture that the general public have of it. Think of the mobile phone network that you use. Do you get the impression that the company is efficient, well organised and business-like or does it look chaotic? Is it trying to attract customers with a lot of money to spend or is it aiming at the cheaper end of the market? Is it lively and fashionable or rather traditional? You can often answer these questions by looking at how a company presents itself to the public through advertising, letters and other publicity.

Many companies wish to appear to be modern and up to date, and this can be achieved by using electronic means of communication. Most customers expect a business to have a website, and if it does not have one then it risks losing credibility. Similarly, many people will want to use e-mail to correspond with an organisation. And everyone today expects a company to produce clear, well-written printed letters.

These means of communication say as much about the company as the actual content of the messages.

Further research – How organisations use IT

Think again about the two organisations that you picked in section 3.1 (page 121). Find out everything you can about how they use IT and why they need IT systems.

Test your knowledge

1   How can IT help to make an organisation more efficient?
2   How can IT help employees to be more productive?
3   List three methods of communication and explain how IT has improved them.
4   Why might a company want to improve its image?

3.4 Data safety and security

The Internet

The **Internet** is used very widely both for business and in the home. It can pose security and safety problems, so we begin with a brief introduction to some of its features.

What does it mean?

The Internet – the Internet is a public network that connects millions of computers across the world.

What are the Internet and the World Wide Web?

The Internet has existed since the 1970s and was used originally by universities, research institutions and the military. Its main function was to enable users to transfer files from one computer to another.

Most of these files could be downloaded and read by anyone. But files which were sent from one person directly to another person became known as electronic mail, or e-mail.

The Internet became widely used by the general public only in the 1990s. The reason for the sudden growth in the use of the Internet was the launch of the **World Wide Web** in 1991. Before then, files could be transferred across the world, but the user had to know where files were stored, and they were not always easy to find.

Webpages can be laid out attractively on the screen and can contain graphics, sound and video clips. Before the Web was invented most files available on the Internet were simple text files. Today all the pages that you visit when you go on the Internet are part of the Web.

The most important feature of the Web is the use of hyperlinks – the hotspots which allow the user to jump to another page. All the pages on the Web are ultimately linked together through hyperlinks, giving a vast network of information.

What does it mean?

World Wide Web – the World Wide Web (WWW or the Web) consists of pages created in a computer language called Hypertext MarkUp Language (HTML). Webpages can contain hyperlinks that enable the user to jump directly to another page located anywhere in the world on the Web.

Is the Internet the same as the Web?

The Internet includes the Web, but has many other aspects as well. The Internet offers:

- e-mail
- newsgroups
- chat rooms
- remote login – this enables users to log into the computer system of an organisation using their IDs and passwords
- search engines, such as Yahoo! and Google
- the Web.

What is the difference between the Internet, intranet and extranet?

As we have seen, the Internet is a public network, which means that anyone can use any of its facilities. In contrast, **intranets** and **extranets** are private systems which can be used only by members of organisations.

What does it mean?

Intranet – a closed system that has many of the features of the Internet but which is accessible only within an organisation.

What does it mean?

Extranet – an extension of an organisation's intranet that can be accessed from the Internet, but only by users who have been given access rights.

Many large businesses encourage staff to use electronic means of communication, and set up internal e-mail systems. Sometimes they also provide a collection of information pages created in HTML. This system is very much like a private Internet and is known as an intranet (note the spelling). The intranet is accessible only to people using the company's own networks and cannot be reached from the Internet.

A large organisation may want its members to view the intranet even when they are not at their place of work. They can make some or all of the intranet pages available over the Internet in an extranet, but members have to use a password to gain access. Extranets are used by a number of businesses, especially if some of their employees are often away on business trips. They can also be used by organisations whose members are spread over a wide area, for example, charities who want to make information available to volunteers.

What is a browser?

A browser is a piece of software which is used to view pages on the Web. The most used browsers at present are Microsoft® Internet Explorer and Netscape® Navigator. When a user visits a webpage the HTML code is downloaded to the person's computer and the browser interprets the code to create the webpage itself. A browser also supports hyperlinks, so that when a user clicks on a link the browser will find the correct page and download it.

What is an e-mail client?

When you send or receive an e-mail you have to use a specialist software package, known as an e-mail client, to do this. The most used e-mail clients are Outlook and Outlook Express, but there are many others. Some Internet Service Providers, such as AOL, supply their own e-mail client software.

Data security

In Unit 2, section 2.3, we saw that software and data must be protected from unauthorised access. In this section we will be looking again at the Data Protection Act and at what an organisation must do to comply with it. We will also look at additional threats to security:

- lack of confidentiality
- loss or damage to the hardware
- Internet use.

Further research – Data protection policies

At your college or place of work, find out what data protection policies the organisation has in place. Do they seem to cover the requirements of the Data Protection Act?

What kind of data is covered by the Data Protection Act?

Most organisations collect and store personal data. For example, they will hold details about their employees.

Many businesses will also have information about their customers and some of this information can be quite detailed. For example, supermarket chains issue loyalty cards to their customers, and the customers can gain loyalty points or other incentives like AirMiles when they do their shopping. Whenever the customer buys anything the system will also be gathering information about the type of goods that the person prefers, what time of the day he or she goes shopping, etc.

The Data Protection Act applies whenever information about living persons is stored, but only if it is possible to identify the individual from the data. So if a survey is done but the names of the people who respond are not collected, then this usually does not count as personal data.

Check your understanding – The Data Protection Act

Let us remind ourselves of the eight Data Protection principles.

1 *Personal data must be processed fairly and lawfully.* Data controllers in organisations must complete a notification form for the Information Commissioner. They must tell the Information Commissioner what data they intend to collect, how they intend to collect it, what they want to use the data for, and who they may pass the information on to. They also have to explain how they intend to keep the data secure. The data subject must give permission for any data to be used.

2 *Personal data must be obtained and processed for limited purposes.* The organisation must use the data only in the way it is described on its notification form and it must not use it for any other purpose.

3 *Personal data must be adequate, relevant and not excessive.* The data must be just what is needed and nothing more.

4 *Personal data must be accurate.* The organisation has to try to ensure that the data is correct, although it cannot be held responsible if the data subject made a mistake when giving the information in the first place.

5 *Personal data must not be kept longer than necessary.*

6 *Personal data must be processed in accordance with the data subject's rights.* Any data subject (that is, the person that the data refers to) is entitled to read the information that is held about him or her. The data controller in the organisation must provide the information so that it is easy to understand. The data subject has the right to ask for his or her name to be removed from any marketing lists.

7 *Personal data must be secure.* The data must be available only to people within the organisation who need to know it. Anything else will count as unauthorised access.

8 *Personal data must not be transferred to countries outside Europe without adequate protection.* This is because all the countries in the European Union (EU) have similar data protection laws, but countries outside the EU vary a great deal.

What is confidential information?

Confidential information is information that should be known only by a limited number of people. For example, patients expect that the information they give to a doctor will be kept confidential, although they will understand that the notes the doctor writes may be read by other staff at the surgery. When something is said 'in confidence' both people should be clear about who is entitled to know the information.

All personal data must be treated as confidential under the Data Protection Act.

However an organisation will also want to keep other, non-personal, data confidential as well.

It will not want its competitors to know how the business is going, or perhaps how it makes its products. This kind of information is 'business sensitive'.

Should customer information be kept confidential?

When one company (a customer) orders supplies from another company (a supplier), the data about the order is not personal data. It will include details of the customer company, and maybe the name of the person who placed the order, but will not include any personal information about an individual.

However, the customer company would still expect that its order remains a piece of confidential information. It would not want another supplier to know who it is buying supplies from, and it would not want a competitor to know how much it is spending on supplies. Indeed, all business transactions are normally treated as confidential.

How can customer information be kept confidential?

Customer information can be kept confidential by:

- using good security procedures (see Unit 2, section 2.3, for more information about these)
- employing reliable staff
- using disciplinary procedures if employees break confidentiality.

Good security procedures will ensure that no one has unauthorised access to information. But what about the people who do have authorised access? How can the organisation make sure that they do not pass the information on to other people?

Staff who deal with confidential information must be selected carefully. The organisation must check references and be convinced that people are reliable before employing them. There will also be clear guidelines about what will happen to an employee if he or she acts improperly.

How can data security be threatened by loss or damage to hardware?

All IT systems have to be protected from loss and damage. This applies to the hardware – the components of the computer system and the network connections – as well as to the software and data held on the system.

An IT system can be damaged by:

- catastrophic events, such as fire, flood or major damage to the building
- environmental problems, such as high temperatures or damp
- electrical and magnetic interference
- minor faults such as damaged cables or broken components
- lost disks, keys or components.

Most of these problems are caused by accidents, but someone who wants to harm an organisation could cause such damage deliberately. Any damage to the hardware puts the software and data at risk as well.

How does the use of the Internet threaten security?

Many business organisations use the Internet for e-mail and remote logins, but these do pose extra security risks.

- *E-mail* – many viruses are carried on e-mail attachments. These can then infect the computer system by deleting or altering files. Many viruses that come via e-mail can also automatically send out new e-mails, with the virus attached, to any addresses in the e-mail address book. Since the process is automatic, viruses can spread from organisation to organisation around the world very rapidly.

- *Remote login* – when employees are working away from the office they can log in to the organisation's network over a modem, using their user IDs and passwords. It is technically possible for someone else to do this illegally and to hack into the system.

Why is data security so important in IT?

The hardware used in organisations can be worth many hundreds of thousands of pounds. If any of it is damaged or stolen then it may take a while to replace it. The cost of replacement will usually be covered by insurance, so the main problem will be the delay in installing the replacement. The delay can mean that business is lost and the company will lose money.

Although the computer hardware in an organisation may be very valuable, damage to software and data is of far greater significance to most businesses. The software can be replaced (as copies will always be available), but the real risk lies in loss of business data. Imagine what could happen if an airline lost all its data about the tickets it had sold for flights in the future. It would not be able to issue the tickets to passengers who had already booked but not yet received their tickets; it would not know whether flights were full, so would not be able to sell more tickets; it would not be able to provide airports with security information about passengers. Data is far more valuable to a business than either the hardware or the programs.

Since business data is so important, it is confidential. Other companies might be very interested to know what it contains, so security is also needed to ensure that information is only available to those with a right to know it.

Data security measures

In Unit 2 we saw that users and network administrators should create backups of files. You also learnt about how they set up access privileges for users. In this section we will look at backup procedures in more detail, and will discuss a number of ways in which access can be controlled.

Why are backups needed?

Hardware, software and data have to be protected, but however good the protection, no one should ever assume that loss and damage will not occur. Damage can be accidental, or it can be caused deliberately. Accidents can and do happen, either through human error or through external events like fire or earthquake. Criminal activity can never be entirely prevented. As a result much of computer security is concerned with how to reinstate a system if it does get damaged.

A backup is a copy of files, which is kept safely apart from the original files. If any programs or data are damaged in any way then it should be possible to go to a backup that was created earlier and install it instead.

Of course, if the backup was created some time ago then it may not be up to date, and some of the data may truly be irrecoverable. Backup procedures should be designed so that as little data as possible is lost if things do go wrong.

How are backups made?

The two main types of backup are:

- *Full backup* – the operating system can be set up so that it automatically makes a backup on a regular basis. Most organisations backup their data every night, at a time when users will not be trying to access it. Some organisations do another full backup at some point during the day as well, but this does mean that the data will not be usable whilst the backup is being performed.
- *Incremental backup* – several of these may be done between one full backup and the next. An incremental backup copies only the files that have been changed since the last backup. Although incremental backups will be done during the working day, they will be much quicker than full backups, so should not noticeably interrupt normal work. If the files need to be restored then the last full backup will be used together with any incremental backups made since.

Some organisations take backups a stage further and make two or more copies of every single file each time it is saved. This means that the system in use will be mirrored by a second system, and perhaps even a third, so if the main system goes wrong the *mirror system* can simply take over.

How should backups be stored?

Backup files should be stored on a medium that:

- makes fast copies
- can be stored in a secure place away from the original.

So if a full backup is taken of all the files on a network server (that is, on the network's hard disk) then it should be stored on a medium that can be removed and locked away in a safe. Digital tape is commonly used for this purpose, as data can be copied to tape very rapidly.

All backup tapes and disks need to be labelled very carefully with the date and time.

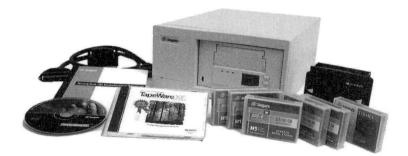

Figure 3.10 Digital tape

What are access controls?

The access to hardware, software and data has to be controlled. This means that people must not be allowed to access any IT resource unless they have a right to do so. It is the responsibility of the network manager to ensure that these controls are in place.

There are three types of access controls:

- physical access control
- procedural access control
- software access control.

What is physical access control?

Access to buildings, rooms and IT systems can be controlled in a number of ways:

- *Locks on workstations* – workstations can be protected with devices that will unlock the system only if a key or keycard is used.
- *Locks on rooms* – all rooms that contain IT equipment or media should have locks. Ordinary keys can be copied, and can be lost by legitimate users, so many organisations now fit digital locks. Some locks can be operated by swiping the user's ID card.
- *Safes* – safes used to store disks and documents should be heavy and fireproof.

Figure 3.11 A digital lock

Figure 3.12 A safe

Procedural access controls

There are a number of procedures that should be carried out to make sure that security is maintained. These tasks should all be recorded, with the date, in a log book.

- *Key control* – keys to rooms containing IT equipment should be issued only to people with a right to hold them. The names of the key holders should be logged.
- *Code control* – the codes for safes and digital locks should be known only by named individuals, who should be logged. The codes should be changed from time to time if possible.
- *Offline storage* – all important disks and documents should be stored in a safe. This will apply to original software, licences and all backups of data. A log should be kept of all the items stored.
- *Password control* – passwords can be changed frequently. Users must be encouraged not to write passwords down.
- *Regular checks* – cables and other vulnerable components should be checked regularly for signs of tampering. Again, a record of all the checks should be kept.

Software access controls

Confidentiality of data and the general security of the software on IT systems can be controlled by:

- *Access privileges* – see Unit 2, section 2.3, for more information about how the network administrator can control access to software and data.
- *Using screen savers* – a screen saver will hide information on a screen if the user leaves the room.
- *Firewalls* – a firewall is a piece of systems software that protects the system from unauthorised access. Firewalls are commonly used to check all the communications between a system and the Internet. If it detects any unexpected attempts to access the system via the Internet it will block them and report them immediately to the system administrator.

Internet safety

The Internet brings enormous benefits to organisations and to individuals, but it is not without risk. The main threats are:

- *Loss of confidentiality* – some of the data stored on the database of an organisation may be displayed on a website. In some cases, data should be shown only to a specific user. For example, if you use Internet banking you should be confident that the bank will not reveal information about your account to anyone else.
- *Receiving offensive material* – Internet users should view only material that they want to see. They should not be presented with material that they find offensive either on the Web or by e-mail. Offensive material would include pornography as well as text and images that promote racism, sexism, violence, illegal drug use, or personal abuse. Possession of some types of material, such as child pornography, is illegal in many countries.
- *Theft and fraud* – credit card fraud can be carried out both on and off the Internet, by people obtaining the details on credit cards and using them illegally to buy goods. The particular problem on the Internet is that the user will not be aware of any electronic 'spying' that is going on.

- *Infringement of copyright* – Internet users may find that they can copy text, images or sounds that are under copyright.
- *Transmission of viruses* – e-mail is the most common medium for the transmission of viruses. One common method is to hide a virus in a macro in a document produced on a general software application, such as a word processor.

How can the Internet be used responsibly by the end user?

The end user can use the Internet responsibly by using common sense and by employing some standard software.

For example, the user is personally responsible for ensuring that he or she respects copyright. Theoretically, the copyright for all text and images on the Web belongs to the person or organisation who produced it. In practice, most material is displayed for public use and the organisation would not object to it being used for personal purposes. Nothing that is displayed on the Web can be used for commercial purposes without permission. This is particularly important in relation to photos, drawings and other images. Some sites do offer copyright-free images, which can be used on other websites provided the source is acknowledged.

These software tools can also be used:

- *Nanny software* – this is software that can be used by network administrators, teachers and parents to control which websites users can access. Nanny software uses key words to detect sites that might be unsuitable or inappropriate in a business, educational or home context, especially pornographic material and offensive language.
- *Browser security settings* – browsers can be configured in a number of ways to control access to websites. They can be used to prevent websites from depositing **cookies** on a computer. They can also carry out some checks whenever the user tries to download software from the Internet.

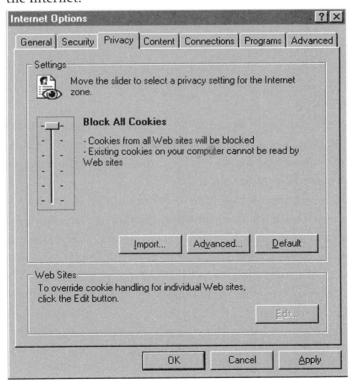

Figure 3.13
Browser settings
in Microsoft® Internet Explorer

What does it mean?

Cookie – a cookie is a short file that is placed on a user's computer system by a website that is visited. Cookies are used to store the user's personal information and preferences that are used by the website to personalise the services that it offers.

■ *Virus protection* – viruses are commonly distributed through the Internet, often as attachments to e-mails. All users should check that their system is covered by up-to-date virus protection. It is the responsibility of the network manager to ensure that all computers on the network are protected, as well as any standalone systems such as laptops. Virus protection data files can be updated automatically, via the Internet, on a regular basis. Many systems will update their virus data files several times each day.

How can services be provided safely through the Internet?

An organisation that offers Internet services needs to be able to reassure customers that they, and their money, will be safe. A number of techniques are used:

■ *Secure server* – when a user provides personal data to a website, he or she needs to know that the information cannot be read by anyone else. This is not only to comply with the Data Protection Act, but also so that the user feels safe about providing credit card details for online shopping. A secure server is used by the website to collect the data. This encrypts all the data so that if anyone does gain illegal access to it they will not be able to understand or use the data. Secure servers are used for all financial transactions over the Internet.

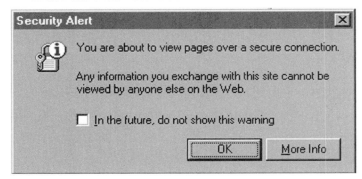

Figure 3.14
Dialogue window that appears when a user is transferred to a secure server

■ *Digital IDs* – there are a number of independent certification authorities who issue digital IDs, after checking the identity of the subscriber. A digital ID can then be added to an e-mail as a signature. If a user receives an e-mail signed with a digital ID, he or she can click on a link to check the identity of the sender.

Figure 3.15 The icon that shows that an e-mail is signed with a digital ID

■ *E-mail encryption* – e-mail sent from an e-mail client can also be encrypted. The person sending the e-mail and the person receiving it must both have digital IDs.

Figure 3.16 The e-mail encryption button in Microsoft® Outlook Express

Test your knowledge

1 Why should a company want to keep its business data confidential even if it is not covered by the Data Protection Act?

2 A small fire at a company destroys the main network server along with the network hard disk storage. Explain how this event could damage the business if it was not able to recover the IT systems. Explain how good security procedures could enable the company to get back into business very quickly.

3 What is the difference between full and incremental backups, and when might each be used?

4 How can a system administrator make sure that backups will not be affected by any disasters that may damage the main system?

🖉 Assessment tasks

This section describes what you must do to obtain a Merit grade for this unit.

A Distinction grade may be awarded if your work demonstrates a deeper understanding of the topics and is of a higher quality. The highlighted sentences indicate the quality of work expected at Distinction level.

How do I provide assessment evidence?

Your evidence will either be all in the form of a written report, or may be a mixture of the following:

- written reports
- printouts from software packages
- material used in a presentation
- witness statements
- observation sheets.

All your evidence should be presented in one folder, which should have a front cover and a contents page. You should divide the evidence into four sections corresponding to the four tasks.

Task 1

Learning outcome 1 – Describe organisational structures and characteristics

Hint – do not simply copy the text from this book, but put it into your own words.

1   Write one or two sentences to define each of these types of organisation and give an example of each:
    - small sole trader
    - partnership
    - private limited company
    - large multi-national company
    - public service organisation
    - commercial organisation.

To achieve a Distinction grade you should give an extensive explanation of each of these types.

2   Choose *two* organisations that you know or have read about. Write a description of each. In your descriptions you should make sure that you have included all the following:
    - describe the organisation's specific purpose
    - describe the organisation's distinct identity
    - from the list in (1) above, identify which type of organisation it is
    - explain who the organisation is accountable to and why
    - describe how the organisation is led

- draw an organisation chart
- explain why the organisation is structured in this way
- describe, with examples, other ways in which organisations could be structured.

> To obtain a Distinction grade, you should also describe the structure and decision-making levels in some detail for at least one of these organisations.

Task 2

Learning outcome 2 – Describe roles of IT practitioners

Chose *two* different jobs in the IT industry. Write at least half a page on each, describing the work.

> To obtain a Distinction grade, you should write a more detailed account of the role of at least one IT practitioner, illustrated with examples of typical responsibilities and tasks.

Task 3

Learning outcome 3 – Explain why organisations use IT

For *each* of the organisations that you identified for Task 1:

1 Describe how the organisation uses IT.
2 Explain why the organisation needs IT.

> To obtain a Distinction grade, you should also explain how these two organisations would have to change if they did not use IT.

Task 4

Learning outcome 4 – Explain the importance of data safety and security

Write several sentences to answer each of these questions:

1 How are browsers and e-mail used in Internet communications?
2 What are the differences between Internet, intranet and extranet?
3 Why is it important to keep customer information confidential?
4 How can data security and confidentiality be maintained within an organisation?
5 Describe additional external threats to an organisation that arise through Internet use.

> To obtain a Distinction grade, you also need to answer these questions:
>
> 6 What might happen if security issues are not considered when using the Internet?
> 7 How can an organisation protect itself against Internet security threats?

UNIT 7: INTRODUCTION TO DATABASES

Success in this unit

What are the learning outcomes?

To achieve this unit you must:

- describe the features and facilities of relational databases
- design a suitable database to satisfy user needs
- provide suitable documentation to support the database design
- evaluate the database.

How is this unit assessed?

This unit is externally assessed. The Examination Board (Edexcel) will set an Integrated Vocational Assignment (IVA), which will be based on all the assessment criteria. This will consist of a series of practical tasks to complete over a period of time.

See the *Assessment tasks* section at the end of this unit for more information about the IVA.

Introduction

About this unit

In this unit you will learn about relational databases and how they are used in business.

The unit is quite practical and you will concentrate on developing your own skills in using a standard database software package. You will also be expected to produce user and technical documentation for your database, and then evaluate it.

Before you begin to learn about relational databases you must make sure that you fully understand the concepts of simple flat file databases. It is a good idea to start by developing some simple databases in a relational database package, as that is the best way to learn to use the facilities that the package offers.

Flat file databases

Databases are organised collections of data. They are widely used in organisations to store information and to help them carry out their business. The simplest kinds of databases are known as **flat file databases**. You will be studying them as a stepping-stone towards understanding how the more complex relational databases work.

? What does it mean?

Database – a database is a collection of data. It is organised so that different kinds of information can be retrieved from it by the users.

? What does it mean?

Flat file database – a flat file database is a simple database in which the data can be written down as a single list or table.

What is a flat file database?

Many software packages include file-handling features. For example, your e-mail client software will include an address book, in which you can store details of people and organisations. The address book is a file, and each entry is a **record**. The e-mail address book will store the data in categories, such as the name of the person and the e-mail address; these categories are known as **fields**. If you use an address book that can be linked to other packages then it may well also contain other fields, such as telephone number, fax number and postal address as well.

? What does it mean?

Record – a record is the data in a database about a single object in the real world.

What does it mean?

Field – a field is a category used for data in a database. The name of the field is its fieldname.

The user is not allowed to change the fields in a built-in file like an address book, but many generic software applications allow you to create your own files and to define the fields that you want to use. You can create a list (in Microsoft® Excel), a datasource (in Microsoft® Word), a table (in Microsoft® Access), or a file (in a programming language). All of these can be called flat file databases, because they are essentially two-dimensional.

Flat file databases are usually printed out as tables. Each row of the table is one record. The headings at the top of the columns are the fieldnames.

Fieldnames

Stock code	Stock description	Sheets per pack	Quantity in stock
P2153	A4 mono inkjet paper	2000	53
P2154	A4 colour inkjet paper	2000	112
P3297	A4 premium inkjet paper	200	32
P4033	A4 glossy paper	50	21
P7122	Banner paper	100	15

Records

Figure 7.1 A flat file database set up in a spreadsheet.

What functions can I carry out with a flat file database?

Flat file databases allow the user to view and browse through the data, and also to add, delete or amend individual records. They often offer you a choice between two ways of viewing the data. The most usual way is to view all the records in a table format, with the fieldnames across the tops of the columns and the records arranged in rows. An alternative is to view one record at a time, presented as an on-screen **form**. Some packages allow you to design your own forms.

What does it mean?

Form – a form is an on-screen user interface designed to view the data in a database.

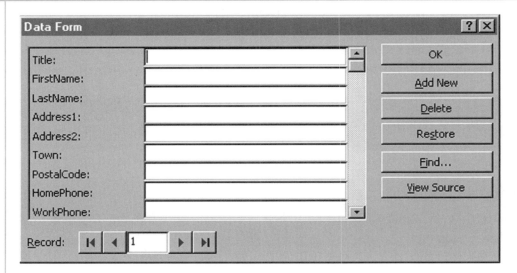

Figure 7.2 A form created by Microsoft® Word for a datasource (flat file database)

The user can normally sort the data as well, using one of the fields as a **sort key field**. For example, the e-mail address book allows the user to sort the records using name as the sort key, or alternatively, using the e-mail address as the sort key. Records can be sorted in ascending or descending order. Similarly, if you create your own list (flat file) in Microsoft® Excel and include the names and date of birth of all your friends, then you will be able to sort the list into alphabetical order by name, or alternatively, in date order using Date of Birth as the sort key.

What does it mean?

Sort key field – a sort key field is used to sort the data into alphabetical or numerical order.

	A	B	C
1	**Surname**	**Forename**	**Date of Birth**
2	Banks	Sophie	21-Apr-87
3	Christofides	Nina	30-Sep-86
4	Cresswell	Chloe	19-Dec-85
5	McDonald	James	04-Oct-85
6	Shah	Indira	03-Jul-86
7			

Figure 7.3 List in Microsoft® Excel sorted by surname

	A	B	C
1	**Surname**	**Forename**	**Date of Birth**
2	McDonald	James	04-Oct-85
3	Cresswell	Chloe	19-Dec-85
4	Shah	Indira	03-Jul-86
5	Christofides	Nina	30-Sep-86
6	Banks	Sophie	21-Apr-87
7			

Figure 7.4 The same list in Microsoft® Excel sorted by date of birth

Files can also be searched (or queried, or interrogated) for data using a **query**. The query would be searching for all the records with data in one particular field that matches some **criterion**. The criterion could specify some text that the data has to match; e.g. it could search for all the names with the surname Jones (Figure 7.5). Alternatively, it could search for data that meets a condition; e.g. a search could be made in the Date of Birth field to find all the records of people born after a specified date. More complex searches can be carried out that check the data in several fields.

What does it mean?

Query – a query is a method for searching and displaying a selection of data in a database.

What does it mean?

Criterion – a criterion is a rule that is used to select data. Note that the plural of criterion is criteria.

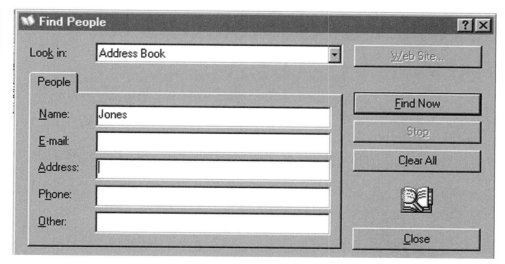

Figure 7.5 This form creates a query that searches an address book

Finally, you can usually print out the data in a file. Any printout like this is known as a *report*. A report can list all the data in the file or can use a query to select specific records and to present data in certain fields only.

Often a flat file database will have one field, the **primary key field**, which uniquely identifies each record. Examples of primary keys are the membership number in a file of club members, the account number in a customer account at a bank, or the stock code in a file of stock held in a shop.

? What does it mean?

Primary key field – a primary key field is the field in a file or table in which the data uniquely identifies each record.

Why do we need relational databases?

A flat file database system can be very useful if the data to be stored is quite simple. It will let the user set up any number of files, each with its own record structure. However it has one overriding problem, namely that the same data may appear in two files, but it is not possible to link the two files together in any way. So data, such as a person's address, may be changed in one file, but be left unchanged in another file.

The relational database was the solution to this important problem.

7.1 Features and facilities of relational databases

Components of a relational database

What is a relational database?

A relational database is a much more complex structure than a simple flat file database. A flat file can hold data about, say, the stock held in a shop. If the retailer wants to store data about orders sent to the suppliers to replenish the stock, or details about customers, he or she will have to create a separate flat file database for each. This is not an efficient way of handling the data.

What are the features of a relational database?

In a relational database, data may be stored in a series of **tables**, each of which has a similar structure to a flat file. Such a database could have one table with data about stock, another of orders and another of customer details. (Note that in some software, the tables are referred to as files.)

What does it mean?

Table – a table in a relational database is a set of records, just like a flat file database. A relational database will have more than one table.

The crucial added feature of a relational database is that it links the tables together. This means that one table can refer to data in another table, so a table of orders could link to the table of stock.

In an organisation, the database should hold centrally all the data required by all the users, so that no separate files need be stored elsewhere. Normally each user will be able to view only those parts of the database which directly affect his or her work. For example, the shop salespersons will be able to view some of the data in the stock file when they make a sale, but only the manager will be able to handle the orders to suppliers.

A relational database system will also hold all the queries, forms and reports that accompany the tables.

Relational database systems are commonly used on networks. The database will be stored on the network server, and several users may be able to access the database at the same time.

How are relational databases managed?

A piece of software known as a database management system (DBMS) holds all the data, as well as all the forms, queries and reports in a database. It organises the data on the backing store, and controls access to the data by users.

Individual users are not really aware of the complexity of the database. The DBMS hides much of it away from them. Users are only aware of the data that they require, which will often appear to them to be a simple flat file. Different users in the company will want to use different mixes of data within the database, and DBMS handles all these needs.

How are relational databases developed?

IT professionals who create databases are known as *database developers*. Their job is to create an underlying database structure that supports all the needs of all the users, and also to provide each type of employee with access to the exact data required, and no more.

The database developer uses the features of the DBMS to build a database, and then the user has to work only with the ready prepared database itself.

What packages are available commercially?

Microsoft® Access is a well-known database management system, which is used by professionals to create complex databases. It was originally intended for use on standalone systems, so that users could create their own small databases. This did mean that some end users found that they became database developers as well, even though they did not have the skills in relational database design that you will be learning in this unit. However, Microsoft® Access is a very flexible piece of software and is also ideal for those learning how to develop relational databases. We will be referring to it throughout this unit.

There are other database management systems on the market which are designed for network use and these do require specialist professional skills. Examples of these are Oracle Database®, and Microsoft® SQL Server.

Further research – Database wizards in Microsoft® Access

You can explore a number of different databases by using the database wizards in Microsoft® Access. They create complete databases for you and can demonstrate a lot of ideas and techniques.

When you first launch Access it asks you whether you want to create a new database using a blank Access database or the Access database wizards, pages and projects. Select the latter, then try out one of the wizards.

Relational database structure

How are tables used in a relational database?

A relational database will have at least two tables, and probably many more. Each table contains data about a single class of objects (sometimes known as an *entity*). On the face of it, each table looks just like a flat file, but as we shall see, one or more of the fields is linked through to other tables.

How is a field defined in a table?

A table is structured around a number of fields. The developer will give each field a fieldname and a data type. The fieldname should be meaningful. For example, 'Field1', 'Number', 'cprptt' are not very explicit, whereas 'Postcode', 'Date of Birth', 'Quantity in Stock' are perfectly clear.

Names should usually be divided into Surname and Forename (or Initials). We often sort names by surname, so it needs its own field and should not be buried in a Name field. If you progress to more advanced database design on another course, you will find that each fieldname may be given a prefix which identifies the datatype. For example, the fieldname 'txtSurname' might be used.

What is a datatype?

The datatype of a field determines two things:

- how many bytes of storage is allocated to each item of data
- what kinds of functions can be carried out with the data; e.g. you can only carry out calculations with data that has a number datatype.

The common data types are:

- *Text* – also known as a 'string'. It allows the user to enter up to 255 characters in a field. Text can include numerical digits, but the database will not be able to calculate with them as it will treat them just like letters.
- *Memo* – also known as 'text' in some DBMS. This is simply a longer text field and can include thousands of characters.
- *Number* – the developer usually has a choice of number types, including:
    - o *Byte* – uses 1 byte of storage to hold an integer (whole number) in the range 0 to 255
    - o *Integer* – uses 2 bytes of storage to hold an integer between −32,768 and 32,767. Use this for most integer fields unless the data is likely to be very large.
    - o *Long integer* – uses 4 bytes of storage to hold an integer in the range −2,147,483,648 to 2,147,483,647.
    - o *Single* – also known as 'single precision real' or 'floating point'. Uses 4 bytes of storage to hold a number with a decimal point. Use this for most decimal number fields.
    - o *Double* – also known as 'double precision real'. Uses 8 bytes of storage to hold a number with a decimal point.
    - o *Decimal* – uses 12 bytes of storage to hold a positive or negative number with a decimal point. This should not be used unless a high degree of accuracy or extremely large numbers are needed.
- *Date/Time* – the developer can usually specify which format the date should appear in. Don't forget that American dates are written in a different order from UK dates, so that 5/10/03 is 10 May 2003 in the USA, and 5 October in the UK.
- *Yes/No* – also known as 'logical'. This can simply hold one of two values – 'yes' or 'no'. As alternatives to 'yes' and 'no', the words 'true' and 'false', or 'on' and 'off', can be entered.

How are records entered?

Figure 7.6 shows an example of a table, with some records entered. Each row in the table contains a record and refers to one specific object in the real world.

The first three fields all use the text data type, whilst the year is an integer. When the data is keyed in the DBMS will not allow the user to enter data which is of the incorrect datatype. So if words are entered in the Year field by mistake the software will display an error message.

Registration	Make	Model	Year
V123 ABC	Nissan	Micra	1999
Y456 XYZ	Fiat	Punto	2001
LD03 LMN	BMW	3 series	2003
AB51 PQR	Skoda	Octavia	2002
R456 CDE	Volkswagen	Polo	1997
T789 JKL	Honda	Civic	1999
C567 RST	Ford	Anglia	1986
P345 TUV	Jaguar	X-type	1996

Figure 7.6 Records entered into a table

Why is the primary key field important?

Each table should have a primary key field. Primary keys are essential in relational databases as we use them to link tables together.

In the example above, the car registration is the primary key field. In each record, the actual registration is unique to that car, and the car can be identified by it. The data in the primary key field for each record is known as the primary key of that record. So 'Registration' is the primary key field for the table, and 'LD03 LMN' is the primary key for the third record.

Check your understanding – Primary key fields

Sometimes it is difficult to decide which field should be the primary key field.

Often, a new field can be created to do the job. For example, a table may hold a list of people's names and addresses. Some people may have the same name, so the name cannot be used as the record key field because the data would not be unique for each record. Also more than one person could live at the same address, so the address could not be used as the primary key field. So a new field would have to be created as the primary key field. This could simply number the records.

In each of these examples, is there a field which can be the primary key field? If not, suggest a new field that could be created for this purpose.

1 bank account details including bank account number, name, address
2 a membership list for a club consisting of names, addresses and the date a person joined
3 a list of the stock held in a warehouse, which includes for each item the stock code, a description of the item and the quantity in stock
4 entries in a telephone book.

A primary key is sometimes simply known as a key, but this can be rather confusing as the terms *sort key* and *foreign key* are also used in databases. You will sometimes see the term 'record key' used – this is simply another term for the primary key.

What is a table definition?

A table definition is a list of all the fields in a table. The primary key should be identified. There are several ways of giving a table definition, but we will do it as a simple list, with the primary key field underlined.

The table definition for the cars table is:

Cars for Sale table

Registration

Make

Model

Year

Figure 7.7 The Cars for Sale table definition

Linking multiple tables

How are the tables in a relational database linked to each other?

This is a magic element of a relational database. We can link two tables together by giving them a common field, that is, a field that appears in both tables. We then tell the DBMS that the two fields are really the same thing, and the software looks after all the effects.

But we do have to choose the linking fields according to some basic rules.

How do we set up the linking fields?

Later we will meet the two tables, in Figure 7.8, in a database. They contain the data about students and their personal tutors at a college.

The college uses the tutors' initials as a code to identify each tutor. They make sure that the codes are unique by adding extra letters if necessary. For example, John Smith has JS as a unique code, but Pete Brown and Philip Black are referred to as PBn and PBk. Each student is given a unique student ID code. So the primary key fields, which are underlined, are the Tutor Initials and Student ID.

Personal Tutor table	**Student table**
Tutor Initials	Student ID
Tutor Forename	Student Forename
Tutor Surname	Student Surname
Department	Date of Birth
	Sex

Figure 7.8 Table definitions for the Personal Tutor and Student tables

There is a relationship between these two tables. Each student has a personal tutor, so if we put a Tutor Initials field in the Student table it will identify the personal tutor for each student (Figure 7.9).

Personal Tutor table	Student table
<u>Tutor Initials</u>	<u>Student ID</u>
Tutor Forename	Student Forename
Tutor Surname	Student Surname
Department	Date of Birth
	Sex
	Tutor Initials

Figure 7.9 Table definitions with the addition of a foreign key field – note the extra field in the Student table

The Tutor Initials field is the only field that is duplicated. In the Personal Tutor table it is the primary key field. In the Student table it is known as a *foreign key field*. A foreign key field should always be a primary key field from another table.

Check your understanding – Choosing a foreign key

You might have noticed that we could have used the Student ID as a foreign key field in the Personal Tutor table instead. Can you see why this was not done, and why the Tutor Initials was used as the foreign key field in the Student table?

We know that each tutor has many students. If we wanted to add data about students to the Personal Tutor table, then we would have to have lots of linking fields, because each tutor would have lots of students.

On the other hand, for each student there is only one tutor. So by adding the Tutor Initials field to the Student table, we have to add exactly one link field. This is a much more efficient way of creating the link.

Look at the table below to see how *not* to do it!

Personal Tutor table	Student table
<u>Tutor Initials</u>	<u>Student ID</u>
Tutor Forename	Student Forename
Tutor Surname	Student Surname
Department	Date of Birth
Student ID	Sex
Student ID	
Student ID	
(etc.)	

Figure 7.10 An incorrect set of table definitions

How does the DBMS know that the two tables are linked?

Just adding the foreign key field is not enough. The developer has to set up a formal relationship between the two linked fields. The relationship is always defined FROM the primary key TO the foreign key.

Facilities in a relational database

What is a form used for?

When the end users work with a database, they should be presented with a user interface that exactly meets their needs. The database developer works with tables and queries, but they should be hidden away from the users. A *form* is an onscreen interface that lets the users do whatever they need to do with the data.

Later in this unit you will create a form for the database of cars that looks something like this:

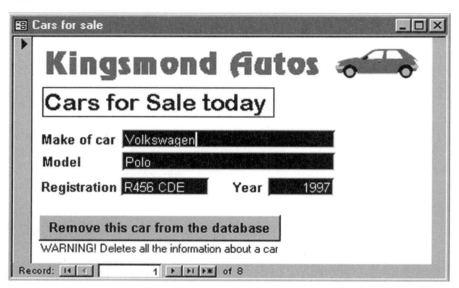

Figure 7.11 A form for the database of cars

Although this is based on the table in Figure 7.6, it provides a much better interface for the user. Forms can be set up to:

- display all the data in one table, or display the data in certain fields only
- display data from more than one table
- allow the user to change the data, or prevent the user from changing the data
- provide extra information and help
- provide buttons to carry out actions, or to switch to another form
- allow the user to search the records.

What can be displayed in a report?

A report is any printed output from a database. These are often printed out as lists of records. Reports can be designed in much the same way as forms.

Later in this unit you will create a report like the one in Figure 7.12 for the database of cars.

Cars for sale

Registration	Make	Model	Year
V123 ABC	Nissan	Micra	1999
Y456 XYZ	Fiat	Punto	2001
LD03 LMN	BMW	3 series	2003
AB51 PQR	Skoda	Octavia	2002
R456 CDE	Volkswagen	Polo	1997
T789 JKL	Honda	Civic	1999
C567 RST	Ford	Anglia	1986
P345 TUV	Jaguar	X-type	1996

Figure 7.12 A report generated by the database of cars

Reports can be set up to:

- display all the data in one table, or display the data in certain fields only
- display data from more than one table
- display only the data that resulted from a search of the records.

How are queries used in relational databases?

A query is a method of searching the database to select certain data only. It uses one or more criteria, which are simple rules for identifying the data it wants. For example, for a simple address list, a query might contain a criterion that selects all the records which have surnames beginning with R. Or it might have two criteria that select all the records that which have surnames beginning with R and also the forename 'Jack'. A query can also limit the fields that it wants to see; for example, it might only display the surname, forename and address fields, and not display other fields, such as phone number.

A query creates a new temporary table which contains only the data that meets the criteria. The tables that you, as the developer, create in the database are known as the *base tables*. The tables created by queries are not saved in the database but are created each time the query is run.

How can data be sorted in a database?

The data in a database can be sorted into numerical or alphabetical order. The tables in Figures 7.13 and 7.14 show the data about cars sorted, first by registration and then by the year of manufacture. Any field can be used as the sort key field. In practice, the database usually keeps the data sorted using the primary key field (in this case, Registration) as the sort key field.

Registration	Make	Model	Year
AB51 PQR	Skoda	Octavia	2002
C567 RST	Ford	Anglia	1986
LD03 LMN	BMW	3 series	2003
P345 TUV	Jaguar	X-type	1996
R456 CDE	Volkswagen	Polo	1997
T789 JKL	Honda	Civic	1999
V123 ABC	Nissan	Micra	1999
Y456 XYZ	Fiat	Punto	2001

Figure 7.13
Data sorted using the Registration field as the sort key field

Registration	Make	Model	Year
C567 RST	Ford	Anglia	1986
P345 TUV	Jaguar	X-type	1996
R456 CDE	Volkswagen	Polo	1997
T789 JKL	Honda	Civic	1999
V123 ABC	Nissan	Micra	1999
Y456 XYZ	Fiat	Punto	2001
AB51 PQR	Skoda	Octavia	2002
LD03 LMN	BMW	3 series	2003

Figure 7.14
Data sorted using the Year field as the sort key field

What calculations can be done in a database?

Numerical data in one or more fields can be used in calculations, and the result held in another field. Just as in a spreadsheet, a formula is entered into a field. And any of the calculations that can be done in a spreadsheet can also be done in a database.

However, the process of creating calculated fields is not as simple as in a spreadsheet. Calculations always give temporary values, so are not held in the usual tables. Instead a calculation can be done in a specially created field in a query or a form.

Case studies

You will be able to find many examples of databases used in industry. Here are some examples:

- *Banking accounts* – all banks and building societies run accounts for customers. A bank account database will have details of the account holder, and then data about each of the transactions (withdrawals and deposits). If the customer has set up standing orders or direct debits, these will be recorded in the database as well. Some of this information can be read by a customer at an Automatic Teller Machine (cash machine).

- *Personnel records* – all businesses keep information about their employees, including names, addresses, etc., qualifications and training, plus department and job title. This information will also be linked into the payroll system, which works out how much each person should be paid each week or month, and then sends out instructions to the bank and payslips to employees.

- *Telephone directories* – these are very large but simple databases, which are used both in the printed form (in telephone books) and also online for directory enquiries. They contain names and addresses of subscribers, with their telephone numbers.

- *Stock control* – the database in a shop stores all the data about all the items that the shop sells. It will include stock codes and descriptions of the items, as well as up-to-date information about how many items are in stock, how many have been sold, and how many should be re-ordered from the supplier.
- *Booking systems* – customers can book tickets for entertainment venues, for flights or for holidays, either by phoning or by visiting an agency. These systems depend on complex databases which keep records of all the seats or vacancies and allocate new bookings. It is very important that these databases be up to date and to the minute, to avoid double booking.

Check your understanding – Databases in industry

You may like to share this out between the members of a group.

Find out one example of each of the types of database listed above. As this is not a complete list, you may find others as well. In each case, try to speak to someone who uses it, either as an end user or as a customer.

Ask these questions:

- How is the data input into the database?
- How is the information displayed on screen?
- What data is printed out?
- How can the data be searched?

Test your knowledge

1 What is the difference between a flat file database and a relational database?
2 For each of these applications, would you use a flat file database or a relational database?
- a list of all your music CDs
- a database for a library, containing information about books and library members
- a database for a video shop
- telephone directory for a large city
- appointments at a hairdressing salon.
3 What would be the best data type to use for each of these fields in a table about people?
- surname
- telephone number
- age (in years)
- height in metres
- sex
- monthly salary.
4 Explain what each of these is used for in a relational database:
- primary key field
- foreign key field
- sort key field.
5 Why is it important for the developer to design forms for the user?

7.2 Designing and building a database

How do I use relational database software?

This section contains a tutorial in the use of Microsoft®Access to build relational databases. The notes all refer to Access 2000, and you may find some minor variations if you are using a later version.

The tutorial is presented in three stages:

- Stage 1 explains how to build a flat file database, and shows you how to design tables, forms and reports. Do not skip this as it introduces you to all the main facilities in the package.
- Stage 2 introduces you to queries, which play a very important role in database design.
- Stage 3 then moves on to show you how to create a relational database.

It is important that you cover all the stages, as you will be expected to create a relational database for assessment.

How do I create a database?

Whenever you carry out a software project there are several steps that you must take. They are:

- identify the problem
- design the database
- build (implement) the database
- provide documentation
- evaluate the database.

In this section you will learn how to design and build a database, for a problem that has already been identified for you. Section 7.3 deals with documentation and section 7.4 with evaluation.

Can I use a wizard?

You may use any of the wizards provided by Microsoft® Access. These include:

- *Database wizards* – these create complete database applications very quickly. It is a good idea to try them out to see what a full database might look like.
  Warning! You should never use a Microsoft® Access database wizard to create the solution to a problem that you are set as part of your course. It will be very obvious to the assessor that you have used a wizard, and it is very unlikely to match the requirements of the problem. This warning applies only to the Access database wizards. Other wizards within Access can be used whenever you wish.
- *Table wizard* – this is not particularly useful, and you would be wiser to create your tables from scratch in the Design view.
- *Form, query and report wizards* – always create a form, query or report using the wizard to begin with. You can then customise them if necessary in Design view.

Stage 1: Creating a flat file database

We will set up a simple database with information about second-hand cars that are for sale at a car dealership called Kingsmond Autos.

How do I get started?

■ Launch Microsoft® Access. Select **Blank Access database**.

Figure 7.15
Select **Blank Access database**

■ You will be prompted to save your database straightaway. All Microsoft® Access databases are given the filename extension .mdb. Call the database 'Kingsmond Autos'. Click **Create**.

■ The database window appears. Note the list of objects to the left – we will be using Tables, Queries, Forms and Reports.

Access will prompt you to save your work whenever you add a new component.

How do I create a table?

■ The database opens in the Tables window. Select **Create table in design view**.

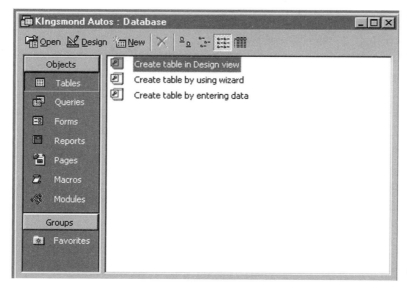

Figure 7.16
The Tables window

■ Enter this information about the fields, exactly as shown here:

Field Name	Data Type	Description
Registration	Text	Car registration e.g. V123 ABC

■ Look at the Field Properties at the bottom of the window, and change the Field Size to 9. This is the maximum number of characters required for a car registration (allowing for spaces). As each character takes up 1 byte of memory this helps to reduce wasted space and make the database more efficient.

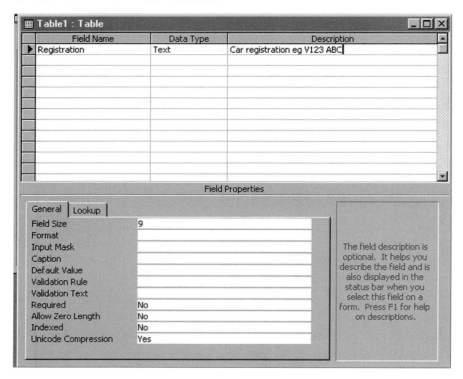

Figure 7.17 Adding a field

■ Add these fields:

Make	Text	Make of the car, e.g. Nissan
Model	Text	Model, e.g. Micra

For each of these fields chose a suitable Field Size.

■ The next field will be numerical.

Year		Year of manufacture

For the Data Type, click on the down arrow and select **Number**. Now change the Field Size to Integer. (Long integers use 4 bytes, but an integer uses 2 bytes.)

■ The table must have a primary key, which in this case will be the car registration. Click anywhere on the row containing the Registration field name. A pointer will appear at the beginning of the row. Now click on the **Primary Key** button in the toolbar (it looks like a door key – see Figure 7.18).

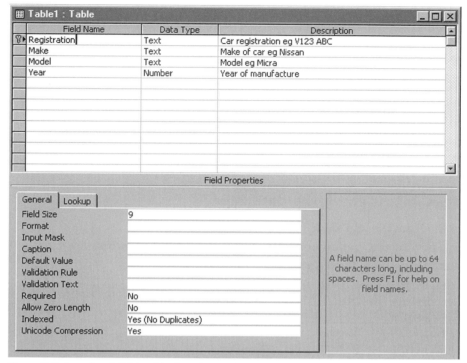

Figure 7.18 Completed fields with the primary key defined

■ Close the window. When prompted to save your table, name it 'Cars for sale'. You will see the 'Cars for sale' table listed in the Tables window.

How do I enter data into a table?

■ From the Kingsmond Autos database window, select **Tables**. Click once on the 'Cars for sale' table and click on **Open** (in the toolbar in the Tables window). This opens the table in the Datasheet view, which allows you to enter data.

■ Enter your own choice of data for six cars. Only enter years after 1980.

Registration	Make	Model	Year
V123 ABC	Nissan	Micra	1999
Y456 XYZ	Fiat	Punto	2001
LD03 LMN	BMW	3 series	2003
AB51 PQR	Skoda	Octavia	2002
R456 CDE	Volkswagen	Polo	1997
T789 JKL	Honda	Civic	1999
			0

Figure 7.19 Data entered in Datasheet view

■ When you close the Datasheet view window the data will automatically be saved.

How can I prevent users from entering the wrong type of data?

It is easy for the end user to make a mistake when entering data. Well-written database software has built-in tests which check whether the data 'makes sense' when it is input. These tests are known as *validation checks*.

Access automatically checks that the data you enter is of the correct datatype. You will have noticed that a number of datatypes can be selected, including text and number.

You can add some further validation checks by checking that data falls within acceptable ranges. Validation checks help to make the database user-friendly.

How does Access check the data type?

- Open the 'Cars for sale' table in Datasheet view.
- Enter a new record, but enter a letter instead of a number into the Year field, then press the **Enter** key. You will get an Access error message.

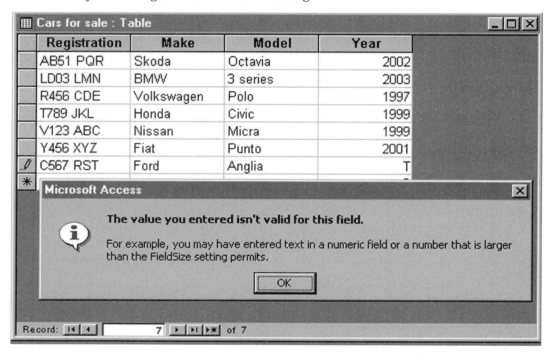

Figure 7.20 A datatype error message

- Correct the data, then close the table. The new data will be saved automatically.

How can I add a validation check?

- From the Kingsmond Autos database window, select **Tables**. Click once on the 'Cars for sale' table and click on **Design** (in the toolbar in the Tables window). This opens the table in Design view.
- Click somewhere in the Year row. In the Field Properties, click in the Validation Rule box and key in >1980. This means that only years from 1980 onwards will be considered valid.
- In the Validation Text box key in Please enter a year from 1980 onwards. Figure 7.21 shows the message that will appear if an invalid year is entered.

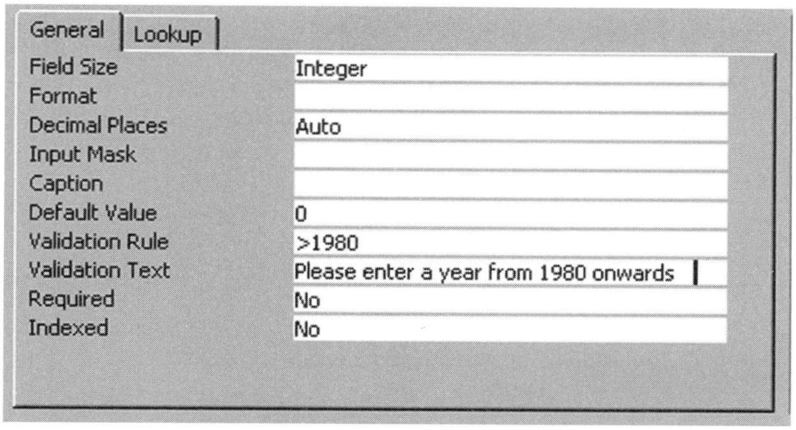

Figure 7.21 Validation rule and text in the Year field

- Close the table. You will be warned that the new validation (or data integrity) rule may make some existing data invalid. Click on **Yes**.
- Open the table in Datasheet view. Add a new record with an invalid Year (e.g. 1066) to see how it is handled.

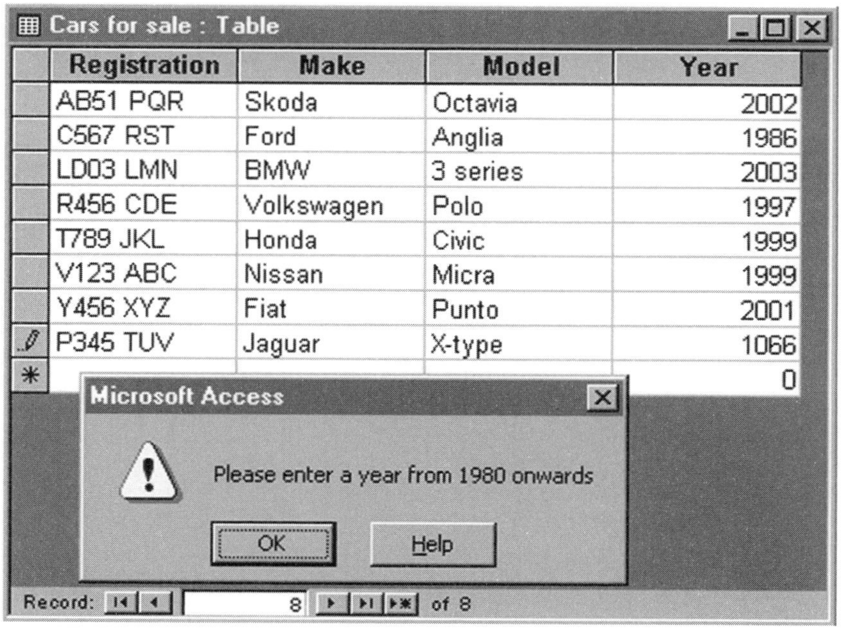

Figure 7.22 Validation text appears in an error box when the validation rule is broken

In future you should always add validation rules *before* entering any data.

How do I create a form?

Tables, in both Design and Datasheet view, are used by the database developer (that is, you) when constructing an application. The end user should not need to see anything you have worked on so far. Instead, you, as developer, should design forms which will give the end user a simple, non-technical view of the database.

- Close the table window if it is still open.
- In the database window click on **Forms**, then click on **Create form by using wizard**.

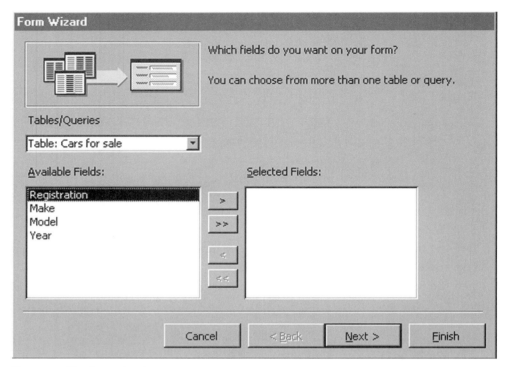

Figure 7.23 The form wizard

- Note that the name of the table 'Cars for sale' appears in the top box, and fields in this table are listed in the Available Fields box. Click on the >> button to select all the fields. (You could select individual fields by clicking on the > button). Click on **Next**.
- Select **Columnar layout** and click on **Next**.
- Select **Standard style**. We will add colour later. Click on **Next** then **Finish**.
- A form appears with all the fields in it. Use the navigation buttons at the bottom of the form to browse through the records. Find out what each navigation button does.

Figure 7.24 A form produced by the Form wizard

- Change the data in one or two fields of existing records.
- Click on the navigation button marked with * to add a new record. Add data in the first field, then use the right cursor (arrow) key on your keyboard to move from one field to the next, and the left cursor key to move back. You can also use the **Tab** key (to the left of Q on the keyboard) to move to the next field.
- Use the form to add a few new records. This is how the end user will enter data.
- Close the form.

How can I rearrange the layout of a form?

The wizard is a quick and easy way to create a form, but you probably want to customise the form further.

A table can be displayed in Design view or Datasheet view. In the same way a form can be displayed in Design view or Form view. Form view is the version that the end user will see, but you need to make any changes to the form in Design view.

▓ In the Kingsmond Autos database window click on **Forms**, then click once on 'Cars for sale'. Click on **Design**.

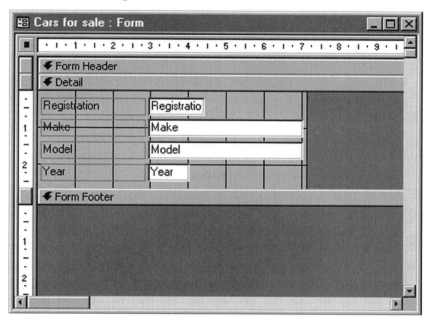

Figure 7.25 Form Design view

▓ The floating toolbox and a small window containing the list of fields will have appeared. You will be using these later.

▓ Enlarge the form by dragging the right-hand edge, just to the right of the text boxes.

▓ Notice the bar with the words 'Form Footer'. To stretch the form downwards, click the top edge of this bar and then drag down.

▓ Each field on the form has two objects – the label and the text box. The label is on the left. The text box is known as a *control* because it controls the way the user can gain access to the data. The text box displays the actual data in Form view.

▓ Click on the Registration label. Now click on the Registration text box. You will note that they are linked. As you move the cursor over the label and text box it will change to a number of different shapes.

▓ When the cursor changes to a full hand (with all the fingers showing) you can drag the label and text box together to another position.

▓ When the cursor changes to a pointing finger you can move the label or text box independently.

▓ When the cursor is positioned over the resizing handles it also allows you to resize the label or text box.

▓ After you have rearranged the form, close it.

▓ Back in the Kingsmond Autos database window, click once on 'Cars for sale' then click on **Open** to open it in Form view.

How can I change the wording on a label?

At first the label contains the fieldname that you used when you designed the table. You can alter the words to make them more meaningful to the user.

- Open the 'Cars for sale' form in Design view.
- Click inside the Make label. The cursor changes to an I-bar. Click again and you can edit the words. Change the label to read 'Make of car'.
- Close the form and open it in Form view to see your changes. (You can also switch directly between Design and Form view by using the button at the left end of the main toolbar.)

How can I add a title and other information to the form?

You can place any other information you like on the form by adding extra labels. This can help the user to decide what to do. You can also use a label as a title for the form.

- Open the 'Cars for sale' form in Design view. You may want to enlarge the window so you can see all the form.
- Click on the **Labels** button in the toolbox. (Move your mouse over the buttons in the toolbox to identify them.) Then click on the form where you want the label to appear, and start typing. Press the **Enter** key when you have finished.

Figure 7.26 Form design floating toolbox

- You can change the font style in any label by clicking on it, then using the buttons in the toolbar at the top of the screen. Note that all the text in one label will have the same style.

How do I add colour and pictures to the form?

- In Design view click anywhere on the background of the form. Then use the **Fill** button on the toolbar to change the colour.
- You can also change the text colour and the fill colour of any label, and add borders. Just click on the label and then use the buttons in the toolbar.

Figure 7.27 Buttons on the toolbar for fill colour, text colour and borders

- To insert a picture, click on the **Image** button in the floating toolbox. Click on the form in the position where you want the image to be placed. Find and select the picture as you would in other software packages.

How can I change the tab order?

The tab order is the order in which the user is guided to enter data onto a form. The user presses either the **Enter** key, the right cursor key or the **Tab** key to move to the next field. The fields will be visited in the same order as they appear in the original table – in our case Registration, Make, Model, Year.

If you have rearranged the fields in the form, as in the example below, then you will want to change the tab order so that the user is taken from one field to another in a sensible sequence.

- Open the 'Cars for sale' form in Design view.
- Select **View** from the main menu, then **Tab Order**, then follow the instructions.

How does the user delete records?

The end users should be able to carry out all their tasks from the form. They can already add a new record, and change data in a record. You should now add a button to the form to let them delete a record.

- Open your form in Design view.
- In the floating toolbox make sure that the **Controls Wizard** button is depressed. Click on the **Command Button** button, then click on the form in the position where you want the button to be placed.
- The Button wizard will guide you through the next steps.
- In the Categories box click on **Record Operations**. In the Actions box click on **Delete Record**, then click on **Next**.
- You can choose whether to have text or an icon on the button. Make your choice, then click **Next**, then **Finish**.
- Switch to Form view to test the button.
- Close and save the form.

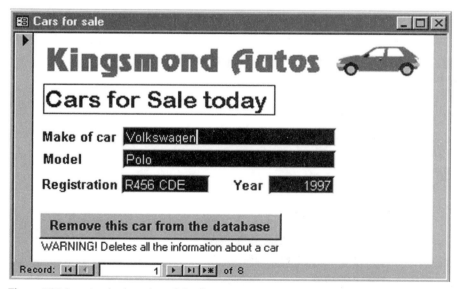

Figure 7.28 A customised version of the form

How do I create a report?

A report is a printed record of data in the database. Access gives you a number of options when formatting a report, but the simplest type is a list of all the data set out in columns.

- Close any tables or forms that may be open.
- In the Kingsmond Autos database window click on **Reports**, then select **Create report by using wizard**.
- Select all the fields by clicking on the >> button, then click on **Next**.
- Click on **Next** in the following two windows. For the layout select **Tabular**, then click on **Next**.
- Choose the style you want for the report, then click on **Next**, then **Finish**.
- You will then view a preview of your report. Print it out or close the window.

Cars for sale

Registration	Make	Model	Year
V123 ABC	Nissan	Micra	1999
Y456 XYZ	Fiat	Punto	2001
LD03 LMN	BMW	3 series	2003
AB51 PQR	Skoda	Octavia	2002
R456 CDE	Volkswagen	Polo	1997
T789 JKL	Honda	Civic	1999
C567 RST	Ford	Anglia	1986
P345 TUV	Jaguar	X-type	1996

Figure 7.29 A report listing all the cars for sale

How does the user print the report?

You need to add a button to the form that allows the user to print the report.

- Open the form in Design view. Use the Button wizard as before. Select the **Report Operations** category, and the **Preview Report** action.
- In the next window, select the 'Cars for sale' report.
- Select text rather than a picture, and use the words 'Print car list'.
- Switch to Form view to see how the button operates.

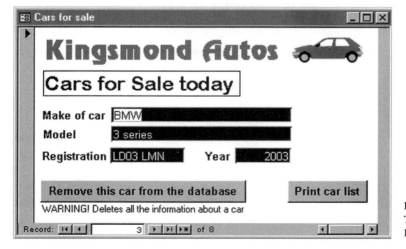

Figure 7.30
The completed form for Kingsmond Autos

How can I change the design of the report?

The report wizard can produce reports in a number of styles. But you may want to make some changes to the appearance and layout of a report. Reports can be viewed in two views – Preview and Design.

■ In the Kingsmond Autos database window click on **Reports**, then click once on 'Cars for sale'. Click on **Design**.

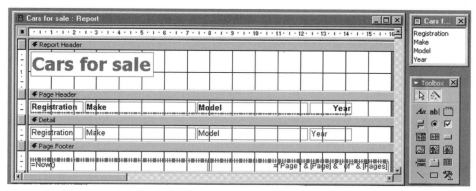

Figure 7.31 The report in Design view

■ Notice that the report is divided into four sections. The Report header appears only on the first page of the report. The Page header will appear on every page, and gives the headings for each of the fields. The Detail section formats all the records that will be displayed in the report. The Page footer appears on each page and contains the date it was printed and the number of pages.

■ The heading 'Cars for sale' in the Report header is a label. Click on this once, then make any changes you want to the text. You can also use the formatting toolbar at the top of the window to change the font, font size, font colour, etc.

■ If you want to add any more information to the Report header you can use the Toolbox to create a new label.

■ To change the appearance of one of the lines, click once on it then use the **Lines/Borders** button in the toolbar. You can use the Toolbox to create a new line.

■ If you decide to make the field columns narrower, do this with care, and make sure that the fieldnames in the Page header line up with the data in the Detail section.

Check your understanding – CD collection

A friend of yours has an extensive collection of CDs. You have been asked to create a database that catalogues them all. Before you use Access you should do these things:

■ Decide on a suitable set of fields for recording information about the CDs, e.g. record label, singer, type of music, when released, single or album. You may like to add a field in which your friend can give each CD a rating.

■ Choose meaningful names for the fields. In some database software you are not allowed to have spaces in a fieldname, so you might have to use TypeOfMusic as a field name. Access does permit spaces.

■ Decide what validation rules you could use.

When you go into Access, then you should start a new database, because the data in the new database is unrelated to Kingsmond Autos. If a database is already open, then close it. Create your own database by following the steps used to create the Kingsmond Autos database.

Stage 2: Adding queries to a database

Users often want to select data from a database. For example, at Kingsmond Autos they may want to see a list of all the cars for sale which were made after 1996. This is carried out by setting up a query within the database.

Another kind of query is one that displays all the records but only gives data in specified fields. For example, at Kingsmond Autos they may want a list of all the cars for sale, but with only the Registration and Year data.

In order to understand how queries work we will set up a new database with some additional features.

The next database will contain a membership list for a gym in Kingsmond, called King Gym. The database will be used for a number of purposes, including printing out lists of members.

How do I create a new database?

- If a database is already open, then close it. You should always start afresh for a new database.
- Select **File/New Database**. Click on **Blank Database**, then click **OK**.
- You will be prompted to name your database. Call it 'King Gym'
- Use 'Create table in Design view' to design a table with these fields and datatypes:

Membership number	Autonumber

Membership number is the primary key field. Autonumber will automatically allocate a number to each member in sequence.

Surname	Text
Forename	Text
Address	Text
Town	Text

Since most of the members live in Kingsmond, we can save the user a lot of typing by making Kingsmond the default value for the Town field. In **Field Properties/Default Value** enter 'Kingsmond'. The user can still type in another town if necessary.

Postcode	Text
Phone	Text
Sex	Text

- Choose suitable field sizes for all the text fields.
- Make *Membership Number* the primary key.
- The Sex field needs a validation rule. The rule is

    ="M" OR = "F"

    and the validation text is

    Please enter either M or F

- Close and save the table as 'Members'.

Check your understanding – Telephone numbers

Telephone numbers are always given the text datatype. Why?

A full phone number in the UK has 11 digits. We should normally store the whole of the number, including the dialling code for a landline number. Mobile phone numbers all begin with 07 and landline numbers all begin with 01 or 02. Find out what happens if you try to store a number that begins with zero, such as 0123. You can try this out on a calculator to see the result.

Should I create a form?

You should always provide your user with one or more user-friendly forms, so that they can interact with the database.

- Create a form based on the Members table using the wizard as before, and save it.
- Rearrange and customise the form in Design view.
- Open the form in Datasheet view and use it to enter details of at least twelve members. Do not enter anything in the Membership Number field. You set the datatype for this field to Autonumber, so the system will give each record a unique membership number.
- Include both males and females and two or three members who do not live in Kingsmond.
- Close the form.

How can I create a query?

We will set up two queries, and will use them for different purposes.

The first query will select all the records in the Members table but will only display certain fields. We will then use it to create first a form and then a report which gives a simple list of all members, giving their names and membership numbers.

How can I create a query that selects certain fields only?

- Close any tables or forms that are open.
- In the King Gym database window click on **Queries**, then select **Create a Query by Using a Wizard**.
- In the Available Fields box click on **Membership Number**, then click on the > to transfer it to the Selected Fields box.
- Repeat with the Surname and Forename fields, then click on **Next**, then **Finish**.
- The query will run and generate a new table, which will be displayed in Datasheet view.

How do I create a form that displays the data in a query?

- Use the Form wizard. In the first window go to the Tables/Queries text box, and select the **Members Query**. Select all three fields using the >> button.
- We want to present the information as a list on screen, so in the next window select **Tabular layout**, and then work through the rest of the wizard.
- Switch to Form view to see what the form looks like.

How can the user change the order in which the records are displayed?

A form automatically sorts the records before displaying them for the first time. It uses the Record key as the sort field, but the user can change the order in which records are displayed.

- In Form view click on one of the names in the Surname column.
- Find the two sort buttons on the main toolbar:

Figure 7.32 Sort buttons

- Click on the left button to sort the records into ascending order using the Surname field as the sort key. This creates a list sorted alphabetically in the normal way. Click on the second button for the reverse order.
- The form will open next time in the chosen sort order.

Can I create a report built on a query?

This query can be used to print a simple membership list.

- Use the report wizard. As with the form, in the first window go to the Tables/Queries text box, and select the **Members Query**. Select all three fields using the >> button.
- The next window asks about grouping records. This is only useful for complex reports so click **Next**.
- The user is not able to choose the sort order for the report so you must do so now. In box 1 select **Surname**, and in box 2 select **Forename**. This means that the records will be sorted first by Surname, then, if the Surname is shared by more than one member, it will sort them by Forename. You may need to add some more records later to see the effect of this.
- In the next window select **Tabular**. Then choose your style and finish.
- Preview the report and decide whether you want to print it.

How can the user see the form and report built on a query?

You can add a button to the Members form to let the user view the Members Query form.

- Open the Members form in Design view and use the Button wizard. Select the **Form Operations** category, and the **Open Form** action.
- In the next window, select 'Members query'.
- Then select 'Open the form and show all the records'.
- Select text rather than a picture, and use the words 'View list of members'.
- Switch to Form view to see how the button operates.

It would be a good idea to give the user the option of printing the list once he or she has viewed it, so we will add a button to the Members Query form.

- Open the Members Query form in Design view. We will put the button in the footer of the form. Drag down the lower edge of the form to open up the Form footer.
- Use the Button wizard and click in the Form footer. Select the **Report Operations** category, and the **Preview Report** action.
- In the next window, select 'Members query'.
- Select text rather than a picture, and use the words 'Print alphabetical list'.
- Switch to Form view to see how the button operates.

How do I create a query that selects only some of the records?

This query will only select the female members.

- Close any tables, queries or forms that are open.
- Use the query wizard as before.
- In the first window make sure that 'Table:Members' is displayed in the Tables/Queries box.
- Select all the fields using the >> button.
- In the last window name the query 'Female Members' then select **Modify the Query Design** (because we have not yet told it to pick out the female members). Click **Finish**.
- The query now opens in Design view. The Design view window shows the fields with the Members table at the top and the query design grid below.

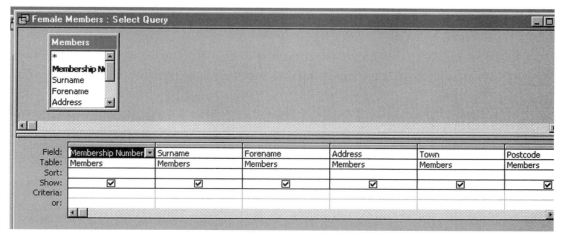

Figure 7.33 Query window with table at the top and query design grid below

- Scroll horizontally through the design grid to find the Sex field.
- Click on the Criteria row in the Sex column and key in:"F" . Do not omit the quotation marks.

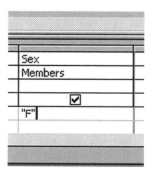

Figure 7.34 Setting up a criterion

- Switch to Datasheet view and check that only female members are listed.

Further research – How can I complete this database?

You will want to add more to this database before moving on to the next stage. Try these:

1 Create a form based on the Female Members query and on the Members form add a button to open this new form.

2 Can you create a query that includes only the name and address fields, but selects only the members who live in Kingsmond?

3 Customise the Members form so that it presents a helpful and attractive user interface.

Stage 3: Creating a relational database

A relational database has two or more tables which are linked together. In other words, we set up relationships between the tables.

All relational databases need careful planning before you build them in Microsoft® Access. You need to work out the best way of representing the information in the real world so that it can be stored and manipulated as data in a database.

The reasons for designing a database carefully are to ensure that data is never duplicated unnecessarily and that queries are carried out efficiently. This in turn will help to keep the data accurate.

How do I decide what data fields to use in the tables?

We will set up a new database containing information about students. At Kingsmond College, each student is assigned his or her own Personal Tutor. Each Personal Tutor looks after up to 15 students.

The database is designed to be used by the staff. It will make it easy to view the data about the students, including the details of their individual personal tutors. It could also list all the students who are assigned to any one tutor. Output will be on screen and printed in varying formats.

We will need two tables – one for the details of the students and another for the details of the tutors. The fields in each table are set out in table definitions like this:

Personal Tutor table	Student table
Tutor Forename	Student Forename
Tutor Surname	Student Surname
Department	Date of Birth
	Sex

Figure 7.35
The initial version of the table definitions

You could add more fields, of course, but we will just work with a simple version.

Each table needs a primary key. The college gives each student a unique student ID code which consists of three letters followed by four digits, so this can be used as the primary key for the Student table.

The Personal Tutors are usually referred to in internal memos by their initials; two initials are usually enough but a third letter may be used to avoid duplicates. Thus John Smith has JS as a unique code, but Pete Brown and Philip Black are referred to as PBn and PBk.

The table definitions (with primary keys underlined) become:

Personal Tutor table	Student table
<u>Tutor Initials</u>	<u>Student ID</u>
Tutor Forename	Student Forename
Tutor Surname	Student Surname
Department	Date of Birth
	Sex

Figure 7.36
The table definitions with primary keys

We usually write the primary key first in each table.

Data fields should appear only once anywhere in the database. If you find that the same field appears more than once in a table, or appears in more than one table, then you should remove one of them. The only exception to this rule is where a foreign key field (see below) is used.

How do I set up a relationship between the tables?

The tables now have to be linked together. What kind of relationship is there between the two tables? We know that:

⟶ For ONE tutor there are MANY students.

The relationship between two tables is always expressed by a sentence in this form. We cannot say that for one student there are many tutors, as it is not true.

The primary key for the Personal Tutor table is now copied into the Student table – that is, from the ONE end of the relationship to the MANY end. It is very important that you do this the right way round.

Remember – copy the primary key from the ONE end to MANY end.

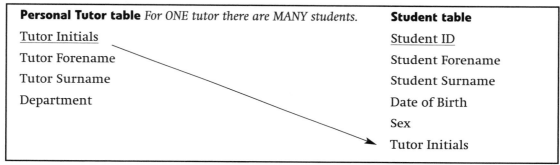

Figure 7.37 The table definitions with the foreign key

This means that the initials of the Personal Tutor will be listed in each record in the Student table.

In the Student table the Student ID field is still the primary key. Tutor Initials is known as a foreign key in the Student table, because it is the primary key in a 'foreign' table.

How do I start building a relational database?

You should start a completely new database. Do not add the Student and Personal Tutor tables to any previous databases you have created.

- Create a new database and call it 'Kingsmond College'.
- Create a table called 'Personal Tutor' with the fields listed above, but do not enter any data yet.
- The datatype for all the fields in this table will be text.
- Choose suitable field sizes for each of the fields, e.g. 3 for Tutor Initials.
- Remember to create the primary key.
- Close and save the table.
- In the same way, create a second table called 'Student' with the fields shown in the list above.
- The datatype is text for all the fields except Date of Birth.
- The datatype for Date of Birth is Date. In the Format box, select **Short Date**.

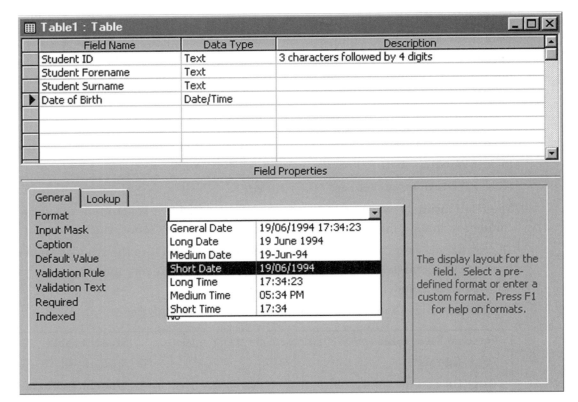

Figure 7.38 Selecting the data type and format for the Date field

- Add validation for the Sex field.
- When you design the Tutor Initials field (the foreign key in the Student table) make sure that it has the same datatype and field size as it has in the Personal Tutor table.
- Create the primary key, close and save the table, but do not enter any data yet.

How do I set up the relationship between the tables?

You must set up the relationship before any data is entered.

- Close any tables that are open.
- Click on the **Relationships** button in the toolbar.
- In the Show Table dialogue box, click on each table in turn, followed by **Add**. Click on **Close**.
- Arrange the two tables so that the Personal Tutor table is on the left and the Student table is on the right, and stretch them so you can see all the fields.
- Click on the Tutor Initials field in the Personal Tutor table and drag it onto the Tutor Initials field in the Student table. Note that you have dragged the primary key to its position as a foreign key, that is, from the ONE to the MANY end of the relationship.
- In the Relationships dialogue box, check that Personal Tutor appears as the heading of the first column, and Student in the second column (as the related table).
- Tick **Enforce Referential Integrity**. This will ensure that the user does not enter Tutor Initials in the Student table that do not already exist in the Personal Tutor table.
- Click on **Create**. The ONE to MANY link is drawn with ∝ representing the MANY end (Figure 7.39).
- Close the Relationships window and click **Yes** to save.

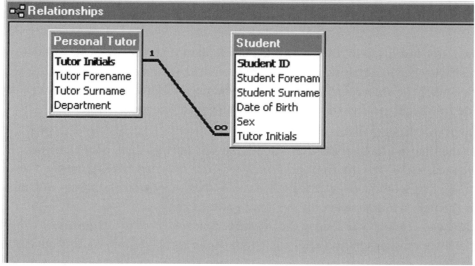

Figure 7.39 The relationship between the tables

How does the user enter data into a relational database?

The user will have to enter the details of all the personal tutors first. Nothing can be entered in the Tutor Initials field in the Student table until the details have first been entered in the Personal Tutor table. This is because you ticked *Enforce Referential Integrity*.

Remember that your user must use a form to enter data.

- Create a simple form using the wizard, based on the Personal Tutor table.
- Enter the data for three tutors. Make a note of the Tutor Initials for each of them.
- Close and save the form.

How do I create a form showing the information about each student?

You want to design a form that can be used to enter and display information about each student. You want to show who each student's personal tutor is. In the Student table the only information about the personal tutor is given in the Tutor Initials field. This is where we use the special facilities of a relational database to extract data from two tables at the same time.

- Use the Form wizard. In the first window go to the Tables/Queries text box, and select the Student table. It is important that you select this table first. You should always start with the table at the MANY end of the relationship.
- Select all the fields in the Student table using the >> button.
- In the Tables/Queries text box, now select the Personal Tutor table.
- Use the >> button to select each of the fields in turn except the Tutor Initials field, as this has already been selected from the Student table. Click on **Next**.
- The answer to the question 'How do you want to view your data?' should be 'by Student'.
- When you have finished the wizard, enter some data about a student. In the Tutor Initials field key in the correct initials for one of the records you entered earlier. You will see that the database automatically looks up and displays the tutor's details for you.

How do I stop the user from keying in non-existent data in the foreign key field?

In the Tutor Initials field, the users must key in data that already exists in the Personal Tutor table. If they key in anything else they are presented with a confusing message when they get to the end of the record. (Try it and see!) So you need to force them to enter correct data. You can do this by presenting them with a drop-down list to choose from.

▨ Open the 'Student' form in Design view.

▨ In the floating toolbox click on the **Combo Box** button. Click on a blank spot on the form (you can move it to the right position later). You may need to enlarge the form first.

▨ In the first window select 'I want the combo box to look up the values in a table or query'.

▨ In the next window select the Personal Tutor table.

▨ The next window will display the available fields. Select **Tutor Initials**.

▨ The next window lets you alter the width of the combo box. It is probably best to leave it unaltered, but you can experiment a bit later. You can see that the user will be given a list of Tutor Initials that have already been entered into the database.

▨ In the next window, select 'Store that value in this field:' and then select 'Tutor Initials'. This means that when the user picks the Tutor Initials from the Combo Box list, the data will be copied into the Tutor Initials (foreign key) field in the Student table.

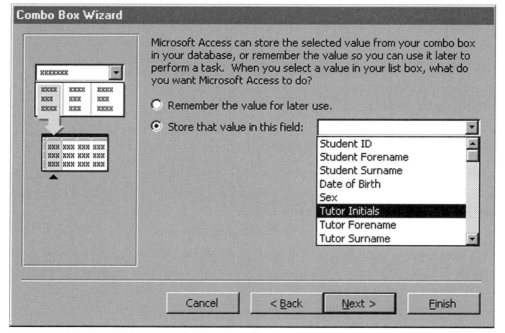

Figure 7.40 Storing the value in the foreign key field

▨ In the final window you should key in a sensible label for the combo box, like 'Select the initials of the personal tutor'.

▨ Switch to Form view to see what it does.

▨ You will probably have to enlarge the label so that all the words can be seen.

▨ Finally delete the label and textbox for the original Tutor Initial field, as the combo box has replaced them (Figure 7.41).

Student

Student ID	ABC1234
Student Forename	George
Student Surname	Matthews
Date of Birth	2/04/1986
Sex	M
Select the initials of the personal tutor	DM
Tutor Forename	Dwayne
Tutor Surname	Montrose
Department	Creative Arts

Record: ◄◄ ◄ [2] ► ►► ►* of 5

Figure 7.41 The Student form with a listbox

How do I create a query based on two tables?

This query will select students born before a given date (01/01/1985), and for each one will display his or her name, date of birth and the name of the personal tutor. You should use the Students form to enter some students with dates of birth in 1984 or earlier, as well as some with later dates, so that you will be able to check that this query works.

- Use the query wizard. In the first window, go to the Tables/Queries text box, and select the Student table (because it is at the MANY end of the relationship).
- Select the Student Surname, Student Forename and Date of Birth fields using the > button.
- In the Tables/Queries textbox, now select the Personal Tutor table. Use the > button to select the Tutor Surname and Tutor Forename fields. Click on **Next**.
- In the last window, name the query 'Students born before 1985' then select 'Modify the query design'. Click **Finish**.
- The query now opens in Design view. The Design view window shows both tables and the relationship between them. The fields you selected are shown in the query design grid.
- In the Date of Birth column enter <#01/01/1985#. You must use the # symbol before and after dates. The 'less than' symbol is interpreted as 'before' when used with dates. Use > for 'after'.

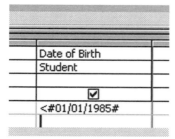

Date of Birth
Student
☑
<#01/01/1985#

Figure 7.42 Setting a date criterion

- Check that the query works. Although you did not include the Tutor Initials field in the query, it has acted as a hidden link between the two tables.
- Create a report based on this query and add a suitable button to the Student form to preview it.

How can I create a menu?

You have created two input forms. Your user should use the Personal Tutor form to change any data or to add a new tutor, and should use the Student form to enter data about students. The data entered on the form is saved when the user goes to a new record or when the form is closed.

You can give the users a menu which lets them choose which form they want to work in. Microsoft® Access uses the term 'switchboard' for a menu.

A menu is simply a form with buttons that opens other forms.

- Close all forms, queries and tables that may be open.
- In the Forms window select **Create Form in Design view**.
- Use the Button wizard to add a button which will open the Personal Tutor form.
- Add another button to open the Student form.
- Add suitable instructions to the form.
- Save the form as 'Main menu'.

When you test the form you will find that it is possible to open all three forms at the same time. This is not a good idea, as new data entered on the Personal Tutor form will not become active on the Student form until it has been saved. The simplest solution to this is to put a button on each form which closes the form.

Open the Personal Tutor form in Design view.

- Use the Button wizard and select the **Form Operations** category, and the **Close Form** action.
- Use the text 'Save all data and return to menu'.
- Create a similar button on the Student form.

Finally, you want the Main menu form to open automatically when the users open the database. This will keep them away from the tables and queries which they should not be looking at.

- From the Access menu at the top of the screen, select **Tools**, then **Startup**.
- In the Display Form/Page box select 'Main menu'. Do not make any other changes in this window at this stage.

Now all that remains is for you to customise the forms.

Check your understanding – Create a new database for a video shop

A video shop is run, for security reasons, as a club.

Customers must enrol as members and complete an application form with their address and phone number. Each is given a membership card which has a unique membership number written on it.

Each video is given an identifying code which is written on the box. The following data must be stored about each video – video code, title and classification (U, PG, 12, 15 or 18). In addition, each film is placed in a category, such as Comedy, Adventure, Cartoon, Children, Horror, Sci-Fi, etc. Although the shop holds several copies of popular videos, each copy will have its own unique video code.

At present, there is no limit to the number of videos that may be hired by a member at any one time (but this may be changed in the near future).

The shop needs a database of the videos, with forms that will allow staff to:

- view all the videos with the name and address of the member who has hired one
- hire out a video, by selecting the person who has hired it from the membership base
- deal with a video which has been returned by removing the name of the person who has hired it (hint: you need to create a member called 'no one', which will be selected when a video is returned)
- print out a list of all the videos, sorted by category and classification
- print out a list of all the videos which are hired out, with the name, address and phone number of the hirer.

7.3 Documentation for a database design

Why is documentation necessary?

When you purchase a software package you are always given some guidance about using the software. This could be in the form of:

- paper-based user manual
- user manual on CD-ROM
- help screens
- links to help pages on the Internet.

These are all referred to as *user documentation*, even though only the first is printed on paper.

There is another type of documentation that is meant to be read by other database developers. When a developer has finished creating a database, he or she has to remember that someone might need to work on it again. For example, some errors may be discovered in the future, or the user might want some new facilities added. The same developer could be asked to carry out the upgrade, or the job could be given to another person. In either case, they need to have full information about the development of the original database. Even an experienced developer can forget how he or she created a particular database. So, a database developer has to assemble *technical documentation* as a record of what has been done.

Further research – Documentation

Try to find examples of each of the types of user documentation.

Which did you find the most helpful and easy to use – and why?

What documentation should I provide?

You should write a paper-based user manual and also provide some of the technical documentation.

User manual

What should be included in a user manual?

A simple user manual should have these sections in it:

- contents
- purpose of the database
- how to use the database.

You may want to subdivide the last section.

How should I explain the purpose of the database?

Describe:

- who should use it
- what it is for.

How should I explain how to use the database?

You should describe how the database should be used, taking the user step by step through it.

- Start with the main menu. You should include a screen shot of the form. Explain what each button/option on the form does.
- Then show what happens when one of the options is chosen. Include screen shots at every stage. Show what happens when data is added to a form. If a report is printed then include a copy.
- Repeat this for all of the options. Make sure that you have covered all the things that a user can do with the database.

How should I present the user manual?

The user manual should be prepared with some care. It should be:

- *Easy to understand* – avoid the use of technical language for a non-technical user.
- *Easy to read* – the layout and presentation of the manual should be attractive.
- *User-friendly* – you should think about using the database from the point of view of a new user.

It is a good idea to ask someone to read through your user manual whilst trying out the database for the first time. The person should be able to identify any shortcomings.

Development log

What is a development log?

A development log is one part of the technical documentation of a database. It is written for other database developers, so you can use technical language (unlike in the user manual).

Anything that is called a 'log' will contain dates. So you need to keep notes on your database throughout the development period, and include the date for each entry.

How do I record the development of the database?

You should record the dates on which you carried out each of these stages, and then write about them in some detail:

▤ *Identify the problem* – for assessment, you will be provided with a problem, so the first stage will simply mark the beginning of the project.

▤ *Design the database* – this may take a while as you try out different ideas. You may find that you make several entries in your log about the design process.

▤ *Build the database* – again, you will want to keep a record of your progress, as you gradually put the database together. This will probably take more time than the other stages. As it develops you will probably want to amend your original design.

How do I record the table definitions?

List the table definitions as explained in section 7.2. For each table you should identify:

▤ the primary key field
▤ all other data fields
▤ any foreign key fields.

You can use an arrow to show the link between two tables, as in Figure 7.37.

How do I consider alternative designs?

The completed database will include menus, input forms and reports, as well as some queries. You will have probably also tried out several alternatives, both as sketches on paper and on screen.

You should use sketches and screen shots to describe the different designs that you considered. Then you should explain why you made your final choice.

Test your knowledge

1 Explain the differences between user documentation and technical documentation.
2 User documentation can be presented in any of the following formats:
 ▤ paper-based user manuals
 ▤ user manuals on CD-ROM
 ▤ help screens
 ▤ links to help pages on the Internet.
 Which format do you find most useful, and why?
3 What should be included in the user manual for a database?
4 What technical documentation should be provided for a database?

7.4 Evaluating a database

What is evaluation?

As you saw in Unit 2, when we evaluate a software application we assess how effective it is in use. A database is a type of software application, so a database developer can ask the same kinds of question to evaluate the database he or she has created.

These are the questions you should be asking about a database that you develop:

- What is its purpose, and is the database fit for its purpose?
- What problems arose when developing the database?
- How easy is it to use?
- How effective is it?

Evaluation

How do I check whether the database is fit for its purpose?

As you saw in the last section, the purpose of a database should state who should use it and what it is for. You should have been told the purpose of the database that you developed when you were set the problem. For example, the purpose of the Kingsmond College database was to make it easy for staff to view the data about the students, including the details of their individual personal tutors.

When the database is finished you need to ask whether it is 'fit for its purpose', in other words, whether it matches the purpose. To do this, you should go carefully through the database and list all the benefits to the intended user, remembering what it was supposed to be achieving.

How do I deal with any problems in using the database?

Problems always arise whenever any software application is developed, and this is just as true of professional developers as beginners. In the process of developing a database you will discover that you are unable to do everything that you would like to do. Some of these problems may be because you do not yet have enough skill. Others may be problems with understanding what is needed, and yet others may be ones that even an experienced developer would not be able to solve.

You should list honestly all the problems with the database. These could include:

- functions that you would like it to have but were unable to provide
- actions that do not work properly
- problems with inputting, outputting or searching the data.

How can I assess how easy the database is to use?

You should try to understand what it would be like for a new user to use the database. The simplest way to do this is to ask other people to use it. Watch them whilst they use it, jot down any problems they have and any questions they ask, then ask them for their opinion and advice. You can then make some changes in the light of their comments.

It should be possible for a new user to use the database successfully with only the user manual as a guide. So you could ask another user to use the database with the user manual, and this time do not stay around to observe. The person should then report back to you any problems that arose.

How can I suggest improvements to the overall design?

Most software can be improved in some way. Often the problem is to know when to stop! You should be able to list some possible improvements to your database by:

- checking against the original purpose and requirements, as stated by the user or described in a scenario
- identifying any problems that could be corrected
- noting what other users have suggested.

You do not have to implement all the improvements that you consider. Remember that most major software applications appear in different versions from one year to the next. Each new version contains improvements to the original software.

Test your knowledge

1 What questions should you ask when evaluating a database?
2 What does 'fit for its purpose' mean in this context?
3 How can a database designer check whether the application is easy to use?

Assessment tasks

Unlike most of the other units in this qualification, this unit is *externally assessed*. That means that you will be set an Integrated Vocational Assignment (IVA) by the examination board, Edexcel. The IVA will consist of a series of tasks, and you will complete them over a period of time. Your evidence will then be submitted to Edexcel, who will assess your work.

The IVA will challenge you to demonstrate that you can meet all the learning outcomes. You will be given a description of a fictitious organisation that requires a new database. You will probably have to do some research into organisations of the same type so that you can develop a database that would meet their needs.

This section describes what you must do to obtain a Merit grade for this unit.

A Distinction grade may be awarded if your work demonstrates a deeper understanding of the topics and is of a higher quality. The highlighted sentences indicate the quality of work expected at Distinction level.

The IVA

Learning outcome 1 – Describe the features and facilities of relational databases

Learning outcome 2 – Design a suitable database to satisfy user needs

Learning outcome 3 – Provide suitable documentation to support the database design

Learning outcome 4 – Provide suitable documentation to support the database design

You should be able to:

1 Understand the function of databases and the distinction between the DBMS and the database content.
2 Analyse the use of a database in an example organisation.
3 Design and build a relational database which has:
    o two or more tables
    o at least one input form
    o user-friendly screen designs.
4 Use the database to:
    o enter sufficient records to enable realistic data manipulation
    o carry out useful sorts
    o generate suitably headed reports
    o design and execute simple queries.
5 Provide a detailed evaluation of the database to include benefits, limitations and improvements.
6 Provide a detailed user guide which is easy to read, user-friendly, well presented and fit for its purpose.

To obtain a Distinction grade, you should also be able to:

7 Provide detailed and comprehensive screen designs, with full justification of their structure.

8 Design and build a fully relational database which is user-friendly and well structured.

9 Design and execute queries which draw on more than one table.

10 Generate reports making good use of design tools (Design view) as well as the standard wizard.

UNIT 5: SOFTWARE DEVELOPMENT

Success in this unit

What are the learning outcomes?

To achieve this unit you must:

- investigate a customer problem
- produce a program design
- create a program from the design
- evaluate the program against the original design.

How is this unit assessed?

This unit is externally assessed and marked using an Integrated Vocational Assignment (IVA). The IVA for this unit will be released each January and you will have to complete it during your Spring term.

See the *Assessment tasks* section at the end of this unit for more information about the IVA.

Introduction

About this unit

While not every IT practitioner is a programmer, an understanding of the process by which programs are written is important. This unit covers all of the main steps in software development, understanding the customer's requirements, designing a program to meet those requirements, writing a program using the design, and then comparing the program produced with the design to check it meets the requirements.

Throughout this unit we will use a case study on Modern Carpets. This is a small company with several shops, which sells carpets and floorings. We will see how a program is developed for them starting with the initial problem, working through the investigation and design stages to the completed program.

What is a computer program?

A computer program is a series of instructions that tells the computer's processor what to do. Programs are what make computers powerful. Unlike a typewriter or a fax machine, which only has one function, different programs enable the computer to carry out any number of different tasks.

Computers, however, can only understand machine code instructions in the form of binary codes (this is covered in Unit 1). Although programs for the very first computers were written using these binary codes, they are very difficult for people to understand, so computer **programming languages** (sometimes called *high-level languages*) were developed.

What does it mean?

Programming languages – have instructions using English-like statements and are therefore easier to understand than binary codes. The English-like statements are converted into the binary codes that the computer understands using a piece of software called *a compiler*.

What computer languages are there?

Since computers first came into general use, a wide variety of languages have been developed, some of which have been aimed at particular applications (Fortran, for example, was designed for doing mathematical calculations). With the dominance of the Microsoft® Windows operating system, many of the most popular programming languages used today are designed to produce Microsoft® Windows applications. In this chapter we will be looking at the Microsoft® Visual Basic programming language.

Further research – Programming languages

There are many different programming languages, but which are currently the most popular in the IT industry? One way you can gauge the popularity of different languages is to check the number of programmer jobs advertised which are looking for each language. Get hold of one of the weekly IT magazines such as *Computing* or *Computer Weekly* and check the jobs section. Alternatively search on the Internet for programming jobs.

What sort of problems can computers solve?

Computers are often used in business to solve problems. For example, a computer program might be written to:

- help a shopkeeper to keep track of how many items of each piece of stock he or she has and when it is time to reorder
- record all of a sales person's customer details
- keep a dairy of appointments for the doctors and nurses in a health centre.

However, the programs are normally written by a programmer, not by the person who has the problem. Therefore the programmer must spend time understanding the exact nature of the problem before starting to write the program.

How are programs written?

Most programs are not written by one person, but by a team of people. In some cases the team of programmers may work in the IT department of the company for whom the program is being produced. Most large organisations like banks or supermarkets have programmers who work in their IT departments and write programs to solve the organisation's particular business problems. However, smaller companies would not normally have their own programmers; instead they would purchase software from companies that specialise in writing programs for other organisations (sometimes called *software houses*). In some cases software houses write specific software for one particular company. In other cases they write software designed to meet the needs of all the companies in a particular type of business.

Although software is written in a number of different ways, the techniques used are broadly similar. Also, you will write programs by yourself, not as part of a team. This will make the process slightly simpler as you will not have to concern yourself with who does what – since you will be doing everything!

What steps are involved in writing a program?

1 The first step in writing a program is to understand what problem or need the program will address. This involves the programmer working with the client (for whom the program is being written) to develop an understanding of what is needed. This stage is sometimes called *system analysis*. It is perhaps the most important stage in software development; if the programmer fails at this stage to understand what the client requires then no matter how well the program is written, it will not meet its purpose. The result of this stage will be a document which describes the requirements in detail.

2 The second step is the design stage. Rather like an architect designing a building, this stage involves planning how the programs will work. Again the outcome of this stage will be a document which describes the way the system is designed.

3 The third step is when the actual program writing begins. Using the design created in the previous step, the program, or in many cases, the suite of programs, are written. As well as being written, the programs also need to be tested to ensure that they do not give any unexpected results.

4 Finally, before the software is handed to the client, it must be checked against the requirements document that was produced in stage one to check that the resulting program really does meet the client's requirements.

Writing programs

Although the first steps in writing a program are to understand the client's needs and to produce a design for the programs, it can be difficult to understand particularly at the design stage unless you have a basic understanding of how programs are written. Therefore in this section we will look at some of the fundamentals of programming.

What types of building blocks can be used to make a program?

We can broadly divide the kind of functions a program performs into three basic building blocks:

- *Sequence* – is where the instructions in a program are followed one after another in sequence.
- *Selection* – is where a choice is made as to which set of instructions to carry out. The choice is made based on criteria such as an option that the user has selected.
- *Iteration* – is where instructions are repeated either a certain number of times or until some criterion is met.

To demonstrate how these different **building blocks** can be used within a program, we will write a very simple calculator program which adds together two numbers. It has three textboxes and a button. You type a number into each of the first two textboxes and then when the button is clicked, it adds together the two numbers and displays the result in the third textbox.

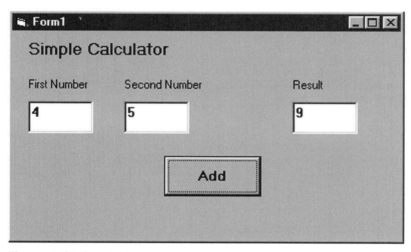

Figure 5.1 Simple calculator program

What does it mean?

Building blocks – Writing a program is a complex process and a program is commonly broken down into 'building blocks' or programming constructs in order to understand how to write it. Just as when constructing a building, walls, doors and roofs etc. are combined to make a complete building, a program is built from different types of program code constructs.

How are programs written using Visual Basic?

When writing a program in Visual Basic, in common with many other Microsoft® Windows programming environments, there are two main steps to creating a program.

■ Firstly you need to create at least one form. This is what you can see in Figure 5.1. It contains the labels, textboxes, buttons and other controls that your program requires.

■ Secondly you need to write sections of programming code (called *procedures*), each of which will run when a certain **event** occurs.

What does it mean?

Events – Visual Basic forms are made up of various objects such as buttons, textboxes and labels. Each of these objects can respond to various *events*. An event is when something happens, for example a button can respond to the *click event*, which occurs when the user clicks the button with the mouse. A textbox can respond to the *text change event* when the text in the box changes. The programmer writes programming code in a procedure that runs when the event occurs to make the program respond in the desired way to the event. Programming languages that work in this way are known as *event-driven* languages.

How can the form for the calculator program be created?

When the Visual Basic **IDE** (Integrated Development Environment) is started, you will first see a screen asking you what type of program you want to create, and if you leave the default Standard EXE selected and click the **Open** button, you will then see the Form editor window with a default form created for you. This is shown in Figure 5.2, although a textbox has been added.

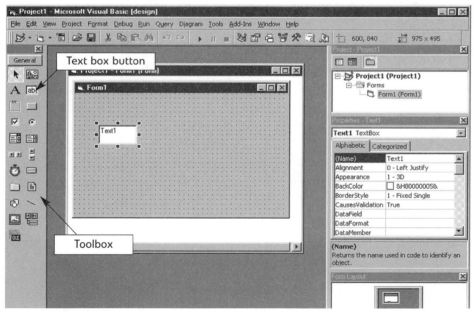

Figure 5.2 Visual Basic IDE

What does it mean?

IDE – most modern programming languages are provided as an IDE. This is a program which includes an editor where you can type the programming codes, a compiler so you can convert the program into binary codes, and a tool called a *debugger* which can help you find errors in the program.

On the left side of the screen is the toolbox from where different controls (textboxes, buttons etc.) can be selected and then dragged out on to the form. In the right centre is the properties list for the currently selected control. Every control has its own list of *properties* that govern how the control looks and behaves. For example, a textbox has a Name property, which sets the name of the control (Text1 in the example above), and a Font property which controls the font, size and any enhancements such as bold, of any text in the textbox. A textbox also has a Text property that sets the text in the textbox. As a default, this is set to the name of the textbox, but you can delete this as there is no reason to have the textbox name appearing in the textboxes in our calculator program.

Add the three textboxes needed for the calculator and add the labels above them:

- ■ To add a textbox you will first need to click the textbox button in the toolbox.
- ■ Move your mouse on to the form and drag out the textbox to the size you require.
- ■ Creating a label is a similar process; the label button is to the left of the textbox button in the toolbox. The property that controls the text that is displayed in a label is called the *Caption property*.
- ■ Finally add the button (the button for creating buttons is the one below the textbox button). The property that controls what text appears on a button is also the *Caption property*.

Your form should now look like Figure 5.3.

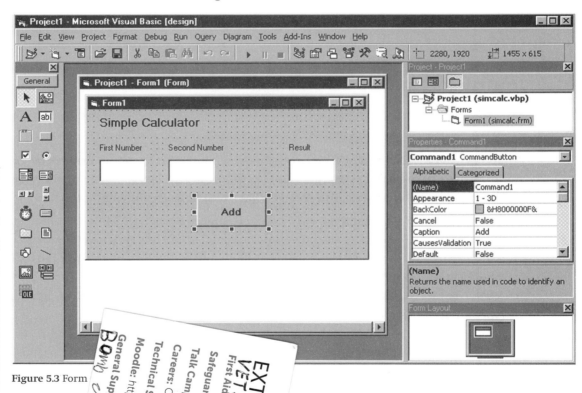

Figure 5.3 Form

Having creat[...] the program instructions or code.

Visual Basic [...] [th]is simple program, the only event that we need to add cod[e...] [A]dd' button. When this happens, the program instructio[n...] [num]bers the user has typed into the first two textboxes, [...] result in the third textbox.

To type th[e...] Add button and a code window is opened. Visual

Basic automatically creates a procedure (a procedure is a small section of code with a specific purpose) called 'Command1_Click'. 'Command1' is the name of the button and 'Click' indicates that this procedure will run when the button is clicked. The procedure begins with the name of the procedure and ends with the instruction End Sub. The code we will type will be entered between these two statements, and is show in Figure 5.4.

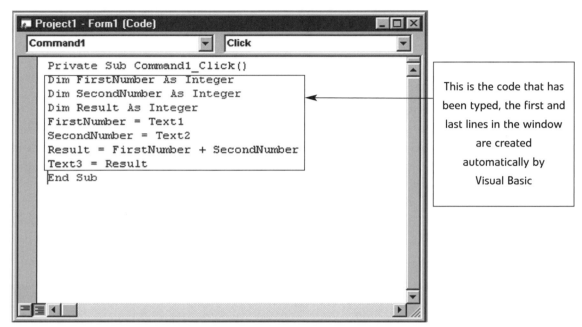

This is the code that has been typed, the first and last lines in the window are created automatically by Visual Basic

Figure 5.4 Code for Command1_Click()

Let us examine this code in detail starting with the first three lines:

```
Dim FirstNumber As Integer
Dim SecondNumber As Integer
Dim Result As Integer
```

Programs need to store data while they are processing it. This program needs to be able to store the two numbers the user enters and the result of adding them. The memory areas where this data is stored are called *variables*. Variables have a number of *attributes*:

- A *name* – given by the programmer. A variable should be given a name that indicates its purpose (for example, 'x' is a valid variable name, but it's not very meaningful 'AccBalance' is a more helpful name for a variable that holds the balance of a bank account). Variable names cannot contain spaces.
- A *datatype* – this indicates the type of data that the variable will hold. Most common data types are *integer* for storing whole numbers, and *string* for storing text.
- A *value* – this is the data that the variable holds. It will change (vary) depending on what the user enters (inputs) and what processing take place, hence the name 'variable'.

These three lines use the Dim instruction to create three variables (called FirstNumber, SecondNumber and Result) all of which have the data type of integer (whole numbers). As yet the variables have no values assigned to them

The next two lines are:

```
FirstNumber = Text1
SecondNumber = Text2
```

These simply take the contents of the two textboxes (called Text1 and Text2) and place them in the variables FirstNumber and SecondNumber.

The next line is:

```
Result = FirstNumber + SecondNumber
```

This adds the values in the two variables together and places the resulting value in the variable called Result.

And the final line reads:

```
Text3 = Result
```

This takes the value in the variable Result and places it in the textbox called Text3, so the user can see the result of the calculation.

You should note that the only programming building block we have used here is *sequence*, since the instructions are followed one after the other.

The program is now complete and can be run using the run button in the toolbar or choosing **Run** from the menu bar and selecting **Start**.

You should remember to save your program, preferably before running it (in case a problem with it causes the computer to crash). With Visual Basic the form in a program is saved in a separate file from the project file, so you will have two files to save.

The program will work fine as long as you remember to type two numbers in the first two textboxes before you click the **Add** button. If you click this button when there are no numbers in the textboxes a dialog box will pop up saying 'Run time error 13, type mismatch'. You will then have to click the **End** button on the box and the program will stop.

This is what is known as a program 'crash'. Your program was unable to continue because it came across a situation it did not know how to deal with. The problem is that with nothing in the first two textboxes the program attempts to transfer these 'nothings' (technically known as null value) into a variable which has a datatype of integer, and this is what causes the program to crash.

To avoid this happening the program needs to be modified so that the contents of the textboxes are tested to ensure they contain numeric values before transferring their values to the variables. To do this we will use the second type of programming building block, *selection*.

First let us write down in **pseudo-code** what needs to happen:

If Text1 and Text2 are numeric then -

move them to the FirstNumber and SecondNumber variables.

Add them together and put the answer in the Result variable.

Move result to Text3.

Otherwise (i.e. they are not numeric) -

display an error message to the user.

? What does it mean?

Pseudo-code – is a kind of 'half-way house' between the actual programming code and normal spoken English. There are no precise rules to writing pseudo-code but it is used to work out the sort of program code needed without having to worry about the exact instructions.

In this case the program code does not follow one instruction after the other as it did when using the sequence building block; instead a choice is made. If the textboxes contain numeric values then one set of instructions is carried out; if they don't another instruction is carried out. The criterion for the choice is whether the textboxes contain numeric values or not.

The modified code is quite similar to our pseudo-code above:

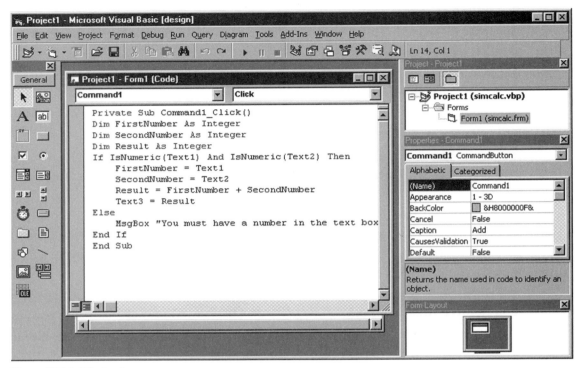

Figure 5.5 Modified code

The first three lines, which create the three variables, remain the same. The next eight lines need some explanation:

```
If IsNumeric(Text1) And IsNumeric(Text2) Then
   FirstNumber = Text1
   SecondNumber = Text2
   Result = FirstNumber + SecondNumber
   Text3 = Result
Else
   MsgBox "You must have a number in the text box"
End If
```

The 'If...Then...Else' instruction is very often used to create a selection building block. The instruction is spread over several lines that begin with If and end with End If. The first line of this block reads:

```
If IsNumeric(Text1) And IsNumeric(Text2) Then
```

The If instruction tests the content of the Text1 and the Text2 textboxes to see whether they contain a numeric value. To do this a function called IsNumeric is used. A function is a special facility that is provided by Visual Basic which performs a task. A function normally has something passed to it; in this case it is the variable you want to test to see whether it is numeric, and it normally returns something. In the case of the IsNumeric function it returns a value of True if the variable you have passed to it is numeric and False if it is not. This might sound rather complex, but think of it as if the above line was written like this and it becomes clearer:

> If it is true that Text1 contains a numeric value and it is true that Text2 contains a numeric value, then do the following instructions.

We have seen the four lines that follow the `Then` before and should need no further explanation. However, suppose either Text1 and/or Text2 doesn't contain a numeric value. In that case the IsNumeric function will return a value of False, and instead of the four lines that follow the `Then` being run, the lines following the `Else` will be run and the MsgBox instruction will display a message box on the screen with the "You must have a number in the textbox" message displayed.

So, the 'If...Then...Else' instruction allows a choice to be made between which lines of code to run. Run the modified program and you will see that if you fail to enter a number into one or both of the textboxes, the message box will pop up.

Check your understanding – Creating a Multiply button

It is not hard to figure out how to add a button which will do multiplication (and others for division and subtraction). See if you can work out what is needed.

How can iteration (repetition) be used in a program?

Finally in this section, we need to look at a simple example of the last of the three programming building blocks, which is *iteration* (or repetition). It is not really possible to demonstrate iteration using the calculator program we have been working on until now, so we must look at another simple example.

The program we will use to demonstrate iteration is shown below in Figure 5.6. When you click on the 'Go!' button the rocket will fly upwards. This program could be the basis for a game.

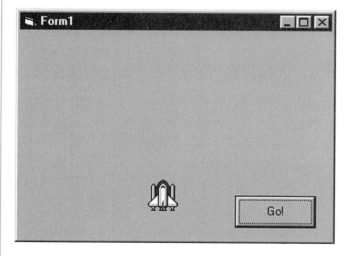

Figure 5.6 Rocket game

In order to understand how a program like this can be written, we first need to understand how Visual Basic positions graphics (and other objects like buttons and textboxes) on a form. Every form is covered by an invisible grid, rather like a piece of graph paper. Each line on the grid is numbered. Every object is positioned on the grid by two properties called Top and Left. The Top property controls the vertical position, the Left controls its horizontal position. This is shown on Figure 5.7, where the grid has been added.

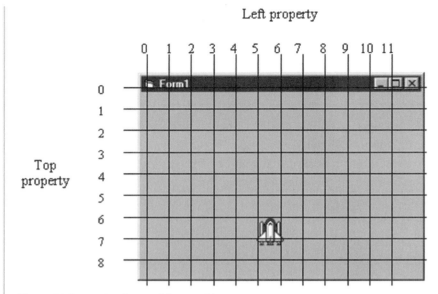

Figure 5.7 Properties that position an object

The rocket picture is placed on the form using an image box. The toolbox on the left of the Visual Basic IDE window has an image box button. By clicking on the button you can then drag out an image box on the form. The picture property of the image box is then set to the graphics file – in this case an icon file – see Figure 5.8.

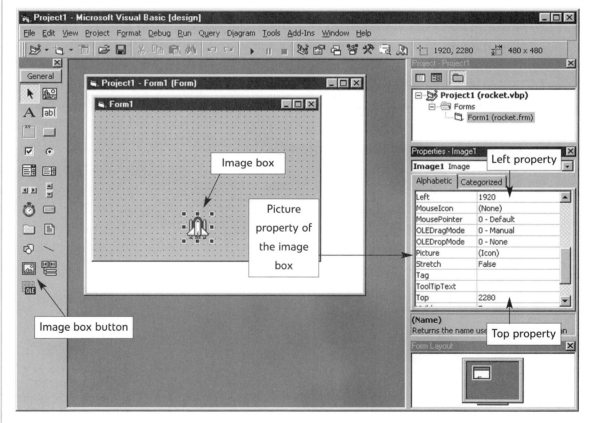

Figure 5.8 Using an image box

To make the rocket fly upwards the Top property needs to be decreased until it reaches the top of the form. To do this all we need to do is repeatedly subtract one from the top property, using what is called a 'For...Next' loop. This loop repeats a certain number of times.

The code for the Go! Button is shown in Figure 5.9.

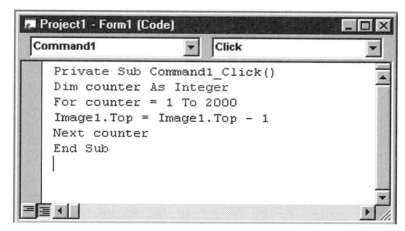

Figure 5.9 Code for the Go! button

Let us look at the code in more detail:

```
Dim counter As Integer
```

This line creates a variable called *counter*. A 'For...Next' loop always needs a variable to count around the loop. This counter is often used within the loop, although not in this case.

```
For counter = 1 To 2000
```

This is the start of the loop. *Counter* is the variable created in the previous line. '1 to 2000' tells the loop to start at 1 and continue looping until the counter reaches the value of 2000. If you position the image of the rocket towards the bottom of a small form like the one shown in the example, its initial top property will be about 2500 or so. So, if the program loops 2000 times, subtracting 1 from the top property each time, by the end of the loop the rocket will be somewhere near to the top of the form.

```
Image1.Top = Image1.Top - 1
```

This line subtracts 1 from the Top property of the picture of the rocket, which is called Image1.

```
Next counter
```

This is the end of the loop. When this instruction is reached, the value in the variable *counter* has 1 added to it and the loop is repeated (unless of course the counter has reached the value of 2000).

Check your understanding – Shoot 'em up game

It is not difficult to work out how to get another image box, perhaps containing a picture of a plane, to fly across the form (try changing the Left property in the loop). The rocket and the plane could be made to collide, creating the basis for a simple 'shoot 'em up' game.

5.1 Investigating the problem

Most commercial programs are written to solve some kind of problem or to take advantage of an opportunity. Clearly it is necessary to understand the nature of the problem or opportunity before you can write a program that will achieve what is required. There are a number of questions that can be asked to gather the necessary information:

- What are the aims of the new system?
- How does the current system work?
- What other systems does it need to interface with?
- What is the scope and boundaries of the system?
- How will the new system work?

We shall look at each of these questions in turn, with the help of a case study.

Case study – Modern Carpets – the problem

Customers who come in to Modern Carpets' shops want to know how much it would cost to buy the carpet for a particular room in their house. To calculate this they need to know not only how large the room is (its length and width) but also how much the carpet costs per square metre. On top of that they also need to add in the cost of the carpet underlay and the cost of fitting (underlay is a foam sheet that goes under the carpet to protect the floor). John Dixon, the company's sales manager, thinks it would be a good idea for the store to have a program on its computers on which the sales people could demonstrate to customers how much different carpets might cost. Modern Carpets buys all its computers and software from a company called Small Business Solutions (SBS). John had a chat with Rajesh Khah, their support manager at SBS, and asked him whether what he had in mind was possible. They discussed using a spreadsheet but decided that writing a simple Visual Basic program would provide a neater solution with an easier-to-use interface.

Rajesh will need to find out exactly what John wants so he can work out how much time it will take him, and from that how much it will cost. John will have to be sure about what, exactly, Rajesh is going to provide them with and how much it will cost. John will then need to go and see Modern Carpet's Managing Director, Sue Francis, and justify the expenditure to her.

Rajesh and John decide that the best way to persuade Sue is to put together a document that will describe the system they have in mind.

Designing a system

What are the aims of the system?

When designing a system, one of the first things that needs to be defined is its primary purposes or aims. This will probably state the problem that it is intended to solve or the opportunity it will take advantage of. It is important to get this clear at the start because sometimes during the process of developing the software people can lose track of the original reason for which the software was required.

Case study – Modern Carpets – the aims

John makes a list of the aims of the Modern Carpets cost calculator program:

1 To provide sales assistants with a simple way of showing customers how much different carpets would cost.

2 To improve the service provided to customers, giving a competitive advantage over other carpet shops in the area.

3 To encourage potential customers to purchase a carpet by quickly providing them with accurate information of the costs involved.

How does the current system work?

In many cases the software to be developed will replace an existing system. It may be a manual system (i.e. using people rather than computers) or it may be an old computer system which has outlived its usefulness. In any case it is important that the current system be thoroughly understood so that the new software can preserve its essential elements and its good features and avoid the problems that it now suffers from.

Case study – Modern Carpets – the report

John needs to explain in his report what currently happens so that Sue can clearly see why the new system will be better. Currently, if a customer asks how much a carpet would cost, the sales person needs to go through the following steps:

- find out the size of the room by multiplying its length by its width
- find the cost per square metre of the carpet
- find out if the customer wants economy or luxury underlay
- multiply the cost of the carpet by the area of the room
- multiply the cost of the chosen underlay by the area of the room
- multiply the cost of fitting by the area of the room
- add together the cost of the carpet, underlay and fitting.

While none of this is particularly difficult, it can be quite time-consuming. If a mistake is made during the process the customer may not be very happy when the mistake comes to light, especially if this means an increase in the cost of the carpet

What other systems does it need to interface with?

No system works in isolation. All systems take input, from the user or another computer system; they also produce some kind of output. Part of understanding the system to be developed involves defining what these inputs and outputs are. At this stage there is no need to go into a lot of detail about these inputs and outputs – that will come later.

Case study – Modern Carpets – inputs and outputs

John's list of inputs and outputs looks like this:

Inputs – the customer using the system will enter the length and width of the room, and the price of the chosen carpet.

The cost of the underlay and the fitting are the same whatever carpet is chosen. At Modern Carpets, economy underlay costs £1.75 per square metre, while luxury underlay costs £2.15 per square metre. Fitting costs £2.00 per square metre.

Outputs – the system will show the total cost of the carpet, including fitting and underlay.

To help develop their understanding of the system, Rajesh draws up a diagram showing the inputs and outputs the system has:

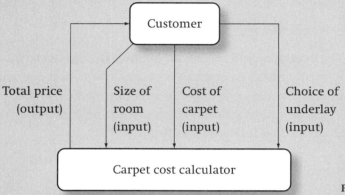

Figure 5.10
Diagram showing the inputs and outputs

What is the scope of the system and what are it boundaries?

The question being asked here is really 'what will the system do, and what won't it do?' This may be an obvious question, but it is an important one. Also, it is important to decide what is to be included and what is to be left out. Computers are very powerful machines and there are many facilities you could include in the software you are developing if you had endless time and money. In some cases you may want to decide what the most important features are (referring back to the aims of the system) and develop the first version of the software with those features, putting the rest on the 'wish list' for future versions.

Case study – Modern Carpets – the prototype program

John and Rajesh decide that the best way to produce the program is to start off with a very simple version. They will show that version to the managers and sales people in the shops and get their opinions on what is good (and bad) about it and what needs to be added and improved.

Based on these comments they will then develop more sophisticated versions. This is known as **prototyping**.

What does it mean?

Prototyping – a method of software development that involves producing a simple or only partially functioning version of the required program and then showing it to the users for them to evaluate how closely it meets their requirements. The process can be repeated several times with each successive prototype adding more functionality and incorporating the users' suggestions. As prototyping involves the user in decisions about how the program should look and work, it often results in a program that matches the users' requirements more closely than more traditional methods of development.

The end result of the investigation stage should be a document that draws together all the information collected and puts the case for developing the software. It should also describe the costs involved. Before the project can go ahead this document will be presented to the manager in the company who is responsible for authorising the expenditure. The decision on whether or not to proceed will most probably be a commercial rather than a technical one. In other words the manager will need to decide whether the cost can be justified and what the return on the investment will be.

Test your knowledge

1   What should the first step be when developing a piece of software?
2   How can the required information be gathered in this first step?
3   What are the three building blocks used in program writing?
4   Give an example of a textbox property. What is this property used for?
5   What are the three attributes of a variable?
6   Why is Account Number not a valid variable name?
7   Which of the programming building blocks is normally created using an IF statement?
8   Give an example of a statement that can be used to start a loop.
9   What function can you use to test whether a value is numeric?

5.2 Program design

Having completed the investigation stage and received the go-ahead from management, the next step is to produce a design. The system design provides more detailed information about the internal working of the software. Much of what is done at this stage involves taking what has already been decided in the investigation stage and adding more detail to it. There are a number of things that need to be designed and planned, such as how the program will look to the user, what data will need to be stored and how it will be processed.

As we have said, programs take some kind of data as input, perform some kind of processing on that data (perhaps a calculation) and produce some kind of output. At the design stage we need to add more detail to what we have discovered about what is to be input, how it will be processed and what will be output.

How will the project be planned?

An important task that must be completed at this stage is to produce some kind of project (or design) plan. This will involve deciding the tasks that must be completed, who will do them and how long they will take. Using this plan, the developers can estimate how long, in total, the program will take to write, and from that they can calculate how much it will cost.

A project plan divides the project into a number of stages. For each stage, the developers estimate how long it will take and how many people will be involved. Estimating the time required to complete software development stages is a notoriously difficult task that is fraught with problems. The software developers will need to use the knowledge of the system they gained during the investigation stage along with their previous experience of other similar projects to be able to make these estimates.

Case study – Modern Carpets – the project plan

To estimate how long it will take to develop this program, Rajesh creates a project plan. He breaks the software development process down into the following tasks:

1. Create design –
   screen form
   variable list
   flowchart
   complete design document.

2. Write the program.
3. Test the program.
4. Write documentation –
   user documentation
   technical documentation.
5. Implement program –
   install at Modern Carpets shops
   train users.

The more detailed the breakdown, the easier the estimation task will be.

Rajesh then works out how long each step will take. He needs to work out the actual number of hours required for each task and also, since he has other work to do, he needs to work out how these tasks can be timetabled with his other work. The end result will be the total amount of hours the project requires (from which he can calculate the project cost), and the elapsed time needed to complete the project (from which he can work out the date the project will be completed).

His completed plan is shown below.

Task	Hours to complete	Scheduled date
1) Create design		
1.1 Form design	2 hours	
1.2 Variable list	1.5 hours	
1.3 Flowchart	2 hours	
1.4 Complete design document	4 hours	
2) Write program	5 hours	
3) Test program	3 hours	
4) Write documentation		
4.1 User documentation	4 hours	
4.2 Technical documentation	3 hours	
5) Implement program		
5.1 Install at shops	3 hours	
5.2 Train users	5 hours	
Total time	32.5 hours	

Figure 5.11 Project plan

When preparing for your IVA, you will need to complete a similar project plan (see the section *Assessment tasks* at the end of this unit). In your case you are not concerned with the cost of the project, but you must complete the work by a given date so you need to make sure you can schedule the work you need to do on the program to fit in with your other work.

Further research – Create your own project plan

Of course, project planning does not only apply to software development, it can be used for almost any task. Planning is an important and useful skill to develop and can help you to complete important tasks, such as finishing an assignment, on time. Try creating a project plan for an assignment you are working on at the moment. By tracking your progress against your plan, you can make sure you are not getting too far behind schedule. Because of the importance and complexity of planning large projects, various sophisticated computer programs have been written to help people produce these plans. Do you have any project planning software installed in your school or college? If so, you could investigate how it works. If not, find out what project planning software is available by searching on the Internet.

How is the user interface designed?

In Visual Basic, one or more forms are used to provide the user with a way of running the program (the *user interface*). The design of the form is a good place to start because it can help you visualise how the program will work. The Visual Basic form editor makes creating forms quite easy, but you need to bear in mind that they need to be neat and clear. They should also be intuitive as far as possible (that is, it should be obvious to the user what they are expected to do with the form).

These objects will need to go on the form:

- labels to inform the user what to do
- textboxes for the user to enter (input) information, and for the program to output information
- list boxes for the user to make choices
- buttons for the user to click to perform various actions.

Design documents previously created, such as the input and output diagrams, provide a guide to objects needed for the inputs and output that the system will have.

Case study – Modern Carpets – designing the form

Using the information from the investigation stage we can see the form will need:

- textboxes to input the length and width of the room
- a textbox to input the price of the carpet
- a way for the user to select the type of underlay
- a button that the user will click to have the calculation done
- a textbox for the program to output the calculated cost.

The initial design for the form is sketched out and is shown in Figure 5.12. A type of list box called a combo box has been used to allow the user to select the type of underlay. A combo box is a drop-down box that displays a list of options (the different types of underlay); the user clicks on the item in the list to select it.

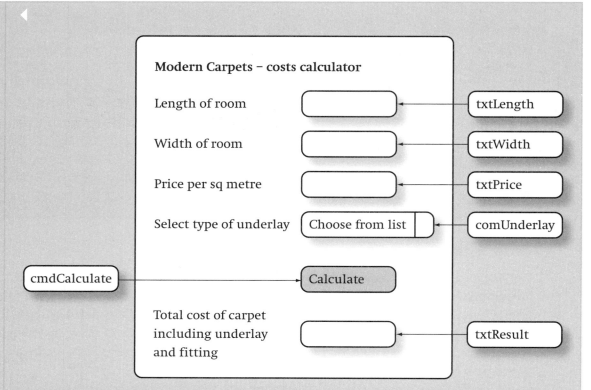

Figure 5.12 Completed form design with object names shown

Previously we left the form objects with their default names (Text2, Command1, etc.) this would work, but as these names give no clue to what the object is used for, it is better to give the objects meaningful names. This is done by modifying the objects' Name property. The names given to the objects are shown above in Figure 5.12. So that it is clear what type of object the name belongs to, textboxes have been given names beginning with txt, combo boxes with com and Command buttons with cmd.

How is a variable list created?

The next thing we can decide upon is the data the program will need to store, using variables, and what those variables' names and datatypes will be. By looking at the form design, we can quickly identify some of the required variables. The textboxes on the form will all require variables to hold the data they input or output

Case study – Modern Carpets – variables

Rajesh begins work on the data design for the program. By looking at the form he can see the following variables will be required:

- length and width of the room
- price per square metre of the carpet
- total cost of the carpet.

These variables are shown in Figure 5.13. The datatype 'Single' stores a single precision floating-point number.

Variable name	Datatype
Length	Single
Width	Single
Price	Single
Total	Single

Figure 5.13 Variables identified so far

However, this isn't a complete list of the variables needed. In order to work out what other variables will be required, Rajesh needs to think in more detail about the processing that will be required.

How can the processing be designed?

So far we have been thinking mainly about the input and output that a program requires. That has helped us complete the form design and also to identify some of the variables the program requires. We shall now consider the processing that has to be done. The starting point for this design will probably be the manual processing that is currently done, which should have been identified at the investigation stage. There are a number of techniques that can be used to design the processing steps required in a program. We will look at a simple technique called *flowcharting*.

How do you draw a flowchart?

As the name suggests, a flowchart is a diagram which shows the steps which must be taken to carry out some task. Flowcharts can be used to design all sorts of processes, not just programming ones.

Flowcharts use a variety of symbols, linked by arrows to indicate the type of step involved at each stage. They start with a circle containing the word *Start* with a single arrow leaving the circle, and end with a circle containing the word *Stop*, with a single arrow entering.

Normal processing steps (a sequence building block), such as doing a calculation, are contained in a rectangle with a brief description of the step inside the rectangle. The rectangle has one arrow entering (from the previous step) and one leaving (to the next step):

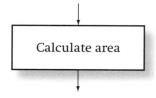

Figure 5.14 Flowchart processing step

Processing steps which involve some input are shown in a skewed rectangle, also with a brief description of the step written in the box, and with one arrow entering and one leaving:

Figure 5.15 Flowchart input box

Output steps, on the other hand, are shown as a box which is meant to look like a torn-off piece of paper:

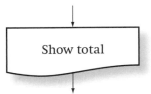

Figure 5.16 Flowchart output box

Where a choice or decision needs to be made (a selection building block), a diamond shape is used, containing a question that describes the choice. While one arrow enters the diamond shape, two leave it: one showing the route taken if the answer to the question is Yes, the other if it is No:

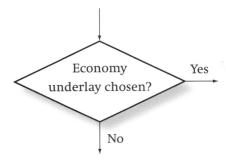

Figure 5.17 Flowchart decision box

Flowcharts are a good introduction to program design methods. However, they are not good for complex problems as the flowcharts themselves then can become complex and difficult to follow.

Case study – Modern Carpets – flowchart and process design

In order to develop the process design for the program, Rajesh refers back to the manual process that the sales people currently go through. This was listed in the document that John produced earlier:

- find out the size of the room by multiplying its length by its width
- find the cost per square metre of the chosen carpet
- find out if the customer wants economy or luxury underlay
- multiply the cost of the carpet by the area of the room
- multiply the cost of the chosen underlay by the area of the room
- multiply the cost of fitting by the area of the room
- add together the cost of the carpet, underlay and fitting.

These steps are shown as a flowchart in Figure 5.18.

Check your understanding – Flowchart skills

Practise your flowchart drawing skills by creating some simple flowcharts for well-known tasks, such as making a cup of tea or getting ready in the morning.

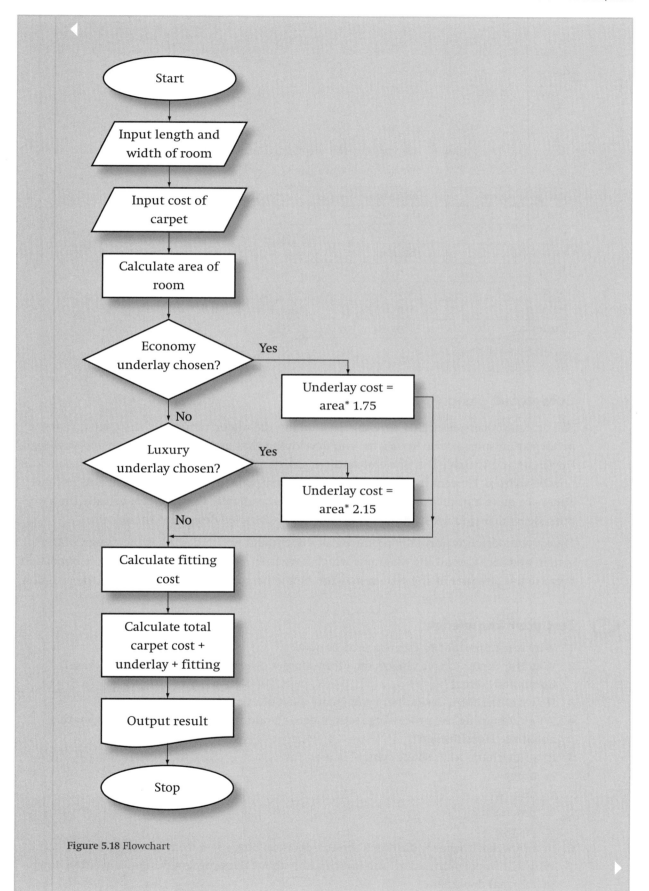

Figure 5.18 Flowchart

On looking at the flowchart it becomes clear that more variables will be needed to hold the results of the calculations, such as:

- area of room
- underlay cost
- fitting cost.

These should be added to the variable list we started earlier. The updated variable list is show in Figure 5.19, with the new variables highlighted in bold.

Variable name	Datatype
Length	Single
Width	Single
Price	Single
Total	Single
Area	Single
Fitting	Single
Underlay	Single

Figure 5.19 Complete variable list

Completed design process

The design process described here involved taking the understanding of the system that the investigation stage provided us with and developing that understanding using a form design, flowchart and variable list. The end result is a design from which the programming code can now be written. Flowcharts are not the only diagrammatic programming design technique. There are quite a number of alternative techniques available. They all have broadly the same purpose, which is to assist in the development of a detailed design for the system.

The system design is normally produced as a document which describes the design of the system and includes all the diagrams which have been produced. The document is important because the designer of the system may not be the person who is going to write the program.

Test your knowledge

1 Why is it important to create a project plan?
2 Why is it better to give objects on a form names other than the default ones (Text1, Command1, etc.)?
3 How can the form design help you create a list of variables?
4 When designing the processing steps, where should you look to find the information about the steps needed?
5 In a flowchart, what shape symbol is used for:
   - inputs
   - outputs
   - processing
   - decisions?
6 In a flowchart, what is different about a decision box, apart from its shape?
7 Why is it important that all the information about the program design be written down in a formal document?

5.3 Create the program

Program writing

Following a considerable amount of time spent on the design, in theory at least, the program writing should be fairly straightforward. The more detailed the design is, the easier the programming should be. However, nothing in life is simple and typically inadequacies and omissions in the design will be revealed at this stage or when the program is tested. The more complex the system, the more likely this is to be the case.

The program form or forms have been created in the design stage, so the steps in creating the program are as follows:

- declare the variables required
- write the code for the event procedures
- test the program to ensure it works correctly.

We shall follow through these steps using the case study.

Case study – Modern Carpets – writing the code

Code needs to be written for one or more events that occur on the form. The most obvious event on the form that has been designed is the click event for the command button cmdCalculate. When this button is clicked the total cost of the carpet will be calculated.

Before writing the code Rajesh needs to have the previous design documents to hand that he will refer to. They are:

- the form design (Figure 5.12)
- the flowchart (Figure 5.18)
- the completed variable list (Figure 5.19).

Rajesh then writes the variable declarations, using the variable list as a guide:

```
Dim Length As Single
Dim Width As Single
Dim Price As Single
Dim Total As Single
Dim Area As Single
Dim Fitting As Single
Dim Underlay As Single
```

He then looks at each of the boxes on the flowchart and works out what code is required to carry out each processing step identified.

The first box in the flowchart is labelled 'Input length and width of room'. This step involves transferring the contents of the textboxes on the form into the variables. He knows the names of the variables from the variable list, and he gets the names of the textboxes from the form design. So the code he writes is as follows:

```
Length = txtLength
Width = txtWidth
```

The next box on the flowchart is labelled 'Input cost of carpet'. Again he knows the names of the textbox and variable so he simply writes:

```
Price = txtPrice
```

The next box is labelled 'Calculate area of room'. This is the length multiplied by the width, so the code is:

```
Area = Length * Width
```

The next part of the flowchart involves making a choice between the two types of underlay, which requires an IF statement. This simply checks the text that has been selected in the comUnderlay combo box. If it is 'Economy' then the underlay costs £1.75 per square metre, so the area is multiplied by 1.75 to give the underlay cost. If it is 'Luxury' then the area is multiplied by 2.15:

```
If comUnderlay.Text = "Economy" Then
Underlay = Area * 1.75
Else If comUnderlay.Text = "Luxury" Then
Underlay = Area * 2.15
End If
```

Then the calculation for the price of the fitting is done. Fitting is charged at £2.50 per square metre, so the code is:

```
Fitting = Area * 2.5
```

The final calculation works out the price of the carpet (area of the room multiplied by the price per square metre of the carpet) and adds the fitting and underlay costs previously calculated:

```
Total = (Area * Price) + Fitting + Underlay
```

The last box on the flowchart is labelled 'Output result'; this simply involves transferring the total, calculated in the last step into the textbox on the form:

```
txtResult = Total
```

The complete code for the cmdCalculate button is shown in Figure 5.20.

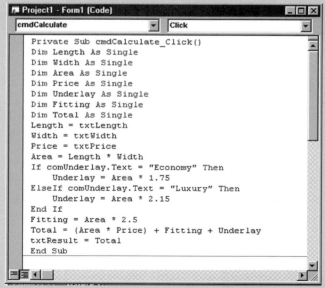

Figure 5.20 The code for the cmdCalculate button.

There is one thing that needs to be done before the program will work. The combo box comUnderlay is used to allow the customer to choose between economy and luxury underlay. The combo box, when the user drops it down, needs to display these two words so the user can select the required one, as shown in Figure 5.21.

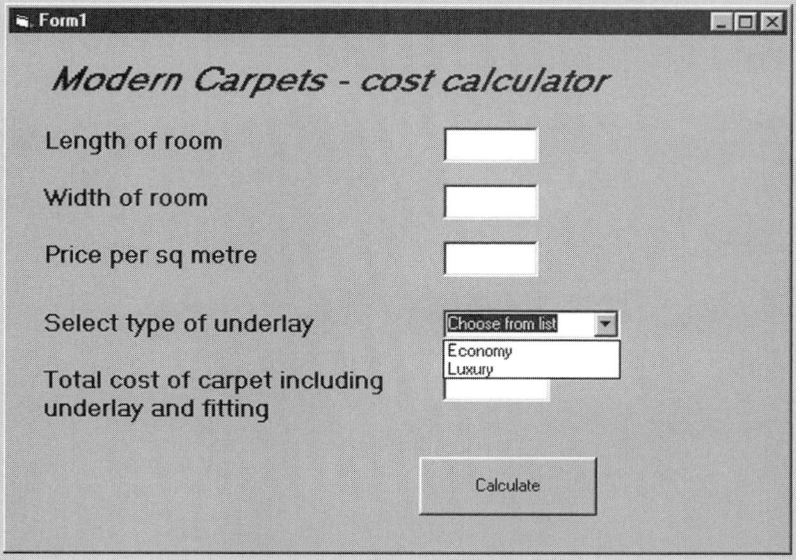

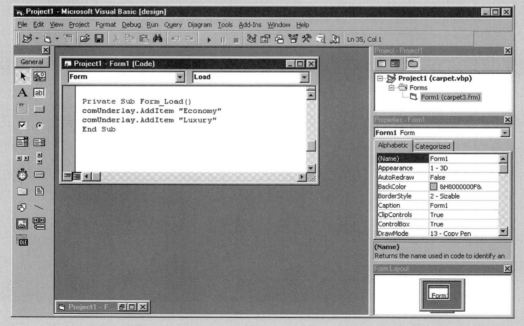

Figure 5.21 List of underlay types in the comUnderlay combo box

The words 'Choose from list' are set by the caption property of the object, but the list of items needs to be added when the form loads. To add code to run when the form load event occurs, you double-click the form background. The code window will then open with a form load procedure created for you. To add items to the combo box list, the AddItem method is used. The required code is shown in Figure 5.22

Figure 5.22 Code required for the form load event

The program is now ready to run. However, when Rajesh runs the program for the first time, he notices a small problem. He enters values for the length and width of the room and the price of the carpet and he selects the Economy underlay. When he clicks the **Calculate** button the total price appears in the txtResult textbox but it is not formatted as a currency value with a £ sign and two decimal places. This is shown in Figure 5.23

Figure 5.23 Total cost of the carpet, unformatted

This is a simple problem to fix as Visual Basic provides a function, called Format, which will re-format values into whatever format is required. The function is used here to format the variable Total (which contains the total price of the carpet) as it is transferred into the txtResult textbox. The modified code is shown below in Figure 5.24

```
Project1 - Form1 (Code)
cmdCalculate                Click

    Private Sub cmdCalculate_Click()
    Dim Length As Single
    Dim Width As Single
    Dim Area As Single
    Dim Price As Single
    Dim Underlay As Single
    Dim Fitting As Single
    Dim Total As Single
    Length = txtLength
    Width = txtWidth
    Price = txtPrice
    Area = Length * Width
    If comUnderlay.Text = "Economy" Then
        Underlay = Area * 1.75
    ElseIf comUnderlay.Text = "Luxury" Then
        Underlay = Area * 2.15
    End If
    Fitting = Area * 2.5
    Total = (Area * Price) + Fitting + Underlay
    txtResult = Format(Total, "currency")
    End Sub
```

Figure 5.24 Modified code for the cmdCalculate button

The program will now display the total price of the carpet formatted as currency.

Modern Carpets - cost calculator

Length of room	4
Width of room	3.5
Price per sq metre	2
Select type of underlay	Economy
Total cost of carpet including underlay and fitting	£87.50

[Calculate]

Figure 5.25 Total price shown formatted

Why does the program need testing?

The next stage in the software development process is to test the program to ensure it works properly. The main reason a program is tested is to ensure it works in the way that is described in the design specification. For example you need to test that the program gives the correct results.

Case study – Modern Carpets – data testing the program

Rajesh needs to check that the program he has written calculates the cost of carpets correctly. The easiest way to do this is to create some test data, in other words some imaginary carpet orders, and then manually calculate the total cost of these orders. Then he can put these orders into the program and see whether he gets the same results as his manual calculations.

Rajesh creates his list of imaginary orders and, using a pen and paper, manually calculates what the total cost should be and puts this data into the table, shown in Figure 5.26.

	Length	Width	Price	Underlay	Manual calculation	Same?
Order 1	2.5m	3m	£2.99	Economy		
Order 2	1.75m	2.25m	£1.99	Economy		
Order 3	5m	3.25m	£4.99	Luxury		

Figure 5.26 Test data

Then he tries these orders in the calculator program and checks the results against the manual calculations. This shows whether the calculator is working properly. If the calculator program comes up with the same result as his manual calculation, then he writes 'Yes' in the 'Same?' column, if not he writes 'No'. If there had been any differences between the manual calculations and the results from the program (i.e. if there are any 'Nos' in the 'Same?' column) then further investigation would be needed. There must either be an error in his manual calculations, or, more seriously, the program is not working properly and must be corrected.

This is only a very brief introduction to the topic of testing, which is covered in more detail in Unit 20.

Test your knowledge

1 What is the Dim statement used for?
2 What previously created document is used as a guide when writing program code?
3 What is the AddItem function used for?
4 What function can be used to display a numerical value as currency?
5 Why is it important to test a program?
6 What is test data? How is it used?

5.4 Evaluating the program

There are two aspects of writing a program that we can usefully evaluate. Firstly we can consider the process; in other words, how it was for you, the programmer. Secondly we can evaluate the outcome; in other words the program itself.

Evaluation

How do I evaluate the process?

Learning to program is not easy. It may well be that your first experiences of programming have been difficult and confusing. Evaluating your experiences can help you understand where you went wrong and where your strengths and weaknesses lie.

One of the most difficult things about software development can be developing a design for a program that makes it possible to produce the program relatively easily. To do this requires a good understanding of programming techniques and the way the programming language in use works. This of course is something that at this stage you probably don't have. It is worth bearing in mind that in industry the people who produce the system design (often called *systems analysts*) normally work for a number of years as programmers before moving on to the more senior post of systems analyst.

Here are some questions you might like to ask yourself:

■ Which parts of the software development process did you understand well?

- Which parts of the software development process do you still not understand well? These are the areas you may need to go over again. However, developing a good understanding of the whole process will take time.
- Did the program development process go according to your plan? If not, which parts of the process took more or less time than you planned?

How do I evaluate the program?

As well as evaluating your experiences in developing software, it is also important to check that the program you have produced meets its original aim.

It is possible, in the excitement and relief of finally getting a program working properly, to forget the original aims of the program. You need to look at the original investigation you did and see whether the program you developed solves the original problem. In particular you need to decide whether the aims of the system that were originally defined in the investigation have been met.

When evaluating a program it can be difficult to be subjective about your own work. One effective method of obtaining constructive feedback about your program is to let other people try it out and comment on it.

Some questions you might ask them to answer are:

- Is the layout and labelling of the form neat and clear?
- Does the program do what you would expect?
- Does it match the program as it was originally specified?
- Does it work properly?
- Is there anything missing from the program?

The result of the evaluation stage should be a report. In the report you need to describe your experiences in developing the software, what the other people who evaluated your program thought about it, and your views on how closely the program you wrote met the original requirements.

Case study – Modern Carpets – user testing

The real test of a program is to give it to the users. After all, they are the people who have to use the program on a day-to-day basis.

Rajesh installs the carpet cost calculator at Modern Carpets shops and shows the staff how to use it. They find it a useful aid in their negotiations with customers but it is not long before they start to think of how it could be made better. This begins the start of another software development process. Rajesh needs to investigate what improvements and additions they would like, then design how these changes can be done and so on.

This is why you will sometimes hear the term *software development cycle*. Just as the software development appears to be complete the process starts again with the development of the next, improved version of the system. The improvements that the staff come up with, and how they are implemented, are described in Unit 20.

Assessment tasks

Assessment for this unit is in the form of an Integrated Vocational Assignment (IVA). This is released each year in November and you will need to complete it during your Spring term. You will normally be asked to write a program to meet a user requirement (not unlike the Modern Carpets cost calculator example used in this chapter). The IVA will describe the scenario (i.e. the problem the user requires the program to solve) and you will need to complete a number of tasks.

A Distinction grade may be awarded if your work demonstrates a deeper understanding of the topics and is of a higher quality. The highlighted sentences indicate the quality of work expected at Distinction level.

The IVA

Learning outcome 1 – Investigate a customer problem

Learning outcome 2 – Produce a program design

Learning outcome 3 – Create a program from the design

Learning outcome 4 – Evaluate the program against the original design

You should be able to:

1 Investigate and analyse the client's problem and demonstrate an understanding of it.
2 Produce a detailed design for the program you will write.
3 Implement the program.
4 Demonstrate that the program meets the original requirements.
5 Provide full documentation for the program, including details of problem areas and what went according to plan.
6 Compare the program to the original design and identify whether or not it follows the design.

To obtain a Distinction grade, you should also be able to:

7 Produce a clear and detailed specification of the problem.
8 Plan the proposed program thoroughly.
9 Evaluate the program according to the original design specification.

These are the steps that have been covered in this unit using the Modern Carpets cost calculator as an example. You will therefore need to cover broadly the same steps, only using the scenario described in the IVA.

You will need to provide evidence of all the work that you do to complete these tasks, including program listings, screen shots, test data and so on. You will need to complete the IVA and hand it to your teacher so it can be checked and sent to Edexcel for marking.

You can find an example IVA for this unit on the Edexcel website, www.edexcel.org.uk.

UNIT 20: VISUAL PROGRAMMING

Success in this unit

What are the learning outcomes?

To achieve this unit you must:

- plan and design a program to meet a given specification
- write the program, ensuring it meets the specification
- test and modify the program
- document the program for users and technical staff.

How is this unit assessed?

This unit is internally assessed. You must provide evidence in the form of a variety of documents that show that you meet the learning outcomes.

How do I provide assessment evidence?

Your evidence will include:

- printed reports of the investigation, design and testing you conducted
- listings of the program you wrote and screen shots of it working
- user and technical manuals.

All your evidence should be presented in one folder, which should have a front cover and a contents page. The section headed *Assessment tasks* at the end of this unit gives you more detailed advice about how to prepare for the assessment.

Introduction

About this unit

This unit follows on from Unit 5, *Software Development*. Before you read this unit you must read Unit 5. The material in that unit about investigating and understanding a problem, and designing the solution to that problem, is not repeated here. Also all the introductory material about writing programs using Visual Basic is not repeated. The case study material follows on from the case study in Unit 5.

What is covered in this chapter is:

■ a summary of the material on planning and designing a program and on the basic features of Visual Basic already covered in Unit 5

■ additional features of Visual Basic not already covered in Unit 5 (including menu bars, adding forms and modifying properties at runtime)

■ more detailed coverage of program testing, which was only briefly covered in Unit 5

■ writing documentation, both user and technical.

You must therefore have a basic understanding of the Visual Basic programming language before you start this chapter.

20.1 Plan and design

A brief summary of planning and designing the software system is given here. Full details can be found in Unit 5.

How can I understand the problem?

Before you can start writing a program, you need to clearly understand what is required. In the IT industry, most programs are not written by the people who will use them. The programmers who write the programs need to spend time investigating what the users of the programs need. The user will generally have some 'problem' that the program will need to solve. For example a clerk working in a bank may need a way to quickly check the balance of a customer's account or a shop assistant may need to be able to check that a customer's credit card is valid. This 'problem' will probably be well understood by the user, but not necessarily by the programmer. The investigation that the programmer will do will generally involve finding the answer to questions such as:

■ What are the aims of the new system?

■ How does the current system work?

■ What other systems does it need to interface with?

■ What is the scope and boundaries of the system?

■ How will the new system work? For example, what inputs, outputs and processing will be required?

The outcome of the investigation stage should be a document which describes in detail (probably with the aid of diagrams) the answers to these questions. Where the problem is large and complex, consideration also needs to be given to how the problem can be split into manageable sections.

The key to deciding how to split up a problem into sections is to choose sections that can be as self-contained as possible. Clearly, when dividing up a system into different sections (or *modules* as they are often called), these modules will need to communicate with each other (probably by passing values, often called *parameters*) to a certain degree. However, this should be kept to a minimum, with each module having a clearly defined purpose and as little interaction with other modules as possible.

Where several programmers are working on the same software development project, dividing the system up into modules is necessary so that each programmer can work on an individual module. Dividing a program into modules also makes the testing easier because each module can be tested as it is completed rather than having to wait until the whole program is complete.

What do I need to do to prepare for programming?

Having investigated and understood the problem and then broken it down into manageable sections, the next step is to design the way the program (or modules) will work. The information required for this process should come from the previous stage.

The first step will probably be defining the input screen forms and the output forms or reports. The data to be input into and output from the system should have been identified during the investigation phase. All that is required here is to sketch out how the forms and/or reports will look and to decide on meaningful object names for the text, list boxes and the command buttons.

Having designed the forms and reports logically, the next step is to start on the variable list, defining names and datatypes for the required variables.

A design for the required processing also needs to be drawn up; commonly techniques using diagrams (such as flowcharts) are used. These should help to identify the programming constructs (or building blocks) of *sequence*, *selection* and *iteration* that are required. Other processing design techniques, such as pseudo-code, may also be used.

Test your knowledge

1 What questions does a programmer need to ask during the initial investigation of the problem?
2 What criteria should be used when splitting a large program up into modules?
3 Why does splitting a large program into modules make the testing easier?
4 What criteria should be used when deciding on object and variable names?
5 What techniques can be used for designing the required processing?
6 What are the three programming constructs that should be identified during the design for the processing?

20.2 Write the program

Visual Basic

Unit 5 contains an introduction to the basic features of the Visual Basic programming language. That material is summarised, rather than repeated, here. The topics covered are:

- creating simple forms with textboxes and buttons
- creating **variables** with the Dim instruction
- transferring the contents of textboxes into variables
- carrying out simple calculations
- using the If instruction so the program can make choices
- using loops to repeat instructions.

? What does it mean?

Variable – is an area of memory that a program uses to store a value while it is running. Variables have names, so that they can be referred to in the program, and a datatype which sets the type of data that the variable can hold, such as text or numbers.

The following simple example program demonstrates these features.

Using a standard Visual Basic EXE file, a form, as shown in Figure 20.1, is created.

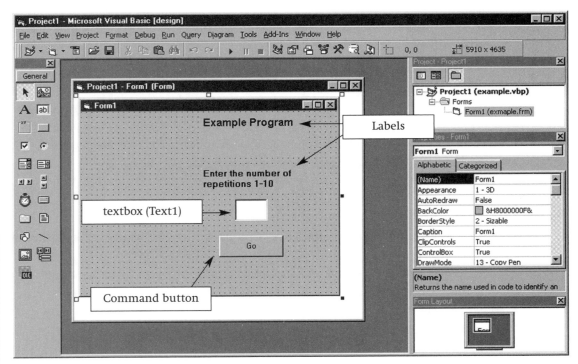

Figure 20.1 Form for the example program

The code for the click event of the command button is shown is Figure 20.2.

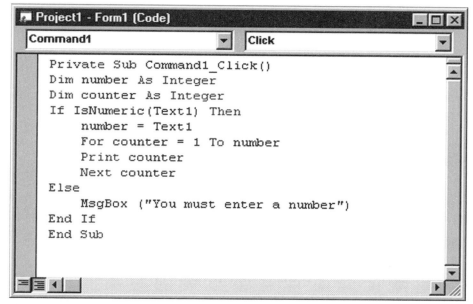

Figure 20.2 Code for the command button

The first two lines of the code are:

```
Dim number As Integer
Dim counter As Integer
```

They define two integer variables: one, called *number*, to hold the value inputted in the textbox; the other, called *counter*, to count the number of repetitions in the loop.

? What does it mean?

Integer – is a whole number with no fractional part.

```
If IsNumeric(Text1) Then
```

This tests the contents of the Text1 textbox to see whether they are numeric. If they are then the next line.

```
number = Text1
```

transfers the contents of the textbox to the variable called *number*.

```
For counter = 1 to number
```

This line starts the loop, which starts at 1 and repeats until it reaches the value in the *number* variable. The variable *counter* counts each loop repetition.

```
Print counter
```

This line prints the value in the *counter* variable on to the form.

```
Next counter
```

This ends the loop and increments (adds one to) the *counter* variable.

```
Else
```

This instruction ends the section of code that is executed if the contents of Text1 are numeric. If the contents of Text1 are not numeric the following instruction is executed:

```
MsgBox ("You must enter a number")
```

This displays a message box on the screen.

```
End if
```

This completes the 'If...Then...Else' instruction.

Remember, if you need more detail about the Visual Basic code shown here, refer to Unit 5. You may also find the following books on the Visual Basic programming language helpful:

- *Visual Basic Made Simple*, Stephen Morris, Made Simple Books; ISBN: 075065189X
- *Visual Basic in Easy Steps*, Tim Anderson, Computer Step; ISBN 1840780290
- *Introductory Visual BASIC*, P.K. McBride, Continuum International Publishing Group; ISBN: 1858052319

Case study – Modern Carpets – running the program

Throughout Unit 5, the Modern Carpets case study was used. This carpet company decided that a program which demonstrated to customers the costs of different carpet and underlay combinations would be a useful sales tool. The running program is shown in Figure 20.3.

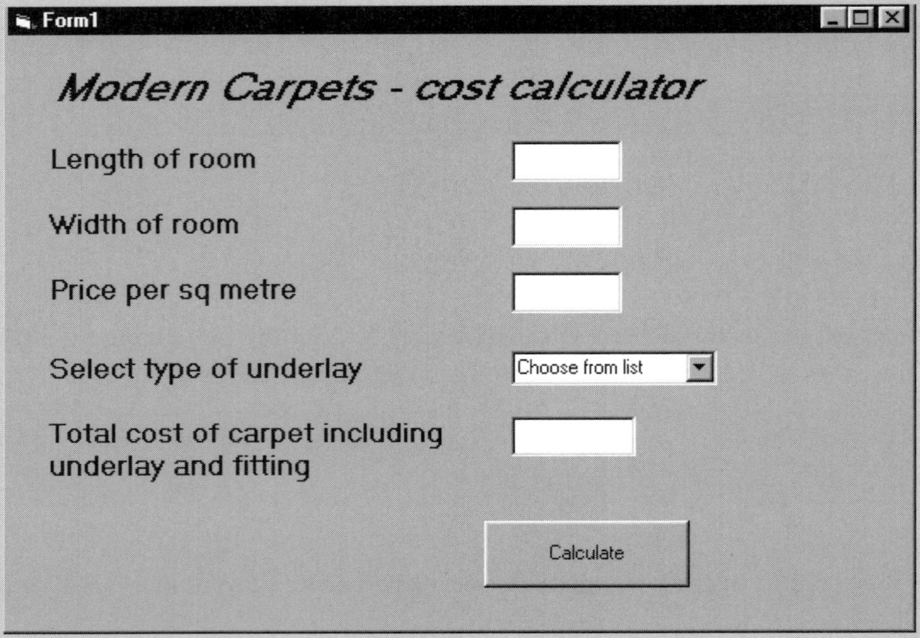

Figure 20.3 Modern Carpets cost calculator

In this chapter we will look at some enhancements to the program.

How can a program be improved?

It is difficult to include all the features and facilities in a program right from the first version. Programs can take quite some time to write and it is often important to have 'something that works OK' available quite soon rather than 'the perfect solution with all the bells and whistles' available much later. Also, many of the ideal features of the program may not become obvious until the first version has been in use for some time. For this reason it is common in the software industry to release new versions of existing programs. These new versions don't just fix faults with the earlier version; they also add new features, often from a 'wish list' provided by their users.

Case study – Modern Carpets – improving on the program

Modern Carpets' shops have been using the carpet calculator for some time now. The sales people in the shop have found it a useful aid in their negotiations with customers. However, there are things about the program that the sales people would like modified. John Dixon, the sales manager at Modern Carpets, has a monthly meeting with the shop managers from every branch. They discuss the program at one of their meetings and come up with a 'wish list' of improvements:

1   Although the prices of the carpet are shown on the form, the name of the carpet is not.

2   The program only shows the total for the current carpet and underlay combination. It would be nice if the program could display a list of all the previous calculations done for a particular customer so the customer can easily make comparisons between the different carpet and underlay combinations.

3   It would be good if, having finished trying the costs of different carpets, the program could print out a sheet showing all the calculations done.

4   They would like to have a menu bar on the program, with shortcut keys, to select options as well as the buttons.

John takes the list of improvements to Rajesh Khan. Rajesh works for Small Business Systems, the company that provides all of Modern Carpets' computers. It was Rajesh that originally wrote the program. Rajesh agrees to investigate what would be required for each of these improvements and get back to John with a price for doing the work.

Improvements

These four modifications can each be dealt with separately, so in this case the problem is already broken down into manageable sections.

How can list boxes be used and properties be modified at runtime?

Rajesh considers the first suggestion. This is a very simple change; all that is required is a textbox where the user can enter the carpet name. He names this textbox TxtName.

Next he moves on to adding a list of the calculations previously done. At first he decides all that needs to be done is to add four list boxes: one for the name of the carpet, one for the price of the carpet, one for the type of underlay chosen, and one for the total price. As each calculation is done, the details are added to the list boxes.

However, as he thinks about how this would work he sees a possible flaw in this way of working. What if, having done a couple of calculations with differently priced carpets and types of underlay, the customer then changed the size of the room and then did another calculation? This would be added to the list but it would not be correct to compare this one with the earlier calculations as the area of the room would be different.

Rajesh decides that when the **Calculate** button is clicked, as well as adding the details to the list boxes, the customer should be prevented from changing the length and width of the room in the textboxes. This can be done by modifying the textbox's Enabled **property**, setting it to False (i.e. so the textbox is not enabled). Any calculations done from then on would be using the same input data and could be comparable. In order to change the size of the room a reset button would be added. This would clear the contents of both the list and textboxes and allow a new set of calculations to be done using different room sizes. It makes sense to include adding the name of the carpet with this modification.

 What does it mean?

Properties – a Visual Basic form has various objects on it such as textboxes and buttons. These objects have *properties* that control how the object looks and how it behaves. For example the Caption property controls the text that appears on a command button. The Enabled property controls whether or not you can type in a textbox. Objects have lots of properties. When you select an object in the Visual Basic IDE, by clicking on it, its properties are displayed in the properties window, in the bottom right of the IDE window. Properties can be set here and also modified within the program code.

Design modification

Rajesh starts on the design for these modifications with the form design. A new textbox for the name of the carpet and four new list boxes (along with suitable labels) and a reset button all need to be added to the form. List boxes are different from combo boxes as they do not need to be dropped down to see the items contained within them. The names Rajesh chooses for the new objects are shown below in Figure 20.4.

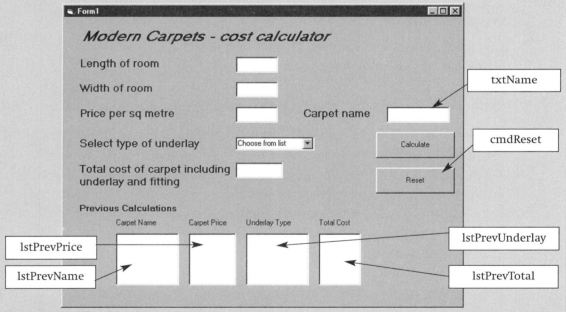

Figure 20.4 Modified form design

Having completed the form design, Rajesh considers whether any changes need to be made to the variable list and the flowchart. All that really needs to be added to the flowchart are two more steps. The first is an output box showing that when a calculation is done the details need to be transferred to the list boxes. The second is a processing step showing that the Length and Width textboxes are disabled. The modified flowchart (with the new steps shown in bold) is shown in Figure 20.5.

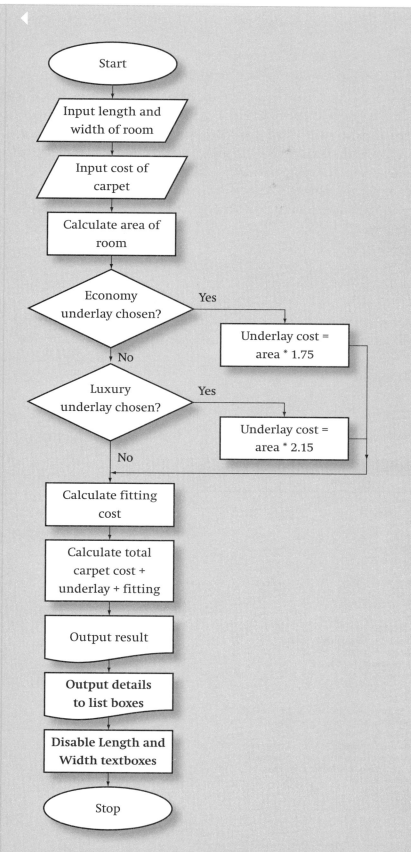

Figure 20.5 Flowchart for the modified cost calculator process

Code modification

With the design modified, Rajesh turns his attention to the modifications to the program code itself.

The first step, shown in the flowchart, involves adding the details of the carpet name, carpet price, underlay type and total cost to the list boxes. The name of the carpet is in the new textbox txtName, the price of the carpet is held in a variable called *Price*, while the total cost is held in a variable called *Total*. The type of underlay chosen is available via the text property of the comUnderlay combo box. These values need to be added to each of the corresponding list boxes. The Price and the Total also need to be formatted as currency. The code required is shown below:

```
lstPrevName.AddItem txtName
lstPrevTotal.AddItem Format(Total, "currency")
lstPrevPrice.AddItem Format(Price, "currency")
lstPrevUnderlay.AddItem comUnderlay.Text
```

The second step involves disabling the Length and Width textboxes so these cannot be changed until the calculations are cleared. Every textbox has a property called Enabled, which is normally set to True. If you set it to False, the user can no longer type in the box. The code required is therefore:

```
txtLength.Enabled = False
txtWidth.Enabled = False
```

The complete, modified code for the cmdCalculate button is shown below in Figure 20.6.

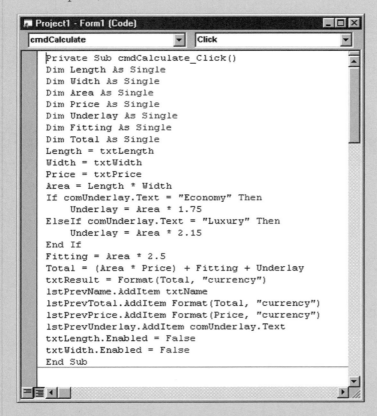

```
Project1 - Form1 (Code)

cmdCalculate                    Click

Private Sub cmdCalculate_Click()
Dim Length As Single
Dim Width As Single
Dim Area As Single
Dim Price As Single
Dim Underlay As Single
Dim Fitting As Single
Dim Total As Single
Length = txtLength
Width = txtWidth
Price = txtPrice
Area = Length * Width
If comUnderlay.Text = "Economy" Then
    Underlay = Area * 1.75
ElseIf comUnderlay.Text = "Luxury" Then
    Underlay = Area * 2.15
End If
Fitting = Area * 2.5
Total = (Area * Price) + Fitting + Underlay
txtResult = Format(Total, "currency")
lstPrevName.AddItem txtName
lstPrevTotal.AddItem Format(Total, "currency")
lstPrevPrice.AddItem Format(Price, "currency")
lstPrevUnderlay.AddItem comUnderlay.Text
txtLength.Enabled = False
txtWidth.Enabled = False
End Sub
```

Figure 20.6 Modified code for cmdCalculate

The second part of this modification involves adding a Reset button. The purpose of the button is to clear the contents of the list boxes and the contents of the Price per sq metre and Carpet name textboxes (txtPrice and txtName). It should also enable the textboxes for the length and width again and move the cursor back to the length textbox (so the user can type in another figure if they wish without having to click in the box). This is all simple sequence code with no choices to be made, so the flowchart shown in Figure 20.7 is very straightforward.

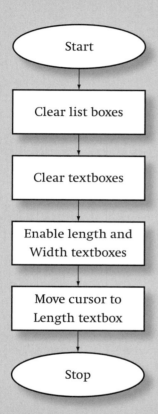

Figure 20.7 Flowchart for the Reset button

To create an on-click event procedure for the Reset button, Rajesh double-clicks the button and the code window appears with an empty procedure. The first step in this procedure is to clear the list boxes. To do this the `Clear` instruction is used:

```
lstPrevName.Clear
lstPrevPrice.Clear
lstPrevUnderlay.Clear
lstprevtotal.Clear
```

Clearing a textbox is also simple, but instead of using a `Clear` instruction the contents of the textbox need to be set to a null (empty) string:

```
txtPrice = ""
txtName = ""
```

Enabling the Length and Width textboxes is done by setting their Enabled property to True:

```
txtLength.Enabled = True
txtWidth.Enabled = True
```

Finally, to place the cursor in the Length textbox the `SetFocus` instruction is used:

```
txtlength.SetFocus
```

? What does it mean?

Focus – the term used in Windows to identify the object that is ready to accept input. Only one object can have the focus at any time. When a textbox has the focus the text cursor can be seen in it. When a command button has the focus pressing the enter key will have the same effect as clicking the button. The focus can be given to an object while a program is running by using the `SetFocus` instruction.

The completed procedure is shown in Figure 20.8.

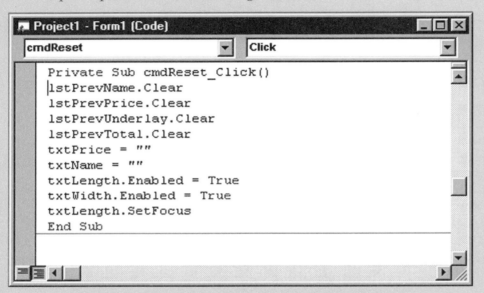

Figure 20.8 Code for the cmdReset button

Running the program

The modified version of the program can now be run. Once the user does a calculation the result is added to the list box, along with the name and price of the carpet and the type of underlay chosen. The user can now try differently priced carpets and a different underlay, and see how the bill compares with earlier ones by looking in the list boxes. The user cannot change the length or width of the room without using the Reset button, which then clears all the text and list boxes so the user can start again.

Figure 20.9 shows that a comparison between the different options can easily be made.

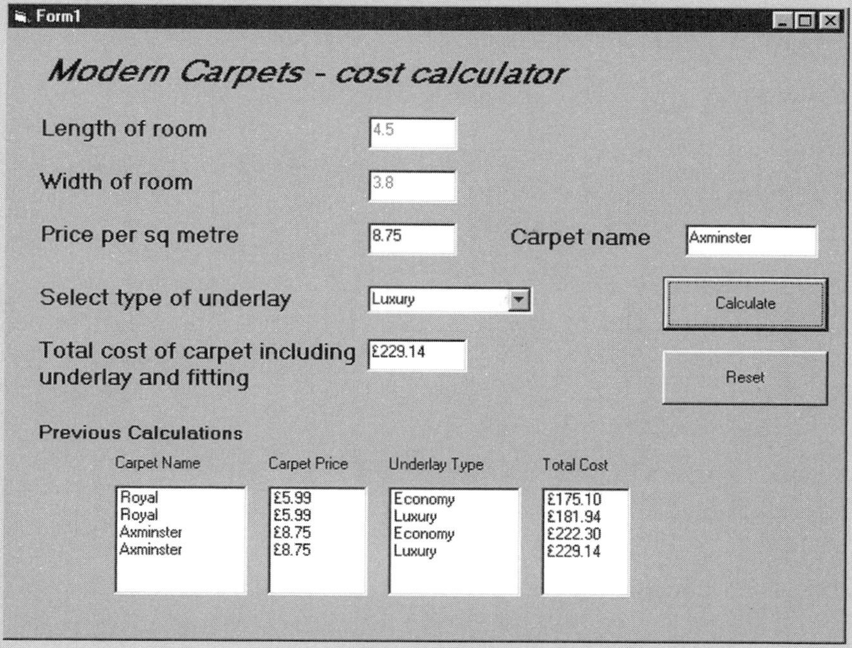

Figure 20.9 Modified program, showing list of previous calculations

This completes the first modification that the users of the program asked for.

How can more forms be added and how can they be printed?

The next modification Rajesh considers is the requirement to be able to produce a printed sheet so that the customers can take it away with them. There are a couple of ways this could be achieved. The simplest would be to print the form as it stands. Visual Basic provides an instruction (`PrintForm`) which prints out a form, and if a Print button is added to the form and a single instruction (`Form1.PrintForm`) added to the button's on-click event procedure, this would print the form. However, this is not a very neat solution as the form is not really designed for printing; it has buttons on it for example. A neater solution would be to design a different form, specifically for printing, and transfer the relevant information on to that form and print it.

As before, Rajesh does the form design first. The only modification needed to the original form is to add a button, with a caption of 'Print' and named cmdPrint. The design of the form that will be printed is shown in Figure 20.10 on the next page. To add a new form to an existing project, you need to go to the **Project** menu, in the menu bar at the top of the Visual Basic program and choose **Add form**. This displays the Add form dialogue box. Leave the default settings and just click **OK**. The default name of the form will be Form2, but Rajesh uses the Name property in the properties box to rename the new form frmPrintForm.

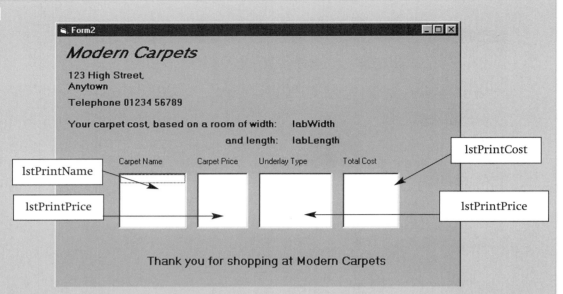

Figure 20.10 Design for the frmPrintForm form

The labels named labWidth and labLength shown in Figure 20.10 will be modified at runtime to show the length and width of the room the user has entered.

Flowchart

Having completed the form design, Rajesh now turns to the flowchart. Transferring the length and width of the room on to the print form is simply a case of moving the contents of the textboxes to the labels on the other form. Transferring the contents of the list box, however, requires a loop (iteration) building block. This is because each item from the list boxes must be transferred one at a time. The flow diagram Rajesh draws is shown in Figure 20.11.

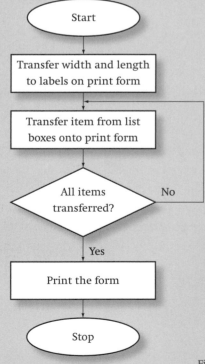

Figure 20.11 Flowchart for the print form process

What coding is needed for the print form?

All the code for the print form is written in the on-click event procedure for the Print button, cmdPrint. Rajesh double-clicks the button to open the code window with the empty procedure already created. He follows the steps in the flowchart. The first step is to transfer the length and width of the room on to the labels on the frmPrintForm. This information is in the two textboxes, txtLength and txtWidth.

When referring to an object on another form, you need to precede the name of the object with the form name. The caption for a label (the text that appears on the label) is one of its properties, so it can be modified like any other property at runtime:

```
frmPrintForm.labWidth.Caption = txtWidth
frmPrintForm.labLength.Caption = txtLength
```

A loop is needed to transfer the contents of the list boxes, but how many times does the program need to go around the loop? Visual Basic provides a function called ListCount which returns the number of items in a list, so the loop needs to be executed ListCount times.

The loop is created using the 'For...Next' instruction. This type of loop needs a variable which is used as a counter (this needs to be declared at the start of the procedure). The number of times around the loop is provided by the ListCount instruction, so to start the loop, the code is (using a variable called *Counter* as the loop counter):

```
For Counter = 0 To lstPrevName.ListCount
```

It does not matter whether we use lstPrevName, lstPrevPrice or any of the other list boxes to get the number of items in the list box as they should be the same. Inside the loop, the AddItem method is used to add items to each of the list boxes on the print form. The items to be added are selected using the List instruction, the counter providing the index number for each one of the items:

```
For Counter = 0 To lstPrevName.ListCount
  frmPrintForm.lstPrintName.AddItem lstPrevName.List(Counter)
  frmPrintForm.lstPrintPrice.AddItem lstPrevPrice.List(Counter)
  frmPrintForm.lstPrintUnderlay.AddItem
                                 lstPrevUnderlay.List(Counter)
  frmPrintForm.lstPrintCost.AddItem lstPrevTotal.List(Counter)
Next Counter
```

The loop is ended with the Next Counter instruction. Remember, *Counter* is just an integer variable. At the start of the loop the value in *Counter* is 0 (because we have 'For counter = 0' at the beginning). Each time the Next Counter instruction is reached the value in *Counter* is increased by 1. When the value in *Counter* is equal to lstPrevName.ListCount the loop ends.

This might seem quite a complex piece of code, but all that is happening is the items listed in the list boxes on the first form are being copied one by one on to the printing form.

The `PrintForm` instruction is used to print out the form (or to save paper while testing the procedure you could use the `Show` instruction instead of `PrintForm`, which simply displays the form on the screen rather than printing it):

```
frmPrintForm.PrintForm
```

OR if you just want to show the form rather than print it:

```
frmPrintForm.Show
```

The complete code for the module is shown in Figure 20.12.

```
Project1 - Form1 (Code)

cmdPrint                                    Click

    Private Sub cmdPrint_Click()
    frmPrintForm.labWidth.Caption = txtWidth
    frmPrintForm.labLength.Caption = txtLength
    For Counter = 0 To lstPrevName.ListCount
        frmPrintForm.lstPrintName.AddItem lstPrevName.List(Counter)
        frmPrintForm.lstPrintPrice.AddItem lstPrevPrice.List(Counter)
        frmPrintForm.lstPrintUnderlay.AddItem lstPrevUnderlay.List(Counter)
        frmPrintForm.lstPrintCost.AddItem lstPrevTotal.List(Counter)
    Next Counter
    frmPrintForm.PrintForm
    End Sub
```

Figure 20.12 The print form procedure

Note that the code within the loop (between 'For Counter ... and Next Counter') has been indented (i.e. the tab key has been pressed at the beginning of each line). This makes the code within the loop easier to spot and aids the readability of the code.

To check that the new button works, Rajesh starts the program, fills in details of the room size and tries the calculation with a couple of different carpets and underlay types. When he clicks the **Print** button, the printer produces a copy of the frmPrintForm with the details of the price plans shown.

How can menu bars be added to a program?

Most Microsoft® Windows programs have a menu bar at the top of the form where various options can be selected. One of the advantages of menu bars is that they provide shortcut keys that allow you to select options from the keyboard without using the mouse. The items in the menu bar have an underlined character, so for example many programs have File as the first option in their menu bar, with the F of File underlined. This means that if you press the Alt key on the keyboard and then (while still pressing Alt) press F, the file menu will drop down. Once the menu has dropped down, the options within the menu are visible and these too have underlined characters. To select a particular option (Save for example) you just need to press the underlined character (S in the case of Save) – once the menu has dropped down you do not have to press the Alt key.

Case study – Modern Carpets – menus and shortcuts

The users of the Modern Carpets cost calculator have asked for menu bars and shortcut keys, so Rajesh is adding them. To set up menus and shortcuts requires very little programming code. Visual Basic provides a Menu editor where most of the work is done.

However, Rajesh first needs to decide what menus and what options need to be provided. In a simple program like this a single menu will be sufficient, which he has decided will be called Options, with a short cut key of O. When the Options menu is selected the following items will appear:

- Calculate – will perform the same function as the Calculate button
- Reset – will perform the same function as the Reset button
- Print – will perform the same function as the Print button
- Exit – will close the program down.

The underlined characters will be the shortcut keys. To create this menu Rajesh makes sure the first form is showing in the Visual Basic editor and then chooses the Tools menu and the Menu Editor option, shown in Figure 20.13.

Figure 20.13 The Menu Editor

First the name of the menu (Options) is typed in the Caption box at the top, with an ampersand (&) preceding the character that is to be the shortcut character, as shown above. Each menu must also have a name that is used within the program. This is entered in the Name box. This menu has been given the name of mnuOptions. You should notice that the name Options also appears in the lower part of the dialogue box.

To create the first of the menu items under the Options menu, Rajesh clicks the **Next** button, which clears the name and caption boxes. He then types the caption for the menu item, &Calculate, and gives it a name of mnuCalculate. To make it a menu item under the Options menu rather than a new menu, he clicks the button with a right arrow on it. In the area at the bottom of the dialogue box the caption &Calculate is now indented under Options. This shows that Calculate is one of the menu items under the Options menu. From now on the Menu Editor assumes that his entries are menu items so Rajesh does not need to click the right arrow button again. He just uses the **Insert** button to clear the Caption and Name boxes and adds the remaining menu items, &Reset with a name of mnuReset, &Print with a name of mnuPrint, and E&xit with a name of mnuExit. The Menu Editor now looks like Figure 20.14.

Figure 20.14 Completed menu

Rajesh clicks the **OK** button on the menu editor to complete the process. The form now has an Option menu at the top of it. However, Rajesh needs to add some code to make each menu item work correctly. He clicks on the **Options** menu and chooses the first item, **Calculate**. This opens the code window, creating an event procedure called mnuCalculate_Click (mnuCalculate was the name he gave the menu item). This is the procedure that will run when someone selects that menu option. However, this menu option should do exactly the same as clicking the Calculate button. The click event procedure for the Calculate button is called cmdCalculate_Click, so all he needs to do is to add the code which will call that procedure, which is:

```
Call cmdCalculate_Click()
```

The same is true for the Reset and Print buttons; their click event procedures just need to call the click event procedures for the corresponding buttons. The Exit procedure needs to end the program. All that requires is a single instruction, End. The four complete procedures for the menu options are shown in Figure 20.15.

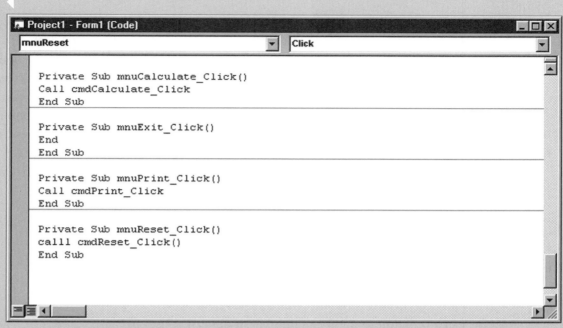

```
Project1 - Form1 (Code)

mnuReset                          Click

Private Sub mnuCalculate_Click()
Call cmdCalculate_Click
End Sub

Private Sub mnuExit_Click()
End
End Sub

Private Sub mnuPrint_Click()
Call cmdPrint_Click
End Sub

Private Sub mnuReset_Click()
call1 cmdReset_Click()
End Sub
```

Figure 20.15 Click event procedures for the menu items

When the program is run, it now has a menu bar with options that can be selected with the mouse or by shortcut keys. The working program, with the menu in use, is shown in Figure 20.16.

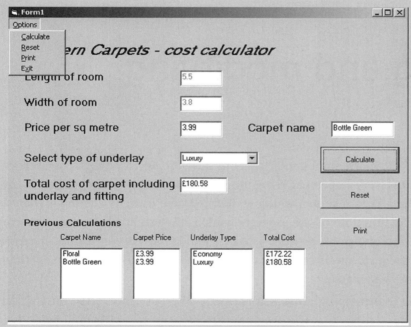

Figure 20.16 Menu bar in use

This completes the modifications to the program.

How can I create an executable version of the program?

Once the coding for the program is complete you will want to create an executable version of your program. At the moment the program can be run only from the Visual Basic IDE, but when you create an executable version a file is created that you can run simply by double-clicking on it. The file can be placed in any folder or on the Desktop. You can also copy the file to any computer (as long as it has Microsoft® Windows installed) where it will run without needing the Visual Basic IDE installed. To create an executable version, go to the **File** menu in the Visual Basic IDE and choose the **Make** option. You will then see a File save dialogue box. Choose the disk and folder where you want to create the executable file, then click **OK** and the file will be created for you. This file is a stand-alone program which will run if you double-click on it. You do not need to load it into the Visual Basic IDE.

Test your knowledge

1 What instruction is used to print a form?
2 What is the difference between a list box and a combo box?
3 How is a loop (iteration building block) shown on a flowchart?
4 What property controls the text that appears in a label?
5 How can a program find out the number of items in a list box?
6 What would the instruction `For X = 1 to 10` do?
7 What instruction is used to end a `For` loop?
8 What instruction will show a form on the screen rather than printing it?
9 Why is it a good idea to indent code within a loop?
10 What does the SetFocus instruction do?

20.3 Testing and modifying

Testing

Testing is a vital (though often unpopular!) part of software development. The users of the software would not be very impressed if the program produced the wrong answers, nor would they be happy if the program kept crashing while they were using it. Testing is the process of checking that all the functions of the program work as they should and give the correct results. The definition of terms like 'work as they should' and 'correct results' needs to come from the original program specification that was agreed by the users and the developers before the program was written.

As well as checking that the program works correctly when used correctly, the software developer also needs to check that the program is robust and can withstand being used incorrectly without crashing. The reason why this is important is because the users of the program are unlikely to be computer experts. They may misunderstand how the program is supposed to be used; they may also make mistakes when using the program, pressing keys or clicking buttons in error or making inappropriate entries in a textbox (a text entry, for example, rather than numeric).

Making sure a program works properly may sound like a fairly simple task, but software testing, except for the very simplest of programs, is a complex and involved task which requires planning.

Testing a program is often split into data testing and event testing. Data testing involves checking that the program can deal correctly with the data that is input by the user and produces the correct output. Event testing involves checking that all the different options, such as button and menu options, produce the expected results. We shall look at data testing first.

How can data testing be done?

The first step in data testing is to produce some test data. This involves choosing some input values and then manually working out what output the program should produce with these chosen inputs (the expected outputs). The program is then run using these input values and the expected outputs are compared with the actual ones the program produces. If there is a difference between the expected outputs and the actual outputs then the program has failed the test and will need to be modified so that the actual and expected values match.

The choice of input values is important. A range of values needs to be chosen in each of the following categories:

- *Normal values* – what would normally be expected as an input value.
- *Extreme values* – would, in the case of a numeric input, be unusually large or small values. In the case of a text value they might be a very large number of characters or very small. For example in a textbox where someone's name is to be entered two extreme values might be 'Ng' and 'Fotherington-Thomas'.
- *Abnormal values* – are incorrect entries. For example 32/10/02 for a date, 205 for someone's age or a text value where a numeric one is expected.

Case study – Modern Carpets – data testing

Rather than testing the program himself, Rajesh asks one of his colleagues, Amy Weston, to test the carpet cost calculator. It is a good idea to get someone other than the original programmer to test a new program. The original programmer may be too 'gentle' with his or her creation. Also, another person may have fewer preconceived ideas about how the program should work. Amy needs to produce a test plan for data testing the cost calculator. For some of the categories in extreme and abnormal test data, Amy needs to check back in the specification to see how it says these values should be dealt with. She needs to know:

- Is there a maximum length and width of room that the program needs to deal with?
- Is there a maximum price of carpet the program should accept?

She looks these questions up in the specification and discovers that 100m is the largest length and width, while £50 per square metre is the highest price the program should accept.

Amy produces a table showing the input data and expected outputs, shown in Figure 20.17.

Test data						
Test no.	Length	Width	Underlay	Price	Expected result	Actual result
Category: Normal						
1	2.5	3.4	Economy	2.50		
2	5.2	4.5	Luxury	5.99		
3	1.4	6.2	Luxury	3.50		
4	6.5	6.8	Economy	7.25		
Category: Extreme						
5	0	0	Luxury	0	0	
6	100	5	Economy	5		
7	101	5	Economy	5	Error Msg	
8	6	100	Luxury	3		
9	4	101	Economy	7	Error Msg	
10	5	7	Luxury	50		
11	6	3	Economy	51	Error Msg	
Category: Abnormal						
12	Five	2.3	Economy	2.99	Error Msg	
13	4.5	Three	Economy	5.99	Error Msg	
14	2.5	4.6	Luxury	Three fifty	Error Msg	

Figure 20.17 Test data table

In order to check that the program is calculating carpet prices correctly, Amy manually works out the correct results for the normal and extreme data where the result should not be an error message. She fills in all the expected results on the test data table and then tries out each of the test calculations on the program, entering the actual results the program produces in the last column. If the entries in the actual and the expected columns are the same then the program has passed the tests. If they are different then there is a problem.

Amy discovers that the program passes the tests with the Normal data fine, but there are problems with both the Extreme and the Abnormal data. She makes a list of the problems:

■ *Extreme data* – the program works as it should with test data items 5, 6, 8 and 10 but it does not produce an error message with test data items 7, 9 and 11. The calculations are done despite the fact that the input data is beyond the ranges listed in the specification.

■ *Abnormal data* – the results are worse with this data. Tests 12, 13 and 14 all cause the program to crash as they contain non-numeric data.

Amy passes the results of her tests back to Rajesh, who is not very happy! When Rajesh wrote the program he forgot that the specification listed maximum values for the room size and carpet price. He also forgot to include code in the program that would check that data input by the user was numeric before attempting to do anything with it. Fortunately neither of these problems are difficult to fix, but it was important that they were spotted before the program was handed over to the users.

Check your understanding

How could Rajesh fix these problems? The solution to a very similar problem can be found in the Introduction in Unit 5. You should be able to work out the required code by having a look there.

How can event testing be done?

Event testing involves testing that the program responds correctly to events such as mouse clicks on buttons and the selection of menu options. These can simply be tested by making a list of all the events that the program is supposed to respond to, and describing what the correct response to those events are. Once the list is made each event on the list can be tried on the program and the actual results compared with what is supposed to happen.

Case study – Modern Carpets – event testing

Amy makes a list of the events the Modern Carpets cost calculator is supposed to respond to. The list, along with the expected outcome of each event, is shown in Figure 20.18.

Event testing			
Event number	Event	Expected outcome	Actual outcome
1	Click on Calculate button	Calculates cost of carpet based on inputs. Also adds details of calculation to list boxes and disables Length and Width textboxes.	
2	Click on Print button	Transferred details of calculations to second form and prints it out.	
3	Click on Reset button	Clears contents of all text and list boxes and enables Length and Width textboxes.	
4	Click on Calculate option under Options menu	Same as Event 1.	
5	Press Alt O then C on keyboard	Same as Event 1.	
6	Click on Print option under the Options menu	Same as Event 2.	
7	Press Alt O then P on keyboard	Same as Event 2.	

Event testing			
Event number	Event	Expected outcome	Actual outcome
8	Click on Reset option under Options menu	Same as Event 3.	
9	Press Alt O then R on keyboard	Same as Event 3.	
10	Click on Exit under options menu	Program ends.	
11	Press Alt O then X on the keyboard	Program ends.	

Figure 20.18 Event testing

Having drawn up the list, Amy tries out each event and checks that the expected outcome is the same as the actual outcome. If it is she puts a tick in the 'Actual outcome' column, if not she writes a description of what actually happens. Fortunately the program passes this test, with ticks for every event.

Modification

How should modifications be done?

Once the tests are complete, the program will need modifying for every error identified during testing. The modifications made should be documented and kept, along with the original test data and event table, in the technical documentation for the program (see section 20.4). The program should then be retested, just to check that the modifications really have been successful and no other errors have been introduced accidentally.

Test your knowledge

1 Why is testing important?
2 Why do you need to check the original specification when testing a program?
3 What is the difference between data and event testing?
4 With an input box for a person's age, give examples of normal, extreme and abnormal data.
5 Why is it not a good idea to get the programmer who wrote the program to test it?
6 How can event testing be done?
7 If a program does not pass any of the tests what should be done?

20.4 Documentation

Simply handing over a completed program on a disk is not sufficient. People need to know how to install the program, how to use it and how to deal with problems that may arise. The completed program must be supported by documentation. Two types of documentation need to be produced:

■ *User documentation* – this explains to the programs' users how they should use the program.
■ *Technical documentation* – this describes the internal working of the software.

Fairly obviously, the contents of these two types of documentation are rather different.

User documentation

User documentation is written for the program's users, and is sometimes called the user manual or guide. There are two main approaches when writing user documentation:

■ *Reference guide* – each function and feature is described, normally in some logical order.
■ *Tutorial* – teaches the user how to use the program in a step-by-step fashion.

Some user manuals combine both approaches. However, whichever approach is taken to user documentation, it must be written in a way that the target audience can understand it. Therefore, technical jargon needs to be avoided and the manual must be relevant to the way the program will be used in the workplace, for example by using realistic examples. Annotated screen dumps need to be used rather than long written explanations, as these are much easier for the user to follow. They can then compare what they see on the computer when running the program with the screen dump in the manual.

What does the user documentation need to contain?

The user documentation needs to contain:

■ Details of how to start the program (how to find the program icon on the desktop or under the Start menu).
■ Comprehensive instructions for using each of the program's features. This should include details of what buttons, textboxes, list boxes and any other objects should be used for. The instructions should also explain how to use any menus and shortcut keys.
■ Explanations of any error messages that the program displays, including an explanation of what to do to correct the problem and how to avoid the error in future.
■ Details of what to do if something goes wrong or the program crashes, such as who to contact (you!).
■ How to exit the program.

It is useful to include a section of Frequently Asked Questions (FAQs), although you will need to use some imagination to decide what questions users may ask. Showing the program to a group of people who are unfamiliar with it and seeing what questions they come up with may help.

Although the term *documentation* tends to suggest a printed book of some kind, it is increasingly popular to do away with the expense of producing user documentation in the form of a book and provide on-line help instead. The Microsoft® Windows operating system provides a way of producing help files in a standard format, with search and index facilities already built in. It is beyond the scope of this chapter to explain how the Microsoft® Windows Help system can be used to provide on-line user documentation. However, you should be aware that this is a common way for user documentation to be provided and has a number of benefits. As well as being cheaper than manuals it is also easier to update and has more powerful search facilities.

Technical documentation

Technical documentation is written for support staff and programmers. Throughout the life of a program changes or improvements may need to be made, and it may be the case that, despite careful testing, some errors surface only after many years of use. The programmers who originally wrote the software will probably have moved to new projects or perhaps different companies. Technical documentation is therefore needed so that the people who need to modify or correct the program can understand how it works.

If the programs are written well in the first place, using meaningful variable names for example, certain aspects will be self-documenting. Also, if the programs follow the design closely, then the design documents can be used to understand the working of the program. It is considered good practice to include comments in the actual code which explain what it does. In Visual Basic comments must begin with a single quote mark (') so the computer knows they are not program code. An example of a well-commented program is shown in Figure 20.19.

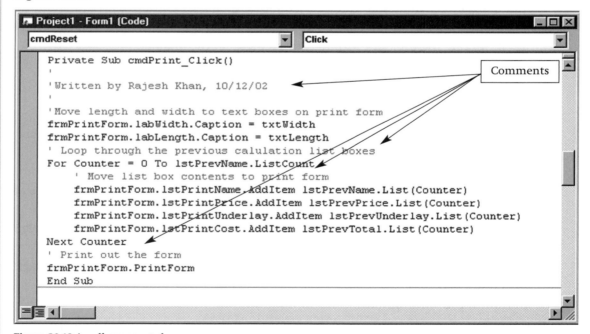

Figure 20.19 A well-commented program

What does technical documentation need to include?

The technical documentation should include the original design documents (variable lists, flowcharts, pseudo-code, etc.) that the program was written from. Diagrams should also be included which describe how the different modules in the program interact. Any special features or complex calculations should be explained.

For each procedure or module in the program the following should be included:

- a listing of the program code, either fully commented or with annotation added
- a printout of the form or forms, including the object names.

Full details of the testing carried out on the program should be in the technical documentation, including the completed test data plan and event testing plan. Notes listing the modifications made as a result of errors uncovered during tests should also be added.

The documentation should also include details of the operating system and version the program will work with, as well as disk space and any other hardware requirements. Instructions on how to install the software should also be included.

When improvements and/or corrections are made to the program, details of these changes should be added to the technical documentation.

Test your knowledge

1 What are the main aims of user and technical documentation?
2 Who are user and technical documentation written for?
3 What sort of information will be included in technical documentation?
4 What are program comments? Why are they important?
5 What are the two main approaches used when writing user documentation?
6 List some of the advantages of on-line documentation
7 Why is it useful to include screen dumps in user documentation?
8 What does the term FAQ mean?

Assessment tasks

This section describes what you must do to obtain a Merit grade for this unit.

A Distinction grade may be awarded if your work demonstrates a deeper understanding of the topics and is of a higher quality. The highlighted sentences indicate the quality of work expected at Distinction level.

How do I provide assessment evidence?

Your evidence will be in the form of a written report, which will describe how you developed your program and will be illustrated with screen shots of your program.

You will need to provide evidence of the process you went through to develop your software including:

- investigations you carried out into the problem
- design documents you produced such as form designs and flowcharts
- printouts of the code you wrote
- evidence of the testing you carried out, including modifications you made
- documentation you produced.

All your evidence should be presented in one folder, which should have a front cover and a contents page. You should divide the evidence into three sections corresponding to the three tasks.

Task1

Learning outcome 1 – Plan and design

Identify a problem that can be solved by writing a program. The problem needs to be sufficiently complex to be broken down into two or more sections, but beware of choosing a problem that is too complex. If possible, choose a real life problem, perhaps a program that you can write for a friend or organisation you know. You will need to investigate the problem finding out as much as you can about it and break it down into manageable sections. You will need to design input and output screens or reports and produce a list of variables required. You will also need to design the processing required.

To gain a Distinction grade, you will need to produce a detailed development plan for your program.

Task 2

Learning outcome 2 – Write the program

Write the program, following the design you created in Task 1.

Task 3

Learning outcome 3 – Test and modify

Learning outcome 4 – Document

1 Create test plans for both data and event testing. You need to plan to test the program thoroughly, with normal, extreme and abnormal test data and test for all possible events. You need to keep evidence of your testing including the completed test forms and screen shots of the program being tested.

2 Investigate the errors identified in the testing of the program and document the modifications you make to correct the program.

3 Write technical and user documentation for the program.

4 Write a report comparing the program you produced with the original specification from Task 1 to see whether it met your original plan.

> To gain a Distinction grade, you will need to evaluate the program (e.g. what is good and bad, what needs to be improved, what would you have done differently, etc.) referring back to the design and to the user's original requirements.

UNIT 4: USER SUPPORT

Success in this unit

What are the learning outcomes?

To achieve this unit you must:

- identify the support needs of IT end users
- take part in end user support
- document the procedures involved with end user support
- evaluate the end user support.

How is this unit assessed?

This unit is externally assessed. The Examination Board (Edexcel) will set an Integrated Vocational Assignment (IVA), which will be based on all the assessment criteria. This will be in the form of simulation, in which you will be expected to work on a help desk.

See the *Assessment tasks* section at the end of this unit for more information about the IVA.

Introduction

About this unit

You will probably have used a help line of some kind in the past. When you have needed advice you may have phoned your mobile phone company, the maker of your computer or an Internet Service Provider (ISP). These organisations are all providing support – that is, help or advice – to the users of their products.

This unit concentrates on the user support that can be offered to the employees within an organisation, helping them with the problems they may have with their IT hardware and software.

In this unit you will learn how to provide user support to other users and will demonstrate your skills through a simulation.

4.1 Identifying the support needs of IT end users

In this unit we will be thinking about IT users in a business organisation, and the support they need.

Home computer users, and people working on their own, also need access to support. If they have any difficulties they will normally contact the makers of their hardware or software. However, in a business the technical staff should normally be able to offer most of the support that employees need.

Users

What is an end user?

An end user is a person who uses a software package on a computer to do a task. In an organisation, an employee who is an end user carries out at least some of his or her everyday work using an IT system.

What is the difference between an end user and a technical user?

An *end user* does his or her work using an IT system. A *technical user* makes sure that the system functions as required for the end user.

If you use a computer at home, then you will sometimes act as an end user and sometimes as a technical user. You will be acting as an end user whenever you print a letter, set up a spreadsheet, play a game, visit a website or send an e-mail. You will be acting as a technical user when you install some new software, move or delete files, do a virus scan, change the screen saver or unjam the paper in a printer.

In a business organisation most of the technical work is carried out by specialist staff. The end user is not normally allowed to install software or make any other changes to the operating system.

How do end users use IT systems?

End users need to be able to:

- access the software they want to use
- use the software to do their work successfully
- print documents
- make files available to another worker.

Who is an end user?

Many, if not most, employees today are end users at some point during their working day. This applies at all levels in an organisation, from the front-line staff to the managing director. Although they may be using different software, their support needs will be very similar.

Here are some end users:

- sales assistant in a shop
- bank clerk
- cinema box office assistant
- office administrator
- parking attendant
- teacher
- police officer
- pharmacist
- finance director
- graphic designer
- recording engineer.

In fact, it is difficult to think of a job which does not require the use of a computer.

How do technical users use IT systems?

The technical users of an IT system are known by a variety of names – systems administrators, network managers, technicians, computer engineers, etc. For most of their work they use systems software, or work directly with the hardware or cabling.

Technical users also need support from time to time when using the systems software, or when installing hardware. They normally contact the manufacturer of the product they are using for advice.

Technical users also have to write reports using a word processor, keep records of their procedures in a database, send e-mails to other employees, and in each of these cases they too act as end users.

How do managers use IT systems?

Managers may use different software from their staff, but they will have very similar support needs. In practice, they may be less familiar with IT systems than their staff, so may need more support. Even the managers of IT systems themselves sometimes have problems with using the IT.

Check your understanding – End users and technical users

If you have a computer at home, or access to a standalone one at your centre, then you can note down all the tasks you carry out on the system in one session. These tasks may include loading software, copying files, changing a printer cartridge, playing a computer game, etc. For each task, write down whether you were acting as an end user or as a technical user.

Support

This unit concentrates on the support given to end users, rather than the specialist support given to technical users.

Who provides support to end users?

A very large organisation will employ a number of people to work as user support staff. They are often referred to as the 'help desk'. All end users will be given the phone number of the help desk – the '**hotline**' number. Someone will always be available to help callers to the help desk.

In smaller organisations the help desk service may be provided by any member of the technical staff, such as the network administrator. In such a case, an end user phoning the hotline may find that no-one is free to help immediately, as they may be doing other tasks. A help desk provides both software support and technical support to end users.

What does it mean?

Hotline – a hotline is a phone number that end users can call when they need IT support.

Case study – Kate Lawler

Figure 4.1 Kate Lawler – winner of Big Brother 2002

MADONNA fan Kate says her main passions in life are sunny days, wine and keeping fit. When the sporty 22-year-old isn't at work on an IT help desk, she's most likely to be found training at the gym or out on the town with her friends.

Lots of things make her angry but her real pet hates are 'putting on weight' and being rained on just after washing her hair!

Do you know anyone who works on an IT help desk? If so, ask the person about the kinds of requests that he or she receives. This service may be offered at your centre, so you may be able to speak to someone there.

©2002 Channel 4 Television Corporation

What is software support?

If an end user does not understand how to use a piece of software, he or she will be given software support. Typical requests might be:

- 'How do I place a picture in my word-processed document?'
- 'How do I change the page size for a document?'
- 'How do I delete a member from a members' database?'
- 'I cannot get the formula to work properly in a spreadsheet.'
- 'The bar code reader will not read this bar code – what do I do?'

What is technical support?

If an end user has a problem with the system itself, he or she will need technical support. Typical requests might be:

- 'The printer is not printing.'
- 'I cannot find a document I was working on yesterday.'
- 'I think I may have a virus on an e-mail attachment.'
- 'I cannot get into the software.'
- 'How can I change the background colour on my screen?'
- 'I cannot get on to the Internet.'

How is the support provided?

A large amount of user support can be provided over the phone, so most organisations have an internal hotline number, but sometimes it is necessary for help to be given in person at the workplace. Occasionally support may be offered by e-mail.

Designing user support procedures

How is information about user requests recorded?

All requests for user support must be recorded in some way. As we have seen, most of these requests will come over the phone, so it is normal for the user support staff to record the details whilst talking to the end user. This information can be collected on a paper form or keyed in on-screen.

Most help desks use standard help desk software, which allows them to record all the information about a user support request. Help desk software is essentially a database which holds all the information about each request for support and about how the problems were solved.

But it is not necessary to use an expensive help desk package. It is not difficult to design your own simple database and forms.

If the problem is solved by visiting the workplace then a paper form will be used.

Further research – Help desk software

Use the Internet to find the names of help desk software packages that are currently on the market. Investigate what facilities each one offers and the cost.

How do I design a form to collect user requests?

The form will record two sorts of information – information about the user request and information about how the problem was solved. These will be recorded whether the form is on paper or on-screen.

The information about the user request will begin with some reference data:

- reference number
- date
- time.

All the remaining data relating to the user request has to be collected directly from the user. This will include the following:

- name of end user
- workstation
- end user request.

What do I add to the form to record the support given?

The form, whether on paper or on-screen, should record the help given and whether it solved the problem:

- name of help desk staff
- nature of the problem
- advice given
- resources used
- date/time problem was resolved
- further action.

It is just as important to record what does not work as well as what does.

Check your understanding – Forms for user requests

Create a form to record user requests for support. This should be designed for printing. Ask a fellow student to act as an end user and to ask for help with an IT problem. Record this on the form.

Revise the content and layout of the form so that it is easier to use.

Keep both the original and revised versions of the form – they may be needed for assessment.

Test your knowledge

1 What do these terms mean?
   - hotline
   - help desk
   - IT support.
2 What is the difference between software support and technical support?
3 Why is it important to record all user support requests on a form?

4.2 Taking part in end user support

This section will give you advice on how to provide end user support yourself. In order to help end users, you need to have gained practical experience of using software, setting up standalone and network systems and solving problems.

You should be able to carry out all the actions listed in this section. Much of the background theory for this can be found in Units 1, 2 and 15, and is not repeated in this unit.

When a problem has been sorted out we say that it has been *resolved*.

How to process support requests

How can common problems be resolved with software support?

End users may be using a software application for the first time, or they may be experienced users. Both may need support, but the help given must be based on the knowledge they already have. Problems are generally of these types:

- *The user does not know how to use some aspects of the application* – support can be given by:
  - o providing immediate advice and demonstrations for straightforward problems (see Unit 2)
  - o referring the user to online Help
  - o referring to manuals
  - o finding suitable training materials, e.g. on CD or on the Internet
  - o suggesting a training course.
- *The software has not been configured to suit the user's needs* – support can be given by
  - o configuring the software (see Unit 1, section 1.2).
- *The software does not provide all the functions that the user needs* – support can be given by:
  - o giving the user access to another version or package on the system (See Unit 15)
  - o installing extra components for the existing software
  - o upgrading the software to a newer version (see Unit 1, section 1.2)
  - o replacing the software with another package (see Unit 1, section 1.2).

How can common problems be resolved with technical support?

- *New consumables are needed* – for example, the paper, ink cartridge or toner may need to be replaced in a printer. Support can be given by:
  - o supplying consumables immediately.
- *The user is unable to carry out basic administrative tasks* – for example, the user may not know how to move and copy files, how to access the CD drive, how to configure the display. Support can be given by:
  - o providing immediate advice and demonstrations for straightforward problems (see Unit 1, section 1.2)
  - o referring the user to online Help
  - o referring to manuals
  - o finding suitable training materials, e.g. on CD or on the Internet
  - o suggesting a training course.

- *The operating system is out of date* – support can be given by:
  - o installing a new operating system.
- *The computers are not networked together* – support can be given by:
  - o setting up a simple network (see Unit 15)
- *The user does not have the right access privileges on a network* – support can be given by:
  - o setting up a new user account (see Unit 15)
  - o changing the password for an account
  - o configuring a user account so that the user has access to the correct software.
- *The hardware is not functioning correctly* – support can be given by:
  - o sorting out the problem on the spot, e.g. unjamming paper in a printer
  - o repairing the hardware if it is faulty, either on the spot or by removing it temporarily
  - o providing a substitute device whilst it is being repaired or a replacement is being acquired
  - o ordering replacement components
  - o ordering a new device to replace the faulty one (see Unit 1, section 1.3).
- *New hardware has to be chosen and installed* – for example, a new printer may have been acquired, or a network interface card must be installed in order to link a new computer to a network. Support can be given by:
  - o selecting suitable hardware (see Unit 1, section 1.3)
  - o installing the hardware and its driver.

Further research – Users' experiences of support

What kind of support is offered to students and to staff at your centre? As a group, create your own log of support requests that you have made over a short period, and how the problems were resolved by the support staff.

Procedures

How should I record the requests and solutions?

You should fill in a form for each request that you receive. This should be one that you designed yourself and could be either paper-based or an on-screen form connected to a database. See section 4.3 for more information about how to complete the forms.

What information should I give to the end user?

The end user should always be told the name of the person who is providing the help, and the reference number for the request. If an end user has the same problem again, he or she should mention the reference number, so the help desk staff can find the original form and check what advice was given before.

How to respond to simple and complex requests

How should I handle user problems in the simulated environment?

Your task is to identify the problem and solve it and this must be done in a way that leaves the user feeling confident and happy. So, here are some basic rules for dealing with users:

- Always accept what the user tells you.
- Never imply that the user is stupid, incapable or has made a mistake.
- Only use words and technical terms that the user understands.
- Never show any signs of annoyance or impatience.

You will be practising these skills in a simulated environment. That means that you may have to use role-play; for example, for the purpose of the exercise, a colleague or lecturer may act as an end user with little knowledge of computers.

How can I identify the problem?

First, make sure that the problem has been described properly by the user. You may need to ask some of these questions:

- What was the user doing on the system when the problem first occurred?
- Has the problem occurred before? If so, what appeared to trigger the problem on that occasion?
- What exactly is happening or is not happening?
- Are there other problems which have not been reported?
- If the problem is intermittent, can I force it to happen again?
- Has this user reported the same problem before?
- Has the same problem been reported on this workstation before?

Next you need to check exactly which hardware and software the user is working on. On most networks, each workstation will have access to a specific operating system, and a record will be kept of what peripherals (such as printers) it can communicate with. Each user will be given access to specific software, and this will be known by the help desk. However in some cases you may need to ask what operating system and which software package (including version number) is being used. Depending on the problem, you may also need to know exactly what hardware is being used, particularly the processor, the printer model, and the specifications of other devices such as disk and CD drives.

Check your understanding – Identifying the problem

You can carry out this exercise in pairs or small groups. Take it in turns to act as an end user and as help desk staff. The end user 'calls' the help desk and describes, very briefly, a problem with a computer. This problem should be based on something that did go wrong with the system in the past.

The help desk staff must complete a user request form for each request. They must then ask questions to find out exactly what the problem is.

Do not attempt to solve the problems at this stage, but keep a note of them as you will be trying to solve them later. However, do realise that a problem cannot be solved unless it has been identified accurately.

How can I investigate a system to find the cause of a problem?

First, check to see whether a similar problem has been reported already by another user or on another machine. If it has, you can look up the form used for that user request and find out how it was solved.

If the problem is new, check out all the advice given in the support resources (see below), and identify the most likely solution. Try this out and note down the result. If this is not successful then decide which is the next most likely solution and try that out.

These attempts must all be documented on the form, so that you can keep track of what has been tried, and what works.

Can I use my own knowledge to respond to simple requests?

Do not underestimate your own knowledge of IT systems. You will probably already be familiar with using a standalone PC as well as a network station. You will have handled basic hardware such as a mouse, keyboard and monitor. You will be able to perform a large number of technical actions, such as deleting and moving files, installing software or checking for viruses. You will also be a competent user of a number of standard software packages.

At the same time, do not overestimate the knowledge that users may have of their systems. Many end users simply know how to use one software package in order to carry out some specific tasks as part of their work. They probably use only a tiny percentage of the facilities within that package. Many end users do not have the confidence to try out anything new.

Check your understanding – Responding to simple requests

In your groups, review the requests that you noted in the last activity. Can you use your own knowledge to solve any of the problems?

Can I use other resources to respond to more complex queries?

If you cannot answer a problem from your own knowledge of the system, you can use support resources provided by suppliers.

There are four types of support resources available:

- manuals
- online help
- product support
- fault diagnosis systems.

You should make a list of all the hardware and software (systems and applications) that you use and identify as many sources of support as you can.

How can I find and use a manual?

A manual is a document traditionally provided as a printed book, but it may also be available in an electronic form, often on CD-ROM, or downloadable from a website. A manual has sections explaining how to use the software step by step, and also has an index so that the user can find relevant topics. Some manuals have a 'troubleshooting' section, which lists a number of common problems and suggests solutions. These can be quite useful for solving relatively straightforward requests to the help desk.

Most major software packages have manuals. If a network version of a package has been purchased it will normally include only one printed copy of the manual, although the electronic version may be made available to all end users on the network. Today, the widespread use of online help facilities has largely made printed manuals obsolete.

How can I find and use online help?

The word 'online' does not necessarily mean on the Internet. Online help is any help system that is built into the software package that is being used. All commonly used packages have a Help menu. Often the help offered is a combination of a manual and a fault diagnosis system.

End users will all be able to access the online help, but not everyone will be able to use it properly. Sometimes users do not know how to describe the problem, and sometimes they do not understand the help they are given.

Online help can be useful to the user support staff as they will be able to search quickly for the topic and then understand the advice. They may then have to explain it in slightly more basic language to the end user, or demonstrate what they have to do.

Check your understanding – Responding to complex requests

In your groups, look again at the unresolved requests. Can you use manuals or online help to solve any of them?

How can I find and use product support?

All the major manufacturers of hardware and software offer support to people who have purchased their products. They all have websites that provide basic product support. These sites will offer free downloads of essential software such as printer drivers. They often provide answers to Frequently Asked Questions (FAQs). These can be very useful sources of information for the user support staff.

Case study – Product support

1   Hardware suppliers

- www.ibm.com/uk
- www.hp.com/uk (Hewlett Packard and Compaq)
- www.dell.co.uk
- www.rm.com (Research Machines)
- www.epson.co.uk
- www.apple.com/uk
- www.iomega.co.uk
- www.toshiba.co.uk

2   Systems software and networking

- www.microsoft.com/uk
- www.cisco.com

3 Applications software

- www.microsoft.com/uk
- www.lotus.com
- www.macromedia.co.uk
- www.corel.com
- www.borland.co.uk
- www.adobe.co.uk

Check this list to see whether it is up to date. Use your usual search engine to find the websites of all the suppliers of hardware and software that you use.

How do I find and use fault diagnosis systems?

A *fault diagnosis system* is a piece of software that helps someone to solve a problem. They are sophisticated troubleshooting systems.

A fault diagnosis system always starts by identifying the problem and then asks one or more questions to establish the cause of the problem. A solution will be suggested, but if this does not work, further questions are asked and more suggestions given. Fault diagnosis systems work in much the same way as an expert would work, and they are a kind of *expert system*.

Professional help desks may purchase fault diagnosis software, which tends to be quite expensive. To find examples of these use your usual search engine on the Internet. There is a surprising number of systems on the Internet that can be used directly from websites for free. Some of the product support sites mentioned above do include full fault diagnosis systems.

Case study – Microsoft® support

Look up http://support.microsoft.com. This site provides support for all the Microsoft® products – both system software and applications software.

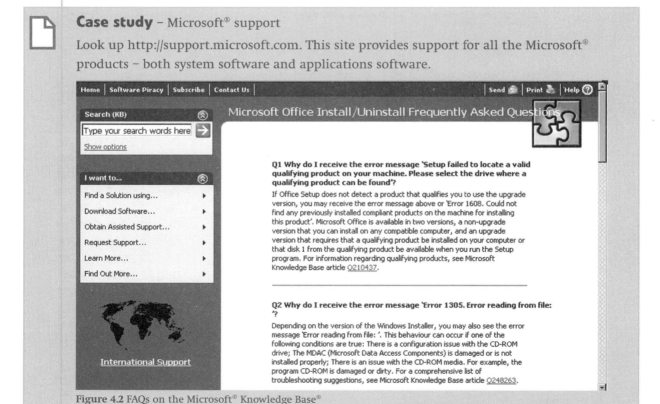

Figure 4.2 FAQs on the Microsoft® Knowledge Base®

The visitor to the site can read Frequently Asked Questions (FAQs) about any software product, search the Knowledge Base for information, or post a problem on a Forum. The FAQ section is organised by product. Figure 4.2 shows some of the questions about installing and uninstalling Microsoft® Office.

The Knowledge Base (which is also known as the Technical Database) contains many articles about software from both the end user and technical point of view. For example, a search for information about templates in Word 2002 resulted in a list of 25 articles. One of them explained where templates were to be found.

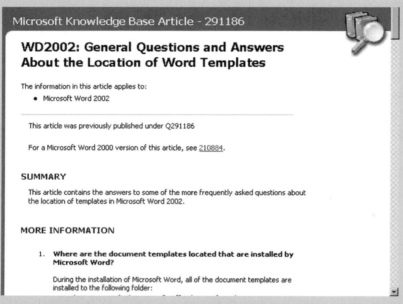

Figure 4.3 An article in the Microsoft® Knowledge Base®

The Forums allow IT support staff to discuss problems with other users across the world. Here is a short extract from the topics that were being discussed in the Forum that deals with setting up Internet Explorer 6.0.

Autocomplete entries will not go awa.	Jason.	Dec 22 2002 6:58PM
Japanese Language Pack.	Frank.	Dec 22 2002 6:56PM
BUG? IE6 & Win XP style buttons gene.	bela.	Dec 22 2002 6:55PM
Auto File Download Pop-Up gone!.	Sajid.	Dec 22 2002 6:19PM
Open in new window.	Donna.	Dec 22 2002 6:18PM
Download any version of IE on any ve.	Rex T..	Dec 22 2002 6:15PM
Text default size setting on MS Expl.	Mark Elenz.	Dec 22 2002 6:14PM
Explorer Stopped Working.	Tim.	Dec 22 2002 4:31PM
Dial-up w/ IE6.0 failing!!.	John HELP ME.	Dec 22 2002 3:50PM
Unwanted links appear in header of I.	Wally.	Dec 22 2002 3:38PM
IE 6.0 update.	A cortes.	Dec 22 2002 3:08PM
driver.	John B. McGuinness.	Dec 22 2002 2:22PM

Figure 4.4 Topics on a Microsoft® support Forum®

Go back to the problems that you identified with your fellow students earlier. If any of them relate to Microsoft® products then use the Microsoft® support to try to solve them.

When should I ask other people to help me solve the problem?

In a large organisation, the user support team will include front-line staff who deal with everyday requests, and other experienced staff who can investigate the more difficult problems. If the person who takes a call is unable to solve the problem, then he or she should always pass it on to a senior member of the team.

In the simulated environment you may be asked to work as a team, and you may find that you can draw on expertise within the team. However, you should not simply allow others to solve the problem for you, but should work with others so that your own understanding grows.

If you need to investigate a difficult problem then you may need to say to the user that you will get back a little later. Or you may be able to visit the user at his or her workplace and try to diagnose the problem on site.

Test your knowledge

1   Why are there so few printed manuals today?
2   Why do help desk staff need access to the Internet?
3   What is a fault diagnosis system?

4.3 Documenting the procedures

Documentation

Help desk staff normally work in a team, and you will probably be working with others in the simulated environment.

Why is documentation important?

It is important that all the records of user requests be available to all members of the team. If a user calls the help desk again about the same problem, he or she may not be able to speak to the same member of the support team, so whoever answers must be able to look back at the history of the problem.

All notes should also be clear – both legible (if handwritten) and understandable. Do not use abbreviations that only you understand.

It is tempting to make very brief (or no) notes of trivial problems, but this should be resisted. This is because the information you keep can be used for a number of other purposes. For example, if one user asks several very basic questions, then it will indicate to the managers that the person needs extra training. Similarly, if the same apparently trivial question is asked by several people then this might suggest that the software or hardware need to be checked and possibly reconfigured.

How should an end user request be recorded?

You should record the full details of the request from the user. You should use the form that you designed in section 4.1.

■ *Reference number* – the form should provide a reference number for each request. If the form is on paper each form should be given a reference number in sequence – the reference number could be pre-printed on the forms. If the form is on-screen then the software will normally assign a unique reference number to each request.

■ *Date* – this is the date when the request is made. An on-screen form may record the date and time automatically.

■ *Time* – again, this is the time when the request is made, not the time when the problem first appeared.

■ *Name of end user* – it may be necessary to check the user's login ID as well. In a large organisation it may be necessary to verify the user in some way – this would be part of the security procedures of the company.

■ *Workstation* – employees may be able to log in on any computer in a network, so the machine that is being used must be identified.

■ *End user request* – this should be written down exactly as said by the end user.

How should the nature of the problem be recorded?

End users do not always explain the problem very clearly.

Suppose the user says 'My printer isn't working.' This could mean:

■ the printer does not do anything at all
■ the printer was working but has now stopped
■ paper goes through the printer but comes out blank
■ the printing is patchy or smeared
■ the printout does not appear as expected.

It is very important that you do not jump to conclusions, so the exact words used should be recorded as the *end user request*. The *nature of the problem* should be described in much more detail. A few simple questions to the user should enable you to describe the problem properly.

How should the actions of the support staff be recorded?

As you work towards a solution you should fill in the remaining sections of the form:

■ *Name of help desk staff* – it is very important to state who worked on the problem. This can be useful if the user wants to speak to the same person again. The manager will also use this information to check on the performance of the support staff.

■ *Nature of the problem* – this is the full description of the problem (see above).

■ *Advice given* – all advice given should be noted down.

■ *Resources used* – here you should list any resources that you referred to in order to solve the problem. See section 4.2 for more information about support resources.

■ *Date/time problem was resolved* – this should be completed only when the end user is satisfied that the problem has been resolved.

■ *Further action* – if the end user calls again later and says that the problem is still present, then further action may be necessary, and this should be noted. You need to work out the best way of recording this further action.

Archiving requests and responses

Where should completed records be stored?

A record of a user request is 'live' until it is solved. Once solved, the records should be stored safely. This process is often known as archiving. An archive is a collection of 'historic' records.

If the data is stored on paper, then it should be stored in a lockable filing cabinet. If the data is stored on specialised help desk software, or on a database created by the user support team, then the datafiles should be backed up regularly.

All records should be stored in shared space – either physically in the help desk room, or in a shared area of the network. Interestingly, if the data is all stored electronically then the user support team does not actually have to share office space, and the team could be distributed around different locations within the organisation.

How should archived records be organised?

Records will normally be stored in reference number order. Since the records are numbered sequentially, this will also mean that they will be in date order as well.

If database software is used, then it will be possible to search the records in a number of ways. The most common search fields will be:

- *Reference number* – when a user calls back with the same problem as before
- *Name of end user* – to try to locate a previous problem if the reference number is not known
- *Workstation* – to check whether the problem has occurred before for that workstation
- *Nature of problem* – to check whether the problem has been encountered before and what the solution was.

Why should I archive old records?

It is very important to keep old records. They may be needed for a number of reasons:

- A user may call the help desk again with the same problem. The reference number will identify the previous request, and the same form will be used to record the additional information.
- Another user may call with a similar problem to one that has already been solved. A quick search through the archives may shorten the time taken to solve the problem.
- The user support manager will analyse the records to find out how effective the user support staff are. They will be able to check how many problems each member of staff managed to solve, how long they took to solve each one, and whether they needed help from colleagues. The manager may decide that a member of the team needs further training, or the analysis may show that a member of staff is not putting in enough effort.

- The user support manager will also analyse the records to see whether certain problems are reported frequently. This may suggest that software or hardware needs to be updated or reconfigured, or it may suggest that end users need additional IT training.

For how long should I store records?

Records are normally kept for two or three years, provided there is space to store them. If a database holds a separate file of users, then these should never be deleted.

Records should not be automatically deleted after a couple of years, but the manager should decide whether they are needed any longer.

What should I do with records that relate to old systems?

If software or hardware has been updated, you may think that you can delete records that refer to the old system. However, the management may well want to compare the number of user requests created by the new system with those generated by the previous system. Usually, user requests increase immediately after new software or hardware are installed, whilst users are learning to use them. But once this initial period is over, the user support team would hope that a new system will generate fewer requests than the old one did.

The records that relate to the old systems should continue to be stored until the managers have no further use for them.

Test your knowledge

1 What is the purpose of the reference number on a user request form?
2 What is an archive, and how should it be stored?

4.4 Evaluating end user support

Evaluation

What is evaluation?

Evaluation is the process of finding out how effective something is. We can evaluate end user support from two perspectives:

- *Individual support* – was the support offered in an individual support session helpful? Did it solve the problem? If so, was it the most efficient way of solving the problem? Was the user satisfied by the service? If the individual support session did not go well, what went wrong and how can it be improved in the future?
- *Team support* – does the team as a whole provide a good service to the users in the organisation? Are they identifying common problems and making changes to the systems to reduce the number of calls?

How can I tell whether the users are satisfied with my support?

Ask them! You can create a short questionnaire to find out what users thought of the support you gave. Normally you would ask them to rate your performance on a number of factors, each on a scale, say from 1 to 5. These are known as *user satisfaction ratings*.

If you do devise a user-satisfaction questionnaire, you should begin by asking the users to give their name, the date and time that they put in a request, the name of the person who helped them, and the reference number if they know it. You will have to think carefully about the topics you ask the users to rate – the wording must be clear and unambiguous. You must also make it clear whether 1 or 5 is the top score. This can be achieved by giving each score a verbal equivalent – e.g. 5 = excellent, 4 = good, etc.

You might like to chose some of the topics (not all) from this list, or devise some of your own:

- attitude of the user support team member
- the solution (did it work?)
- time taken to solve the problem
- overall satisfaction.

How can I evaluate my performance?

When you solve a complex problem you would be wise to evaluate your own performance, by asking:

- What went well?
- What went badly?
- How can I improve my performance?

You will obtain some insight into this by:

- reading the user satisfaction ratings
- going back over the things that you did and asking yourself whether you could have done them in another, more efficient way
- discussing it with other team members involved.

Evaluating trends

What is a trend?

Over time the user support team will gather information about a wide range of problems and about many end users. An important part of the team's job is to watch out for repeated problems. So if they note that a particular problem occurs several times, they may be able to suggest something that can be done to prevent it from happening again.

For example, several users may report that a particular software package seems to hang (stop responding) when large files are used. The support team may realise that the package has not been configured properly for all users, so they can prevent this problem happening again by making some changes to the system.

A trend is an emerging pattern. If several users report the same problem then this can be seen as a trend. Of course, it could be completely coincidental, but the pattern suggests that it is worth investigating the problem further to see whether the occurrences are connected in any way.

How should I summarise user requests?

In order to see patterns, the user requests have to be summarised in some way. If all the user requests are recorded on paper forms then a summary table can be drawn up. You should group the problems into categories, such as problems with the network, printers, software package, Internet, etc. The summary table has one line for each request. The headings on the summary table should include, as a minimum:

- date
- name of user
- workstation
- nature of the problem (in brief).

You may also want to include other headings, such as:

- time taken to solve problem
- operating system
- software package (including version number).

If you are using a database package then you can set it up so that it produces these summary reports for you. If you are using a specialised help desk software package then it will automatically generate reports.

How can I make a report on trends?

The summary table is a very useful tool for you, but if you are asked by your manager to evaluate trends then it still contains too much detail. You should write an analysis of the information, in which you provide answers to these questions:

- What is the most common type of problem?
- Are certain types of problems increasing?

To illustrate the report you will want to produce charts and graphs. These can be generated by specialist software or in a database, or you can prepare them in a spreadsheet. Here are some examples of the types of charts you might produce:

- a pie chart showing the proportion of problems of each category
- a line graph showing the number of problems of a particular type that were reported each month.

Action arising

The summary table and charts will identify for you the most common problems that are reported to the help desk. They will also flag up problems that are being reported at an increasing rate.

How can I propose a strategy to deal with trends?

A strategy is a plan to solve a challenge. The challenge in this case is to make the best use of the highly qualified help desk staff.

Help desk staff are always very busy, and they would like to give time to solving complex problems. Sometimes they find that they are spending a lot of time helping with very simple problems, which could be prevented.

The help desk should review the trends on a regular basis – in a large organisation this could be once a month. They should then take preventative action to deal with common problems. Preventative action prevents the problems from occurring in the first place, or they enable the end users to correct problems themselves without calling the help desk. You should ask:

- Are there any obvious explanations for these problems?
- What can be done to reduce the number of problems reported?

How can the most common problems be prevented?

Preventative action will depend on the kinds of problems that are commonly reported. Here are some suggestions for dealing with frequent problems:

Forgotten password

- Advise users on how to select a password that they can remember without writing it down.

Consumables

- Place a supply of paper, cartridges, toners, disks, etc. in each department, according to usage.
- Check and top up the supplies each week.
- Train users in each department to change toners, etc.
- Paper jamming in a printer:
  - o if this happens to particular users, check that they are loading paper correctly and that they know how to deal with paper jams
  - o check whether one particular model of printer is causing the problem.

Problems with using standard software

- Check what software training has been given and recommend additional training if necessary.
- Produce a short guide to the software – this could be in the form of FAQs based on the ones most commonly asked of the help desk.

Access to software denied

- Reconfigure user access to the network so that all users can access the software they need.
- When new software is installed, find out who should have access to it.

In general, problems can often be prevented by:

- configuring the systems correctly
- proving information
- providing training.

Test your knowledge

1 What is a user satisfaction rating?
2 Why is it a good idea to spot trends in user requests?
3 From your own experience, what do you think might be the most common problems reported to the help desk at your centre? You might be able to check this with the technical staff.
4 Why is it a good idea to reduce the number of support requests?

Assessment tasks

Unlike most of the other units in this qualification, this unit is externally assessed. That means that you will be set an Integrated Vocational Assignment (IVA) by the examination board, Edexcel. The IVA will consist of a series of tasks and you will complete them over a period of time. Your evidence will then be submitted to Edexcel, who will assess your work.

The IVA will challenge you to demonstrate that you can meet all the learning outcomes. You will be asked to work through a simulation, in which you will be acting in the role of a member of a help desk support team for a company.

This section describes what you must do to obtain a Merit grade for this unit.

A Distinction grade may be awarded if your work demonstrates a deeper understanding of the topics and is of a higher quality. The highlighted sentences indicate the quality of work expected at Distinction level.

The IVA

Learning outcome 1 – Identify the support needs of IT end users

Learning outcome 2 – Take part in end user support

Learning outcome 3 – Document the procedures involved with end user support

Learning outcome 4 – Evaluate the end user support

You should be able to:

1 Create and use forms to identify and record the nature of a series of problems reported by users.
2 Respond to requests which you can solve from your own knowledge and by looking up information from a variety of sources.
3 Undertake extensive systems investigation of a complex problem, including taking an active part with others in finding a solution.
4 Provide detailed records of user problems and related solutions, including details of the analysis done to determine the true nature of the problem.
5 Identify basic trends which emerge from the simulation, and carry out a detailed analysis of records with use of charts and diagrams.

To obtain a Distinction grade, you should also be able to:

6 Provide comprehensive records of user problems and user support solutions, including dates and times, identity of user support staff involved and times taken to effect a solution.
7 Respond to requests quickly and effectively to the satisfaction of users.
8 Take an active part in finding a solution to a complex problem and evaluate the process.
9 Make a suggestion for a preventative action for the most common problems.

UNIT 15: NETWORKING ESSENTIALS

Success in this unit

What are the learning outcomes?

To achieve this unit you must:
- describe the application of networks in organisations
- understand basic local area network (LAN) technology
- understand basic local area network conventions
- examine the uses of wide area network (WAN) technology.

How is this unit assessed?

This unit is internally assessed. You must provide evidence in the form of a variety of documents that show that you meet the learning outcomes.

How do I provide assessment evidence?

Your evidence will probably be a mixture of the following:
- written reports
- answers to questions
- witness statements and screen shots.

All your evidence should be presented in one folder, which should have a front cover and a contents page. The section headed *Assessment tasks* at the end of this unit gives you more detailed advice about how to prepare for the assessment.

Introduction

About this unit

This unit introduces you to the basic theoretical concepts of networking. Topics covered within this unit will be dealt with in more depth in other units.

You will look at networks in organisations and how communications play an important part in the activities of organisations.

You will look at different topologies of networks for both LANs (local area networks) and WANs (wide area networks) to see how best to use networks to enhance the communications within an organisation.

Whilst the assessment for this unit is of a theoretical nature, it would be best if you could gain some practical experience of networks. Try talking to the technical people within your centre and asking if they could show you a simple network. Your centre may even be able to let you try setting up a simple network between two standalone computers.

15.1 Networks in organisations

Communication in organisations

How do organisations communicate?

Communication is an essential part of the day-to-day running of an organisation. Without the correct communication channels, organisations would find themselves lacking in information, holding out-of-date information and maybe even losing business opportunities.

Networks aim to help people with much of this communication. If electronic communications are in place, it can help make communication easier, quicker, more reliable, less expensive and less stressful for people. It must also be remembered that electronic communications and networks can save paper, making them more environmentally friendly.

Case study – Video conferencing

If we take as an example a networking capability called **video conferencing**, the use of networks to help people will become more obvious.

An organisation that has offices in Australia, America and the UK needs to hold a meeting to discuss a product launch. Each of the offices has a team of six people that has been working on the new product. Instead of hiring a venue, paying for flights and accommodation and any other expenses such as meals or car hire, the organisation can set up a video conference. Each team can stay in their own country, meet at an agreed time, and link to the other teams electronically. This not only saves money for the organisation but also saves time – the teams are working rather than travelling. It is easier to set up than arranging a face-to-face meeting. An **electronic whiteboard** can also be used. This means that each team can look at and work on the same document or diagram at the same time, ensuring that all teams have the latest versions available. Any relevant documentation, such as an agenda, can be e-mailed to each team member around the world, saving on paper.

? What does it mean?

Video conferencing – video conferencing is the term given to a meeting between two or more people when they can see and talk to each other through a computerised video link. The computer screen is the visual link and speakers are used for the sound link. A video camera, attached to each computer, sends the images through telephone lines, whilst a microphone sends the sound at the same time.

? What does it mean?

Electronic whiteboard – an electronic whiteboard is a shared work area in a window on the monitor of a networked computer. It is designed to be used whilst video and/or voice contact is taking place. More than one person at a time, in different locations, can see the window and change drawings or documents that are on view..

You can see that for organisations today a networked system can be invaluable. Because the main aim of a network is to help with communication, we need to understand the different types of communications in organisations and how they are used before looking in detail at networks.

Communication in an organisation is carried out at two levels:

- internally
- externally.

What is internal communication?

Internal communication is any communication within an organisation. It does not involve any people outside the organisation. There are several different forms of internal communication, including:

- discussions between staff members
- exchanges of information or ideas between staff members
- internal orders for items such as stationary
- meetings within departments to discuss issues such as budgets
- project meetings involving people from different departments
- group presentations to show the latest sales figures
- internal telephone calls
- posting of company events on a notice board
- chats around the coffee machine.

Internal communication can involve members within the organisation at any level, from a receptionist to a managing director.

What type of communication could individuals be involved in?

Individuals within organisations communicate constantly. It could be a case of them just having a chat about the latest sales figures between themselves, or it could be that someone in the personnel department needs to know how many hours someone has worked the week before. Whatever the situation is, individual communication would be when just two people are talking or sharing information and ideas.

What type of communication could teams of people be involved in?

In most organisations, teamwork is an important part of the working environment. For example, if an organisation is involved in the manufacture of mobile telephones, they could have a team of people working together to design a new mobile telephone for them to make. This would be known as a 'project team' and it may be that the people within the team are not from the same department, building or even country. Project teams are often made up of people who do not always work together within an organisation on a day-to-day basis. Many organisations have more than one site in different places within the country in which they are based. Lots of organisations even have different sites spread around the world. It is important that communication systems be in place to enable these people to be in touch easily and quickly.

How are functional areas affected by communications?

A functional area is the overall name given to different departments within an organisation. For example, a sales office would be the functional area for most jobs to do with sales within an organisation.

Functional areas need good communication systems to enable them to share information. For example, if a good communication system has been set up, the accounts department within an organisation will be able to access a customer's record easily to see what the customer has ordered, whether the customer has had the goods or services ordered, and whether the goods or services have been paid for. This will make sure that the organisation does not wait too long for payment for the goods or services it has provided to that customer.

What is external communication?

External communication is any communication that involves someone inside the organisation being in contact with anyone from outside the organisation. There are lots of reasons why organisations need to communicate with people externally, including:

- placing orders with suppliers
- taking orders from customers
- dealing with government departments, e.g. on tax issues
- ensuring they are up to date with new legislation
- keeping an eye on competitors.

Why do organisations need to communicate with customers?

Good communication with customers is essential. If customers feel that they are important to an organisation, they are more likely to buy goods or services from that organisation again. Good communication would involve things like contacting the customer to see whether they were happy with goods or services. It might be that an organisation wants to let their customers know about a special offer they have on some goods or services.

Whatever the reason why an organisation wants to communicate with customers, it is important that the communication channels be easily accessible and that all information is up to date. If an organisation rang one of their customers and used the wrong name, it would not be very professional. It would be likely that the customer would not use that organisation again.

Why are public relations important when talking about communications?

Public relations is the overall name given to how organisations are seen by their customers and how the organisation deals with their customers. Good public relations are important to organisations because they need to be able to have a good reputation with their customers to ensure that customers trust the organisation and will buy goods or services from them.

If an organisation is easy to contact, has good customer service, and seems to care about their customers, then it is likely that the organisation will be successful.

How is research important when talking about communications?

Let us use a case study to explain this.

Case study – Modern Mobiles – product research

Modern Mobiles, a new mobile phone company, is thinking of introducing a new telephone into its product range. It has set up a project team to design this.

One of the first things that the project team will have to do is to look at all the mobile telephones that are currently available to customers. This would be part of the initial research into the new product. There would be no point in producing a mobile telephone that is identical in its design and the functions as a mobile phone that is already available.

Two of the project team have been given the task of researching the mobile telephones currently available. One team member is using leaflets from other mobile telephone companies and a telephone directory to talk to other mobile phone manufacturers to see what is currently available. The other team member is using the Internet to search for mobile telephones currently available. Neither of these methods of research can guarantee that all currently available mobile telephones will be found, but the team member who is using the Internet for research will be able to complete the task much quicker than the one using leaflets and making telephone calls.

The Internet is a form of communication (you will learn more about this later in this unit). This is one reason why good communication systems are important to organisations when they need to carry out research.

Why are information resources important when talking about communication?

Information resources are used in one way or another constantly by organisations. Information resources are obtained in different ways and come in different formats. Within an organisation these could include:

- telephone directories
- customer records
- supplier records
- sales invoices
- order forms
- supermarket loyalty cards.

All of these are sources of information for an organisation. The information they collect from external sources is important, amongst other things, in building up a picture of the organisation's customers. It is essential that any external resources used are accurate and up to date.

Let us use the same case study to explain this.

Case study – Modern Mobiles – mailshots

If our mobile telephone organisation wanted to send a **mailshot** to inform people of their new product, they could source the names and addresses of people who already own mobile telephones from a market research company holding that information. If the listing of names and addresses that the organisation used was out of date, then it is possible that the organisation could lose potential customers, as they would not receive the mailshot.

Obtaining this listing of names and addresses would be a form of communication. If the correct communication systems were in place, then it would easier and quicker for the organisation to ensure that they were using up-to-date information, sourced from a reliable market research company.

What does it mean?

Mailshot – a mailshot is a leaflet, letter or brochure that is sent from an organisation to a wide range of customers. The listing of customers that are to be sent the mailshot will be collated by the organisation and all those on the listing will be sent exactly the same information. Sometimes organisations will 'target' certain customers only. For example, if we think about the mobile telephone company, a new product with extra functions could be available. The organisation might only want to let people who already own mobile telephones know about this new product. Therefore, they will target existing mobile telephone owners. They will not include any people in the mailshot who do not already own a mobile telephone.

Check your understanding

In groups, research the methods of communication within your centre. Think about as many things as you can , from how a lecturer might communicate with a class, to how the centre might use communication to recruit new students. Once you have made a list of methods of communicatrion that you could research, it is a good idea to split the list between your group members, so that each person is researching a different area of communication.

Once your research is complete, design a presentation to deliver to the rest of the class. When you have seen all the presentations, you can compare your findings with the rest of the groups in the class. It is likely that some groups will think of different ways of communication within your centre than you do.

Networks

What is a network?

As you can see from the above, communication within an organisation is fundamentally linked with information. Computer networks are used to share information and resources. A network is a system that allows people to share information with each other. It could be as simple as a communication network between two people or a computer network between millions of people.

If you think about a simple communication network then the probability is that you have used one at some stage in your life. Anything from children's toy walkie-talkies to the mobile telephone are forms of communication network.

Figure 15.1 A walkie-talkie can be part of a simple communication network

Computer networks are made by connecting one computer to another computer. One way of making the connection between two computers is to use cables to link them. We will look at other ways of connecting computers later in this unit. This is the simplest form of computer network, but computer networks can involve hundreds, thousands, or even millions of computers being connected.

When lots of computers in different locations need to be connected to form a network, the use of cables alone is not a feasible solution. If two computers in the same room need to be connected, it would not be a problem to link them using a cable. But if two computers at opposite ends of a country, or even in different countries, need to be connected, it would be impossible to link them using a cable across this many miles. This is when other connections are needed, such as telephone lines and broadband connections. We will look at ways of connecting computers in more detail later in this unit.

There are two basic types of computer network that are used today:

- local area networks (LANs)
- wide area networks (WANs).

What is a local area network (LAN)?

A local area network (LAN) consists of computers connected across a small geographical area. The example of two computers in the same room being connected would mean that they have a LAN connection.

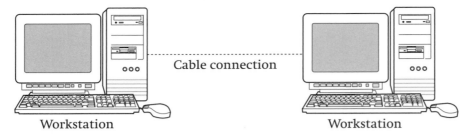

Figure 15.2 A simple LAN connection

What is a wide area network (WAN)?

A wide area network consists of computers connected across a large geographical area. If we take Modern Mobiles as an example, they have more than one location in the country. They have an office in London and an office in Birmingham. Because of the distance between these two offices, it would not be possible to connect computers between the offices by using a simple cable connection. The organisation needs to use other types of connection, for example a telephone line, to connect the computers.

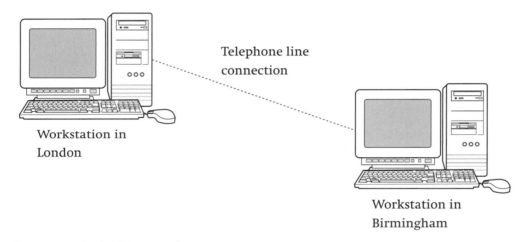

Figure 15.3 A simple WAN connection

In both LAN and WAN connections, the **workstations** are usually connected to a **server** that holds the hardware, software, information and resources that the computers can share.

?

What does it mean?

Workstation – a workstation is a computer that is linked to a network. It may or may not have its own hard disk. In some types of network the workstation is just the monitor and keyboard. Workstations that are linked to a network are able to use the hardware and software of the computer that is acting as a server on the network.

?

What does it mean?

Server – a server is the name given to a central computer that stores the hardware, software and data on a network. It is capable of managing multiple users at workstations. Servers often manage and prioritise the use of peripherals that workstations can share, such as printers. The server then 'serves' any other users, known as '**clients**', with any resources needed.

What are the different types of operation for networks in organisations?

There are two basic types of local area network that organisations use:

- **client**–server
- thin client.

? What does it mean?

Client – a client is the name given to a workstation connected to a server. It is also the name given to software that has been designed specifically to work with a server application. For example, web browser software is client software. It is made to work with web servers, like the Internet.

What is a client–server network?

A client–server network consists of one computer acting as a server for one or more clients. This means that one computer holds most of the information, resources and software. Other computers that are networked to it can access what they need without having the software or hardware installed on hard disks.

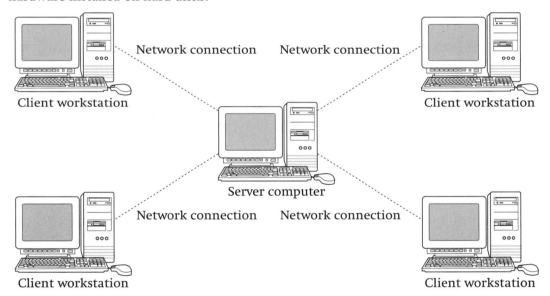

Figure 15.4 Client–server network

If you think about how you access documents and software on your school or college computers, this is easier to explain.

It is likely that you use a computer in the classroom that you have to log onto. Once you have logged onto the computer, you will be able to access work that you have stored on the hard disk in your own work area. You will not be able to access work that a friend has stored on the hard disk in another work area. This is because you are not accessing the hard disk of the computer you are physically using, but the hard disk of the server computer.

The computer you are using *does* have its own hard disk. This can be used to store things temporarily during the session, to install software that is needed only within that classroom, or to process information you are working with.

The important thing to remember is that when you save something during your lesson, you are not saving it to the computer you are working on, but to the main server computer.

What is a thin client network?

A thin client network consists of computers connected to a network, but each workstation does not need to have its own hard disk. There will usually be a server within the network of computers that contains all hardware, software and information that is needed (Figure 15.5). The individual workstations will not usually store any software, but will temporarily download software from the server, as and when it is required.

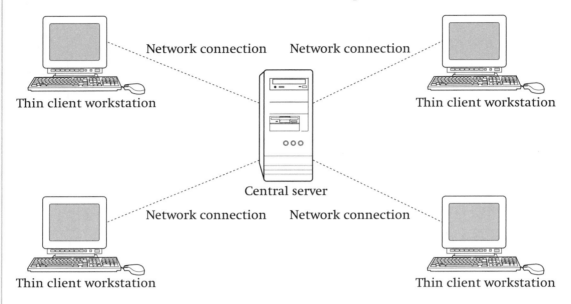

Figure 15.5 Thin client network

Is there an alternative to relying on a single server?

In some smaller organisations, where there are not many workstations that need to be networked (usually less than 20), it is sometimes preferable not to have a single server. This means if there are problems with the server, they will not affect other workstations and the majority of people can carry on working. A network can still be set up between the workstations but, because they each have an individual server, they are all equal. For this reason, this type of network is known as *peer-to-peer*. The workstations can still share resources, but can also each use printers and store files individually without having to pass the data and/or instructions through a central server. In other words, each workstation manages its own section of the network.

Peer-to-peer networks do not cost much to set up and run, as only ordinary workstations are needed. Organisations will not need to invest in a powerful server. However, it must be remembered that a peer-to-peer network is suitable only for a small number of workstations, as the system can run very slowly if more than one person tries to access the hard disk at the same time.

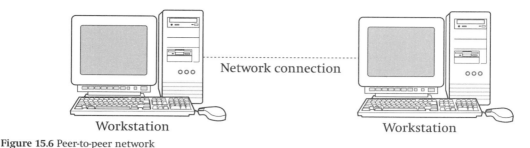

Workstation   Network connection   Workstation

Figure 15.6 Peer-to-peer network

Check your understanding

A small company selling comic books needs to networks its computer system. It has an office in Manchester and an office in New York. The company's basic requirements will be that some members of staff, in both offices, will need to be able to use the same data and it is vitally important that the data be up-to-date. There is an unlimited budget.

Look at the different types of operation for networks that could be used, e.g. peer-to-peer. Give a recommendation for a network for the company to install, and justify your choice.

The use of networks for communications in organisations

Earlier in this unit, we looked at the different ways in which organisations might communicate, both internally and externally.

Organisations can use networks to ensure that communication is carried out efficiently and effectively. Networks are a way of sharing resources and information. Let us now look again at the areas of communication within organisations and see how networks could enable an organisation to run more efficiently.

How can networks help internal communication in an organisation?

We have looked at communications between individuals, teams and functional areas. We now need to look at these again and see how a network in an organisation could help these types of internal communication.

An organisation that has a local area network in place has the capability of sharing information and resources internally. There are many ways in which this can be done, including:

- *Setting up a drive to store shared files, resources, etc.* – this will then enable people to access the drive from their own workstation, and use whatever is required. One example of this would be to have a folder on the shared drive to hold product leaflets or brochures. This could then be easily accessible by any member of staff, to either look at or print off the information needed.
- *Setting up software on the LAN so that it can be shared throughout the organisation* – one example of this would be if word processing software were shared. Under the templates in the word processing package, the organisation could have outline documents, such as sales invoices,

that could be called up on individual workstations and used. Once completed, these could then be saved into a common folder on the shared drive so that records of the sales invoice are kept.

- *Setting up a company intranet* – an intranet is a type of website that is accessible only within the network it has been set up in. No one from outside the organisation can access it without access rights being set up. Its main purpose is to share organisational information confidentially. This can then be used to design easy access routes to any organisational data that needs to be accessed by more than one individual. One example of this would be to have a link to the organisation's IT Security Policy.

- *Setting up e-mail accounts* – these can then be used by individuals or functional areas to communicate electronically within the organisation. One example would be if the accounts department was having a staff meeting. The accounts department could e-mail everyone else in the organisation to let them know in advance that they would be uncontactable at that time. Also, e-mails can have attachments. This would mean that once the accounts department had finished their meeting, the minutes could be e-mailed as an attachment to anyone who needed a copy.

- *Setting up a bulletin board* – a bulletin board is like an electronic notice board. Notices can be posted on a bulletin board, which can then be accessed by anyone with the correct level of access rights. Bulletin boards are normally static – this means that things can be posted onto them, but responses are not in **real-time**. This can then be used to post information that a wide range of individuals may need to know. One example of this would be if an organisation were organising an outing. The date and time of this could be posted on the bulletin board to save the organisation sending individual notes to each person.

- *Setting up a newsgroup* – a newsgroup is an interactive area on a network where users can communicate in real-time. They are different from chatrooms/sites in that the discussion topics on a newsgroup can normally be viewed after the discussion has taken place, as well as in real-time. Newsgroups are usually set up with specific subject areas in mind, so that like-minded people can join in. This can then be used for groups of people to communicate electronically. One example of this would be to have a newsgroup for the project team that is designing a new mobile telephone. It would be a way of them keeping in touch and keeping each other up to date with the progress of the project. It could also be used to discuss ideas or problems without having a physical meeting.

? What does it mean?

Real-time – real-time means that each user is accessing and using information simultaneously. Users are able to respond immediately to something someone else is typing.

How can networks help external communication in an organisation?

When we looked earlier at external communication, we looked at communication between organisations and customers, communicating for public relations purposes, communicating for research purposes and communicating in relation to information resources. We now need to look at these again and see how a network could help these types of external communication.

When an organisation needs to communicate externally on a regular basis, it is likely that as well as having the intranet, they will set up access to the Internet. This will then enable them to use extra facilities to help with their external communication needs.

Ways in which networks can help external communication in organisations include:

- *Having access to external websites* – if an organisation has access to websites, they can carry out research, check on competitors, and access other external websites, for example government websites to ensure they are up to date with new legislation. One example of this could be the project team member researching currently available mobile telephones. Searching competitors' websites will give a good idea of what is available, the designs, functions and features.

- *Having a website for their own organisation* – this could help the organisation in gaining a good reputation, provided their website is kept up to date and looks professional. It is good public relations to have a website, as existing or potential customers can access this to look for products, find out more about the organisation and even contact the organisation easily through the use of forms, e-mail buttons, etc. One example would be for Modern Mobiles to have a customer feedback form on their website, so that they can get valuable comments from their customers.

- *Having EDI (electronic data interchange) facilities available* – this would enable the organisation to send orders to suppliers electronically and take customer orders electronically. For example, Modern Mobiles could have a customer order form on their website, which would save the customers time in ordering products. The orders would be received much quicker than if being sent in by normal postal services, and could be actioned immediately by the organisation to give a good customer service.

- *Having e-mail facilities available* – organisations could use the e-mail facilities to send mailshots electronically to customers and keep in touch with customers and suppliers. An example would be if Modern Mobiles had a special offer on a new product. They could create an e-mail listing of existing customers and send them the information electronically. An advantage of this would be that it is usually cheaper than sending out printed mailshots, thereby saving the organisation money.

- *Creating newsgroups which can be accessed from the organisation's website* – for example, Modern Mobiles could create a newsgroup for their customers, whereby customers could find out information on products from people already using them. If someone was thinking about buying a new mobile telephone, they could go to the newsgroup and type up a message to see what other users thought of the product they were thinking of buying.

- *Creating bulletin boards which can be accessed from the organisation's website* – for example, Modern Mobiles could set up a bulletin board for its customers. They could post information about new product ranges, special offers, etc. instead of sending e-mail mailshots.

Networks and resource issues

Can networks cause problems?

As well as saving the organisation money and time, networks can also create problems. Imagine that any of the people in your class could access your personal record from their workstations. There may well be information on there that you do not wish to share with people. It may be that you do not wish people to have your home address and telephone number, unless you choose to give it to them. You would not be very happy if everyone in your class could access that information.

Another problem could be in the way that software is shared. In your school or college, you might have software available for certain courses that is not licensed for everyone to use at one time. Although this software might be available on every workstation in the school/college, it would be breaking the law if more people than the license covered were to access it at the same time.

Another problem might be in the sharing of hardware. If your school/college had a small server to run the network, the people in charge of the IT facilities would need to be careful that not too many people tried to use the system at the same time. This could result in the server running very slowly, and users becoming frustrated. It could even mean that the system cannot cope with the number of users, and crashes so that no one can use the system until the problem has been dealt with.

When using a network, there are ways in which these problems can be addressed.

How can a network manage information in an organisation?

One of the best ways of making sure that only the people who are allowed to see information held on the system actually see it is to set up what are known as *access rights*. Setting up access rights also enables an organisation to make sure that certain information is not altered by anyone who is unauthorised to do so.

There are several different levels of access rights that can be set up:

- *Read only* – this is where someone is allowed to view the information held on the system, but cannot alter it in any way. It also means that users with read-only access cannot delete information. One example would be the product information leaflets for Modern Mobiles. Once they have been issued, the organisation will not want anyone to be able to delete or alter them, unless they are authorised to do so. By making the file a read-only file, the organisation knows that only someone with the correct access rights can update the leaflet.
- *Write* – this is where someone is allowed to alter the information held on the system, for example the person mentioned above who is allowed to update a product leaflet. He or she can call the leaflet, update it, and save it back to the directory/file it was downloaded from.
- *Create* – this is where someone is allowed to create new files, folders or directories on the system. Looking at the example of the product leaflet, it may be that Modern Mobiles will want only one person to be able to produce a new product leaflet. This will save duplication and confusion. Anyone who does not have the correct access level of creating within that folder/directory will not be able to do this.

■ *Erase* – this is where someone is allowed to erase files, folders or directories on the system, for example if a mobile telephone became obsolete for Modern Mobiles. It would not be wise to still have the product leaflet available to everyone, so the person with the correct access rights could delete it to ensure that no one was recommending that product to a customer.

■ *Modify* – this is where someone is allowed to change the names and attributes of files, folders and directories. As an example, Modern Mobiles could have a folder for their product leaflets that is named 'Product Leaflets'. When a product becomes obsolete, they might not want to delete the leaflet from the system completely but keep it on the system somewhere for future reference. Someone with the correct access rights could change the name of the existing folder to 'Current Product Leaflets', and create a new folder called 'Obsolete Product Leaflets' to store the old product leaflet in.

■ *Copy* – this is where someone is allowed to copy work from one area to another, or from the hard drive to a disk. For example, a person from Modern Mobiles who has been given the task of creating a new product leaflet might want to take a product leaflet template home to work on it over a weekend. If the correct access rights have been set up, the person can copy the template to a disk for this purpose.

Why are standard ways of working within organisations important?

It is important that organisations have some control over the communication that takes place. You have already seen some of the problems that can arise from members of staff not being able to easily share information or resources, or not keeping other members of staff informed when working together as a team. It is also important to have this control so that the organisation can ensure that computers being used are *secure* and are not being used for anything that would be illegal or against the organisation's IT Security Policy.

A network can help communications with coordination, collaboration, keeping staff informed and helping with research. By having a central server where common folders for files can be held and accessed easily, the job of coordinating communication in an organisation can be better managed.

If we think about the Modern Mobiles project team, they could have a common folder for their research, design sketches and other information they require. By the use of **version control** they can ensure that any documentation they are retrieving from the folder is the most up-to-date version. This would then ensure that no one from the project team is looking at or working on out-of-date material, even if more than one person is working on a design, for example.

?

What does it mean?

Version control – people agree a code to put on documentation to tell them which is the most up-to-date copy of that information. For example, when you are working on portfolio documentation, it may be that you keep more than one copy so that you can see where changes have been made and anything has been added. If your first draft of your work is coded V1 and the next time you work on it you change the coding to V2 and save it under a different file name, you will know that the most recent copy is the one marked V2. This will then be the one that you retrieve and continue to work on.

If the documentation within the folder is passworded, this will also ensure that the ongoing project is secure and that no one who should not be accessing the information has the ability to do so.

Using a common folder on a shared drive also helps with research. If you remember, two of our project team have been given the task of researching mobile telephones currently available. If any information found is stored in the common folder then any team member can look at it. Not only does this save team members from having to send photocopies of information found to the other team members, it also means that the team members are not wasting time by searching for the same information. They can access the folder, see what has already been found, and know which mobile telephone companies the other person has already researched.

An example of how a network can help collaborate communications would be in the use of newsgroups and e-mails. We have already looked at how a newsgroup could help our project team.

When thinking about the use of e-mail, the project team could have a **distribution list** of the other team members set up on their e-mail account. This would mean that if they needed to share some information or let the team know about something, the e-mail would be sent to every member of the project team. The use of a distribution list would also help in keeping people informed of the current stages of work, ideas and information for the project.

What does it mean?

Distribution list – a distribution list is used on an e-mail account to set up a list of e-mail addresses under a given group. When an e-mail needs to be sent to that group, the person sending the e-mail can address it to the name of the distribution list. This means that there is only one 'address' to put in the 'send to' section of the e-mail. The e-mail software will have stored the individual addresses that you put in when creating the distribution list and will send the e-mail to each person on that list.

Managing resources in organisations

When an organisation is using a network system, it is important that all aspects of that system be correctly managed.

Organisations will want to ensure that their systems are not being overloaded with information and documentation that is not required. They will also want to know that the data held is as secure as possible and that any hardware and software are being used correctly. Sometimes there might be legal issues to take into consideration.

Most organisations will employ someone to manage the network overall. Their job role will include aspects concerning information, network hardware and software, overall administration of the network, security aspects and legal issues. This person usually has the job title of Network Manager.

In large organisations, there may be other people employed for specific jobs that result from the organisation having a network computer system. We will look at these in more detail shortly.

How can information be managed on a network?

We have already looked at some of the ways in which information can be managed on a network. Recall that we looked at users logging into a network system. From the user login, the network administrators can tell which person is using which workstation, what hardware and software he or she is using, and even which websites are being accessed and if any information is being downloaded from them. Access rights can be set up individually for all users by programming the access rights against the user login.

How can hardware be managed on a network?

The hardware that is connected to a network is likely to be shared for some, if not all, of the time. It is important to manage hardware such as printers, storage devices and scanners to make sure users do not encounter unnecessary problems.

Hardware such as printers can be set to a queuing system, known as 'job queues'. When a user sends a document to the printer, it may not be first in the queue, so it may not print out immediately, even if the printer appears to the user to not be busy. It is important that users know whether any hardware is on a queuing system, otherwise they might think that their instruction has not been read. This can result in the same document being printed out lots of times. Most network systems will have an icon or a facility in the 'Start' menu to enable a user to check the print queue. This way, they can see that their instruction has been sent, but that they will have to wait to get their printed document until they are at the front of the queue. Figure 15.7 shows a printer menu and an empty print queue.

Figure 15.7 A printer window and empty print queue

How can software be managed on a network?

When a network system is set up in an organisation, the management of software is important for several reasons.

Most organisations will have different types of software available on the network for different types of job within the organisation. For example, someone working in the accounts department might need to use a financial management package but it is unlikely that he or she will need to use a desktop publishing package. However, someone working in the marketing department might need to use a desktop publishing package but would not have much use for a financial management package. The network can be set up so that, after logon, the person in the accounts department has access to the financial management package and the person in the marketing department has access to the desktop publishing package.

There are two main reasons for the organisation restricting who uses the packages held on the system.

- The first is that when you buy a software package for use on a network, you have to buy more than one licence for it. By restricting who has access to the package, the organisation can buy fewer licences and be certain that they are not using packages illegally by having more users accessing the package than they have licences for.

- Secondly, software packages that use a lot of memory to run can slow down the system. If you only allow those people who need to use it to access the software, then there should be fewer problems with the network system.

Another way in which software needs to be managed on a network is to make sure that there is no illegal software on the system. When the network is set up, programming can be used to allow only certain people to install software. This way, a member of staff cannot install any software that the organisation is not licensed to use.

How can a network be administered?

When a network is installed, it is usual for an organisation to appoint a Network Administrator or Network Manager. This person will be responsible for monitoring the network and its resources. The job will involve many aspects of monitoring the network, including:

- recognising where there might be potential problems
- fixing any problems that do occur
- making sure the network is running smoothly and performing to its maximum capability
- backing up data
- setting policies on the use of the network and all its resources
- providing security for the network and the data held on it.

Further research – Standards for network administration

As networks have become more commonly used, software tools have become available to help the Network Administrator. To make sure that all network management tools are capable of helping to administrate the most important functions of a network system, an organisation called ISO (International Standards Organisation) developed a model to show the five major functions of a network management system. All companies developing network management tools use this model. The basic functions of a network system that the ISO recognised are:

- performance management
- configuration management
- accounting management
- fault management
- security management.

Research some of the software tools that are available for network administration to find out what these five functions do.

Is the software you found able to help in the performance of these five functions?

How can personnel be managed on a network?

We have already looked at managing personnel on a network by setting up access rights through user logins and passwords. Once this has been done, an **audit trail** can be used by the Network Administrator to keep track of what each user is accessing on the network.

An important way of managing personnel in an organisation is to have an IT Security Policy and to make sure that all staff are aware of the policy. Most organisations will ask their staff to sign a copy of the IT Security Policy, stating that they will comply with the rules that the organisation has laid down about using its network system.

What does it mean?

Audit trail – an audit program can be installed onto a network system and an audit trail set up. This is not just used for keeping track of individual users, but also, for example, to trace transactions as they go through a system. The audit trail can tell the network administrator where a transaction is in the system at any time, or where a user is logged on and what he or she is accessing, downloading or printing.

What legislation and security issues do you have to consider on a network?

You have already looked in some detail at legislation and security in Unit 2. Re-read pages 94-100 and consider which ones relate to networks.

In Unit 2 you saw that software and data must be protected from unauthorised access. Look again at the sections on copyright, software piracy, hacking and the Computer Misuse Act. Also remind yourself about the software risks to IT systems and how security procedures can protect software and recover data.

Check your understanding

Write a short report for the comic book company, detailing how the installation of a networked computer system could help them in the following areas:

- improving internal communication
- improving external communication
- management of their information
- security of their information.

Test your knowledge

1 List *three* examples of internal communications and *three* examples of external communications.
2 What is the difference between a LAN and a WAN?
3 What is a client–server network?
4 What are the functions of access rights?

15.2 Local area network technology

Hardware for local area networks

What are the hardware components required for networks and what are their objectives?

Some hardware components for LANs will be needed no matter which type of network is set up on the system.

Just as in any type of computer system, the main hardware components required will be the *hard disk*, *monitor* and *keyboard*. There may be other types of *data capture devices* on the system, depending on the nature of the organisation. Supermarkets, for example, will normally have a **bar code scanner** as an input device, as well as a type of keyboard known as a **concept keyboard**. The computer system that you work on at school or college is likely to have a mouse as an additional data capture component along with the keyboard.

> **?**
>
> **What does it mean?**
>
> Bar code scanner – a bar code scanner is an input device which reads a series of lines of different thickness and shading. The scanner is passed over the bar code on a product and a light on the scanner is read. The bar code is then processed automatically and converted to a code. It is this code that identifies the product. If you look at a bar code on a product, you will see that because scanner systems are not one hundred percent reliable, the code that the bars represent is printed underneath the lines.

> **?**
>
> **What does it mean?**
>
> Concept keyboard – a concept keyboard has different keys to that of a QWERTY keyboard. An example of a concept keyboard is the keyboard attached to weighing scales in a supermarket. The customer places produce on the scales, then presses the button that represents the food being weighed.

Some types of network will not require all their workstations to have individual hard drives but other types of networks use both the server and individual hard disks for each workstation.

To be able to access the network, each workstation will require a *network adaptor* (often referred to as a network card or NIC – network interface card). This will be installed into an expansion slot inside the computer and acts as an interface for connection to the network. The type of network card used will depend on the network topology being used.

Once these basic components are present, other kinds of hardware will be required to connect the workstations to the network. Different types of *cables* and *wires* are required, again depending on the type of network that is being set up. The main type of cable used for networking is made of copper wire. The most common types are:

Figure 15.8 A network card

■ *Coaxial cable* – this is similar to the cable used for television aerials.

■ *Unshielded twisted pair cable* (UTP cable) – the wires are twisted together in pairs and held together by a plastic covering.

■ *Fibre optic cable* – this is a cable which is made up of glass or plastic fibres and carries a digital signal through a laser light. Because there is no conversion from analogue to digital, it is a much faster way of transmitting data.

Depending on the type of network being installed, you may also need a *hub*. This is a type of electronic switching box, and its purpose is to control the traffic flow around the network. It can also give workstations some independence from the other connected workstations. This is useful if, for example, one computer on the network develops a problem. With the use of a hub, other workstations can carry on working normally – unaffected by the problem.

If **peripherals** are to be a shared resource on the network, then these are items of hardware that will also need to be taken into account.

Other hardware components that can be used in networks include:

■ *Repeaters* – these are electronic devices that boost signals before sending them along the network. They are also used to connect two cables together in a LAN if the cable needs extending.

■ *Bridges* – these are used to extend a network by linking two LANs together.

What does it mean?

Peripheral – this is the name given to a hardware component that is connected to a computer. For example, printers are often shared on a network system. A printer is a peripheral.

Check your understanding

Produce a diagram showing the hardware components that will be required to set up a simple LAN between two workstations. Include any peripherals you think may be required. Clearly label each piece of hardware and show, through the use of arrows, how the hardware will connect to the workstation, and which way the data will flow.

Topology

What are the different types of networks that can be used?

Instead of saying that a network is a 'type', it is usual to speak of network *topology*. The hardware components that are connected on a network are often referred to as *nodes*. So the pattern of a network connection consists of a certain topology, where the servers are connected to nodes. Remember, not all hardware components connected on a network are workstations. There could be printers, scanners, speakers and digital cameras, just to name a few.

There are many different network topologies. The most common topologies that organisations use are known as *bus*, *star* and *ring*.

Bus topology

This topology has been given the name 'bus' because it works in a very similar way to how a bus would follow its route on the road. All the nodes are connected to a central cable. When data is sent from one computer it is carried by the 'bus', visiting each node in turn, until it reaches the correct destination. The central cable used is not joined up, so the 'bus' has to travel backwards and forwards along the length of the cable to let data on and off the bus.

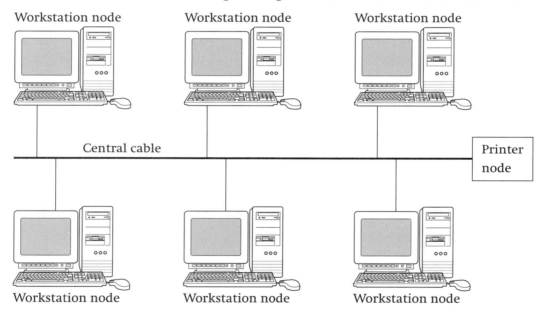

Figure 15.9 A bus network

With a bus topology, there is no main computer as it is easy to connect all nodes to the central cable. There is no level of priority between the nodes. All nodes have equal status for transmitting data. For this reason, if the central cable is busy elsewhere, other transmissions have to wait their turn.

The main problem with a bus topology is that only one node at a time can send or receive data. For this reason, bus topologies are normally used for small LANs, where not many workstations are connected to the network. If more workstations are added to the network as the organisation grows, the network topology may need to be changed. If too many workstations are connected to a bus topology, the system will become very slow and the work rate will not be efficient.

The main advantages of a bus topology are that it is easy to set up, it is a reliable network connection, and – because only one main cable is required – it is not as expensive to set up as other network topologies.

Star topology

This topology has been given the name 'star' because it consists of a central controlling computer, connected to nodes by individual cables. Each workstation user can send and receive data from the central computer when required, without having to wait his or her turn. This means that it is a faster network than the bus topology.

The central computer is sometimes known as a *hub node*, as it is responsible for controlling the flow of data between the other nodes.

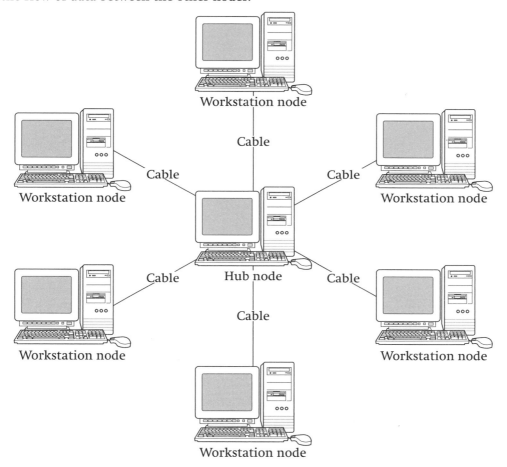

Figure 15.10 A star topology

One of the main problems with a star topology is that if the hub node has a problem or crashes, the entire network will be affected. It is likely that no one will be able to work. However, as each node is connected by its own cable, if one of the nodes has a problem then the rest of the network will be unaffected.

Ring topology

This topology has been given the name 'ring' because all the nodes are connected together in a circle. There is no one controlling computer, and all workstations have equal status. There is one computer that holds all the files for the network, including all the programs and software that are required.

The way in which data is transmitted in a ring topology is by using 'tokens'. There are tokens travelling around the ring and a node has to have the use of a token before it can send data. The node waits for the token to reach it, captures the token and then sends its data. The token then passes around the ring, holding the data, until the correct destination is reached. The node that has been sent the data then downloads it, and releases the token so that it can continue passing around the ring waiting to be used again.

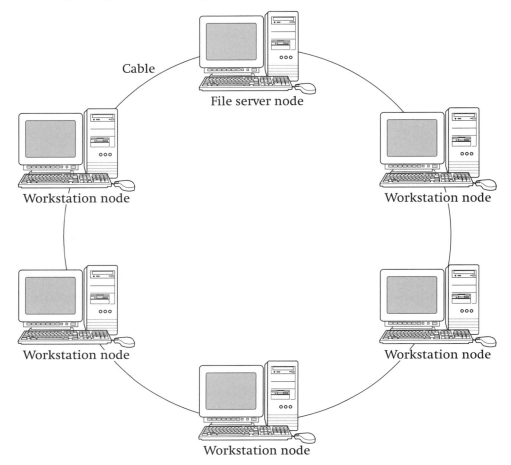

Figure 15.11 A ring topology

The main problem with a ring topology is that if one node has a problem then it affects the whole network. Another problem is that if nodes need to be added or removed, or new hardware or software put onto the network, then the whole network will be unusable while this is being done.

The main advantage with using a ring topology is that because all nodes have equal status and can use a token as it passes around the ring, there should not be any situation where one user is holding up the other users.

How do wireless links work?

Networks today do not have to be physically linked by cables. It is possible to set up a network using a wireless link through the following technologies:

- *Satellite communication* – this uses a two-way transmission beam via a satellite.
- *Infra-red communication* – this uses infra-red waves to transmit and receive data. Infra-red waves are longer than light waves but shorter than radio waves.

■ *Microwave communication* – this uses short-wavelength electromagnetic radio transmission, operating at high frequencies. It can be used only over very short distances, as both the 'sender' and 'receiver' components must be able to 'see' each other.

You will no doubt be aware of wireless technology, even if you do not know that this is what it is called. Mobile telephones use wireless technology.

One of the main problems with wireless technology is that the connection is not as fast at the moment as when using cabling. Also, wireless connections are not as reliable as cabled connections.

However, the use of wireless connection for LANs is becoming more popular. This is because a wireless connection is easier to install, as cables do not need to be laid. This can often make it a cheaper alternative for a network connection too.

An example of a LAN using wireless technology is when stock checks are being carried out in supermarkets. You may have seen people carrying portable devices with keypads. These are terminals that have a wireless link to a central computer. When they are out on the shop floor, the stock checkers can enter codes and numbers of products into the terminal and the information is then sent through to the central computer. Many supermarkets use this method to enable automatic stock orders to be made.

Further research – Standards of network protocols

There are several groups of people who are helping to set up protocols and standardise the use of wireless technology. These include Bluetooth, the Infrafred Data Association (IrDA) and HomeRf.

Research each of the above groups and prepare a short presentation for your class outlining how each is involved in wireless technology.

Check your understanding

Write a short report explaining the differences between cabled networks and wireless networks. Make sure you include clear indications of where the advantages and/or disadvantages are.

Selecting a suitable type of network

Selection factors are the things you have to take into account when deciding which network topology and which type of network (peer-to-peer or client–server) you are going to set up. We will now look at the factors that must be considered when making the decision on the topology and type of network required.

How many workstations will need to be connected?

If your organisation is likely to grow and you will need to add extra workstations to the network, this must be taken into account. This is called *future proofing*. Remember that some topologies are easier to add workstations to. Some topologies might mean that if too many workstations are connected, the data transmission rate will be too slow for efficient working.

Do you need (or want) one central computer to control the network?

If a hub node is going to be used, this will affect which network topology you choose.

What distance does the network system need to cover?

Is the network being set up in one room or over a wider distance? Some network topologies are feasible only for very short distances.

What is your budget for setting up the network?

Some types of network and some topologies are cheaper to set up than others.

How essential is it that your network system is never totally unusable?

If your organisation can cope with no one being able to access the network system for a while if problems arise, then you might decide on a set-up that uses a central control computer. If, however, it is vitally important that at least some staff can access the network system at any time, then it is likely you will take the option of setting up a system where there is less risk of the entire network failing.

What about maintenance and upkeep of the network system?

You will need to consider how easy it is to add or remove workstations. You will also need to consider how easy it will be to work on the actual cabling if something goes wrong – how easily can you get to the cable?

How important is it that your network system is secure?

Some types of networks and topologies are more secure than others. If it is important to your organisation that the system is secure then you will need to research this.

Test your knowledge

1   What hardware will be required to set up a basic LAN between two workstations?
2   What are the main differences between a bus topology and a right topology?
3   Apart from the use of cables, what other ways are there of networking computers?

Check your understanding

The comic book company has looked at your previous proposals, and have noticed that they forgot to tell you that, although there are only a few computers that require networking at present, they expect to expand rapidly over the next 18 months. Look again at your recommendations for their networking system and see whether this needs to be changed

Prepare a short presentation for the company to explain your decisions following the new information you have received. Explain why certain topologies are not recommended when a large number of workstations need to be connected, and new workstations need to be added on a regular basis.

15.3 Local area network conventions

Network software protocols

What are the protocols for network software use?

A protocol is a set of rules that determines how data is transmitted between computers. Groups of protocols usually work together for different types of networks. One of the main protocols used for LANs is called *Ethernet*. This uses a bus topology and what is known as 'carrier sense multiple action with collision detect', abbreviated to CSMA/CD, for its access method. We will look at this later in the unit.

What is the purpose of network software protocols?

Protocols have been produced to ensure as few errors during the transmission as possible by all networked data being managed in a common way. The protocol will tell the computers that are trying to communicate when to send and receive data. The protocol also needs to understand addresses so that it can direct the data to the correct destination.

Further research – Examples of the purpose of network software protocols

Look at the information given above concerning the purpose of network software protocols. Think about what could go wrong if the protocols were not followed. Research network software protocols to give you a better understanding if you cannot think of anything.

Prepare a brief scenario of how a business could be affected when sending data through a network that has not set up a correct protocol. One or two paragraphs are enough.

Network access methods

What are network access methods?

Network access methods are ways in which users can gain access to the network without interfering with other users on the network. The purpose of the chosen method is to stop nodes from attempting to gain access at the same time, thereby resulting in what is known as a 'collision'.

There are two main network access methods; token passing and CSMA/CD (carrier sense multiple access with collision detection).

What is a token ring network?

When we looked at ring topology, we mentioned the fact that usually a 'token' is used to carry the data around the network. To recap, a workstation must have use of a token in order to transmit any data. The token then carries on around the ring and stops at the correct destination for the data to be passed to another workstation or node.

What is CSMA?

CSMA is the abbreviation for 'carrier sense multiple access'. This is where devices attached to the network cable can 'listen' to sense if the network is busy. The network sends a certain sound, known as a 'carrier tone', when it is in use. Unlike the token ring access method, this means that users do not have to wait their turn for the token, but can transmit data across the network when they know the network is free.

What is collision detection?

Collision detection works in conjunction with CSMA. Because CSMA is a multiple access method, more than one node at a time might sense that the network is clear for use and try to send data at the same time. This causes a collision of data on the network. When this happens, the nodes stop trying to transmit the data and wait a random amount of time before trying again. By using collision detection with random times for trying to send data again, it prevents the network from failing completely.

However, if the network is constantly busy, then the collision detection aspect could slow the network down dramatically. Nodes could be randomly trying to send data for a long time after their initial attempt. Collision detection means that the nodes are no longer 'listening' to see when the network is free, but repeatedly and randomly trying to send their data.

Check your understanding

Produce a short report detailing the differences between the two network access methods discussed above. Include a diagram for each method to show how it works.

Test your knowledge

1 Why is it important to follow network protocols?
2 Explain how ARCNET works.
3 What are the advantages and disadvantages of using CSMA.CD?

15.4 Wide area network technology

Wide area network (WAN) technologies

A WAN is a network that is distributed over a large geographical area. The best known WAN is the Internet. WANs have to be connected in a different way to LANs because of the problems (or sometimes impossibilities) of connecting nodes through a simple cabling system.

We will start this section by looking at some of the wide area communication technologies that are available.

What is voice–band PSTN (public switched telephone network)?

Voice-band PSTN is a type of modem. It was one of the first modems and started to become available in the late 1950s. Voice-band modems work by transmitting data through the public telephone network, along the usual telephone communication line that a landline based telephone uses. There are advantages and disadvantages to using a voice-band PSTN connection.

One of the main advantages is that the telephone lines needed to connect the network are normally already available. If you think about standalone home PCs, many of these are connected to the Internet. Whilst some use newer technology, there are still many that use either an internal or external modem, connected to an ordinary telephone line, which in turn will dial a number for an Internet connection to enable access to the Internet. For this reason, it is often a cheap way of setting up a WAN.

One of the main disadvantages, however, is that the ordinary telephone line is what is know as an 'analogue' transmitter. We will look at the difference between analogue and digital signals a bit later on, but what this basically means is that the data being transmitted has to go through two conversions in its format to get from one computer to another. This means that the transmission rate is often very slow in comparison with other connection methods.

What are leased lines?

A leased line is a permanent or switched connection which links a user's computer to a service-provider WAN. The line is usually leased on the basis of how often and for how long the user connects to the WAN. Users will normally pay a monthly or annual fee for the use of the line, and will probably pay extra each time they connect to the WAN.

An example of a switched-connection leased line is the situation we looked at in the above section where an ordinary telephone line is used to connect. By using an adaptor, you can connect both a telephone and a modem to the same line. When you want to use the Internet, the modem will connect to the telephone line, and when the modem is not connected the line can be used for the telephone.

The main disadvantage of this is that you cannot use both the telephone and the modem at the same time. So, if you are on the Internet for long periods of time, people will not be able to reach you on that telephone number. You can buy gadgets nowadays that will let you know if someone is trying to telephone you when you have your modem connected, so that you can still take your telephone calls without having to pay for an extra line to be installed.

What are dedicated lines?

Dedicated lines are those where a permanent connection to a WAN is set up. They are usually still leased lines – the user pays to be able to use the dedicated line.

The biggest advantage of using a dedicated line is that it is much quicker than using a switched line. Your telephone will never be engaged just because you are using the Internet.

How does satellite communication technology work?

With satellite communication technology, satellites in the Earth's orbit receive and retransmit data that has been sent from a device on Earth. The signal being transmitted is known as an 'uplink'. Once the satellite has read the destination address, the signal can be sent back down to the correct location on Earth. This retransmission of the data is known as the 'downlink'.

Because the satellite is above the Earth, the transmission can be made over many thousands of miles, as there is always a line of sight between the sender and receiver.

The main disadvantage of using satellite communications is that, because the data has to travel to the satellite and then back again, the connection is not always reliable and there is normally a visible time delay.

How does microwave technology work?

Microwave transmissions use a short-wavelength signal, an electromagnetic radio transmission that operates at a high frequency.

One problem with using microwave technology for networking is that data can be sent only over fairly small distances, up to about 50 kilometres. This is because the nodes require line of sight to be able to transmit to each other, and the Earth's curvature can affect the line of sight.

How does cellular radio technology work?

Cellular radio transmission works through a dedicated radio channel being allocated to a single transmission. Whilst this is an efficient way of transmitting lengthy and continuous data, it can prove a waste of the dedicated bandwidth. Once a bandwidth has been allocated for a transmission, if the transmission is sent in bursts of data, then the bandwidth will remain unused during those times.

What is the difference between a digital line and an analogue line?

Digital and analogue are two different types of transmission system. Data cannot be sent directly between them unless an analogue-to-digital converter is used.

Analogue signals are a continuously varying set of electromagnetic waves. An example of an analogue signal would be the voice data sent along a telephone landline.

Digital signals are discrete voltage pulses, measured in bits per second. An example of a digital signal would be the data sent into a television via a digital cable.

Computers cannot deal with analogue signals, and some types of cabling cannot deal with digital signals. For this reason, when a node is transmitting data via an analogue line, it is converted from digital to analogue before travelling along that line. However, the user at the other end of the network would not be able to read the analogue signal, so the analogue has to be converted back to digital again before entering the computer system.

You can see why digital technology is quicker and more reliable than analogue technology. This is why digital technology is one of the fastest growing areas within the communication sector.

What is a modem and how does it work?

When using analogue transmission, a process known as 'modulation' carries out the conversion process. In order to do this, a modem is involved in the process.

The word 'modem' is made up from the two processes involved in this conversion: modulator and demodulator. When the digital signal is leaving the computer, the conversion into analogue is known as the *modulation process*. When the analogue signal is being converted back into a digital signal, the process is known as *demodulation*.

Modems can process asynchronous and synchronous transmissions.

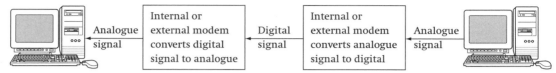

Figure. **15.12** How data is sent between computers using modems

With asynchronous transmissions, the data is sent at irregular intervals. So that the receiver knows when a transmission starts and stops, asynchronous transmission uses what are referred to as 'start bits' and 'stop bits'. These extra bits are added to the beginning and end of the data being transmitted.

With synchronous transmissions, the computer sending the data and the computer receiving the data can keep up with each other during the transmission. The data transmission is one continuous flow of data, with no irregularities. This is a quicker and more reliable method of transmission than using asynchronous transmission.

What are broadband technologies?

Broadband is the wider name given to any communication method that has a faster transmission rate than that of the fastest telephone line.

Broadband is becoming more popular as a network connection as it usually provides a permanent connection. Most broadband technologies work through a digital signal, so it is also a fast way of connecting to a network as no conversion of data is required. Broadband technologies are capable of using a wider bandwidth than other connection technologies.

The most commonly available broadband technologies are:

- *ADSL (asymmetric digital subscriber line)* – this is a high-bandwidth digital service that is normally offered by telephone companies, although some ISPs (Internet Service Providers) can supply an ADSL. Depending on the service provided, these can supply an extremely high transmission rate.
- *ISDN (integrated services digital network)* – this is a digital connection that can be set up using existing copper telephone cables. Until the introduction of ADSL, ISDN was one of the most advanced communication technologies to be introduced recently. ISDN has a lower transmission rate than ADSL.
- *Fibre optic cables* – these are cables consisting of glass or plastic fibres. They carry a digital signal and can have a very high transmission rate. They are also one of the most secure ways of networking. Fibre optic cables do not give off any electromagnetic radiation, so remote sensing equipment cannot detect them.

Check your understanding

In groups, prepare a short presentation to give to the class, showing the differences between using a modem to connect to a network and using broadband technologies to connect to a network. Include diagrams where appropriate, for example of the different types of cabling used in broadband technologies.

Issues concerning WAN technology

When considering using WAN technology, there are many issues that need to be taken into account.

What are data rates?

Data rates are the speed of transmission over the network. The data transfer rate is calculated on the basis of its transmission through a channel per second. In the section above, we have already looked at the advantages a broadband connection can give in relation to data rates.

Factors that determine data rates include:

- *Bandwidth* – this refers to the capacity that an information channel has, i.e. how much data can be carried at one time. Analogue transmissions are measured in cycles per second. Digital transmissions are measured in bits per second.
- *Delays* – these can affect the speed of a system. Delays are caused by a variety of factors. Some of the most common causes of delays are:
  - o   the distance that the transmission has to travel
  - o   errors occurring during transmission and error recovery programs running to deal with errors
  - o   the amount of 'traffic' on a network, i.e. the *congestion factor*
  - o   the processing capabilities of the systems involved in the transmission.
- *Throughput* – this refers to the amount of work done by a system. In a network situation it means taking into account possible delays and then measuring system performance including delays.

What about security?

You have already covered the security aspects of networked systems in Unit 2. Also, refer back to the 'data security' information on page 282.

What dictates the speed of webpage loading?

The speed of webpage loading will depend on several factors. The main factor is the type of connection you are using. You have already seen how much quicker a digital broadband connection is than a telephone line/modem connection.

Another factor will be the speed of your CPU. If your processor is slow then the downloading of information will be slow. Also, the speed will depend on the amount of information being downloaded. If the file you are downloading is very large, then logically this will take longer than if you were downloading a small piece of information.

Software use with wide area network technology

WAN technology uses different software to that used on standalone computers or LANs.

What are Internet browsers?

You looked at browsers in Unit 2. As a reminder, an Internet browser is a package that displays pages that have been created in Web format. The two most common Internet browsers available are Microsoft® Internet Explorer and Netscape® Navigator.

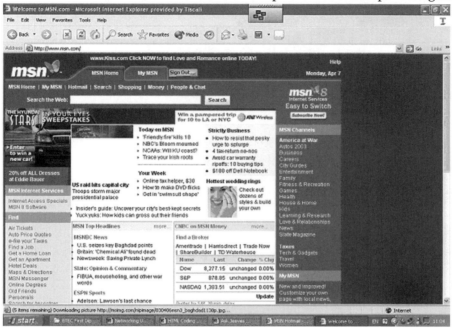

Figure 15.13 A Microsoft® Internet Explorer browser

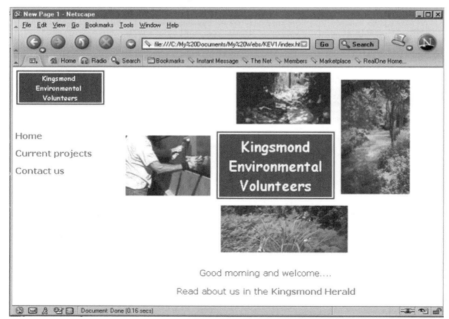

Netscape browser window © 2002 Netscape Communications Corporation. Used with permission.

Figure. 15.14 A Netscape® Navigator browser

Internet browsers run on **TCP/IP networks** and transfer **HTML coding** to a user-friendly front end. They are capable of presenting the information to the user in many formats apart from text, including animation, graphics and videos.

? What does it mean?

TCP/IP network – TCP/IP is an abbreviation for 'transmission control protocol/internet protocol'. This protocol dictates the way in which networked computers are named and addressed, how different networks can be connected together, and how messages are sent across a wide variety of networks that are linked together to make up the Internet. For example, not everything you see on the Internet is held on a main, centralised computer. Many people have developed websites in their homes and have 'uploaded' them onto the Internet. So, if you were to contact the developer of that website, you would contact them via the Internet but the message would be sub-routed to their computer.

? What does it mean?

HTML coding – HTML is an abbreviation for Hypertext Mark-up Language. This is the coding that is used to create webpages. It is a standard programming language that the browser will be able to easily convert into the front-end pages that you look at. From any webpage on the Internet, you can look at the HTML coding behind it by selecting 'View' on the toolbar and then 'Source'.

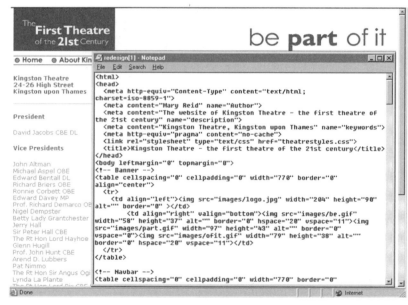

Figure 15.15 HTML coding

What is a WWW site?

WWW is an abbreviation for World Wide Web. The terms 'Internet' and 'World Wide Web' have become interchangeable, but they are actually different. The Internet is the collection of networks worldwide. The WWW is the viewable resources held on those networks. Without the WWW the Internet would be a collection of text-only documents. It is the WWW that allows you to view the webpages as a mixture of text, graphics, animation and videos.

What is a WAP site?

WAP is an abbreviation for 'wireless application protocol'. A WAP site is one that is accessible without a physical cable connection to a network, for example through a digital mobile telephone.

WAP sites are accessed using a WAP browser, and instead of using HTML to code the information held on the site, another language called 'wireless mark-up language' (WML) is used.

For example, if you asked for the balance of your bank account (which is £100) to be sent to your mobile phone by text message, the coding for the message would read:

```
<P>Your balance is £<wml:getvarname="X"/>.</p>
```

This would be displayed on your mobile phone screen as: Your balance is £100.00

What is the difference between WWW sites and WAP sites?

WAP sites are much more limited in the information and functions that can be accessed compared with WWW sites. There is currently a new technology about to be launched at the time of writing for WAP sites that will enable videos to run on mobile telephones, and the technology to combine a digital camera and recorded sound is already on the market. However, the technology for WAP sites is still in its early stages and is far from perfect. It will be some time, if ever, before we can have the same access via WAP technology as we can via cabled access.

How do you choose your Internet browser?

The choice of Internet browser can often be dictated by the computer and network you are accessing the Internet from. It used to be the case not long ago that the two main browsers available were not compatible. This meant that sites that had been developed for, say, viewing with Microsoft® Internet Explorer could not be viewed properly with Netscape® Navigator. The compatibility aspect has improved recently and there is now a standard way of developing websites that can be fully viewed and accessed whichever browser you are running the Internet on.

If you have a free choice of which browser to choose, you need to look at the functions and features available on each. Some features are available, whichever web browser you are using. These include:

- *Plug-ins and Helper Applications* – these are programs that can be downloaded so that different kinds of content can be displayed or played. For example, RealPlayer by RealNetworks will enable you to play music and videos in what is known as RealTime or RealMedia formats.
- *Storing or bookmarking favourite webpages* – once you have found a webpage you like and would like to go back to regularly, you can store it in 'Favourites' on Microsoft® Internet Explorer, or 'Bookmarks' in Netscape® Navigator.

- *History lists* – this is a feature that will keep a record of all sites you have visited over a given period. It does not save the site itself but saves the address so it is easy to access another time.
- *Back and forward buttons* – these are available on the toolbar of all browsers and enable you to move quickly from one page to another that you have already visited during that browsing session.
- *Searching* – all browsers have the capability of allowing you to search the Internet for specific information.

These are just a few of the common functions and features available. You will need to research to find others that are common, and also to see any that are available in one browser but not in another.

What is e-mail and how does it work?

E-mail is an abbreviation for 'electronic mail' and is available through an e-mail client, as you saw in Unit 2. It is used for sending messages from one user to another via electronic communications. On a computer, file attachments can be added of any format, e.g. you can attach a simple document or a complex jpeg graphic.

When the message has been typed, the sender has to give the computer the **e-mail address** of where the message is being sent. The message is then processed through your network connection telephone line or cabling, passing through different servers until it reaches its destination. It is placed into the 'inbox' of the person it has been sent to, and that person can access the message next time he or she logs on.

What does it mean?

E-mail address – an e-mail address is a string of data that identifies a user. It will enable the user to receive e-mail. For example, hp123@bod.co.uk would be an e-mail address if the ISP you had your e-mail account with was called 'Bod'.

Most e-mail packages have several functions available as standard. For instance, there is usually a 'reply' button, whereby you can simply click on this and the e-mail address you want to send the message to is automatically notified to your computer.

What software is required to use e-mail facilities?

To be able to use e-mail facilities, you will normally need an e-mail client software package. If your computer has a browser loaded, this will normally mean that you already have an e-mail package. Microsoft® Internet Explorer uses an e-mail client called 'Outlook Express'; Netscape Navigator uses an e-mail client called 'Netscape Messenger'. There are other e-mail clients available, and they will usually work with the most common browser software.

Further research – Choosing an e-mail client

Research commonly available e-mail packages. Try to find three different ones.

What differences are there between the e-mail packages? Do they all offer the same facilities?

What is FTP?

FTP is an abbreviation for 'file transfer protocol', which uses TCP/IP. This enables you to download information onto your computer from other computers that are within the same network. The most common use of FTP is in loading webpages onto a server so that they are accessible over the Internet.

What software do you need to connect to FTP sites?

You will need an FTP client to enable you to connect to FTP sites, such as CuteFTP. There are many FTP clients available, some of which can be downloaded free from Internet sites. A quick search on the Internet for FTP clients will show you what else is available.

How does downloading from FTP sites work?

To download from an FTP site, TCP/IP is used. When you start up your FTP client and connect with an FTP server, a connection is opened between your computer and the computer that you are accessing. This connection remains open until you give the 'close' command. There is another connection that is open when you request a file transfer, but this one will automatically close when the file's data has finished being transferred. For each file that you transfer, a different connection is opened. So, if you request more than one file to be transferred, there could be more than two connections open at one time between your computer and the computer you are accessing.

What are virus checkers and how do they work?

You have already looked briefly at virus checkers in Unit 2. As a reminder, a virus checker (also known as virus protection software) can be installed on your computer to check for incoming viruses. This will make sure that the data on your computer does not get corrupted.

Virus checkers work by scanning incoming data and comparing it with information that the virus checker has stored about all known viruses. It will be able to tell whether data has been infected. It will then let you know if it detects a virus, so that you can choose what to do, i.e. not accept the data into your system.

What software do you need to check for viruses?

You will need to install a virus protection program, such as Symantec™ Norton Antivirus. This can then be programmed not only to check incoming data, but also to scan your hard disk each time the computer is booted. You must remember that new viruses are being created all the time, so it is essential to update your virus protection software regularly. Most virus protection programs have the facility to automatically download updates direct from the Internet as soon as they are created.

What is a firewall and how does it work?

A firewall is another type of security system, and is used primarily to protect networks from external threats. This means that if someone tries to hack into your network system from outside your organisation, a firewall will detect this and, hopefully, prevent it from happening. Firewalls are usually a combination of a piece of hardware and some software to monitor and manage the firewall.

Firewalls work by putting an invisible wall between your network file server and the actual external network. When someone tries to connect to your network server, the firewall will check to see whether the person is authorised to access the network. Any attempts at connection that the firewall does not recognise as being from an authorised user are just ignored and thrown off the system.

All communications in and out of the network system are checked by the firewall. This means that if you are trying to connect to a network that the organisation does not want you to visit from their network, this can also be blocked. Users within the organisation will usually receive a message telling them that they are not going to be allowed to access this site.

On another level, firewalls can be programmed to block only part of an access or retrieval process. A good example of this is that a lot of organisations will let people access most websites, but will block the network system from letting '**cookies**' into the system.

Firewalls are a good way of organisations easily keeping control of what is coming into and going out of their network system.

What does it mean?

Cookie – a cookie is a small file that will remember whether you have visited a site before from the same computer. It will store personal information so that you do not have to keep putting the information in every time you visit the same site.

What software is required to have a firewall on your system?

You will need a firewall software package and you might need some firewall hardware in order to have a firewall on your system. There are two main types of firewall:

- *Network-level firewalls* – these are usually built into a router and can be used to check:
  - o content of incoming/outgoing data
  - o whether or not the correct protocols are being used for data transfer
  - o which port number is being used to transfer data and whether it is the correct one
  - o what the address is of the sender of the information.

- *Application-proxy firewalls* – these act as a proxy for the connection, translating the data before allowing it into or out of the network system, rather than just running a standard set of checks.

Check your understanding

Look at the common features and functions listed on pages 303 and 304 that are available through browser software. Research other features and functions that are available for the Microsoft® Internet Explorer and Netscape® Navigator browser software. Produce a table showing what is available for each, and give a brief explanation of what the feature or function provides for the user.

Test your knowledge

1 How does voice-band PSTN differ from leased lines with regard to connection to a network?

2 What is the difference between analogue and digital lines? Which one can be used to send data through a network connection?

3 What factors need to be considered when choosing a browser?

Assessment tasks

This section describes what you must do to obtain a Merit grade for this unit.

A Distinction grade may be awarded if your work demonstrates a deeper understanding of the topics and is of a higher quality. The highlighted sentences indicate the quality of work expected at Distinction level.

How do I provide assessment evidence?

Your evidence will either be all in the form of a written report, or may be a mixture of the following:

- written reports
- answers to set questions
- material used in a presentation.

All your evidence should be presented in one folder, which should have a front cover and contents page. You should divide the evidence into four sections corresponding to the learning outcomes.

Scenario for assessment tasks

A small marketing company has decided that it needs to network the computers in their offices. The company has 35 people working for them, most of whom need access to information that could be held on the network. This information is currently held on each standalone computer. Factors they have already considered are:

- They are going to employ a Network Manager and one Network Administrator.
- They do not want to spend a lot of money on setting up their network system.
- They are willing to purchase a central controlling computer if this is felt necessary.
- The company holds personal information on members of the public, so security is important for them.
- Most of their work is done on the computers:
  - o customers are contacted by telephone, but the customer details are called up from a large database in order for the staff to do this
  - o mailshots are sent out on a regular basis to a mailing list held on a computer
  - o leaflets and questionnaires are designed in-house to be sent in mailshots
  - o the company administration tasks are performed on computer, e.g. the payroll details for all staff.

Task 1

Learning outcome 1 – Describe the application of networks in organisations

1 Explain how a networked system would aid the marketing company's internal and external communications. Use specific examples to demonstrate your understanding.

2   Explain how a networked system can help manage information and resources for the marketing company. Use specific examples to demonstrate your understanding.

3   Explain the role of the Network Manager and the Network Administrator in the marketing company once the network system has been installed.

To obtain a Distinction grade, you should critically evaluate the way in which the application of networks in organisations could help the marketing company rather than just explaining things to them. The use of examples and justifications in how company's resources should be managed should also be included.

Task 2

Learning outcome 2 – Understand basic local area network (LAN) technology

1   Look at the marketing company's requirements. Prepare some questions for an interview with the marketing company to investigate any needs that have not been covered in the scenario. Remember to think carefully about the future requirements, the level of maintenance and upkeep that might be required, and ask questions relating directly to setting up a network system.

2   Ask either your lecturer, another person in your class or someone who is knowledgeable about network systems to answer the questions you have prepared. Following the responses you get, write a report giving a recommendation for the type of network you think will be required. Compare your recommendation with other types of network systems to highlight to the marketing company the reasons for your choice. Include in the report the following considerations:

   ▪ the topology that would best suit the marketing company's network setup

   ▪ security requirements.

3   Produce your report in a presentation format, with diagrams, to present your recommendations to the marketing company.

To obtain a Distinction grade, you should include in your report an analysis of all the ways LANs are organised, accessed and operated. Your comparison with other types of network systems and topologies should be in-depth to show your understanding of the differences.

Task 3

Learning outcome 3 – Understand basic local area network conventions

The marketing company has some further questions that you need to answer and explain to them.

   ▪ They are aware that certain protocols should be followed but have not looked at the different protocols or thought about how and why they should be followed.

   ▪ They are aware that there are different access methods, but do not understand what this means, or what choices are available.

1   Write a short report explaining what network software protocols are, what their purpose is, and the advantages and disadvantages for using them.

2   Explain what is meant by the following terms:
   - ■ token ring network
   - ■ CSMA/CD.

To obtain a Distinction grade, your report (1) must show that you have carried out further research into network software protocols and refer to other protocols, as well as Ethernet. Your explanation for part (2) should show that you have also researched other access methods, e.g. ARCNET.

Task 4

Learning outcome 4 – Examine the uses of wide area networking (WAN) technology

The marketing company is thinking of opening offices in other areas of the country, and maybe even in different countries. They would like to know about wide area networking technology so that this can be considered in their final decision of how to set up their network system.

1   Compare the different technologies available for connection of WANs. Produce a table to show the following:
   - ■ list the different technologies currently available
   - ■ give a basic explanation of how each technology works
   - ■ state any advantages or disadvantages of using each technology.

2   Prepare a presentation for the marketing company, including diagrams where relevant, to look at the issues concerning WAN technology. You must include at least one issue under each of the following headings:
   - ■ data rates
   - ■ security
   - ■ browser selection, e.g. different features and functions that may be required
   - ■ software that may have to be bought.

To obtain a Distinction grade, you must give a recommendation to the marketing company of a connection method for (1) and have directly related the issues in (2) to the given scenario.

UNIT 8: BUSINESS APPLICATIONS

Success in this unit

What are the learning outcomes?

To achieve this unit you must:

- describe the importance of business software applications
- use different document styles and layouts
- produce and print a range of business documentation
- deliver a presentation to an appropriate audience.

How is this unit assessed?

This unit is internally assessed. You must provide evidence in the form of a variety of documents that show that you meet the learning outcomes.

How do I provide assessment evidence?

Your evidence will include:

- printed documents
- evidence of a short presentation that you have given.

All your evidence should be presented in one folder, which should have a front cover and a contents page. The section headed *Assessment tasks* at the end of this unit gives you more detailed advice about how to prepare for the assessment.

Introduction

About this unit

This unit is an opportunity for you to gain new skills with standard office software, and to learn how they are used in business contexts.

You should have already acquired basic skills and will have been revising and practising them in Unit 2. As Unit 8 is a specialist unit you are expected to extend your skills considerably, and to learn new techniques.

Standard software packages offer a very wide range of facilities, and we will be looking at some of them in this unit. It is said that most users use no more than 10 per cent of the facilities in their software. So it is a good idea to explore the applications that you use and see what you are missing.

8.1 The importance of business software applications

The function of business applications

Why are software applications used in industry and commerce?

Before desktop computers became widely available, office technology was limited to phones, typewriters, calculators and some specialist printing machines. ICT has transformed the way businesses carry out their day-to-day operations. It has also altered the job opportunities and career paths for most employees. Today almost all employees in business have to have IT skills.

ICT hardware and software is expensive, but businesses have invested heavily in them because they make them more efficient; in other words, they cannot only make enough profit to cover the cost of the investment, but can do even better than that and generate extra profit.

Today businesses also use business applications because they would appear unprofessional to the general public if they did not do so. Customers do not place much confidence in a handwritten quote or invoice for a job, and a poorly produced letter is considered discourteous.

The types of business software applications

Both general and specialist software applications are used in business, and many of these were considered in Unit 2.

This unit concentrates on the common applications that are used in most offices. They include:

- *word processing* – used for letters, reports, simple publications, mail merge, labels, presentation of information
- *spreadsheets* – used for statistical tables and analysis, graphs and charts, financial records, financial forecasting, modelling engineering problems
- *database* – used for storing and retrieving records, reports, labels, creating rotas, target mailings
- *desktop publishing* – used for publications that require complex layouts and a combination of text and graphics
- *graphics* – used to create, manipulate and compress images (both drawings and photos)
- *presentation* – used to create presentation graphics
- *communications* – used to access and search the Internet and to create, send, receive, store and organise e-mails.

8.2 Document styles and layouts

Documents used in business

What kinds of documents are produced in business?

Very many types of documents are produced in business. Templates for many of these are given in relevant software packages. The following list is a limited selection.

- *Report* – a report is any document that is written to explain a project, provide facts or generally convey information. Internal reports will be used by managers to help them make decisions. Companies may also have to produce reports, such as an Annual Report, for the general public. Reports are usually written in a formal structured style, with heavy use of headings, subheadings and numbered points.
- *Memo* – a memo is a short note to someone else in the same organisation. It can be hand-written, sent by e-mail, or printed out and delivered by hand. Memos are usually informal in style.
- *Letter* – a letter is a form of correspondence from an organisation to an external client or other contact (the recipient).
- *Invoice* – an invoice is a bill sent to a customer after the goods have been delivered. When you buy something in a shop you will normally pay for it on the spot, and when you order something from a mail order company you are usually expected to pay for the goods before you receive them. If a business orders supplies, such as stationary, the supplier will deliver the goods, then send an invoice, which should be paid within a month. An invoice should have a business heading.
- *Notice* – a notice will be displayed on notice boards around the organisation, or can be used as a form of external publicity. The company logo and contact details should always appear somewhere on the notice.
- *Article* – an article may be written for the staff newsletter, or for a national or local newspaper. In style, an article falls between a report and an essay. It will have a heading and one level of subheadings.
- *Graph* – a graph or chart can be printed out as a single document or it can be embedded

into a word-processed document. In either case it must have a heading and be properly labelled.

■ *Graphical image* – an image can be used to illustrate text, can be used in a logo or can be used as decoration. Either bitmapped or vector images can be used. Be very careful about the use of images in business documents, especially as decoration, as they can look amateurish. Always ask yourself whether the image is necessary and whether it adds to the meaning.

■ *E-mail message* – an e-mail is normally treated as an informal form of communication so is more like a memo than a letter, but in business it is still important to write clearly, and you should avoid the use of the abbreviations used in text messaging.

■ *Webpage* – information can be retrieved from webpages, either by copying the text or printing out a complete page. Printing can sometimes cause problems as the page width may be fixed so that the page cannot fit on to A4 paper. Use Print Preview (in the File menu) to check what the page will look like, and if necessary, change the paper orientation to Landscape.

■ *Database report* – information can be retrieved from a database and then printed out as a report. Database software allows you to format a report. For more information, see Unit 7.

■ *Directory* – most organisations produce their own internal directories, which will list the names, rooms, phone extensions and e-mail addresses of all employees. The data can be set up in a database and the list printed out as a report.

Check your understanding – Writing business letters

Business letters normally have a standard structure and should include:

■ Business heading – this could be pre-printed on the stationary or included in a letter template. This will include the name, address, phone and fax numbers, e-mail address, etc. of the organisation. It will probably also have a company logo.

■ Address of the recipient – this is often placed on the left side of the page below the heading.

■ Date letter was written – this can be placed on either side depending on the design of the business heading.

■ The salutation – normally 'Dear Mr Jones', or if the name is not known, then 'Dear Sir or Madam' may be used.

■ The text of the letter, written in clear English. Do not be tempted to use a very formal, old fashioned style of language, as today it is considered pompous.

■ The ending – normally 'Yours sincerely', although 'Yours faithfully' is used with 'Dear Sir or Madam'.

■ Signature of the sender.

■ The printed name of the sender.

■ A copy list – this is a list of anyone else who is being sent a copy of the letter, and is written 'Cc: Jane Davies, Gerry Smith' at the bottom of the letter.

Find some examples of business letters and check them against this list.

How are multi-page documents produced?

Reports are often longer than one page. Some information, such as page number, author and the date it was written, should appear on almost every page and the headers and footers can be used for this purpose.

A title page may be required, although some reports simply have a heading on the first page instead.

Sections of the document may be numbered 1, 2, 3, etc. Then subsections within each section can be numbered 1.1, 1.2, 1.3, etc. A contents list should give the page numbers of each section, and possibly each subsection as well.

The first version of a long document is known as a *draft*. This should be printed out and checked, and corrections should be made. An important document may go through several drafts before it is ready for the final printing.

Further research –Collecting business documents

Try to find an example of each of the documents listed in this section.

Style of documents

Should I use a style list?

In Unit 1 you saw how you can create your own text styles and save them in the style list. You should create styles for every business document that you create.

Should I create templates?

Templates and wizards were also discussed in Unit 1. You should certainly set up templates for any business documents that are likely to be used more than once. For example, headed stationery should be set up in a template.

Check your understanding – Exploring templates in Microsoft® Word

1. Use a template

■ Create a new Microsoft® Word document.

■ The template dialogue will open and you will be able to choose from a number of templates. Some of these can be selected by clicking on the tabs. The choice available to you will depend on how the software has been installed.

Figure 8.1 A selection of templates and wizards in Microsoft® Word

■ Try out some of these templates. Each one has a pre-set page size and page layout, and font styles have been created in the Style list.

In the General tab, the Blank Document is also a template, which usually has an A4 page layout and some basic styles.

2. Create a template

- Select **New** from the **File** menu, and select an existing template.
- Set up the page layout and create styles to add to the style list. If you need a header or footer then add these. If you need a letterhead then create this. Remember that any text on the page will be saved in the template.
- Select **Save As** from the **File** menu, and in the Save As Type box choose **Document Template**. All Microsoft® Word templates have the file extension .dot. Your template will be saved with the other templates.

What is corporate style?

Many organisations use a logo on all their printed materials. Their documents will also often have a very specific style. This will be achieved by always using the same fonts, font sizes, text and page colours and page layout. This is known as the *corporate style* of the organisation.

The managers in an organisation will probably produce some templates that match the rules of the corporate style. All employees will be expected to produce documents using the templates, or that conform to the same style.

Electronic 'documents' such as webpages and presentation slides should also be produced in the corporate style.

Further research – Corporate style

Collect examples of several printed documents that are produced by the same organisation. Can you work out what the corporate style is?

Collect and analyse documents for two other organisations. Compare the documents of the three organisations. Are the corporate styles applied consistently? Which corporate style is the most effective?

Have the organisations used the corporate style in their websites?

Facilities within software applications

This section should introduce you to some new skills, and get you to think about the software packages that you use in a new way.

Many packages offer very similar facilities so if you can do something in one package it is worthwhile seeing whether you can do the same in another. This similarity is most noticeable if you use software applications that are produced by the same company.

The examples in this unit all come from commonly used Microsoft® products – Word, Excel, Access, Publisher, PowerPoint, Paint and Outlook Express. You should be able to find similar functions in other packages.

How can I edit text?

You will already be very familiar with using word processing software to create and edit text. You should know how to copy, cut, paste, delete and move text around.

In many packages text is created within a textbox, which can then be positioned anywhere on the document. Here are some examples:

■ In Microsoft® Publisher, click on the Textbox button 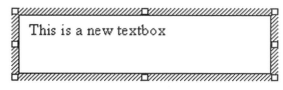 then draw a textbox (also known as a text frame) anywhere on the document. You will notice that a text toolbar appears, which gives all the usual font options. Start typing your text in the box. You can apply all the usual text formats to the text in the textbox.

■ You can also create a textbox in Microsoft® Word or PowerPoint. In the **Insert** menu, select **Textbox**. Drag out the shape of the box on the document, then enter your text.

> This is a new textbox

Figure 8.2 A textbox in Microsoft® Word

You can change the appearance of the textbox by right-clicking on it and selecting **Format Textbox**.

■ Textboxes can also be created on a form in Microsoft® Access, where they are known as *labels*. See Unit 7 for more details on how to do this.

■ Charts and graphs can be produced in Microsoft® Excel, and these need to have clear labels on the axes. A legend identifies what each colour represents on the chart. Labels and legends are special types of textboxes, and you can read more about them in the later section on charts and graphs.

The advantage of using a textbox is that it can be moved around the document. You can normally do this by moving the mouse to the edge of the textbox until the Move pointer appears, then dragging it to its new position.

A textbox can also be resized by dragging on any of the handles around the edge of the box. A textbox does not automatically get larger when it is full, so you need to enlarge it to display all your text.

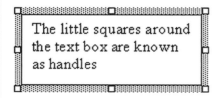

> The little squares around the text box are known as handles

Figure 8.3 Handles on a text box

How can I edit images?

All bitmapped and vector graphics packages allow you to edit an image. Each package offers its own choice of functions that can be applied to an image. You might like to explore several different packages to see what they offer.

■ *Copying and pasting* – when you create an image in Microsoft® Paint, you can copy or cut areas of the picture. First select an area using one of the selection tools ⬚⬚, then copy or cut it in the usual way. The selected area can then be pasted onto the same document, and can be moved around to a new position.

With all bitmapped graphics packages, once a selection has been placed it merges into the rest of the image and cannot be picked up again.

Vector graphics store each line or other element on the page as a separate item, so each can be copied and pasted individually within the drawing area.

■ *Cropping* – when you crop a bitmapped image you cut off the parts that you do not need, often using a selection tool. This is sometimes known as 'trimming'. In Microsoft® Paint you simply drag on one of the handles at the edge of the image to crop it. In some packages you use the selection tool to outline the area that you want to keep, then select **Crop** from a menu.

You cannot crop a vector graphic.

■ *Resizing* – an image can be resized without cropping any part of it. This is also known as 'stretching', although you can 'stretch' an image by making it smaller as well as larger. In Microsoft® Paint you should select **Image**, then **Stretch/Skew**. Change the percentages in the Stretch boxes – the figures should normally be the same. For example, if you enter 50 per cent for both horizontal and vertical, the image will be halved in size along each edge. You can stretch or squash the image in one direction by entering different horizontal and vertical percentages.

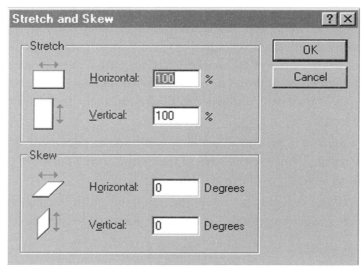

Figure 8.4 The resizing dialogue box in Microsoft® Paint

When you click on an object in a vector image, handles appear at each corner and along each edge. The object can be stretched by dragging on the handles. To keep the shape in proportion, try holding down the **Shift** key whilst dragging on a corner handle.

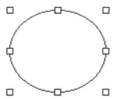

Figure 8.5 The corner and edge handles on a vector object

A whole vector image can also be resized in the drawing tool in Microsoft® Word by clicking once on the image and then dragging on one of its handles.

■ *Rotating* – sometimes you want to rotate an image, or part of an image. In Microsoft® Paint you are limited to rotations of 90°, 180° or 270°, and angles are measured anticlockwise. You can rotate the whole image or you can outline an area with one of the selection tools. Use **Image**, then **Flip/Rotate**.

The objects in a vector image created in the Drawing tool can be rotated by any angle you choose. You will find the **Rotate** or **Flip** option in the **Draw** menu at the left end of the Drawing toolbar.

Check your understanding – Calculating the storage requirements for bitmap images

A bitmap image 800 pixels by 600 pixels consists of 480,000 pixels – nearly half a million. Each pixel needs one, two or three bytes of storage depending on the quality of colour needed.

Number of bytes per pixel	Storage space needed for a 800x600 image
1 (8 bits)	480,000 bytes = 480Kb
2 (16 bits)	960,000 bytes = 960Kb
3 (24 bits)	1,440,000 bytes = 1,440Kb = 1.44Mb

Figure 8.6 Storage requirements for images

Can you calculate the storage requirements for each of these images?

1   a photograph, 1,000 by 1,500 pixels, using 24-bit colour
2   an icon drawn with 8-bit colour and only 15 pixels square.

How can I add interest to a document?

You can improve the appearance of any document by adding bullets, lines, borders and shading, but do not overdo them. The careful use of one or two features can make a document look professional, whereas a jumble of unrelated additions can look messy and amateurish.

Depending on the software used, bullets, lines, borders and shading can be added to a highlighted selection of text, to a textbox, or to a cell (or set of cells) in a table or spreadsheet. You first select or highlight the item, then choose the feature you want.

■ *Bullet points* – the square at the beginning of this paragraph is a bullet point. It is used to separate the paragraphs and to draw attention to them. Bullet points are found in many documents and are widely used in Microsoft® PowerPoint presentations.

In Microsoft® Word, Publisher or PowerPoint, highlight the text then click on the **Bullets** icon ⬚. A new bullet point is created every time you have used the Enter key.

You can choose a different image for the actual bullet, by selecting **Format**, then **Bullets and Numbering** in Microsoft® Word or PowerPoint, or by simply selecting from the options when you click on the **Bullets** icon in Microsoft® Publisher.

■ *Shading and patterns* – in Microsoft® Word select **Format** from the main menu, then **Borders and Shading**, then select the **Shading** tab and start experimenting! In Microsoft® Excel select **Format**, then **Cell**, and then select the **Patterns** tab.

You can see that the Format menu normally offers you shading options for plain text. Textboxes can also be decorated in a number of ways by using the buttons on the Drawing toolbar in Microsoft® Word, Excel and PowerPoint. In Microsoft® Publisher, select **Format**, then **Fill** or **Fill Patterns and Shading**.

Graphics packages usually provide a Fill button, which can be used to fill a selected area or shape with a colour or pattern.

- *Lines* – straight and freeform lines can be drawn on most text documents and images. In Microsoft® Word, Excel and PowerPoint you can use the line tool from the Drawing toolbar. Microsoft® Paint and Publisher also have line tools in their toolboxes.

- *Borders* – a border can be placed around a selected section of text, a cell or a textbox. Again for simple text or cells use the Format menu in Microsoft® Word and Excel, and for textboxes use the Drawing toolbar in Microsoft® Word, Excel and PowerPoint or the Format menu in Microsoft® Publisher. Most packages allow you to choose the style, colour and thickness of the border.

- *Backgrounds* – a complete document can be given a suitable coloured or patterned background in Microsoft® Word and PowerPoint. Just select **Format**, then **Background**.

How can I find and handle data?

Large amounts of data are stored in company databases, and even more can be found on the Internet, but the right information has to be extracted, by sifting and sorting it from the data. It must then be presented in a way that makes it meaningful to the user.

- *Retrieving data* – you retrieve data from the Internet when you successfully download the information that you need. There are a number of tools that can help you to find the right information, the most common being **search engines**.

?

What does it mean?

Search engine – a search engine is a software tool that can be used to find pages on the Internet. Search engines track millions of webpages and create an index, based on the text appearing on the pages, or on the keywords provided by the Web designer. The user enters search terms (one or more words) and the search engine then finds and lists relevant websites. Well-known search engines include Google and Yahoo!

- *Searching for information* – sometimes you need to search for information within a specific document. For example, to find where a phrase appears within a Microsoft® Word document, select **Edit**, then **Find**, then key in the words.
  Databases are designed to make the process of searching very easy. Most databases will offer a Find button, or more complex search facilities on the user interface. These can be used to select one or more records which meet specific search criteria. For example, a shop manager may be able to search a database of stock held in the shop to find out which items are low so that he or she can re-order from the suppliers.

- *Sorting data* – some software applications allow you to sort data into alphabetical or numerical order. Databases and spreadsheets always offer you this option.

How do I merge documents?

Two documents are merged when they are joined together to form one document. There are several ways of doing this and we will just touch on three methods.

- *Inserting a file* – if you are working in a word processing or desktop publishing file you can often bring in a different type of file and make it part of your current file. This is sometimes known as *importing* a file.

Desktop publishing packages usually allow you to combine files from many different sources into one document. In Microsoft® Publisher, draw a textbox then select **Insert** from the main menu, then **Text File**. You will then be able to search for a file created in a word processing package and drop the contents into the box.

You can also insert picture files. In Microsoft® Publisher select **Insert**, then **Picture**. You can then find an image file – which can be a bitmapped or vector image – and place the image on the page. When you click on the image, handles will appear which will allow you to resize the image.

A similar facility is found in most other packages. In Microsoft® Word, Excel and PowerPoint, select **Insert** then **Picture**, then **From File**.

■ *Inserting an object* – once a picture is inserted into another file it becomes 'embedded' which means that it cannot be changed, except in size. But Microsoft® packages also allow you to insert a file along with the application that supports it. In Microsoft® Word, Excel, PowerPoint, Publisher or Access you can select **Object** from the **Insert** menu, then select **Bitmap Image**. A small window will appear on the page, surrounded by the familiar Paint tools. Use them to create an image in the window. When you click anywhere on the document outside the image the tools will disappear, but you can bring them back at any time by double-clicking on the image.

You will probably now realise that when you were creating a drawing using the Drawing tool in Microsoft® Word, you were also inserting an object.

■ *Mail merge* – you will probably have received a letter, addressed to you, but you will know that very similar letters will also have been sent to thousands of other people. These letters are generated by a process known as *mail merge*. The name and address data is held in a simple database, which is then merged with a standard letter document to produce thousands of personally addressed letters. The data can be stored in a database, in a spreadsheet, or in another document.

Check your understanding – Mail merge in Microsoft® Word

Mail merge allows you to create a simple database of records that can be used in conjunction with a main word processed document. Mail merging can be used for direct marketing mailings, club membership mailings, billing, etc.

You need a *main document* and a *data source* attached to it. A data source is another Microsoft® Word document that contains a simple flat file database. The steps are:

1 create a main document
2 create or identify a data source
3 merge the data with the main document to produce a set of printed documents.

In this activity you will be setting up a mail merge letter to the customers of a small business telling them about a new product.

1. Create the main document

■ Make a new document in the usual way and create a simple letter heading, with the name and address of the business with its logo. This is your main document for the mail merge. Save it as 'Letter'.

■ Select **Mail Merge** in the **Tools** menu to bring up the Mail Merge Helper dialogue window.

■ In Step 1, click on **Create**, select **Form Letters** and then click on **Active Window**.

- Click on Step 1, **Edit** to do more work on your main document.
- Start by including today's date by selecting **Date and Time** from the **Insert** menu. If you tick **Update Automatically**, the date will be updated each time the document is opened. Save again.
- The Mail Merge toolbar has appeared either immediately above the document or as a floating toolbar. Check what each button does by placing the pointer over each for a few seconds. You will be using **Insert Merge Field**, **View Merged Data**, the browse buttons and the **Mail Merge Helper** button.
- Click on the **Mail Merge Helper** button.

2. Create the data source

- In the Mail Merge Helper dialogue window click on Step 2, **Get Data**, then select **Create Data Source**.
- The Mail Merge Helper provides you with a standard set of fields, but you can remove or add to these to meet your requirements. You will need the following fields: Title, FirstName, LastName, Address1, Address2, City, PostalCode. Make sure that you have removed any others. Note that Address1 and Address2 are for the separate lines in an address, not for two separate addresses.
- Click **OK** when you have finished. You will be prompted to save your data source. Call it 'Customer data'.
- You have not yet entered any data. Click on **Edit Data Source**.
- Add data to the fields in the data input window. Click on **Add New** to create the next record. Create three records in all.
- Scan between the records with the browse buttons. Click on **OK** when finished.

3. Merge the main document and the data source

- You should be viewing the main document (called 'Letter'). If you have already closed this document then you should open it in the usual way. Microsoft® Word will automatically find the data source ('Customer data') that is associated with it.
- You want to position the name and address of each customer on the left side of the letter. To do this you will insert the fieldnames from the data source. Select **Insert Merge Field** from the Mail Merge toolbar and then select the relevant fieldnames one at a time, adding spaces and returns where needed.
- Add the salutation ('Dear ...') followed by the relevant fieldnames.
- Write the rest of the letter telling customers about your new product. Save it.

Figure 8.7 Merge fields inserted into the main document

◀

- Click the **View Merged Data** button to see what your merged documents will look like. Use the browse buttons to check all the records. Click the **View Merged Data** button again to return to the main document.

Mrs Jenny Hughes
29 Oak Tree Court
Station Road
Kingsmond

Dear Jenny Hughes

Amazing new offer!

Figure 8.8 One of the merged documents

- To print out the merged documents, click on the **Mail Merge Helper** button, then click on Step 3, **Merge**.
- In the Merge To box select **Printer**. Click **Merge**.

Character and paragraph formats

How can I select a font?

A font is a style of character that can be used on screen and for printing. Different fonts have been around since the invention of printing. Many more have been designed for use on computers, and there are now thousands to choose from.

The *size* of each font is measured in points – another old printing term. There are 72 points to an inch, or approximately 29 points to a centimetre. A font size of, say, 12 points measures the length from the top of the highest character to the bottom of the lowest character. But some fonts are long and thin and others are short and fat, so fonts with the same font size may look very different on the page.

Using the font Architecture
Using the font Bernard Fashion
Using the font Rockwell
Using the font Vivaldi

Figure 8.9 These fonts are all displayed in the same font size

Generally speaking you should not use less than 12 points for normal text, although smaller sizes can be used for footnotes and captions.

There are three main kinds of *typeface* used for fonts:

- *Serif* fonts have extra marks (serifs) at the ends of the strokes. These imitate the chisel marks left when letters are carved into stone. The most widely used serif font is Times Roman – so called because it was used by the *Times* newspaper and imitated the lettering used in ancient Rome. Serif fonts are often very easy to read (see Figure 8.10).

Using Times New Roman
Using Bookman Old Style
Using Century School Book
Using Calisto
Using Poster Bodoni

Figure 8.10 A selection of serif fonts

Serif fonts create a definite impression for the reader. They suggest tradition, stability, honesty and good old-fashioned values, so they are sometimes used in logos when a business wants to appear to be substantial, long established and trustworthy.

■ *Sans serif* fonts lack the extra marks and appear much plainer, but you will find a greater variety of shapes amongst sans serif fonts.

Using Arial
Using Verdana
Using Futura
Using Graphite Light

Figure 8.11 A selection of sans serif fonts

Sans serif fonts look modern and friendly. They are often used to give an impression that a business is up-to-date, customer centred and forward looking.

■ *Cursive* fonts imitate handwriting, although some of them are based on handwriting styles from over a century ago.

Using Bradley Hand
Using Lucida Calligraphy
Using Signet Roundhand
Using Viner Hand

Figure 8.12 A selection of cursive fonts

Cursive fonts look warm and informal, but should be used with great care. They are not as legible as the other fonts, so should not be used for large areas of text. One obvious use would be for mock signatures, but they can also be used for headings.

How are you going to choose which fonts to use? It is a good idea to analyse printed materials and work out what looks professional and what looks amateurish. Here are a few suggestions:

■ Think carefully about the impression you want to give. Choose fonts to convey a hidden message to your reader.

■ Use a maximum of two fonts in a simple document like a letter or a report – one font for the main text and another one for headings.

■ If you use a serif font for the main text, then you can use either a serif or sans serif font for headings.

■ If you use a sans serif font for the main text then a serif font will often look odd when used for headings.

■ Only use a third font for special emphasis, or for text in a separate section such as a footer.

■ For the main text use at least 12 point, and larger sizes for headings.

How can text be laid out on a page?

Text can be positioned on the page using a number of different tools.

Text *alignment* arranges text in relation to the margins of the document or the textbox. Normally the text is highlighted then aligned. In some packages all the text in a textbox is automatically given the same alignment. In many packages the alignment buttons can be found in the formatting toolbar. Alignment is sometimes referred to as *justification*.

This text is aligned to the left, which means that it is lined up against the left margin of the page. Left alignment is commonly used for all kinds of documents, although it does mean that the text looks 'ragged' along the right margin. This can be overcome by using fully justified text (see below) instead.

This text is aligned to the right. Right alignment is normally only used for positioning addresses on letters. It is sometimes used to create special effects, but generally it looks rather odd and is difficult to read.

This text is aligned to the centre.
Headings are often centre aligned, but otherwise use it with care, as eyes find it difficult to dart from one starting point on a line to another.

This text is fully justified. The characters have been spaced out so that they line up on both the left and the right margins. This looks neat in formal printed documents, although you may find that some words are stretched a little too much.

Text can also be *indented*.

This text has been indented. The section of text is highlighted then moved to the right or left using the Text Indent buttons. Indented text can also be aligned in any of the available ways.

Tabs can be used to indent individual words.

If you press the tab key on the keyboard (above the Caps Lock key), as I did at the beginning of this sentence, the cursor moves a short distance to the right.

If you press the tab key more than once, the cursor makes a number of jumps.

You can	use tabs	in the same line	to space out words
and then	use them	on the next line	to keep them in columns.

The tab positions are set, by default, at fixed intervals. In Microsoft® Word you can set the tab positions by highlighting a block of text (use **Edit** and **Select All** for the whole document) and then clicking on the top ruler at the points where you want the tabs to be.

How can I format whole paragraphs?

When you write a new paragraph you may want the first word to be indented. You may also want to increase or decrease the spacing between one paragraph and the next. These settings can be made in Microsoft® Word. First highlight one or more paragraphs, or the whole document (using **Select All**), then select **Paragraph** from the **Format** menu.

This paragraph has been formatted with line spacing before the paragraph and with the first line indented by 1 centimetre.

First line indenting is used in documents which do not have any spacing between the paragraphs, such as newspapers. If spacing is used between paragraphs then indenting is often not used.

Further research – Formatting characters in Microsoft® Outlook Express

You can format the characters in an e-mail created in Microsoft® Outlook Express, although you must realise that some recipients will not be able to view the formats in their e-mail software.

Create a new e-mail in the usual way. Select **Rich Text** from the **Format** menu. This brings up a Formatting toolbar, which you can use just as you would in any other package. You can even insert pictures using the **Insert** menu.

How do I create a table?

Spreadsheets are naturally arranged as tables. Although they are designed for numerical calculations, they can be used to arrange information neatly even where no numbers are included.

	A	B	C
1	Task	Deadline	Completed
2	Write to Jones Ltd about contract	28th Feb	28th Feb
3	Fix meeting with Margaret		27th Feb
4	Order more pens	2nd March	
5	Write report	4th March	
6			

Figure 8.13 A simple table created in a spreadsheet

Individual cells, or groups of cells, can be shaded or given borders. In Microsoft® Excel, highlight the cells, from the **Format** menu select **Cells**, then use the **Border** and **Patterns** tabs. The text in each cell can be formatted in the usual way.

Task	Deadline	Completed
Write to Jones Ltd about contract	28th Feb	28th Feb
Fix meeting with Margaret		27th Feb
Order more pens	2nd March	
Write report	4th March	

Figure 8.14 The same table printed out with formatted cells

Tables can also be created in Microsoft® Word, PowerPoint and Publisher, although they work in slightly different ways. In Microsoft® Word or PowerPoint click on the **Insert Table** button in the main toolbar, and then highlight the number of cells that you need.

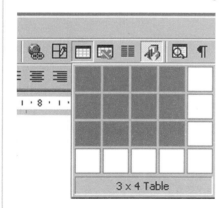

Figure 8.15 Creating a table in Microsoft® Word or PowerPoint

In Microsoft® Publisher, click on the **Tables** button in the toolbox, drag an outline of the table on the document, then follow the instructions in the dialogue box.

You can then add data to the cells. Cells can be formatted by highlighting one cell or a set of cells and using the options in the **Format** menu. Drag the edges of the cells to make them bigger or smaller.

How can I format the data type?

Spreadsheets allow you to specify the type of data that appears in each cell. You can format the data as:

- *Text* – this is the default format, although Microsoft® Excel is clever enough to recognise a number when it is entered. Text is always aligned to the left and numbers to the right, unless you format them otherwise.
- *Integer* – this rounds any decimal numbers to whole numbers.
- *Decimal number* – this displays the numbers with decimal places, and you can specify how many digits there should be after the decimal point. Any numbers entered with more decimal places will be rounded.
- *Currency* – this is a number formatted with two decimal places (or none, if you want whole pounds only), and with a £ sign at the front.
- *Date* – when you format data as a date, the software converts it into a 'hidden' number called a serial value. The serial value is the number of days from 1 January 1900 to the date entered. This means that you can carry out arithmetic with dates, such as adding one day to a date, or finding how many days there are between two dates. Although all dates have a serial value, you can choose how you want the date to be formatted.

Formulae

How can I use basic formulae?

Spreadsheets are essentially designed to carry out calculations. A cell can contain either a *value* or a *formula*. A value is simply keyed in by the user, whereas a formula in a cell calculates a value, which is then displayed in the cell.

You can click on a cell to see whether it contains a value or a formula. The contents are shown in the formula bar. All formulae begin with an = sign.

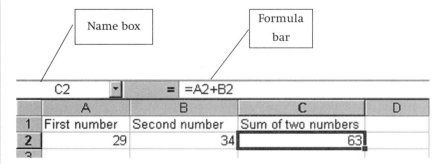

Figure 8.16 A formula in a cell – all the other cells contain values

- *Addition* – The example above shows a formula that adds the contents of two cells. The cells containing the values are referred to by their cell names, A2 and B2. You can create a formula that adds the contents of as many cells as you like.

■ *Subtraction, Multiplication and Division* – You can also use the -, * and / keys for subtraction, multiplication and division within any calculation. Notice that if you try to divide a number by zero you will get an error message.

Similar calculations can be carried out in database software, but you do need some in-depth understanding of how database queries work before you can attempt them.

How can I use functions?

A function is a shortcut that enables you to carry out complex calculations quite simply.

■ *Sum* – with this function you can add all the numbers in a column or row. A formula could look like this:

=SUM(A1: A7)   or   =SUM(A1: F1)

A1: A7 means all the cells in a column from position A1 to A7, and A1: F1 means all the cells in the row from A1 to F1.

A9	▼	=	=SUM(A1:A7)
	A	**B**	
1	34		
2	17		
3	39		
4	206		
5	6		
6	62		
7	167		
8			
9	531		

Figure 8.17 Cell A9 displays the result of the calculation using the SUM function

■ *Average* – the mean average of a set of numbers can be calculated directly, using a formula.

A10	▼	=	=AVERAGE(A1:A9)	
	A	**B**	**C**	
1	34			
2	17			
3	39			
4	206			
5	6			
6	62			
7	167			
8				
9	531			
10	133			
11				

Figure 8.18 Cell A10 displays the average (mean) of the set of numbers in A1: A9

Check your understanding – Working with dates in Microsoft® Excel

1. Formatting dates

■ Highlight the cells, or the column, that you want to have in date format. Select **Cells** from the **Format** menu, then click on the **Number** tab. Select the Date category. You will see a list of date formats listed under Type.

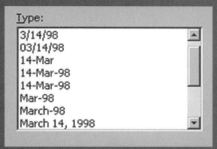

Figure 8.19 A selection of date formats in Microsoft® Excel

Remember that the date format 9/11/01 means 11 September in America, whereas it means 9 November in the UK.

■ Once you have selected a format you can enter a date into a cell in any format you wish and it will be converted to the format you have chosen.

2. Calculating with dates

Sometimes you will want to produce a list of dates – maybe all the dates in one month, or the first day of each week in a year. It would be very tedious to type these all in by hand, but you can use a formula.

■ Set up a column with a date format. Enter a date in the first cell. In the next cell enter a formula that adds 1 to the date in the first cell.

A2	▾	=	=A1+1	
	A	**B**	**C**	
1	1-Jun-03			
2	2-Jun-03			
3				
4				

Figure 8.20 Entering a formula for a date

Now copy this formula down the column. You do this by dragging on the fill handle in the bottom right corner of the cell containing the formula.

	A
1	1-Jun-03
2	2-Jun-03
3	3-Jun-03
4	4-Jun-03
5	5-Jun-03
6	6-Jun-03
7	7-Jun-03
8	8-Jun-03
9	9-Jun-03
10	10-Jun-03
11	11-Jun-03
12	12-Jun-03
13	13-Jun-03
14	14-Jun-03
15	15-Jun-03
16	

Figure 8.21 A list of dates generated by a formula

- If you want a list of weekly dates, then simply add 7 in the formula.
- You can subtract one date from another to give the number of days between the two dates.
  Warning: the cell containing the number of days must be formatted as a number, not as a date.

B5	▾	=	=B3-B1

	A	B	C
1	Start date	12-Dec-00	
2			
3	End date	19-Jun-02	
4			
5	Number of days	554	
6			
7			

Figure 8.22 Calculating the number of days between two dates

3. Using a date function

- A cell can display today's date using the function
  =TODAY()
  The value in this cell will change from day to day.

Charts and graphs

Charts and graphs can be created easily in a spreadsheet. They can then be copied and pasted into another document.

This is by far the simplest method of handling charts but there are two further approaches that you might want to explore, if you already feel confident with the software.

- In Microsoft® Access, when you are designing a form, you can insert a chart by selecting **Chart** from the **Insert** menu. The numerical data must already exist in a table in the database.
- In Microsoft® Word, PowerPoint and Publisher you can insert a special Chart Object by selecting **Object** from the **Insert** menu, then selecting **Microsoft® Excel Chart**. This displays a workbook with two sheets – the first one contains the chart and the second one contains the data. Enter your own data in the spreadsheet. A Chart toolbox appears when you click on the chart, and you can use this to select the type of chart you require. When you click elsewhere on your document only the chart remains. When you double-click on this again you can edit the data and chart directly.

How do I create a bar chart?

A bar chart allows you to compare the *values* for a number of different *categories*. For example, Figure 8.23 shows the daily sales for six newspapers in the UK in November 2002.

	Nov-02
Times	688,480
Telegraph	965,208
Guardian	404,801
Sun	3,541,198
Mirror	2,148,058
Mail	2,420,301

Figure 8.23 Daily sales for six newspapers

Source: Audit Bureau of Circulations

In this case the names of the newspapers are the categories, and the numbers of sales are the values. We can enter this data into a spreadsheet, then create a bar chart which shows very clearly how the sales compare with each other.

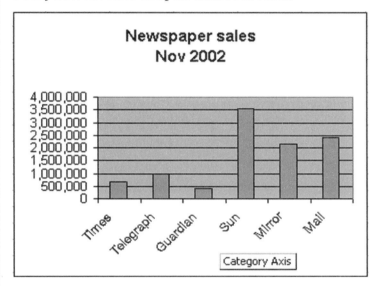

Figure 8.24 Bar chart produced from the data in the table

Bar charts can display the bars either horizontally, or vertically (when they are sometimes known as column charts). In the chart shown, the bottom axis is the category axis, and the vertical axis is the value axis. The axes should be clearly labelled. Labels are textboxes which identify the categories and the scale for the values.

It is also possible to create a bar chart that compares two parallel sets of values. For example, we might want to compare the sales in November with the sales a year earlier. So we could add another column of values to the table.

	Nov-02	Nov-01
Times	688,480	715,022
Telegraph	965,208	1,012,698
Guardian	404,801	410,664
Sun	3,541,198	3,377,906
Mirror	2,148,058	2,107,606
Mail	2,420,301	2,466,370

Figure 8.25 Comparing daily sales for six newspapers over two years

Source: Audit Bureau of Circulations

We can now draw a comparative chart which shows visually which newspapers have increased their sales and which have decreased. We use colour or patterns to distinguish the values for the two years. The short list that identifies the colours is known as a *legend*. A comparative chart is meaningless without a legend.

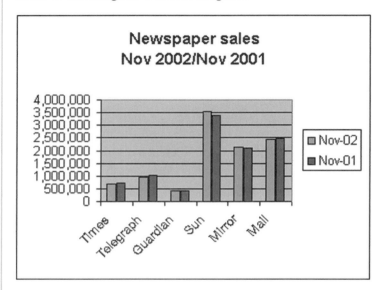

Figure 8.26 Comparative bar chart showing newspaper sales in two periods

How do I create a pie chart?

A pie chart demonstrates how the values of each category contribute to the total. It makes it easy to see what share of the total each has.

You can draw a pie chart only if you have data available for all the categories. In the tables above we had data for only six newspapers, and we need data for all the national daily newspapers to get the full picture.

	Nov-02
Times	688,480
Telegraph	965,208
Guardian	404,801
Sun	3,541,198
Mirror	2,148,058
Mail	2,420,301
Independent	221,597
Financial Times	451,790
Star	736,186
Express	988,136

Figure 8.27 Daily sales for ten national newspapers

Source: Audit Bureau of Circulations

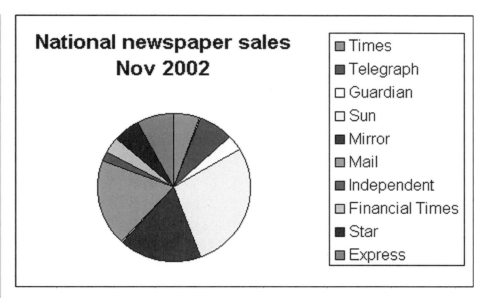

Figure 8.28 Pie chart drawn from the data in the table

In this case, the legend is essential. You will notice that there is always a problem when printing a pie chart in monochrome (one colour) only. It is difficult to distinguish between the sectors, especially if there are quite a number of them. Patterns can be used instead of colours, but they often look very similar.

It is possible to produce pie charts which appear three-dimensional or 'exploded'. Avoid these, as they do not add anything to the information you are giving, and can, in fact, be more difficult to understand.

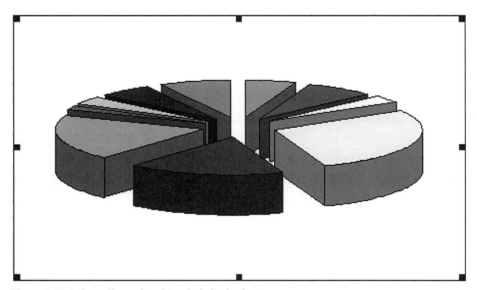

Figure 8.29 A three-dimensional 'exploded' pie chart

How do I create a line graph?

Both bar charts and pie charts are drawn to illustrate values given to a set of categories. In the examples, the newspapers' titles were the categories.

Line graphs have numerical values along both axes. They show how the values along one axis change in relation to the other.

One very common type of line graph is a time series, which has a timeline along its horizontal axis. A timeline could show days, months or years. For example, we might have data for the sales of just one of the newspapers over a period of time.

This table shows the pre-tax profits made by the retailer Carpetright.

	Profits £M
1998	29.2
1999	23.5
2000	36.6
2001	44.6
2002	52.5

Figure 8.30 Carpetright pre-tax profits

Here is the line graph drawn to illustrate the data.

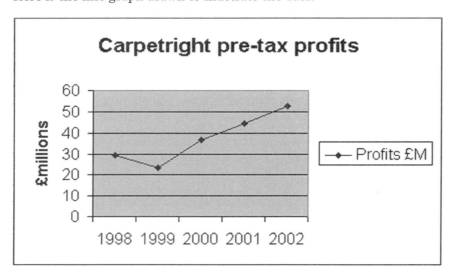

Figure 8.31 Line graph for a time series

Note that the points have been plotted as though they applied at the middle of each year. As the timeline is continuous we can join the points together. The line shows clearly how the profits are changing. You can see at a glance that profits have been rising since 1999.

✓ **Check your understanding** – Creating charts and graphs in Microsoft® Excel

The purpose of any chart or graph is to bring the data to life by turning it into a diagram. You need to choose the type that is most appropriate for the data you have.

You can create a wide variety of charts and graphs in Microsoft® Excel. Do not be tempted to produce more than one chart for a set of data, or to draw a fancy one when a simple chart would do.

■ Enter the data in Figure 8.23 into a new spreadsheet and save it. You may want to format the cells containing the numerical data.
It is possible to enter the data in rows instead of columns, but it is more common to set it out as shown.

■ Highlight all the cells shown in the table, including the heading Nov-02. Then click on the **Chart Wizard** button in the main toolbar.

▶

■ In the Chart Type box select **Column** for a vertical bar chart. In the Chart Sub-Type box select the first option in the top left hand corner. Then click on **Next**.

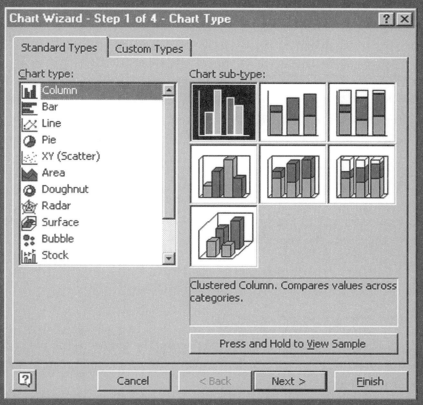

Figure 8.32 The Chart Wizard in Microsoft® Excel

■ The next screen will show you what the chart will look like. Click on **Next**.
■ In the Chart Title box key in 'Newspaper Sales in November 2002'. You can put in a label for the category axis, although in this case it is not necessary – it could be 'Name of newspaper'. You could also add the label 'Daily sales' to the value axis. Click on **Next**.
■ In the next page you can choose whether the chart will be placed on the same sheet or on a new sheet. Click on **Finish**.
■ The chart will appear on the sheet and you can move it to the correct position.

At Step 1 of the Chart Wizard you could choose bar (for a horizontal bar chart), or pie for a pie chart. In each case select the first option in the Chart Sub-Type box.

Page layout

How do I change the size of the page?

Paper is produced in International paper sizes from A0 (largest) down to A10 (smallest). The normal paper used in most printers is A4, which is 210mm by 297mm.

One special feature of the International sizes is that if you cut any standard sheet of paper in half as shown you get two sheets of paper in the next size down (Figure 8.33).

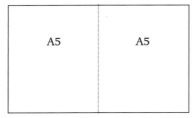

Figure 8.33 One A4 sheet can be cut into two A5 sheets

This means that you can print out two A5 pages side by side on one A4 sheet of paper.

In the US, an alternative set of paper sizes is used. You need to know about these as some software may be set up for American papers. The US sizes are A (smallest) to K (largest). Size A is also known as Letter size, and at 8.5 inches by 11 inches (216mm by 254mm) it is the nearest to A4.

Other specialist paper sizes are used, and special sizes are used for envelopes.

You can choose the paper size in most software applications, by going to the **File** menu and selecting **Page SetUp**. Select the **Paper Size** tab, and then make your choice from the list. The default is usually set as A4, but it is worth checking that it has not been set at Letter (US) size instead.

How do I select the page orientation?

You can arrange a document so that the text runs across the length of the paper (landscape) or across its width (portrait). This is the orientation of the paper, and it can be set in the Page SetUp dialogue, in the **Paper Size** tab.

How do I start a new page?

In most applications you can usually insert a page break or create a new page from the **Insert** menu.

How do I set the size of the margins?

Margins can be set at the left, right, top and bottom of the page in most applications. This is usually done through the Page Setup dialogue. The left and right margins should normally be the same size, but if you are producing a document in which pages are to be printed back-to-back and then bound as a book, you will probably want a larger margin on the inside edge – this will be on the left edge of odd numbered pages and on the right edge of even numbered pages.

The top margin and bottom margins contain the header and footer so you need to make them large enough to hold whatever text you want there.

How do I number pages?

Most software packages will automatically number pages for you, although they vary in how this is achieved.

In Microsoft® Word, select **Page numbers** from the **Insert** menu. You can choose to have the number at the top or bottom of the page, and positioned to the left, right or centre. A common position is at the bottom of the page in the centre.

What are headers and footers?

A header is an area at the top of each page, and a footer is at the bottom. The content of the header or the footer is usually the same on each page. Text in a header or footer is normally smaller than the main body of the text, to distinguish it from the rest of the document.

If you have set up page numbering, then the numbers will appear in the header or footer. You can add extra information to the header or footer. For example, you might want the name of the document, the date it was written or your own name to appear on each page.

In Microsoft® Word, Excel and PowerPoint select **Header and Footer** from the **View** menu. The three packages have different dialogue boxes so you would be wise to check out all three.

Microsoft® Word opens directly in the Header section with a floating Header and Footer toolbar. Check what each button does by passing the mouse over each.

Figure 8.34 The header section and the Header and Footer toolbar in Microsoft® Word

Text typed into the header section will appear on each page. You can insert the date or page numbering, or you can choose from the Insert AutoText list. Text can be formatted using the usual formatting toolbar.

You can switch to the footer by clicking on the **Switch** button .

Microsoft® PowerPoint allows you to place the date, the slide number and some extra text on each slide at fixed positions at the bottom of each slide. You can also add headers and footers to the printed notes that the package can create to accompany your slides.

You can create headers and footers on forms or reports in Microsoft® Access. They can be seen at the top and the bottom in Design view.

How can I set up columns?

Many documents arrange the text in columns. This can easily be seen in newspapers and magazines, but many businesses also use a column layout for publicity leaflets, newsletters and staff information.

In Microsoft® Word, select **Columns** from the **Format** menu, then select the number of columns that you want (Figure 8.35). You can add a line between the columns if you like.

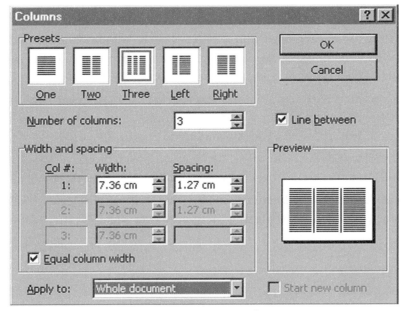

Figure 8.35 The columns dialogue box in Microsoft® Word

As you enter your text it will flow from the bottom of one column to the next.

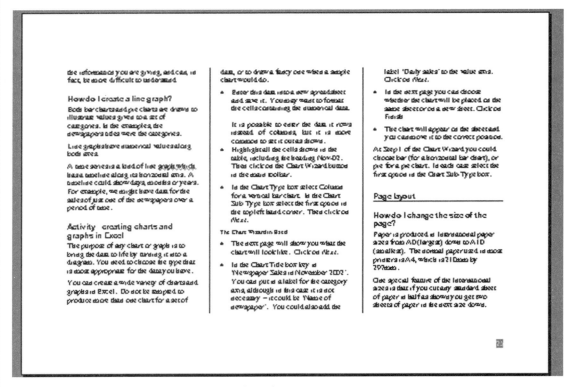

Figure 8.36 Three-column layout in landscape orientation

In a desktop publishing package you have a lot of freedom to place textboxes anywhere on the page, and these could be laid out as columns. You can make the text flow from one textbox to another.

Check your understanding – Text flow in Microsoft® Publisher

Textboxes are called text frames in Microsoft® Publisher. You can make the text flow from the end of one text frame over to the beginning of another frame. The frames can be on the same page or on different pages.

■ Create a new blank document, and then use the Text button  to draw two text frames.

■ Start typing into one of the frames. You will notice the Connect Frame button at the bottom of the frame, and this will display a white diamond.

Figure 8.37 Empty text frame in Microsoft® Publisher

■ Carry on typing until the text frame is full up. You can continue to type but the extra text will not be visible. The Connect Frame button changes to this:

Figure 8.38 Full text frame

■ Click on the **Connect Frame** button. The pointer changes into a jug (or pitcher) . Now click inside the frame where you want the text to flow, and the extra text that has overflowed from the first frame will appear in it.

■ Now go back and add more text in the middle of the first frame, and you will see its effect on the second. You can now change the size and positions of either frame.

■ You will notice that the Connect Frame button on the first frame has changed again.

Figure 8.39 Connected text frame

The chain icon shows that the frame is connected to another one. If you click on the new arrow button it will jump to the connected frame.

Test your knowledge

1 Do you know the difference between a report, a memo and an invoice?

2 What is the corporate style used by your school or college?

3 What is a clipboard, and how can you use it to copy and move text?

4 What is the difference between resizing and cropping an image? Explain how you resize bitmapped and vector images.

5 What are bullet points used for?

6 What might a business use mail merge for?

7 Select a number of fonts and describe what each might be used for.

8 How can text be aligned?

9 Give an example of data which it would be appropriate to represent in a:
- bar chart
- pie chart
- line graph.

10 Given that an A4 sheet is 210mm by 297mm, what are the dimensions of an A2 sheet?

8.3 Produce and print documents

Produce a range of documents

What kind of documents should I produce?

For the purposes of assessment in this unit, you should be able to produce a wide range of printed business documents. Some of these documents should include numbers and images as well as text.

You need to demonstrate that you can choose the right software to produce each document, so you should be familiar with all the types of business software applications listed in section 8.1.

The assessment requirements are given in more detail at the end of this unit.

What kind of printer can I use?

In Unit 1 we noted that there are two main types of printer that are used for business applications – inkjet and laser printers.

To work effectively, all printers need:

- *a printer driver* – this is software that allows the CPU to communicate with the printer
- *suitable paper*
- *ink supply* – toner is needed for a laser printer and ink cartridge(s) for an inkjet printer.

Most office printers will take paper up to a maximum of A4 size, although these can usually be adjusted to take the slightly larger width of US Letter size.

Large-format printers can also be purchased that will print A3 paper, or even larger. The largest printers can print A0 posters.

How can I improve the quality of printing?

Generally, laser printers produce better quality printouts than inkjet printers. But most people will find it difficult to distinguish between the output from a laser printer and high-quality output from an inkjet printer, at least for normal text printing.

Printouts of photographs and other graphics can look very different when produced by different printers, or by the same printer using different settings.

The quality of printing depends on two factors:

- *The resolution* – this measures how closely the dots of ink lie to each other, in dots per inch (dpi). Resolution ranges from 300 to 3600 dpi.
- *The quality of the paper* (see next section).

Print a range of documents

What kind of paper can I use?

Printer papers are identified as being suitable for use in either a laser or an inkjet printer, or both. Do not use other papers, as they may contain fibres that can come loose and damage the printer.

The weight of paper affects its look and feel. Paper is weighed in grams per square metre (gsm or g/m^2). Here is a selection of printer papers:

- *Business quality* paper is everyday paper for internal use, is usually 80 gsm and can be obtained in a number of tints.
- *Letter quality* papers are often 100 gsm and can be tinted, or given a more interesting surface to imitate woven papers or parchment.
- *Photo quality* papers can be heavy and glossy and produce prints that look just like normal photos. Other photo-quality papers give good images on high-quality matt papers.
- *Card* can be used in most printers, and is available in many colours and up to 250 gsm.
- *Label stationary* is used to print out sticky labels for mailings.

Some papers, such as glossy photo paper, can be only printed on one side. Make sure that you load the paper the correct way up in the printer tray.

What print options are offered by the software?

Most software applications have a print button 🖨 . When you click on this, one copy of your document is sent to the printer, using the current settings. You can customise the printing in a number of ways, by using **Print** from the **File** menu instead.

The print dialogue that appears varies depending on which software you are using. In Microsoft® Word, for example, you can make these choices:

- *Pages to print* – you can specify which pages in a multi-page document should be printed.

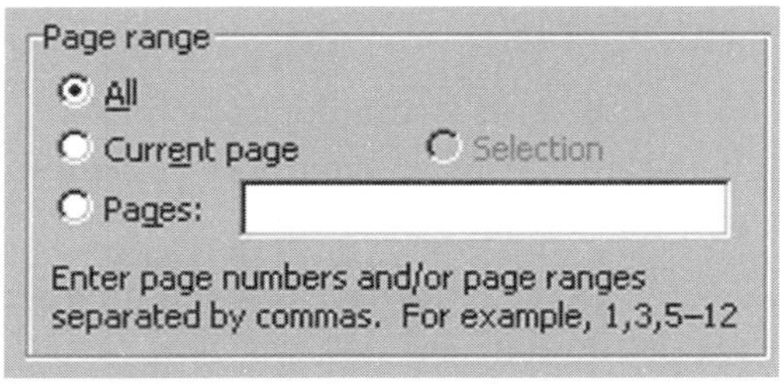

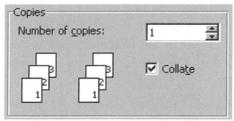

Figure 8.40 Selecting the range of pages to print

■ *Number of copies* – if you need several copies of a document, it is a good idea to print one copy and check it before trying to print the rest.

■ *Collate* – if the document has more than one page, and you are printing more than one copy, you then need to decide whether to collate the pages. When pages are collated one copy of the whole document will be printed in sequence, then the next copy is printed. If pages are not collated then all the copies of the first page will be printed, followed by all the copies of the next page.

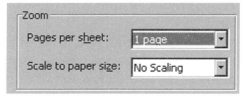

Figure 8.41 Selecting number of copies and collation

■ *Pages per sheet* – you can print two or more pages on one sheet of paper. The printer will reduce the size of the pages to fit.

Figure 8.42 Selecting how many pages to print on one sheet

What print options does the printer offer?

Each printer offers a number of options, using its own dialogue box. In the main print dialogue, click on the **Properties** button alongside the name of the printer.

Printer
Name: HP OfficeJet T Series Printer | Properties

Figure 8.43 Printer properties

The illustrations are from the properties for a Hewlett Packard inkjet printer. You can select the following options and you should be able to find similar options for other printers:

■ *Print quality* – you can choose between Best, Normal and Fast (sometimes known as Draft) mode. Draft mode uses a lower resolution, with fewer dpi, but produces a fast printout, so is useful for doing a quick check. Best mode uses a high resolution, but takes much longer to print, and uses more ink. You will be able to see a difference in quality between photos printed in Best and Normal mode, but the differences for text will be barely noticeable.

Figure 8.44 Print quality options

■ *Paper type* – you can identify the type of paper you are using, and the software will automatically select the right settings.

Figure 8.45 Selecting the right paper

■ *Last page first* – this option prints the pages of a multi-page document in reverse order. If you have already chosen to collate the pages, this means that when the printing is complete all the documents will sit in the out tray in the correct order.

Figure 8.46 Changing the order in which pages are printed

How do I use colour?

Colour printers use mixtures of the three standard colours, cyan, magenta and yellow, to reproduce any colour at all. They also use black ink for pure black printing.

Documents that include colours can be printed in full colour or in shades of grey.

Grey is, in fact, produced by mixing colours, so true grey scale can be achieved only on a colour printer.

If you are using a monochrome printer, it will print grey shades with a stippled effect, that is, with dots of black ink spaced out to give the impression of a grey colour.

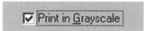

Figure 8.47 Printing in greyscale

Note that the American spelling of grey ('gray') is often used in applications.

Test your knowledge

1 Suggest a suitable type of paper for each of these business documents:
   ■ letter to a job applicant inviting him or her to an interview
   ■ invoice to a customer
   ■ three-fold publicity leaflet, with photos
   ■ internal memo
   ■ printout of e-mail
   ■ notice for staff noticeboard.
2 You want to produce a four-page leaflet made by folding a single sheet of A4 page in half, with printing on both sides. Draw a sketch to show how the pages will be numbered. Suggest two ways in which this could be achieved.

8.4 Delivering a presentation

Presentations

What is a presentation?

When a member of an organisation needs to explain a project to a wider audience, he or she will often do this through a presentation. This means that the relevant people will meet together and the person giving the presentation will give a talk.

The talk will be illustrated with projected images and text. In the past, photographic slides were used, and today we still refer to the individual projected pages as slides. Today, of course, we use digital methods. There are three main ways of creating the display for a presentation:

- *Transparencies* – these are sheets of acetate (slides) which are placed on an overhead projector (OHP) and projected onto a white or silver screen. The presenter is able to face the audience whilst changing the slides. Traditionally people wrote directly on the transparencies, but it is now possible to print them from software.

  Transparencies can be prepared using any document software, such as Microsoft® Word or Publisher, or by using specialised presentation software like Microsoft® PowerPoint. But it is essential that the correct transparency slides are used, as the wrong kind of slide can melt in a printer.

Figure 8.48 Photo of an OHP

- *Projecting from a computer* – a multi-media projector is installed on a PC or laptop. This projects onto a screen whatever is shown on the computer monitor. Again, the presenter is able to face the audience whilst controlling the presentation.

Figure 8.49 Photo of a data projector

■ *Viewing a computer display* – the presentation can be viewed directly on a computer screen. A large display screen can be added as a second monitor, so the presenter can still control the presentation from a PC or laptop. For a presentation to a couple of people it is possible to simply view the display on a PC's normal monitor.

The last two methods display the output from a computer in real time. This means that the presentation can include animation and video. It can also include sound, provided suitable speakers have been installed.

What are the advantages of making a presentation?

A presentation is a combination of live talk and ready-prepared graphical materials (a slide show). The alternative could be a video on its own, or a simple talk without illustrations. Combining visuals and speech into one presentation has many advantages:

■ The slides add impact to a talk – the audience is much more likely to listen and understand if the message is reinforced by text and pictures.
■ The presenter can feel confident that the main points of the talk are included in the slide show.
■ The presenter can take the presentation at his or her own speed.
■ The presenter can respond to the audience as the presentation proceeds, going back to earlier slides if necessary.

How do I plan the content of a presentation?

You need to plan the presentation carefully, and you should complete this on paper before you begin to work with the software. Assuming that you have already been given a subject for the presentation, you should:

■ break the subject down into a number of topic areas
■ for each topic, work out the main points that you want to make
■ add an introduction, explaining who you are and what the presentation is about
■ at the end, add a summary.

You should start thinking about the slides only when you have completed your planning.

How do I design the slides?

Here is a suggested sequence of slides:

■ title
■ introduction – your name and position
■ what the presentation is about
■ first topic – heading plus main points
■ more about the first point in this topic
■ more about the next point in this topic
■ ...
■ second topic
■ more about the first point in this topic
■ more about the next point in this topic
■ ...
■ third topic

- ▨ more about the first point in this topic
- ▨ more about the next point in this topic
- ▨ ...
- ▨ summary.

How do I create the visual design of the slides?

It is a good idea to check the templates and wizards provided with presentation software, as they will give you ideas for your own. You can use any of the backgrounds, lines, bullet points and other graphics that are provided with the software. Alternatively you can find or create your own images.

The slides must be designed to suit your audience. In a business context you can assume that your audience will expect a sophisticated presentation, so avoid bright clashing colours and confusing animations. You may be expected to use corporate colours or a logo.

How do I choose the basic features?

- ▨ *Background* – choose a background that does not interfere visually with the text or any images that you want to use. Generally speaking, a simple background is preferable to a busy one, although colour shading can be very effective.
- ▨ *Logos* – if you want to use a logo, place it in the same position on every slide.
- ▨ *Font* – you should give some thought to the fonts that you use (as discussed in section 8.2). Fonts make as much impact as the other graphics, so choose them carefully.
- ▨ *Font size* – make sure that you do not include too much text on a slide. Generally speaking you should use a font size of 24 to 32 points, with larger sizes for headings.
- ▨ *Colours* – use a very limited range of colours on the slides. Too many colours can confuse the audience. The font colour should balance the background colour, and be easy to read. A dark background should have light text and vice versa.
- ▨ *Bullet points* – these are often used in slides, and you can add interest by choosing a suitable graphic to replace the standard dot.
- ▨ *Lines* – can be added in a variety of styles. They help to break up the slide, or separate the heading from the rest of the text.

How about printed materials?

Presentation software often has features which allow you to print out supporting materials. These include:

- ▨ Speaker notes on the slides, which you can print out as a script for the talk.
- ▨ Handouts for the audience, containing pictures of the slides. You may want to give these out at the end of the presentation as a reminder of the content.
- ▨ Handouts for the audience, containing pictures and with space for notes. These can be given out at the beginning of the presentation so that the audience can make notes as they go along.

Using presentation software

What software can I use?

Microsoft® PowerPoint is the most widely used presentation software package. You can use it to print slides onto transparencies for an OHP, or you can create a digital slideshow for a multi-media projector. Although it is possible to demonstrate the slides on a desktop PC, you would be wise to learn how to make a presentation with a talk supported by slides.

You can also use other applications. It is possible to create a slideshow for a multi-media projector using Web design software. If you decide to do this, you must remember to restrict the page size to the area that can be viewed on screen. You do not expect to scroll down the page. Read Unit 13 if you would like to explore how you could use webpages for this purpose.

It is even possible to design a series of slides in a word processor, although again you need to be careful about the page size. You can add hyperlinks to the pages to take you from one page to the next.

There is no doubt that a specialist presentation software package like Microsoft® PowerPoint offers you superior features, and automatically sets up slides and a full slide show for you.

How can I get started in Microsoft® PowerPoint?

The Microsoft® PowerPoint package includes an online tutorial. If you have not used the software before, you are advised to work through the tutorial before you try anything else.

You can create a presentation in three ways:

- use the AutoContent Wizard to create a slideshow that you can then customise for your needs
- use a design template
- start with a blank presentation.

You will probably want to start with the AutoContent wizard, but you will not want your slides to look just like everyone else's so you should move on to the other two methods as soon as you feel confident.

Check your understanding – Using the AutoContent wizard in Microsoft® PowerPoint

1. Get started with the wizard

- Create a new Office document, and select **AutoContent Wizard**.
- Click on **Presentation Type**, and then click on **All**. You will see a list of standard presentation topics, such as Business Plan and Company Meeting. You can check them all out, but start with Generic.

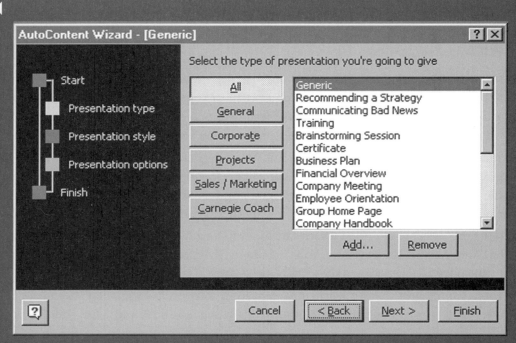

Figure 8.50 The AutoContent wizard in PowerPoint

- On the next screen select **On-Screen presentation**.
- Next, choose a title for your presentation (e.g. Improving the company website) and make sure that your name is inserted in the footer.

When the wizard has finished, a complete presentation will be displayed. The Slide Pane on the right shows the first slide. The Outline pane on the left shows the structure of the complete slideshow, with all the text that each slide contains.

To view another slide, click on one of the numbered slide icons in the Outline Pane, e.g. 3 ☐.

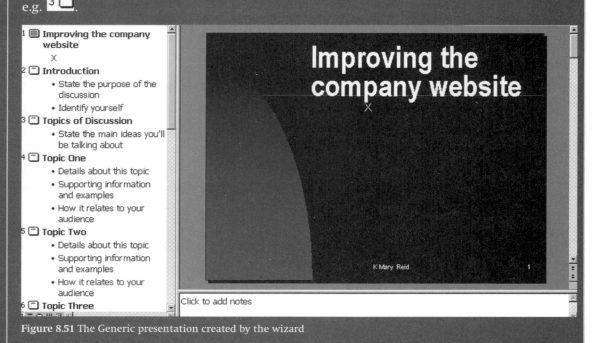

Figure 8.51 The Generic presentation created by the wizard

2. Customise the presentation

The sequence of the slides is quite similar to the one suggested earlier, but you will want to put in your own words and add new slides.

- You can change the text on any slide by typing over the text in the Outline Pane. Alternatively you can type directly onto the slide itself, replacing the existing text.
- You can move text by dragging and dropping it either in the Outline Pane or directly on the slide.
- You can delete a slide by clicking on the slide icon in the Outline Pane and then selecting **Delete Slide** from the **Edit** menu.
- You can add a new slide by clicking on the slide icon immediately before the point where you want the new slide. Select **New Slide** from the **Insert** menu, then select the style of slide that you want from the AutoLayout options. The boxes on each slide are known as **placeholders**.

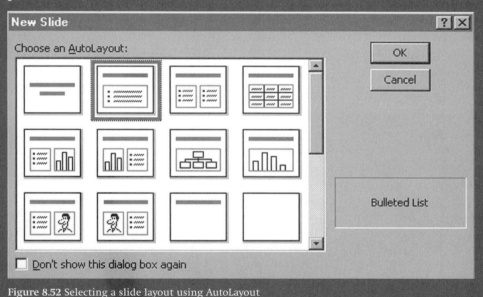

Figure 8.52 Selecting a slide layout using AutoLayout

How can I view the slides?

In the View menu, you can switch between four different 'views' of the slides.

- *Normal* – view displays three panes – the Outline Pane on the left, the Slide Pane on the right and the Notes Pane under the Slide Pane. The Outline Pane lists the slides and the text on them. To view a slide, click on the slide icon in the Outline Pane. The text in the Notes Pane will be printed in the speaker notes.
- *Slide Sorter* – shows thumbnails (small pictures) of all the slides. If you want to change their order you can drag and drop a slide to a new position.
- *Notes Page* – displays a document with the slide at the top and the notes from the Notes Pane underneath. These can be printed as the speaker notes.
- *Slide Show* – (or F5) displays the slides full screen as they will be seen in the presentation. Click anywhere on the screen to move to the next slide. You will also find a button at the bottom of each slide which presents a pop-up menu that allows you to go back to previous slides or end the slideshow.

How can I use a design template?

You can select a complete look for a presentation by choosing one of the design templates that are provided by Microsoft® PowerPoint. The templates specify for you:

- background
- colour schemes
- font style and sizes
- font colour
- bullet style.

The elements of the template are stored in the Slide Master, and you can change any of them if you wish.

In the **View** menu, select **Master**, then **Slide Master**. You will be able to view the details of the template that you are using. You can change the fonts, font sizes and colours in the slide master by highlighting as usual and selecting **Font** from the **Format** menu. From the Format menu you can also experiment with Bullets and Numbering, Background and Slide Colour Scheme.

Check your understanding – Using design templates in Microsoft® PowerPoint

- Create a new Document and choose one of the Design templates.
- You should then choose the page layout for the first page from the AutoLayout dialogue.
- Insert new slides when needed, choosing a suitable layout for each slide. Experiment with different page layouts – some provide bulleted lists, some include placeholders for graphics, tables, charts, video or sound.
- To change the layout of an existing page, click on the slide icon, then select **Slide Layout** from the **Format** menu.

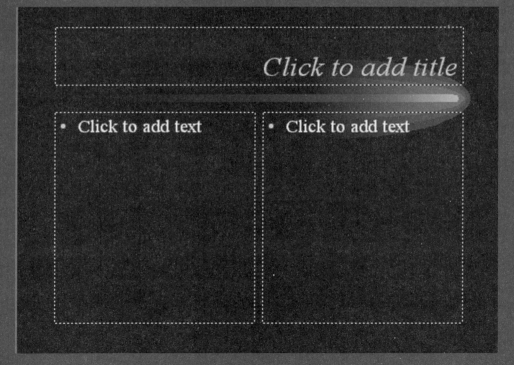

Figure 8.53 A page layout created with a Design template

How can I use a blank presentation?

If you start a new presentation and select **Blank Presentation**, you will still be able to select the page layout for each page.

You will then be able to use the Slide Master to create a complete design for your presentation.

You can also add an image, such as a logo, to the Slide Master.

How can I add extra effects?

After you have created your slides and made sure that the text is correct, you may want to add extra features to the presentation. But you should use them to enhance the message that you are trying to get across to your audience. A badly chosen feature can simply be a distraction.

- *Slide animations* – you can animate the text, by letting it fly onto the screen one line at a time. On a slide, click on the placeholder that you want to animate, then select **Preset Animation** in the **Slide Show** menu. Make your choice, then select **Animation Preview** from the **Slide Show** menu to see the effect.
- *Slide transitions* – the switch from one slide to another can be made more interesting by applying a transition effect. For example, the next slide could appear to move in from one side, or the previous slide could dissolve away. Click on the next slide, then select **Slide Transition** from the **Slide Show** menu. You can apply the transition to the chosen slide, or to all the slides. **Select Animation Preview** to see the effect.

Figure 8.54 The Slide transition dialogue

- *Sound effects* – some of the slide animations have sound effects. You can add sounds to slide transitions – just make your choice in the dialogue box.
- *Sound and movie clips* – if you have digital sound or movie files you can add them to the presentation, by selecting **Movies and Sounds** from the **Insert** menu.
- *Buttons* – you can add buttons to a slide. These can be used to move from one slide to another, or to the end of the slide show. Select **Action Buttons** from the **Slide Show** menu, and then choose a suitable button icon. Click on the slide in the position where you want the button to be. The Button dialogue will appear, and you can select the action associated

with the button. Normally it will be a hyperlink to another slide, and you can select which slide from the list.

Can I create masters for printed notes?

The master slide for a presentation contains all the elements that will appear on each slide. Similarly, the software allows you to customise the master documents for the speaker and audience notes.

In the **View** menu, select **Master**, then **Handout Master**. A document layout appears with the Handout Master floating toolbox. Click on each button to see what it does.

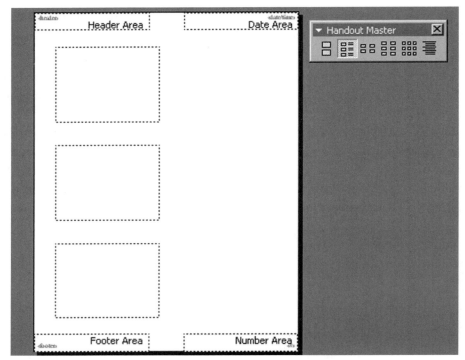

Figure 8.55 The Handout Master with the floating toolbox

In the same way, you can change the layout of the speaker notes by selecting the Notes Master.

How do I print out notes or slides?

Select **File**, then **Print**, and in the Print dialogue box you will see a Print What: list. You can choose to print thumbnails of all the slides, or to print Handouts for the audience, or to print the Notes Pages (speakers notes), or to print an outline of the whole presentation.

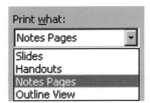

Figure 8.56 Part of the print dialogue in PowerPoint

The appearance of the Notes Page or the Handouts will reflect any changes you have made to the Notes Master and the Handout Master.

✏ Assessment tasks

This section describes what you must do to obtain a Merit grade for this unit.

A Distinction grade may be awarded if your work demonstrates a deeper understanding of the topics and is of a higher quality. The highlighted sentences indicate the quality of work expected at Distinction level.

How do I provide assessment evidence?

Your evidence will in the form of:

- at least six documents *plus*
- evidence of a short presentation that you have given.

All your evidence should be presented in one folder, which should have a front cover and a contents page. You should divide the evidence into two sections corresponding to Tasks 2 and 3.

Task 1

Learning outcome 1 – Describe the importance of business software applications

Describe three types of business applications software packages (e.g. word processing, desktop publishing).

For each type of package, describe two examples of how it could be used in a commercial environment. In each case, describe the software facilities that are needed for the suggested use and explain whether the type of software is appropriate.

You may like to illustrate your descriptions with samples of real commercial documents.

Present your descriptions:

- *either* – as a report (as one of the documents for Task 2)
- *or* – as a presentation (for Task 3)

To obtain a Distinction grade, you should compare and contrast the business software in more detail. You should also report the research that you have done on how the software is used in industry and commerce.

Task 2

Learning outcome 2 – Use different document styles and layouts

Learning outcome 3 – Produce and print a range of business documentation

Create and print at least six different types of business documents. These could all be for the same real or imagined business.

One of these documents could be a report covering the requirements of Task 1.

Within the documents you should include:

- at least two bitmapped images that you have created
- at least two vector images that you have created
- a line graph, a bar chart and a pie chart (for different data)
- at least one multi-paged document
- at least two documents that combine text, numbers and graphics
- at least one document that has been produced using a template that you have created.

Between them you should demonstrate that you can use all these features successfully:

- merge documents
- retrieve, sort and search data
- import files
- copy and move text and images
- resize and rotate images
- combine text, different sized images and shapes into single images
- use shading, lines and borders
- use bullet points
- use labels and legends for charts
- format text using bold, underline, italics, fonts
- arrange text using indents, tabs and paragraphs
- create tables
- use basic formulae, including addition, subtraction, multiplication, division and average
- format data as currency, integers and dates
- layout pages using page size, orientation, page numbering, headers, footers, margins and columns.

Write handwritten notes on the documents to identify all these features.

Include in your folder any extra documents (such as a template and a data source) that provide evidence that you can do all this.

To obtain a Distinction grade, the quality of the work produced will be high and should be appropriate for the commercial need. You should also ensure that:

- at least one of the documents is produced from a database
- at least one document is in columns.

Images should use colour, shading, patterns and lines.

Task 3

Learning outcome 4 – Deliver a presentation to an appropriate audience

Select a topic and prepare a presentation to an audience. You may wish to present the material for Task 1 in this way.

Your presentation should include around 15 slides.

UNIT 13: WEB DEVELOPMENT

Success in this unit

What are the learning outcomes?

To achieve this unit you must:
- identify the uses of websites
- evaluate a range of websites
- create a suitable website
- test and problem-solve a website.

How is this unit assessed?

This unit is internally assessed. You must provide evidence in the form of a variety of documents that show that you meet the learning outcomes.

How do I provide assessment evidence?

Your evidence will probably be a mixture of the following:
- written reports
- screen shots of websites
- witness statements.

All your evidence should be presented in one folder, which should have a front cover and a contents page. The section headed *Assessment tasks* at the end of this unit gives you more detailed advice about how to prepare for the assessment.

Introduction

About this unit

In this unit you will explore and analyse a number of existing websites. You will learn to distinguish effective sites from poor ones, and you will discuss the design features that make a site easy to use.

Websites have joined the traditional **media** of newspapers, radio and television as an important means of communication between individuals and organisations. In the past the media offered one-way communication only, although digital interactive television is now changing that. But websites can be used very easily for two-way communication, so had a clear advantage over the other media when they first appeared in the 1990s.

In this unit you will be concentrating on the use of websites by organisations, such as businesses. Personal websites are also significant because they give individuals a platform to express their opinions and share their interests, but personal websites will not be discussed in this unit.

? **What does it mean?**

Media – the traditional ways of providing news to the general public, such as newspapers, radio and television, became known as communication media (or simply, 'the media'). The word 'media' is the plural for 'medium', i.e. the means whereby information is transmitted. Websites, e-mail, interactive television and mobile phones are referred to as the 'new media'.

Will I create my own site?

You will have the opportunity to design and build a website for an organisation.

What resources do I need?

In order to succeed in this unit you will need to have easy access to the Internet and a good search engine. You should also have the use of one or more web design packages.

13.1 Identifying the uses of websites

Main uses of websites

What are websites used for?

Websites can:

- *Inform* – all websites provide some information, which is one reason why the Internet became known as the 'Information Superhighway'.

- *Sell* – websites can be used to promote products and services to visitors.
- *Interact* – websites can easily offer interactivity, allowing the visitor to send information and ideas back to the organisation and engage in dialogue.

It is interesting that we use the terms 'reader', 'listener' and 'viewer' for people who use newspapers, radio and television, whereas a person who goes to a website is referred to as a 'visitor'. Visitors, of course, do not just passively accept what is given to them, instead they make choices about what they want to see and where they want to go. It is the interactive nature of websites that distinguishes them from the traditional media.

Types of website

Websites created by organisations can be placed in four categories:

- **e-commerce**
- marketing
- external communications
- internal communications.

What does it mean?

E-commerce – e-commerce is the use of the Internet for selling goods and services to customers.

How are websites used for e-commerce?

As the Internet has grown, so more and more businesses have emerged that exist only on the Web. There are many examples of online banks, shops, travel agencies and insurance companies. These companies sell goods and services directly to customers.

Customers normally pay for products online with a credit card, and they need to be reassured that their payments will be safe. Online payments are usually routed through a secure server which encrypts all the data.

Goods have to be sent to the customer either by post or using a distribution company, and successful online businesses usually guarantee delivery in 24 hours or a few days.

Case study – Amazon, the online bookstore

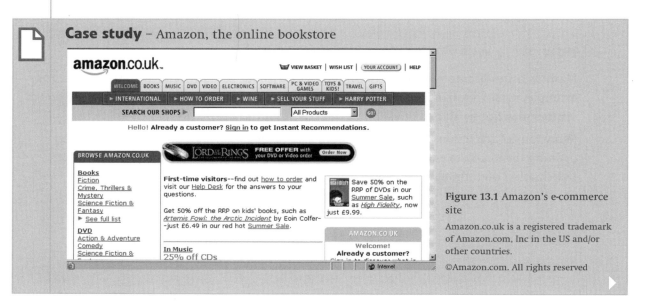

Figure 13.1 Amazon's e-commerce site

Amazon.co.uk is a registered trademark of Amazon.com, Inc in the US and/or other countries.

©Amazon.com. All rights reserved

Amazon describe themselves in this way:

Who We Are

Amazon.co.uk is the trading name for Amazon.com Int'l Sales, Inc. and Amazon.com International Auctions, Inc. Both companies are subsidiaries of Amazon.com – a leading online retailer of products that inform, educate and inspire. The Amazon group also has stores in the United States, Germany, France, Japan and Canada. Amazon.co.uk has its origins in an independent online store, Bookpages, which was established in 1996, and subsequently acquired by Amazon.com in early 1998.

What We Do

Amazon.co.uk offers a catalogue of more than 1.5 million books, thousands of CDs, DVDs and videos, a wide range of software and PC & video games and a great selection of children's products in Toys & Kids! The site also hosts online auctions and brings independent buyers and sellers together in zShops, our online marketplace. In addition, customers have access to a variety of other resources including customer reviews, e-mail personal recommendations and gift certificates.

Source:www.amazon.co.uk

Further research – other e-commerce sites

Use your usual search engine to find other e-commerce websites. Can you work out which kinds of business have gone in for e-commerce? And what kinds of business are rarely to be found on the Web?

Some Internet businesses offer services, which avoid the need to deliver goods. For example, online banking has grown very rapidly, and customers can view their balance, make payments and generally manage their accounts at any time of the day. Similarly, travel companies can send documents, such as ticket confirmations, by e-mail and may not need to use the post at all.

In addition, many high street chains now have online e-commerce operations as well. Large supermarkets offer a home shopping service which can be very helpful for people who are housebound, have young children, or lead busy lives.

How can a website be used for marketing?

Many websites promote a service or product but without actually offering online sales. For example, most rock bands have websites which promote the band and their music, although visitors may not be able to buy albums directly from the site.

Many tourist attractions use the Internet to give people information about location and opening times and to encourage people to attend. Similarly, hotels often provide basic information even though you may have to phone up to book a room.

Case study – Disneyland, Paris

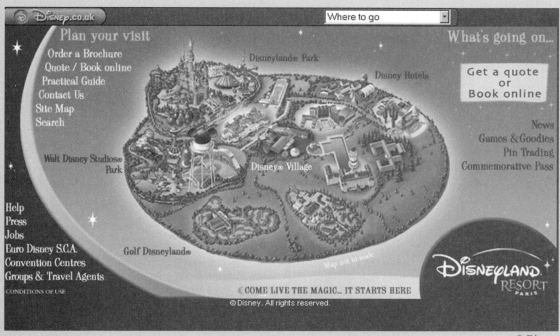

Figure 13.2 Marketing Disneyland Paris © Disney

Disneyland Paris uses its website to show what it offers and to encourage people to visit. Can you find other leisure attractions that market their services on the web?

Here are some other organisations that use the Internet for marketing:

- schools, colleges and universities
- charities
- political parties
- churches and other religious organisations
- theatres and cinemas.

All these organisations are trying to persuade the visitor to do something in response and are not simply providing interesting information.

Some marketing sites also offer some online sales, and start to develop an e-commerce angle. The dividing line between marketing and e-commerce sites is not precise; the category depends on what is the main purpose of the site.

How can a website be used for external communications?

Websites are an ideal means of providing information, so it is not surprising that some of the most visited sites are those that specialise in giving information to the general public. External communications are those directed primarily at people outside the organisation.

These include the traditional media such as newspapers and magazines, which have developed their own online versions, and television and radio channels. Whilst it is possible to listen to radio and watch television over the Internet, these sites have taken on a life of their own, exploiting the specific qualities of the new medium.

Case study – NHS direct

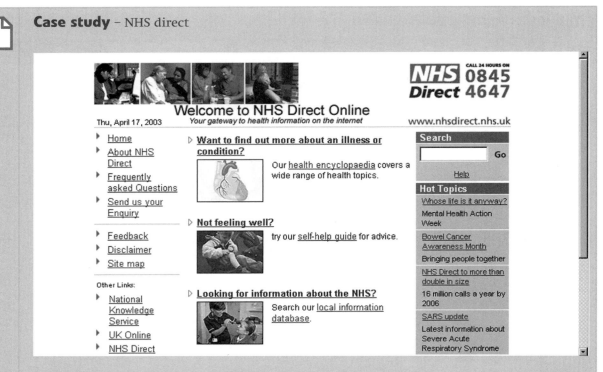

Figure 13.3 The site for NHS Direct is used for external communication   Source: www.nhsdirect.nhs.uk 2003

The NHS Direct site provides health advice and information to the general public. If you are not feeling well it will ask you a series of questions to pinpoint the problem and then advise you on what to do about it. You can search the site for all kinds of information on the National Health Service

Many public services have sites, such as the well used NHS-Direct (www.nhsdirect.nhs.uk), that specialise in communicating information to members of the public.

There are also a few online organisations which have built huge databases of articles and external links, which they then provide as service to visitors. One example is About (www.about.com).

You may wonder how an organisation can finance a free information service. You will usually find that sites are sponsored by other businesses and their advertisements will appear in banners and pop-up screens. Some information sites, such as the Government's site, UKOnline (www.ukonline.gov.uk), are paid for out of public taxation.

How can a website be use for internal communications?

Sometimes an organisation will use a website primarily as a means of communicating with its own members, rather than for the general public. Sites for internal communication can be kept private, but many sites used for internal communications are quite happy to exist in the public domain.

Case study – official website of the Scouts

Figure 13.4 A site used mainly for internal communication.   Reproduced by permission of the Scout Association
Licence no. 0203

ScoutBase UK is the official Members Website of The Scout Association, and has been running since the summer of 1996. It is primarily a collection of resources for Leaders and other adults involved with Scouting and related youth organisations.

Source: www.scoutbase.org.uk

The site for the Scouts in the UK provides support to scout groups around the country. It is not a private access site as it hopes to attract some new members and leaders, but it is primarily designed for internal communications within the organisation.

How can websites for internal communications be kept private?

The Internet is essentially a public access network, so that anyone can visit any site they chose. An organisation may want to maintain a site for internal communications that can be accessed only by employees or members. To do this they can set up an intranet or an extranet. (See Section 3.4 in Unit 3 for more information about intranets and extranets.)

Check your understanding – Visit websites

Use a search engine or portal sites to find a wide range of websites developed for organisations. Keep notes on all the sites that you visit. You will need them later for the assessment tasks.

For each site you visit, jot down:

- the Web address (URL) and name of the organisation
- the purpose of the site
- the type of site – e-commerce, marketing, external communications, internal communications
- a brief description of the content.

Eventually you will have to select at least six of these sites, and write about them in more depth. However, it is still useful at this stage to build up a list from which you can choose.

History of the Internet

What is the Internet?

The Internet has been described as a network of networks. It links computer networks across the world, enabling them to communicate with each other. It is essentially a vast public network. Not only can any computer be linked to it via a Web server, but any computer linked to the Internet can send data files directly to any other.

A number of methods of data communication are used within the Internet – ordinary phone lines, broadband cable connections and satellite links.

It is important to remember that the Internet is not simply a collection of websites. In fact, the Internet was used long before the World Wide Web was invented. The Internet offers a number of communication services including:

- e-mail
- newsgroups
- chat rooms
- remote login – this enables users to login to the computer system of an organisation using their IDs and passwords
- search engines, such as Yahoo! and Google
- the World Wide Web (the Web, or WWW).

Today, the most common types of data files sent over the Internet are e-mails and webpages.

How did the Internet begin?

The Internet began in 1969 when the Advanced Research Projects Agency Network (ARPANET) was set up by the US Defense Department to link it with university research centres. This was during the Cold War period, and the system was designed so that centres could continue to communicate with each other even if one or more of them were destroyed in a nuclear attack.

E-mail was invented in 1971, and the following year users were able to chat to each other from their computers. University College, London, linked to the ARPANET in 1973 and the idea of a global network began to be discussed. The Queen first sent an e-mail in 1976.

Usenet, the basis for all newsgroups, was invented in 1979 and researchers in Essex created the first multi-user game.

Many of the networks were already described as internets (with a small i). When the common data communication protocol, known as TCP/IP, was formally launched in 1982 it became possible for any network to join in, and the linked networks together became known as the Internet (with a capital I).

In the 1980s many countries set up academic research networks; amongst these was the Joint Academic Network (JANET) in the UK. By 1984 there were over 1000 hosts worldwide and organisations (mainly universities) began to register domain names.

In 1986 the US National Science Foundation set up NSFNET which provided a basic 'backbone' which supported any research or educational institution. Its data transmission speed was 56Kbps – the speed of a dial-up modem today – and this supported all the traffic across the US. Within two years the speed of NSFNET had been increased thirty-fold.

This resulted in many more connections, rising to over 100,000 host computers by 1989, with many thousands more connected to these hosts.

The first recorded Internet worm (a type of virus program) affected 6,000 hosts in 1988. Internet Relay Chat (IRC), the technology used by chat rooms, was invented in the same year.

How was the Internet used before the 1990s?

In the early years of the Internet all the files that were transmitted were text files. This was ideal for researchers who wanted to download and read research papers written by colleagues around the world. Electronic mail was simply a method for sending text files directly to a named person.

All files created on a computer consist of binary codes, so in practice any file at all can be transmitted through the Internet. That meant that files created in a word processing package, or graphics, or sounds could all be transferred through the Internet from one computer to another. The problem lay in interpreting those files once they arrived at their destination. To do that, both computers would have to be using the same software packages.

By the end of the 1980s there was a growing interest in **multimedia**, combining several different data types (text, sound, images) within one document, and specialist software packages were produced to handle these.

What does it mean?

Multimedia – refers to any computer-based source of information that uses a combination of text, graphics, animation, video and sound.

Since the Internet is a global system, it is unrealistic to expect all users to use the same software packages, so there was a need for a standard method of producing, transmitting and viewing multimedia documents via the Internet. This was the need that was met by the invention of the World Wide Web.

When was the World Wide Web developed?

In 1991, Tim Berners-Lee developed the World Wide Web whilst he was working at CERN (the European Organization for Nuclear Research). He was a computer scientist whose job was to ensure that physicists got the very best use out of the Internet.

The World Wide Web (also known as the Web, or WWW) very rapidly became the universal standard way of displaying and linking documents on the Internet.

What is the Web?

The Web (short for World Wide Web) is a **hypermedia** system. Like all multimedia systems it handles data in a variety of formats, such as sound, graphics and animation. It also embeds hyperlinks to other webpages. All the pages on the Web are ultimately linked together.

What does it mean?

Hypermedia – a multimedia system that includes hyperlinks to other pages.

Case study – Tim Berners-Lee

Figure 13.5 Tim Berners-Lee

In late 1990, Tim Berners-Lee, a CERN computer scientist, invented the World Wide Web. The 'Web' as it is affectionately called, was originally conceived and developed for the large high-energy physics collaborations which have a demand for instantaneous information sharing between physicists working in different universities and institutes all over the world. Now it has millions of academic and commercial users.

Source: Conseil Européen par la Recherche Nucléaire, www.cern.ch

To find out more about the origins of the Web, visit the CERN website.

Tim Berners-Lee developed three important elements that together make the Web work for users:

- *Hypertext Mark-up Language (HTML)* – the code which is used to create all webpages.
- *HyperText Transfer Protocol (HTTP)* – the rules for transferring HTML files from one computer to another
- *browsers* – software applications which enable the user to view webpages.

Since 1991 HTML has been extended quite considerably, so that it can now include snippets of programming languages, known as **scripts**. At the same time a number of different browsers have been launched, and they are frequently updated to reflect the new developments in HTML.

What is a browser?

The most commonly used browser is Microsoft® Internet Explorer, but other browsers, such as Netscape® Navigator, are also used. A browser does a number of tasks:

- It sends a request for a page to the Web server where the website is stored. The request identifies the page by its Uniform Resource Locator (URL) – often referred to as its web address. The HTML code for that page is then transmitted over the Internet.
- It interprets the HTML code and displays the webpage.

- It sends requests to the Web server for additional files that are referred to in the HTML code for the page – these could be for graphics or sounds. Each image or sound is transmitted as a separate file.
- When the user clicks on a hyperlink, it sends a new page request to the Web server.

Browsers have been updated to match the developments in HTML, but it is important to realise that not all users use the latest versions. Webpages can appear differently in different browsers and in different versions of the same browser.

What effect did the Web have on the growth of the Internet?

The Web had a dramatic effect on the use of the Internet. Today most people in the UK have access to the Internet, and it is used in all countries in the world. The Web's development is guided by the international World Wide Web Consortium (W3C).

Up until 1994 there had been very little commercial interest in the Internet. The Web was designed so that information could be shared freely across the world. Businesses began to understand that they could use the Web to market themselves and to sell goods, and the first commercial sites appeared.

E-commerce was a risky enterprise at first, as it was difficult for a company to predict what the response would be. Some businesses were overwhelmed with orders which they did not have the capacity to deal with. Others enthusiastically invested large sums of money in developing online businesses, only to find that trading developed very slowly. There were some spectacular online business failures, and some notable successes as well.

The Internet continues to be a means of communication between individuals, and has not been taken over completely by businesses and other organisations. Over the years many lively online communities have developed. An online community is a group of people who have a common interest and want to share information through the Internet, usually using a combination of websites, e-mail, newsgroups and chatrooms.

Case study – Guillain-Barré Syndrome Support Group

The Guillain-Barré Syndrome website (www.gbs.org.uk) offers support and information to people suffering from this rare illness. People can communicate directly with others through the online forum, and can search the site for personal and professional advice. This is a good example of an online community which connects people who live all over the UK.

Can you find other examples of online communities on the Web?

Test your knowledge

1 All kinds of media – explain what these words and phrases mean:
   - the media
   - traditional media
   - new media
   - multimedia
   - hypermedia.
2 What is the difference between internal and external communications in an organisation?

▶

3 If you book a ticket through a website how could you:
- pay for it
- receive the ticket?

4 In each of these categories, name one organisation (different in each case) that uses its website for:
- e-commerce
- marketing
- internal communications
- external communications.

5 What is the difference between an intranet and an extranet?

6 What other services does the Internet offer besides websites?

7 When did the Internet start, and how?

8 When was the World Wide Web invented, and by whom?

9 What is a hyperlink?

10 Name two browsers.

13.2 Evaluating a range of websites

How can I evaluate a website?

When you evaluate a product you judge how effective it is. A website is a product of an organisation like any other, and its effectiveness can be judged by referring to its purpose.

It would not be sensible or fair if all websites were assessed against the same standards. A website that is designed for a fan club will be very different from one for a company selling computer supplies.

Before evaluating a website you need to decide:

- *Its purpose* – this may be stated somewhere on the site, or you may have to make an intelligent guess.
- *Its intended audience* – you need to know whether the site is aimed at the world in general or at a specific section of the population, e.g. young people, car owners, parents, football supporters, women, members of a particular religion, residents in a particular town. Most sites are built with a typical visitor in mind.

Once you have decided what these are, you can then ask whether the content and the visual design are appropriate, and whether the site has been designed well technically. You will then be in a position to form a judgement about the quality of the site and how it could be improved.

Evaluation criteria

What evaluation criteria should I use?

You can evaluate the design of a website by looking at it in three different ways:

- *Content design* – is the information appropriate and is it presented clearly?
- *Visual design* – does the site portray the right image, and is it laid out well?
- *Technical design* – is it easy to navigate, and does it work properly?

What content design criteria can I use?

Here are some questions you can ask about the content of a website. Not all the questions will be relevant for all sites.

Information

- Does the site provide the information that I was expecting?
- Is there too much information or too little? The right amount will depend on the purpose of the site.
- Am I given basic information about the organisation, who it includes and what it does?
- Does the site tell me how to contact the organisation? This information should always be provided somewhere on the site.
- Does the site allow me to contact the organisation directly? This may be offered through an online form, or an e-mail address may be given.
- Is there a privacy policy? This is a statement about how the organisation will handle any information given them by a visitor. This is necessary to comply with the Data Protection Act and to give the visitor the confidence to do business with the organisation.

Language

- Does it use language in a style that is appropriate to the subject matter? Business sites will tend to use more formal language than sites devoted to leisure interests; the age of expected visitors is also relevant.

Appearance of text

- Is the text easy to read on screen? Short paragraphs are easier to read than long ones; text which spreads itself across a wide screen can be difficult to read.
- Can the text be downloaded or printed so I can read it offline?
- Is the text presented in a consistent style? Sites will probably use a number of different text styles, but they should be used consistently.

What visual design criteria can I use?

Impression

- What impression is the site trying to give to visitors? It could be businesslike, friendly, busy, formal, casual, etc.
- What impression did I form of the organisation from the site?

Colour and images

- Does the site use an appropriate colour scheme? Sometimes an organisation will have corporate colours; in other cases a set of colours should be chosen to convey the desired impression.
- Do the colours of the text and background make it easy to read? Dark text on a light background is best.
- Is the colour scheme used consistently?
- Do images convey additional information? Images such as photos or drawings often impart information.

- Do images enhance the impact of the site? Some images are used as decoration, and to create a mood or style.
- Are the images appropriate for the site? The purpose and audience must not be forgotten.
- If flash, video or other animations are used, do they add to the quality of the site? Lengthy introductions can be very irritating.

Home page

- Does the home page give a good idea of what the site contains?
- Is the home page informative and interesting?
- Are the most important items on the home page visible without scrolling down? Some visitors never use the scroll bar, so all the most important items should be towards the top of the page.

What technical design criteria can I use?

Navigation

Navigation refers to the way a visitor finds a way around a site, using links provided on the pages. Text or images can act as navigation links, and image links are often called *buttons*. Some of the most important links may be positioned together in a navigation bar (navbar).

- Is it easy to find my way around the site? The main navbar is often along the top of the screen, or it may be down the left-hand side; other links may be provided anywhere on the page.
- Are the methods of navigation consistent? The navbar should be in the same position on each page, and the colours and images which identify them should be consistent throughout the site.
- Can I find most of the information I want with no more than three mouse clicks? The 'three click rule' should apply to almost all information, as visitors leave a site if they cannot find information quickly.
- Does the site offer a search box? A visitor can enter a key word in a search box and a list of possible pages will be displayed.
- Does the site offer a site map? A site map is a diagram which shows how the pages link together; a complete site map cannot be provided for large and complex sites.

Downloading

- Do pages download quickly? A page should normally download in less than a minute on the slowest communication channel at the busiest time of day.
- Are visitors warned in advance if a page is likely to take some time to download? Visitors may want to view pages with high-quality photos, or to download a file in a graphical format like pdf; in these cases they should be warned about the size of the download.
- Do images have alternative text? When you pass the mouse over an image a short text description may pop up; this is the alternative text for the image and should always be provided to support users of non-standard browsers and for visitors with visual impairment.
- Does the site appear the same in different browsers? There can be surprising variations in appearance of a webpage in different browsers and in different versions of the same browser.

Case study – NHS Direct

NHS Direct provides a site map for visitors. This is a separate page laid out as shown.

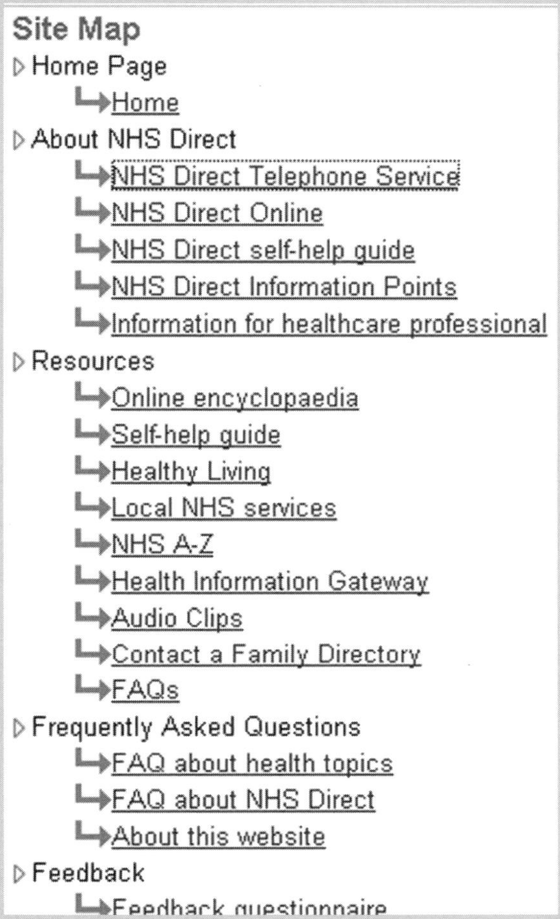

Figure 13.6 Part of the site map for NHS Direct

Source: www.nhsdirect.nhs.uk 2003

Have you seen site maps on other sites? Do they help the visitor?

Maintenance

Maintenance refers to updating the site with new material. Some sites are updated many times a day, whilst others are updated only monthly or less often.

- Is the site kept up to date? Sites should be maintained as frequently as appropriate; for example, a news site will be updated every day, whilst a site which gives advice on buying a kitchen freezer needs to be updated only when new freezers come on to the market.

Check your understanding – Evaluating websites

Visit at least six websites and evaluate them using the evaluation criteria given in this section. Keep notes on all the sites you visit.

For the assessment tasks you will have to select at least six, and you should aim to have a wide variety of sites. It is a good idea to pick some poor-quality sites as well as good ones for analysis.

Evaluating websites

Once you have assessed a site using the evaluation criteria, you should be able to form some judgements about its quality and effectiveness.

How can I assess the strengths and weaknesses of a website?

Most sites have both good points and bad. Do not forget that what counts as a strength or a weakness depends on the purpose of the site. For example, the chatty style adopted in a site devoted to a computer game would not be appropriate for a site that lists the proceedings in Parliament – informal language would be a strength in one case, but a weakness in the other.

It is quite interesting to compare two sites that have the same purpose and intended audience and to give them each a score (say from 1 to 5) under each of the evaluation criteria above.

How can I make suggestions for improvement?

One important reason for evaluating anything is to see whether it can be improved. The evaluation criteria and your lists of weaknesses should provide some ideas on how to improve a site.

Test your knowledge

1 What information should *always* be included on a website?
2 What is a privacy policy, and why is it needed?
3 What is a navigation bar (navbar)?
4 What is a site map?

13.3 Creating a website

This section does *not* provide a tutorial in the use of any particular software package, but instead highlights the general principles that you should understand. You are advised to check the Help file on your chosen package or to visit its associated website. There are also many tutorials available on the Web.

How can I view the HTML used to create a website?

When you download a webpage into a browser, the HTML code is transferred to your computer. This is referred to as the *source code*. HTML code is always stored and transmitted in a simple text file (ASCII file). It usually has a file name with .htm or .html as its file extension, for example, homepage.htm

In Internet Explorer you can view the HTML by selecting **View** then **Source**. This usually opens up Notepad and displays the code. Notepad is a text editor, and is the simplest means of viewing and creating text files. If you use a different browser, then you should also be able to view the source code from the View menu.

Must I learn HTML in order to create a website?

No. Many websites are created using specialist Web authoring software packages. These let you create a webpage in much the same way as you would create a document in a word processing or desktop publishing package. The Web authoring software then generates the HTML for you. You are free to look at the HTML code at any time, and to change or add to it directly. But it is perfectly possible to create a straightforward website that meets its purpose without knowing any HTML.

However, professional Web developers often work directly in HTML. Some of the advanced features of websites can be created only in this way.

How can I use a Web authoring tool to create a website?

There are a number of useful Web authoring packages available, such as Microsoft® FrontPage and Macromedia® Dreamweaver. Another Web authoring tool, Netscape® Composer, can be downloaded free with Netscape® Navigator (the browser).

How can I use templates to create a website?

A number of templates and wizards can be used to create complete websites. Although some of the results can be quite pleasing, you will find them rather limiting. Websites produced in this way are difficult to modify and update, and they do look very similar to each other.

You can find web templates and wizards in a number of Microsoft® products.

You may enjoy looking at some of these website templates for ideas for websites of your own, but you are advised *not* to use them for completing your assessment tasks. You may, however, use individual webpage templates when building your own site.

Using a Web authoring tool to create a website

How do I create and save a page?

In your chosen Web authoring package, type in some text, as you would in a word processor, and then save the page. All webpages are saved with either .htm or .html as the filename extension. Your Web authoring package will usually allow you to display the page in three views:

- page layout (normal)
- HTML
- page preview.

You create the page in page layout, then you can check what it will look like when displayed by a browser in the page preview. Have a look at the HTML that the package is generating for each page.

How do I handle text?

You will want to add variety to your page by using different font styles.

A word of warning – a visitor's browser will only be able to display a font that is already resident on the visitor's computer. So although you may want to use an attractive but obscure font for a heading, the visitor will be able to see the characters displayed in the font only if they already have the font on board. If they do not have the required font then the browser will display the text in the default font for that browser; on a Microsoft® Windows system the default font is normally Times New Roman, but the user can change the default font to whatever he or she wishes.

To begin with you would be wise to stick to Times New Roman, or Arial fonts, as they are widely used. You can format text styles in much the same way as you would in a word processor. Your package probably offers a Format Font function which shows you all the options you can use.

How do I use images?

When we use a computer graphic we can refer to its size in two senses:

- *The memory needed to store the image* – most computer graphics use a very large amount of memory. For example, a photograph taken with a digital camera will be 2Mb or more. On a slow connection, a picture this size could take half an hour or more to download from the Internet!
- *The dimensions of the image measured in pixels* – images are composed of many tiny spots of colour known as pixels. The width and height of an image are measured in pixels. It is very important that when you create an image for a webpage that you make it exactly the right size for the space it is going to occupy. That ensures that it has no more pixels than it really needs.

Because of the size problems, all images used on websites are stored in a compressed format. The two compressed formats commonly used on the Web are:

- *jpg* – used mainly for photos
- *gif* – used for most other images.

Compression reduces significantly the amount of memory needed to store an image of given dimensions.

How can I obtain images for a webpage?

There are many ways of finding or creating images to use on a website:

- *Create an image in a graphics package* – you can use a simple package like Microsoft® Paint or a more sophisticated one like Adobe® Illustrator. Once you have designed your image you should reduce the dimensions (number of pixels) to the exact ones needed on the webpage. Finally, save the image as a gif.
- *Use a photograph* – you will either take a photo with a digital camera or scan in a photo print. This will normally be stored as a bitmap (.bmp), which is a non-compressed pixel format. You can then load it into a photo manipulation package, such as Microsoft® Photo Editor, Corel® Photo House, or Adobe® PhotoShop.

Once again reduce the dimensions to the number of pixels needed on the webpage. Then save the photo as a jpg. The package will offer you some choice over the level of compression. A more compressed photo will take up less memory, but will also display less detail. If you are asked to choose the *quality* select 75%; on the other hand if you are asked to specify the *degree of compression* select 25%. These two choices have exactly the same effect as each other, but unfortunately software packages are not consistent in the way they ask the question.

- *Obtain an image from the Web* – you should never simply copy images on existing websites as the images will probably be protected by copyright. Fortunately, there are many sources of copyright-free Web images online. In many cases the creators do ask you to acknowledge the source of any image you use. A search through a search engine will produce a bewildering choice, but you might like to start with www.freefoto.com and the portal site www.freegraphics.com.

Once an image has been saved in a compressed form, gif or jpg, you should not try to manipulate it any further. If the image is compressed for a second time the quality may suffer noticeably. Always go back to the original version before it was compressed if you want to make any more changes.

How do I create a layout on the page?

You can insert an image on a webpage, but you will soon realise that it is not always easy to arrange items on the page where you would like them to be. There are several ways of controlling the layout of text and images:

- *Use the picture properties* – if you click on an image in the page layout view you can usually display the image (picture) properties either by right-clicking or by selecting from the main menu. The alignment of the image can be set as 'right', left', 'top', etc. – these are relative to the text. You can also set a border, or create horizontal or vertical spacing around the image.

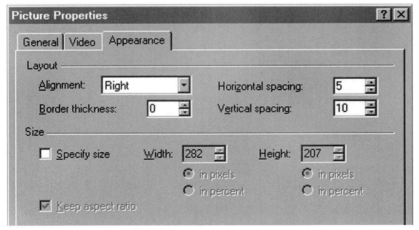

Figure 13.7 Setting the picture properties in Microsoft® FrontPage.

- *Use a table* – tables can be created on a webpage, just as they can in a word processor. But although a table can be used to display data in boxes in the traditional way, tables are more commonly used on webpages as a way of arranging text and images on screen. Often the tables are created without borders, so when the page is viewed in page preview, the dividing lines are not visible. You can specify many of the properties of a table by clicking on it, then right-clicking or selecting the table properties from the main menu.

Case study – Size of images

Figure 13.8 An image-rich webpage

Source: www.guardians.net

This page consists entirely of images. You can check the size of each one by right-clicking on the image, then selecting **Properties**. For example, here are the properties of the Egyptian eye image in the middle of the screen.

Figure 13.9 Properties of the image of the Egyptian eye

This shows that the image has been saved in the compressed jpg format. The memory required is 26488 bytes (around 26Kb) and the dimensions are 367 pixels wide by 221 pixels high.

Links

How do I display a hyperlink?

Any section of text or any image can be used as a hyperlink to another webpage. You can find out how to do this in any Web authoring package. But how does the visitor recognise that text or an image is a link? Originally text links were all identified by underlining.

Text can, in fact, be used as a link without underlining, but this can only be done if the visitor is left in no doubt that this is, in fact, a link. Usually a different colour is used for the link, or all the links are placed together in a navigation bar.

Images can also be used as links. Buttons are image-based links which look like the kind of buttons that you might press in the real world, but any image can be used as a link.

Should I use text or image links?

If you use an image as a link then the image has to be downloaded into the browser before it can be used as a link. If a page has many image links then it may take some time for them to appear on a slow Internet connection, and the visitor may become impatient.

As a general rule, images used as links should be as small as possible, in terms of memory. Images in gif format usually take less memory that photos stored in jpg format. Text links do not suffer from this problem, and they can be customised to appear quite interesting. Sometimes buttons created as image links can be replaced by text links with no loss of visual style.

Case study – Text and image links

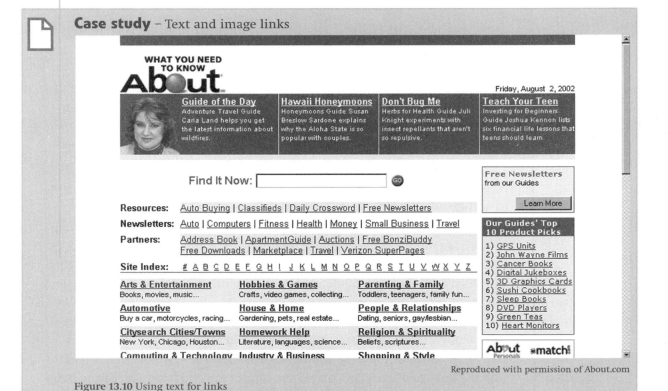

Reproduced with permission of About.com

Figure 13.10 Using text for links

The About site has a great many text links on one page. In comparison, lastminute.com prefers to use images as links.

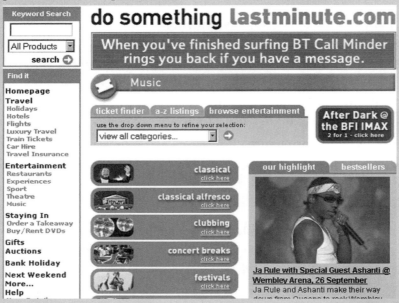

Figure 13.11 Using graphics for links

Almost all the graphical elements – photos and boxes – on this page are links. Colour is used to identify the text links in the navigation bar on the left.

Which do you prefer, and why? Find and compare other sites that make heavy use of either text or image links.

How can I use internal links?

Internal links allow visitors to find their way around the site. No one is going to find a page unless it is linked from another page. Unless the site is very small you will not be able to provide links from any one page to all the other pages, so you have to think about how the pages are related to each other and work out what pages a visitor might want to see next.

Visitors can be divided into two types: those who are looking for specific information, and those who just want to look round. The site must provide links to suit both. A site can use either, or both, of these linking styles:

■ *Linking by structure* – the website may naturally fall into a number of main sections, and links to the first page in each section should be given in the main navbar. The main navbar should then be visible on every page on the site. Each section may then have its own secondary navbar. Each page should always carry a link back to the home page and this is usually included in the main navbar. Linking by structure helps the visitor who knows exactly what he or she is looking for (See Figure 13.12).

■ *Linking by theme* – not all sites can be as tightly structured as Tesco's. The Web allows visitors to browse to any page they like and in any order they like, so it is sometimes helpful to provide links to other pages that cover similar topics. Linking by theme helps the visitor who just wants to surf.

Many sites use a mixture of linking by structure and linking by theme.

Case study – Linking by structure at Tesco

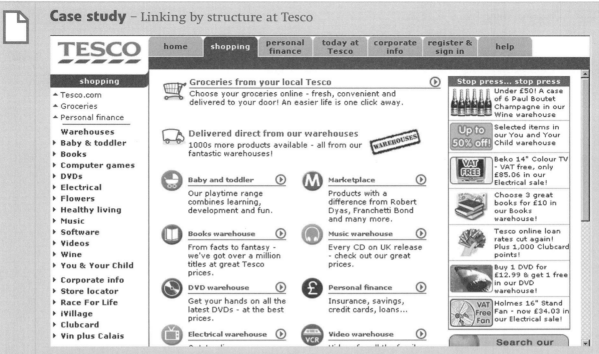

Figure 13.12 Linking by structure on Tesco's site
Source: www.tesco.com

Tesco uses a strong structure to link its pages. The main navbar is shown as a series of tabs along the top of the screen and it appears on every page. The Shopping link has been selected and the first page of this section is displayed. The secondary navbar is down the left-hand side of the screen and shows the links within the Shopping section. The secondary navbar is displayed on every page in the Shopping section.

Further research – Combining linking styles

Visit the BBC News homepage at news.bbc.co.uk. You will find that the page has a main navbar along the top and a secondary navbar down the left side, but it also has some thematic links in the right-hand column. These link to other news stories.

How can I use external links?

One of the great advantages of the Web is that it allows websites to provide links to other related sites. External links like these help to join all the sites on the Web into one vast network.

Some very useful websites are specifically designed to provide lists of external links arranged by subject matter – these are known as *portal sites*. However, some sites, especially commercial ones, would prefer visitors to stay on their site so give few, if any, external links.

Case study – A portal site

Figure 13.13 Yahoo! – a portal site

Source: www.yahoo.co.uk

Yahoo's site provides many thousands of links to other sites and acts as an online directory.

Check your understanding – Creating a website

Use a Web authoring tool to create a simple website to meet a specific need. Do *not* use a template.

Read through this section again, and make sure that you have thought about:

- fonts and font sizes
- sources of images
- size of images – in bytes and in pixels
- layout
- hyperlinks
- internal linking structure.

Test your knowledge

1 What is HTML?
2 What is a Web authoring package? Name one example.
3 What is a webpage template?
4 Sometimes the Web designer creates a webpage, but it appears differently to a visitor. Why might that happen?
5 The 'size' of an image can be measured in Kb or in pixels. Explain the difference.
6 Name two compressed image formats used on the Web.
7 Name one website that offers free Web images that you can use on your own sites.

13.4 Testing and problem solving

All websites should be fully tested before they go live. They should then be tested again after they have been uploaded to the Internet. Similar tests should also be done whenever a site is updated.

Testing a website before uploading

How do I test my site before uploading it?

Before the site is uploaded the homepage should be opened in a browser. These tests should be carried out:

Internal links

- Check that each of the links from the main navigation bar loads the correct page.
- Check that the links in the main navigation bar on all other pages behave as expected.
- Check all the internal links on each page.

Images

- Check that each image occupies the intended space on the screen and is positioned correctly.
- Select the properties of each image to check how much memory each uses. Do not forget to include any graphical buttons or bullets that you have used. Calculate the total memory used by all the images on each page. Aim to keep the total to under 60Kb per page.
- If you want to use a larger image (for example, if you want to offer your visitor the chance to see a full size photo), you should warn visitors before they link to the page that it will be a slow download.

Layout

- Check that each page appears as intended in your usual browser.
- Check the whole site on an earlier version of the browser you are using.
- Check the whole site on a different browser.

How do I record the testing?

It is important to document the tests carried out on a site as you do it. It is very easy to lose track of the tests you have done, and then to repeat tests unnecessarily, or even leave some out.

- *Internal links* – when you check links you can create a table like this:

products.htm

Link to	OK?	Notes
contacts.htm	✓	
home.htm	✓	
cartridges.htm	Bad link	Update this

■ *Images* – you can keep a record of all the images on a page with a table like this:

products.htm

Image	Size in pixels	Memory	Notes
homebutton.gif	120 × 30	4Kb	
contactsbutton.gif	120 × 30	4Kb	
office.jpg	350 × 160	63Kb	Can photo be compressed further?
Total memory		71Kb	Must reduce this

■ *Layout* – you can provide screen dumps of pages to show what they look like.

Publishing your site to the web server

Once you have tested your site you will then want to publish (upload) it to the Web server. A Web server is a computer that is permanently online to the Internet and which makes your website available to others.

In order to put your site on the Web you must have some Web space available for your use on a server. You will also be given a Web address (URL) that identifies the space.

If you are working on a network at your place of study then the network administrator will provide instructions on how to upload your site to the Web server.

If you are working from a standalone computer at home then your Internet Service Provider (ISP) should be able to offer you space on its Web server.

Most Web authoring packages provide you with a simple tool for uploading the webpages to the server. If you are using an HTML editor then you will have to use FTP (file transfer protocol) software, which can be downloaded free from a number of sites.

Testing a website after uploading

How do I test my site after uploading it?

You should check your site again immediately after uploading it to the Web server. The most common mistake at this stage is to forget to upload a page or an image, so you need to repeat all the tests that you did earlier.

You should make some extra checks at this stage as well.

External links

Check that each external link loads the correct site.

Download times

Check how long it takes to download each page, including all the images. You should, if possible, carry out this test on a number of different computers. In particular, try to check the download times on both slow dial-up connections and fast broadband connections

How do I record the testing?

Use the same tables as before to record the tests you do for internal links. You can then create a similar table for the external links.

▪ *Download times* – you might like to create a table to record the download times for each page. If possible, find out the speed of the broadband connection that you are using and insert it into the table where indicated by ??Kbps.

Page	Download time with 56Kbps dial-up modem	Download time with broadband working at ?? Kbps	Notes
home.htm	95 secs	10 seconds	Too slow
products.htm			
contacts.htm			
cartridges.htm			

Check your understanding – Testing a website

Use the techniques mentioned in this section to test a simple site that you have created. It is a good idea to work on a practice site before starting the assessment task.

Test your knowledge

1. What is the difference between an internal and an external link?
2. How can you upload pages to the Web server on the system that you are using?
3. Why do some webpages download faster than others?
4. Why should a website be tested after uploading as well as before?

Assessment tasks

This section describes what you must do to obtain a Merit grade for this unit.

A Distinction grade may be awarded if your work demonstrates a deeper understanding of the topics and is of a higher quality. The highlighted sentences indicate the quality of work expected at Distinction level.

How do I provide assessment evidence?

Your evidence will in the form of a written report, which will be illustrated with screen shots of the websites that you have visited.

You should also provide evidence of the website that you create. This should also be a report about the creation and testing of your site, illustrated with screen shots and possibly supported by witness statements.

All your evidence should be presented in one folder, which should have a front cover and a contents page. You should divide the evidence into two sections corresponding to the two tasks.

Task 1

Learning outcome 1 – Identify the uses of websites
Learning outcome 2 – Evaluate a range of websites

Find at least six websites that are different in style and purpose. You should include at least one example from each of these categories:

- e-commerce
- marketing
- external communications
- internal communications.

You might like to include examples of websites for both large and small organisations; websites with a wide variety of visual styles, websites aimed at different audiences and websites that have been developed by amateurs as well as professionals. You may include poor-quality sites as well as successful ones.

For each website you should provide:

- the URL and name of the organisation
- the purpose of the site
- the type of site, from the categories above
- a description of the content
- an assessment of the content, referring to its purpose (see section 13.2 for more details)
- an assessment of the visual design, referring to its purpose (see section 13.2 for more details)
- an assessment of the technical aspects of the site, referring to its purpose (see section 13.2 for more details)

- strengths and weaknesses of the site, including whether the site achieves its purpose
- suggestions for improvements.

You should provide screen shots to illustrate all aspects of the site.

You might like to give each site a score against the different assessment criteria, so you can compare their effectiveness.

Task 2

Learning outcome 3 – Create a suitable website

Learning outcome 4 – Test and problem-solve a website

You should create a website using whichever Web authoring software you have available. You are strongly advised not to use one of the standard website templates that are provided in a number of software packages – these do not offer enough challenge or flexibility, and are easy to spot.

Your website should have at least four linked pages. You may decide you need more pages, but remember that the site will be judged on quality not quantity.

You are advised to follow these steps and include evidence in your report.

Step 1: Specification

Identify an organisation that needs a website. This should not normally be for yourself, unless you run a small business and need a site.

If you know someone in the organisation, then discuss their needs with them. If you do not know anyone in the organisation then do some research and establish why they might need a website, or why they might need a new website to replace the one they have already.

Describe:

- the organisation
- the purpose of the site and its intended audience
- the type of site – e-commerce, marketing, external communications, internal communications
- user requirements – what the organisation wants the site to achieve
- the impression you want to give.

Step 2: Design

Design the site using notes, diagrams and sketches. Explain why you have made your choices. For more ideas read section 13.2 again. You should cover the following:

Content design:

- information that should be included
- style of language to be used
- text styles.

Visual design:

- how the required impression is to be created
- colours to be used for backgrounds, text and graphics
- images to be included
- detailed design of the home page, and of other specimen pages.

Technical design:

- methods of navigation
- site map.

You should try to include a selection of pictures, internal and external links, and a variety of text formats.

> To obtain a Distinction you must provide evidence of a thorough plan of the website before production using project management techniques. This applies particularly to the quality of your work in Steps 1 and 2.

Step 3: Implement

Provide evidence of all aspects of your site. This will normally be in the form of annotated screen shots. You may also include witness statements as evidence that the site navigation works as intended.

Step 4: Test and problem-solve

You should test your site both before and after uploading it to a server. You must provide evidence of each test and the results you got. The evidence can be in the form of tables of results supported by screen shots. For more detailed advice on testing, see section 13.4.

Tests should include:

- test all internal navigation links
- check that all text and images appear as intended
- check appearance and layout of each page
- test all external links (may only be possible after uploading)
- check download times.

The website should be checked:

- on the original computer
- on another computer in a different location
- using, if possible, more than one browser, or different versions of the same browser.

Comment on any problems you found.

> To obtain a Distinction you should be able to propose a range of solutions for problems that may be encountered with your website.

Step 5: Evaluate

Assess your website. For more advice about evaluating websites, see section 13.2.

> To obtain a Distinction you should be able to show whether the site matches the purpose and user requirements described in the specification in Step 1, and whether it matches the design described in Step 2.

INDEX